CITY OF DREAMS

CITY OF DREAMS

DODGER STADIUM
AND THE BIRTH
OF MODERN
LOS ANGELES

JERALD PODAIR

PRINCETON UNIVERSITY PRESS
PRINCETON AND OXFORD

Copyright © 2017 by Princeton University Press
Published by Princeton University Press, 41 William Street,
Princeton, New Jersey 08540
In the United Kingdom: Princeton University Press, 6 Oxford
Street, Woodstock, Oxfordshire OX20 1TR
press.princeton.edu
Jacket design by Kathleen Lynch/Black Kat Design
Jacket image courtesy of iStock
All Rights Reserved
ISBN 978-0-691-12503-9
Library of Congress Control Number: 2016955221
British Library Cataloging-in-Publication Data is available
This book has been composed in Sabon LT Std
Printed on acid-free paper. ∞
Printed in the United States of America
1 3 5 7 9 10 8 6 4 2

For Caren and Julie

CONTENTS

ACKNOWLEDGMENTS

This book owes its existence to one of the many wonderful conversations I had over the years with my late friend Bill Reel, one of New York's greatest journalists and chroniclers. What individual, he asked me, most affected the histories of America's two most important cities? My answer—Walter O'Malley—launched me on the road to writing this book. Along the way it became more of a Los Angeles story than a New York one, but I know Bill would understand.

In 1986, Robert Merring took me to Dodger Stadium and gave me my first look at America's greatest ballpark. At the time, I had no idea that thirty years later I would be completing a book about it, but thanks just the same, Robert, for the introduction. I don't recall the score of the game, but I certainly remember the experience.

I am grateful, as always, for the support Lawrence University offers for my scholarship and writing. Thanks in large measure to Provost David Burrows, Lawrence is a model for liberal arts colleges in encouraging faculty research. The funding provided by my Robert S. French Chair in American Studies has made possible everything I have written during my time at Lawrence.

Also at Lawrence, I appreciate the help of the staff at the Seeley G. Mudd Library, especially research librarian Gretchen Revie, and that of my student research assistants over the years: Alyson Richey, Caitlin Gallogly, Hayley Vatch, Jennifer Sdunzik, Emily McLane, Sarah Golden, Michael Sze, and Emma Saiz. Lori Rose and Valerie Carlow of Lawrence's Main Hall office personify efficiency, dedication, and good humor.

Thanks also to Jon Shelton, Jerry Seaman, Park and Katie Drescher, Paul Cohen, Tim Spurgin, Jake Frederick, Marty Finkler, Mary Meany, Vin Cannato, Max Lane, Dianne Mesa, Gary Gerstle, Robert Klein, Don Tobias, Jane Latour, Kevin Fogarty, and the late Richard Warch, Margot Warch, William Chaney, and Robert French.

James McPherson and Alan Brinkley continue to inspire me, both as historians and as human beings.

In Los Angeles, my time at UCLA's Charles E. Young Research Library was spent productively thanks to its responsive staff and student workers.

Also in Los Angeles, I owe an immense debt to Peter O'Malley, Brent Shyer, and Robert Schweppe for their generosity as I worked on this project. Without the incredibly rich collection of materials related to Dodger Stadium and Walter O'Malley that they opened to me, this book would not exist. They responded to my queries and inquiries with an attention to detail worthy of the nation's best research libraries; no item was too small or trivial for their interest and assistance. They also offered a welcoming atmosphere in Los Angeles that made me greatly look forward to my visits to the city.

Thanks as well to those who consented to be interviewed for this book: Peter O'Malley, Terry Seidler, Vin Scully, Rosalind Wyman, Fred Claire, Bob Smith, and Carol Jacques.

At Princeton University Press, it was a great joy to work with Brigitta van Rheinberg, who has made the press a place where ideas are valued and history has a true home. Thanks also to Quinn Fusting, Lyndsey Claro, and Amanda Peery for their knowledgeable professionalism.

My greatest debts of all are to my family, including my mother-in-law, Florence Benzer, and my late parents, Simon and Selma Podair. I hope my brother, Lee, will enjoy this book, even if it is not about his favorite baseball team. My daughter, Julie, and wife, Caren, sustain me in more ways than they can know. This book is for both of you.

PREFACE

OPENING DAY IN
LOS ANGELES

On April 10, 1962, amid ceremony and celebration, Dodger Stadium, major league baseball's modern showpiece, opened in Los Angeles, California. It was a day of pride and accomplishment for Walter O'Malley, the fifty-eight-year-old owner of the Los Angeles Dodgers, who had moved his team from Brooklyn, New York, in 1957 in order to build the ballpark of his dreams, one with every possible amenity and convenience. Now here it stood in the former Chavez Ravine neighborhood, a beautiful setting overlooking downtown Los Angeles to the south and the San Gabriel Mountains to the north.

The city of Los Angeles also had reason to be proud. It had attracted the Brooklyn Dodgers, a storied and successful baseball franchise, with the promise of the finest stadium in America. Here it was, adorned in vibrant earth-to-sky colors, with unobstructed field views and the biggest and most technologically advanced scoreboard in the game. It was already being called the wonder of the baseball world, a grand civic monument befitting a world-class city. O'Malley, the Dodgers, and Los Angeles had done it.

But at what cost? Between 1957 and opening day 1962, Dodger Stadium divided Los Angeles in deep and profound ways. It raised

the question of the city's modern identity. How would it best serve
and govern its citizens? How would it present itself to the nation
and world? Opponents of the stadium objected to what they
viewed as a giveaway of public property—the land at Chavez
Ravine on which the stadium would be constructed—for the personal gain of a private individual. Supporters argued that the public benefits derived from the stadium in the form of property tax
revenues, jobs, entertainment, and civic improvement justified
O'Malley's profits. They also envisioned Dodger Stadium as an
important step in revitalizing Los Angeles's lackluster downtown
area and as one of the cultural amenities that marked the emergence of a sophisticated and modern city. Stadium critics rejected
the idea that a great American city required a central core studded
with civic monuments. They argued instead for a Los Angeles that
performed the basic tasks of urban life, concentrating tax resources
on neighborhoods in need of schools, streets, sanitation, and safety.

The disagreements over Dodger Stadium and these larger issues
were fought out across the political and social landscape of Los
Angeles between 1957 and 1962. There was a citywide referendum on the stadium project, a series of taxpayer lawsuits filed
against the stadium contract, and a racially charged eviction of
residents from the land on which the stadium was to be built. The
battles took place in City Council chambers, at the ballot box, in
newspapers and over the airwaves, in the courts, and sometimes
in the streets. In the end, Dodger Stadium was built. But the arguments surrounding it did not end on that gala opening day. The
questions it raised about the relationship between public and private power, the respective roles of urban core and periphery, and
the modern identity of Los Angeles itself would remain long
after April 10, 1962. Dodger Stadium was not the only venue on
which the battle between differing visions of the city was contested. But as one of the very first such battlegrounds, it holds
both tangible and symbolic importance. If the questions Dodger
Stadium presented to the citizens of Los Angeles have not been
answered definitively in the succeeding five decades of the city's
history—and they have not—here is where they began. It is where

an understanding of Los Angeles as a modern American city begins as well.

The struggle over Dodger Stadium made for unlikely political allies. In part this can be attributed to the vagaries of Los Angeles's nonpartisan electoral system, which blurred party distinctions in the minds of voters. But it was also a product of differing views of the city's identity and destiny, which crossed lines of race, class, and ideology and brought strange bedfellows together. Opposition to the Dodger contract united a white conservative Republican small businessman and a Latino liberal Democrat on the Los Angeles City Council. Among the contract's most ardent supporters were the city's mayor—the classic representative of business-oriented "Downtown" Republicanism—and a Jewish left-of-center Democratic councilwoman from Downtown's rival power center, the Westside.*

What drove proponents and critics of the 1957 City Council ordinance providing for the transfer of publicly owned land at Chavez Ravine to the Dodgers for the construction of Dodger Stadium were as much cultural visions as political ones. Dodger Stadium became the locus for an argument between those who envisioned Los Angeles as an everyday city of neighborhoods and services and others who saw it as a modern, growth-focused city with a vibrant central core featuring civic institutions that announced themselves to the nation and world.

They also disagreed over the role of the state in the life and culture of Los Angeles. Again, Dodger Stadium crystallized the differences between growth advocates who believed it was appropriate to offer state resources to private businesses that promised to generate taxable revenues and public benefits for the city—in addition to the substantial profits envisioned by their owners—and those who opposed public sector gifts to entrepreneurs which made the

---

* The term "downtown," as used in this book, refers to its geographic area. When capitalized as "Downtown" it denotes a locus of political, economic, cultural, and social power in the affairs of the city of Los Angeles.

rich even richer. What kind of city would Los Angeles be? One built around the provision of basic services to communities and average citizens? Or a city with global dreams and the physical structures to match them? The battle over Dodger Stadium, Los Angeles's first truly modern entertainment venue, would be crucial in answering these questions.

The issues of where to build the Dodgers' new ballpark, who would build it, and who would pay for it thus extended beyond sports and into the bloodstream of the city as a whole. Dodger Stadium, perched on a hill only a mile from City Hall, would be the most significant addition to the downtown area in decades. By 1957, the year of the Dodgers' arrival, downtown Los Angeles was a work-and-flee zone, a place in which white middle-class Angelenos earned a living by day and then abandoned at night. The city's business establishment, notably the Chandler family of the *Los Angeles Times*, owned a substantial amount of real estate in the downtown area, and thus had much to lose from declining property values there; between 1920 and 1950, downtown's share of the city's retail trade had dropped from 90 percent to 17 percent.[1]

Bunker Hill, downtown's main residential neighborhood, was home to a diverse working- and lower-class population. Municipal government officials, headquartered in the adjoining Civic Center, and downtown business and professional leaders, from their nearby offices, regarded Bunker Hill as an embarrassing eyesore. They viewed Dodger Stadium as the first step toward the revitalization of downtown, which they envisioned in the image of more established cities—New York, Chicago, and even San Francisco, Los Angeles's rival to the north. These downtowns combined commerce, culture, and leisure. They also offered close-in residential neighborhoods—Greenwich Village, the Gold Coast, Nob Hill—that permitted middle- and upper-class white urbanites to enjoy the richness of downtown metropolitan life. Supporters of the Dodger Stadium project filtered their hopes for Los Angeles's new downtown through this lens of cosmopolitanism.

But their opponents feared the implications of a revitalized downtown for their own Los Angeles. In the neighborhoods on the city's peripheries, the defining issues were more practical and prosaic. They concerned basic services—roads, schools, sanitation, police, and housing. Here there were no great visions for Los Angeles's downtown, only worries that their needs and their neighborhoods would be sacrificed in the name of downtown's rebirth. Dodger Stadium, which in their view exacted an extraordinarily high price in diverted public resources, epitomized that unjust sacrifice. The battle against the construction of Dodger Stadium symbolized the revolt of the margins—geographic, social, economic—against perceived centers of power and, indeed, the idea of a center itself.

In keeping with the breadth and complexity of the alliances for and against the stadium, the term "margins," as applied to Dodger Stadium opponents, took on a similar multidimensionality. It included both racial and ethnic minorities in positions of social and economic disadvantage and those we are less accustomed to view as marginalized—white middle-class homeowners and apartment dwellers residing in peripheral areas of the city. These Angelenos felt cut off from the downtown area in the literal sense, living miles away with little geographic connection to it. But they also felt disconnected from what that area represented: the wealthy, the powerful, and the insiders whose successes and privileges seemingly had come at their expense.

There were a number of ways to be marginalized in the Los Angeles of the 1950s and early 1960s, and the deal to build Dodger Stadium came to embody the resentments and anxieties of a diverse group of citizens. For Latinos, the construction of the stadium on the site of a long-standing, traditional Mexican American community at Chavez Ravine that had originally been uprooted in the early 1950s for a never-built public housing project engendered strong feelings of disempowerment and loss. The forced removal in 1959 of the last of Chavez Ravine's families from the land by sheriff's deputies, televised live across the city, served as an impetus for the political and cultural radicalization of the broader Latino community in the 1960s and beyond. The working- and lower-class residents of Bunker Hill who lost their dwellings to a massive redevelopment project that, like Dodger Stadium, was supported by Downtown political, business, and real estate interests were estranged from power centers whose offices they could see from their own windows. Even the middle-class white homeowners and small businessmen of outlying areas such as the rapidly growing San Fernando Valley had reason to resent the Downtown establishment, which spent their tax money on projects that redirected resources from their neighborhoods.

All of these marginalized constituencies channeled their anger at perceived elites into the movement to stop Dodger Stadium from being built. This anger was expressed variously in racial, cultural, and class-related terms, but its common denominator was a rejection of a government-business nexus of special accommodation that excluded them. It found a voice in an anti-stadium movement that would employ a citywide referendum, a series of taxpayer lawsuits, and acts of civil disobedience against a stadium that had come to embody a vision of a modern Los Angeles from which they also felt marginalized.

The term "modern," of course, can carry a host of meanings, some so theoretically dense as to render them almost useless. Los Angeles in the 1950s and 1960s was a rapidly growing metropolitan area with an ambitious civic and business class eager for it to shed its provincial reputation and take on the attributes associated with the modern and with the more established American cities to which its members aspired. These included civic edifices and cultural institutions situated in vibrant and sophisticated central core areas. Their understanding of modern was thus somewhat derivative, based as it was on what other cities had achieved. It can be argued, of course, that the modern encompasses more than buildings arrayed around a newly reconfigured downtown area. But civic leaders, be they businessmen or elected officials, are rarely theoreticians or philosophers. They live in the world of the possible and the tangible, and define ideas through what they can see and touch. For Los Angeles's political and economic leadership class, this meant physical structures, of which Dodger Stadium would be the first to appear.

Realizing the desire of Los Angeles's leadership class for the city to be modern, to possess what New York, Chicago, and San Francisco already had, would come at a cost in spending, tax revenues, land, housing, and broken community bonds. These costs would largely be borne by others, notably minorities and working- and middle-class whites who opposed Dodger Stadium and with it Los Angeles's rise to modernity. Their vision of a workaday city that provided basic services for its neighborhoods was at odds with the grander dreams of the modernists. The struggle over Dodger Stadium between 1957 and 1962 was their battle as well.

Dodger Stadium was the type of entertainment venue that modern cities possessed. It was the kind of civic venue that modern downtowns possessed. Los Angeles voters had rejected a proposed bond issue for a municipally constructed baseball stadium in 1955. The only viable alternative was a privately financed ballpark built by the owner of an existing major league team willing to relocate. By October 1957, Los Angeles had that owner and team, in Walter O'Malley and the Brooklyn Dodgers. But O'Malley did not have the financial resources to build a stadium without at least some form of government assistance. He would require a favorable land deal, with property made available at a price he could afford. He had left New York, his lifelong home, because municipal officials there had refused to take steps to allow him to build on the ballpark site he favored. Chavez Ravine, the site O'Malley desired in Los Angeles, was owned by the city. If city officials offered this property to the Dodgers on favorable terms, the new stadium could be built and the city of Los Angeles could have its first modern icon.

But was it fair for the city to make what some viewed as a gift of valuable land to a private businessman to use for his personal benefit? One that would, moreover, enhance real estate values in the adjoining downtown area, rewarding business elites such as the Chandlers? And one that would inevitably siphon off resources that could have been used to pave a road in a San Fernando Valley neighborhood or build a school in East Los Angeles? The battle over Dodger Stadium was thus a debate over whether Los Angeles would become a modern city of grand civic monuments and a vital downtown or a decentered city of functioning neighborhoods and communities. When Walter O'Malley made the decision to move his team to Los Angeles, a city he had visited only three times in his life, he did not intend to animate such a debate. He wished merely to build a baseball stadium. But however inadvertently, he made that stadium the center of a struggle over the future of his adopted city, one that would shape its identity for decades to come. This is the story of that stadium and that struggle.

1

ROADS WEST

The road west to Dodger Stadium began with Walter O'Malley's birth in New York City on October 9, 1903. The son of a Democratic politician who served as the city's commissioner of public markets in the 1920s, O'Malley attended the University of Pennsylvania and Columbia and Fordham Law Schools, graduating from Fordham in 1930. Entering the world of law, business, and politics at the height of the Great Depression, the young O'Malley was forced to live by his wits.

He soon established connections in the Tammany Hall Democratic Party organization in which his father had served. Despite the ascendancy of reform mayor Fiorello La Guardia, a staunch foe of Tammany Hall, a potent machine culture with a distinct Catholic influence still existed in 1930s-era New York. The astute, gregarious, and Irish Catholic O'Malley thrived in it, building a successful law practice around corporate reorganizations and bankruptcy, two of the few growth areas in commercial law during those economically difficult times. But O'Malley wanted more than a career spent working for others as a respected and well-compensated attorney. Only business and entrepreneurship could offer the independence and control over his own destiny that he sought. O'Malley invested in the New York Subways Advertising Company, in which he became the largest single stockholder, and produced a popular legal guide and register for building projects.[1]

O'Malley would have remained a prosperous commercial lawyer with a midsized law firm and a happy family life in Brooklyn and Amityville, Long Island, if not for a beleaguered and debt-ridden National League baseball team named the Brooklyn Dodgers. In 1913, the team's half owner and chief operating officer, Charles Ebbets, opened his eponymously named ballpark in the Flatbush section of Brooklyn.[2] Ebbets Field was the state of the art for its time, featuring steel grandstands and an upper deck. But the cost of constructing the ballpark forced Ebbets to sell a half interest in the Dodgers to two building contractors, Edward and Steven McKeever.

The team enjoyed success in Ebbets Field's early years, winning National League pennants in 1916 and 1920, but declined thereafter. By the 1930s, with Ebbets and Edward McKeever dead, debts accumulating, and Ebbets Field itself deteriorating, the Dodgers had become the laughingstock of baseball. Known as the "Daffiness Boys," the team's consistent second-division finishes were punctuated with farcical occurrences such as three men on a base simultaneously and an outfielder hit on the head by a fly ball. Attendance shrank and the virtually bankrupt team was taken over by its major creditor, the Brooklyn Trust Company, which held the shares belonging to the Ebbets and Edward McKeever estates as collateral for its unpaid loans.[3]

Brooklyn Trust was a client of O'Malley's law firm, and bank president George McLaughlin asked him to organize the team's debt structure and corporate management. In 1943, O'Malley began serving as the Dodgers' general counsel. From there, it was a short step to buying part of the team, which he did in 1944 in partnership with Dodger president and general manager Branch Rickey. By the next year O'Malley, along with Rickey and pharmaceutical magnate John L. Smith, owned 75 percent of the Dodgers, in equal shares, with an option for a partner to match any outside bid for the purchase of a share. O'Malley was now in the baseball business.[4]

For O'Malley, who lacked the independent wealth of John L. Smith, baseball was truly a business. Unlike with other major league team owners, the team was his primary source of income.[5] This view of baseball as a business venture and not an avocation, hobby, or public service would govern O'Malley's conduct as a team owner for the rest of his career.[6]

The idea of the national pastime as a bottom-line affair ran counter to every received myth about it. According to this nostalgic and sentimental tale, players played for the love of the game and its American spirit of competition and fair play. Owners operated teams to bring the sport to the fans; profits, if they came, were only an incidental consideration. But O'Malley was a businessman, not a dilettante sportsman. Although he had loved the game from his childhood days—ironically, as a New York Giants fan—he understood that it was governed by the classic rules of capitalism: overhead, investment, payroll, profit, and loss. Every other baseball team owner understood this as well, of course, but given their independent wealth, they could pretend otherwise or at least avoid the subject.[7] O'Malley, by necessity, confronted it head-on. This did not help him with New York's sports media, who were perhaps the most active abettors of the for-the-love-of-the-game myth.

It also hurt his public image in comparison to that of his partner, Branch Rickey, who, despite his prowess as a nickel-squeezer, had successfully sold himself as a true baseball man, with goals loftier than merely improving his team's balance sheet. Rickey was a devout Methodist from Ohio. He had spent two decades running the St. Louis Cardinals organization, where he developed the game's first farm system as a source of major league talent, before joining the Dodgers as general manager in 1942. The avuncular Rickey viewed himself as something of a moral philosopher as well as a talent evaluator and deal maker, expounding on baseball's role in instilling American values of hard work and team play and advising young players that marriage would help their careers by stabilizing their personal lives. Rickey was also of course a civil rights pioneer, bringing Jackie Robinson to the Dodgers in 1947 with the approval of O'Malley and Smith.[8]

Rickey's public pose as a teacher, sage, and social visionary almost inevitably brought him into conflict with the more practically minded O'Malley. There were arguments over spending, as when Rickey's plan to invest in a Brooklyn Dodgers professional football team went awry and cost the partnership hundreds of thousands of dollars.[9] There were also clashes of a more personal nature, involving culture, religion, and outlook. Rickey was a midwestern Protestant, O'Malley an urban Catholic. Rickey wore his religious values on his sleeve, to the point of refusing to attend games on Sundays. O'Malley's faith was expressed in less public ways, and he was discomfited by what he considered Rickey's sanctimony. Rickey, in turn, was discomfited by O'Malley's apparent ease in the milieu of Democratic Party machine politics, where contacts and friends in high places could open doors in ways that merely being in the right could not.[10] But what may have doomed their working relationship was not their differences but their similarities. Each desired to be his own boss. Rickey had worked for many years under Cardinals ownership, not always comfortably, and had come to Brooklyn largely for the opportunity to run the entire organization. Moving up the ladder to partial team ownership, he believed, would solidify his management position.

But O'Malley had even less experience working for others than did Rickey, and he was just as determined to place his own stamp on the Dodgers. He had not come up in the game, as Rickey had, but O'Malley had built a legal and business career largely on his own and believed he had the ability to shape the direction of the franchise. He had in particular decided on the necessity of replacing Ebbets Field, a project in which Rickey was less interested.

By the late 1940s, the park was deteriorating physically. It featured dirty bathrooms, narrow aisles, rusting pillars, and a general down-at-the-heels raffishness that charmed only those who did not patronize it regularly.[11] Since it had been constructed to fit the contours of an already existing city block, the stadium lacked symmetry, with a deep left field topped by double-decked grandstands and a shorter right field with a thirty-eight-foot fence that played havoc with fly balls. Ticket sellers and ushers were notoriously surly, often behaving like panhandlers. Seats did not always face home plate, creating less-than-optimal sightlines. Poles also blocked many views. The park was built from ground level up, forcing upper-deck fans to walk up ramps to their seats.

Ebbets Field was also geographically inconvenient. No highway ran near it. Automobile parking was challenging, with only 700-odd spaces available. Even subway service was not as accessible as it could be, with the nearest line stopping four blocks from the ballpark. Ebbets Field held only 32,000 spectators, making it one of the smallest parks in the major leagues and particularly size-challenged in comparison with the homes of the Dodgers' New York City rivals, the Giants (Polo Grounds, capacity 55,000) and Yankees (Yankee Stadium, capacity 67,000). Almost from the moment he bought an interest in the Dodgers, it was clear to O'Malley that Ebbets Field had to be replaced. As early as 1946, he was writing to architect-engineer Emil Praeger—who would later design Dodger Stadium—requesting advice about "enlarging or replacing our present stadium."[12] In 1948, O'Malley began what would become a ten-year campaign for a new facility in Brooklyn, one that would lead circuitously and controversially to Los Angeles and Chavez Ravine.

The atmosphere was tense between O'Malley and Rickey by 1950, when the latter's contract as Dodger general manager came up for renewal. After John L. Smith's death from cancer that year, his widow inherited his partnership share and aligned herself with O'Malley. When it became clear to Rickey that he would be reduced to a partnership without power, he decided to make the best deal possible. Taking advantage of O'Malley's desire to control the club, Rickey solicited wealthy real estate man William Zeckendorf to bid on his share of the team, knowing O'Malley would be forced to match it. Zeckendorf's bid, never intended to be a serious one, was $1 million, almost three times what Rickey had originally paid for his share.[13] O'Malley would not forgive Rickey for this maneuver. But if he wanted the Dodgers, he would have to come up with the money. Liquidating some of his outside business investments to raise capital, he did so.[14] At an October 26, 1950, press conference, Walter O'Malley was introduced as the new president of the Brooklyn Dodgers. Rickey, about to join the Pittsburgh Pirates as their general manager, may have had O'Malley's money, but O'Malley had his team.[15]

O'Malley never pretended to know the intricacies of scouting, trades, the minor leagues, and the everyday work of assembling a winning on-field product. So, unlike Rickey, he delegated these functions to others. Veteran baseball man Emil "Buzzie" Bavasi was made responsible for major league operations as the Dodgers' general manager. Another astute talent evaluator, Fresco Thompson, was placed in charge of scouting and minor league development. Both men spent more than a quarter century in the Dodger organization. Their long tenures exemplified O'Malley's management style, which emphasized identifying talented personnel and giving them the independence to do their jobs over the long term, riding out ups and downs in the interest of stability and loyalty. During the almost thirty years he controlled the Dodgers, O'Malley employed only three general managers and three field managers. One of the managers, Walter Alston, served for twenty-three years on a series of one-year contracts. Vin Scully, the Dodgers' lead radio announcer, worked for the team all but one year of O'Malley's tenure as controlling owner.[16]

Organizational continuity translated into on-field success. During the first seven years of O'Malley's controlling ownership, all in Brooklyn, the Dodgers won four National League pennants (losing another in a playoff), as well as the franchise's only New York World Series.[17] The Dodger players, later immortalized as "the Boys of Summer" by the author Roger Kahn, were some of the most beloved athletes in New York City sports history, replete with affectionate nicknames—Pee Wee (shortstop Harold Reese), Campy (catcher Roy Campanella), Duke (center fielder Edwin Snider), and Oisk (pitcher Carl Erskine). The presence of Jackie Robinson gave the team an air of historic gravitas. Many baseball fans considered the Dodgers more compelling as losers than the all-conquering Yankees were as perennial winners.

The Brooklyn Dodgers, indeed, were the people's team of New York. The roots of its fan base were proudly and consciously in the city's working class. The Dodgers' tumbledown ballpark in an off-the-beaten-path section of an off-the-beaten-path borough stood in contrast to monumental Yankee Stadium, home of champions, and even to the Giants' Polo Grounds, which was located in Manhattan, the center of the American sports universe.

The Yankees were a patrician team, drawing fans from the city's professional and business classes and the wealthy suburbs. Yankee fans viewed their team as a proprietary trust, expecting to win the World Series each and every year. When they did—one out of every two years between 1923 and 1962—they were greeted not with rapture but smug satisfaction. "Rooting for the Yankees," quipped an observer in the 1950s, "is like rooting for U.S. Steel."[18]

The Giants and their fans also harbored lordly attitudes, especially toward their hometown National League rivals. They viewed the Dodgers as akin to country cousins desperately seeking to climb the social ladder. In the early decades of the twentieth century, before the rise of the Yankees, the Giants had dominated the New York sporting scene; the Yankees, in fact, had been their tenants at the Polo Grounds before opening their own stadium in 1923. Managed by the legendary John McGraw, the Giants were the toast of Manhattan's "smart set," a Broadway team that in the 1920s attracted the likes of New York's dapper mayor, "Gentleman Jimmy" Walker.

Even after McGraw's retirement in 1932, the Giants' mystique continued, with future Hall of Famers Bill Terry, Mel Ott, and Carl Hubbell leading the team to three National League pennants and one world championship in the 1930s. During this time, the Dodgers were largely irrelevant on the field and in the city's sports culture. When asked about the Dodgers' chances before the 1934 season, Terry replied sardonically, "Are they still in the National League?"[19] Although the Dodgers improved in the 1940s, the Giants continued to view them as upstarts who never could win the big one. The Dodgers' record of late-season futility appeared to bear this out. Between 1946 and 1954, the Dodgers featured four future Hall of Famers and their players earned ten All Star team selections. Yet during that period, they lost the National League pennant to the St. Louis Cardinals in a playoff in 1946; lost to the Yankees in the seventh and deciding game of the World Series in 1947; lost to the Yankees in five games in the World Series of 1949; lost the pennant to the Philadelphia Phillies on the last day of the 1950 season; lost the 1952 and 1953 World Series to the Yankees in seven and six games, respectively; and lost a pennant race to the Giants in 1954.

Worst of all was 1951. That year, the Dodgers led the Giants by a seemingly insurmountable thirteen games in mid-August, only to see the Giants win thirty-seven of their forty-four remaining games to overtake them. The teams were tied on the last day of the regular season; a two-out-of-three-game playoff would decide the pennant. The Giants took game one and the Dodgers game two. The champion would be crowned on October 3, 1951, at the Polo Grounds.

The Dodgers took a 4–1 lead into the bottom of the ninth. Three outs from the pennant, the unimaginable occurred. A lead-off single for the Giants and, after an out, another single and a double made the score 4–2 with runners on second and third. A pitching change brought in Ralph Branca—number 13—for the Dodgers. Giant third baseman Bobby Thomson hit Branca's second pitch on a low line drive into the left field seats for a pennant-clinching three-run homer, a blow that traveled into history as "the shot heard round the world." It was somehow fitting that the Brooklyn Dodgers would be on the losing end of what is generally considered to be the most dramatic moment in baseball history. It was especially humiliating to fall to the team's bitter interleague competitors.

Neither the Dodger players nor their fans knew at the time that the Giants had been surreptitiously using a telescope mounted in their center-field clubhouse at the Polo Grounds to steal signs from opposing catchers, passing them along to Giant batters through a series of buzzers and signals.[20] The advance knowledge afforded by this subterfuge gave the Giants a huge advantage when playing at home, and their 24–6 record at the Polo Grounds after the telescope began to be used testifies to its value.[21] For the Brooklyn Dodgers, the perpetual team of the underdog and of working-class New York, it seemed always to end this way—with a heartbreaking defeat at the hands of one of the other two local teams. As the 1955 season began, the Dodgers' recent history included five

World Series defeats at the hands of the Yankees and two losses to the Giants for the National League pennant.

That history made 1955 one of the most satisfying and redemptive seasons any sports team had experienced. After winning the pennant easily, the Dodgers squared off against the Yankees in the World Series for the third time in four years. With the Dodgers defeated in the first two games, it appeared that history would repeat itself yet again. But the Dodgers stormed back to win the Series in seven games. When left-hander Johnny Podres recorded the last out in a 2–0 complete-game shutout at Yankee Stadium on October 4, 1955, the Brooklyn Dodgers were world champions at last. In Brooklyn that night, the atmosphere rivaled that of V-E Day ten years earlier, as long-suffering fans thronged in the streets throwing confetti and banging pots and pans. "Who's a Bum!" crowed the front-page headline of New York's working-class newspaper, the *Daily News*, above a cartoon image of the Dodgers' mythical mascot, the Bum—a disheveled, virtually toothless hobo—sporting an ear-to-ear grin.[22]

Even this moment of catharsis was short-lived, as events surrounding the Dodgers' impending move began to crowd out lingering good feelings from the 1955 championship. A loss to the Yankees in the 1956 World Series appeared to bring a more familiar order to the New York baseball universe. Still, the bond between the Brooklyn Dodgers and their fans was a uniquely deep one, rooted in the ethnic neighborhoods of the borough where many Dodger players made their homes and in the working-class culture of the city. In addition, with six African American players on their roster by 1957—the Yankees had taken until 1955 to grudgingly integrate their squad—the Dodgers were the major league team most closely associated with racial egalitarianism. New York was a city of workers in the 1950s. The Brooklyn Dodgers were their team.

But while the Yankees were the team of the suites and the Dodgers that of the streets, this did not always translate into packed houses at Ebbets Field. Only during the first two years of O'Malley's Brooklyn ownership, 1951 and 1952, did the Dodgers lead the National League in home attendance; they were second three times

Walter O'Malley and his beloved wife, Kay, at Yankee Stadium for a 1955 World Series game. While Walter tended to daily Dodger business, Kay always kept a scorecard at games and had two team-owned airplanes christened in her honor. Photo courtesy of walteromalley.com.

and fourth and fifth the other two years.[23] In no year did they come close to surpassing the Yankees, who enjoyed the advantage of a more easily accessible stadium with more than twice as many seats as Ebbets Field.

Revenues from over-the-air television broadcasts of Dodger games enabled O'Malley to turn profits each year he was in Brooklyn, but an ominous threat appeared on the horizon in 1953. That year, the moribund Boston Braves became the first major league baseball franchise to move in over half a century, shifting to Milwaukee, a baseball-starved city that gave them a rapturous welcome. The Milwaukee Braves led the major leagues in attendance every year from 1953 to 1957, outdrawing even the Yankees despite playing in a ballpark with almost 25,000 fewer seats.[24]

Ebbets Field, September 29, 1956. Dodger shortstop Pee Wee Reese bats against Pittsburgh Pirates pitcher Bob Friend. Despite winning the National League pennant, the Dodgers averaged less than sixteen thousand fans per home game at the aging ballpark in 1956. Photo by Peter O'Malley, courtesy of walteromalley.com.

During that period, the Braves attracted almost twice the number of home fans as the Dodgers.[25]

The terms of the stadium deal the Braves received when they relocated to Milwaukee deeply concerned O'Malley. Milwaukee County Stadium was a 43,000-seat facility with approximately 11,000 more seats than Ebbets Field, giving the Braves a built-in advantage in ticket income. More fans in the stands meant more money spent on concessions, almost all of which also went into the Braves' coffers.[26] The Braves paid a total rental of $250,000 for 1953 and 1954.[27] County Stadium was directly accessible from a major highway and boasted a 10,000-space on-site parking lot.[28] The Braves also adopted a policy of not televising any of their games, which further stimulated attendance by making it necessary to go to County Stadium in order to see Milwaukee's favorite team.

The Braves' enormous financial success at County Stadium accentuated Ebbets Field's shortcomings. Looking uneasily to the future, O'Malley envisioned a time when the Braves would use their advantages in attendance and revenue to bury the Dodgers competitively. With the free market still governing player signings, the Braves could outbid the Dodgers for the best young prospects.[29] They could afford to hire the best scouts and front office personnel. They could spend whatever was necessary—and what the Dodgers could not afford to spend—to bring in the best managers and coaches at both the major and minor league levels. This increased spending would eventually allow the Braves to overtake the Dodgers on the field, using the revenue from multiple pennants and world championships to further consign the Brooklyn team to second-place status or worse.

From his vantage point at Ebbets Field, O'Malley could see this nightmarish scenario taking shape year by year. The Braves increased their home attendance by 600 percent in 1953 after they moved to Milwaukee.[30] They improved their won-loss record from 64–89 (seventh place) in 1952, their last year in Boston, to 92–62 (second place) the next year in Milwaukee.[31] They followed with a third-place finish in 1954 (85–69) that left them three games behind the Dodgers and second place in 1955 (85–69). They lost the pennant to the Dodgers on the last day of the regular season in 1956 (92–62).[32] In 1957, the Braves bested the Dodgers by eleven games in winning the National League pennant (95–69) and defeated the Yankees to win the World Series. Thanks to a new stadium on favorable rental terms in a new city desperate for major league baseball, the Braves had gone from next-to-last place and an average of 3,650 fans per home game to a world championship and baseball's best attendance in the space of five years.[33] Even before that 1957 World Series, O'Malley could see the challenges facing him. He now viewed a new Brooklyn stadium as a matter of competitive survival.

It was clear that any road to that new stadium would run through the good offices of Robert Moses, who in 1950s New York City determined what would be built, who would build it, and where it would be built. Moses had famously combined a series of appointive administrative positions heading public authorities and agencies with the power to issue bonds, collect revenues, condemn and sell land, and award construction contracts. Moses had never won an election on his own. In his only run for public office, in the 1934 New York governor's race, he had been defeated decisively. But the wily Moses packaged his bureaucratic positions—by the 1950s he served simultaneously as chairman of the Triborough Bridge and Tunnel Authority, the New York City Parks Commissioner, the New York State Power Commission chairman, and the New York City coordinator of construction—into a position of command and influence that outweighed that of any elected official. Governors, senators, and mayors bent to his will.

Perhaps Moses's most potent source of power in the 1950s came from his control of the administration of what was known as Title I of the Federal Housing Act of 1949. Under Title I, local governments would use federal funds to condemn blighted or slum properties, then sell the land at a subsidized price to private developers for projects that would serve or relate to a public purpose or use, such as schools, hospitals, roads, parks, or housing. Residents of these areas, often members of minority groups, would, at least theoretically, be relocated to better accommodations elsewhere.

As New York City's Title I coordinator, Moses had almost untrammeled power to greenlight a project. This enabled him to build a personal machine of banks, construction firms, architects, and real estate firms beholden to him for business and referrals.[34] While not a grafter himself, Moses still fell prey to the all-too-human impulse to reward friends and allies. He developed a coterie of favored individuals and entities to serve his interests and receive his largesse. Often these friends of Bob Moses reflected his own culture and outlook, which were very much in the good-government mode of public-service-oriented reformers. Moses was born Jewish but identified as an Anglo-Saxon Protestant. He had fought his earliest political battles against a venal Tammany Hall Democratic machine that pursued its own narrowly selfish goals without regard for the public good. Moses never lost his distaste for those he considered vulgar and grasping Tammany politicians. While there is no indication that Moses was bigoted against Irish Catholics, it was well known that the Tammany machine was dominated by them.

It was thus almost predictable that Walter O'Malley would have a great deal of trouble convincing Robert Moses to help him build a new stadium for the Brooklyn Dodgers. O'Malley was an outsider to Moses, not part of his club of friendly colleagues. O'Malley was an Irish Catholic. He had connections to Tammany, both through his father and via the contacts he had established over the course of his years as a local attorney and businessman. Moses, moreover, was notoriously uninterested in spectator sports. He considered them a waste of time, preferring more active and participatory forms of recreation such as swimming.

Perhaps most important, Moses viewed a privately owned baseball stadium as just that—a private enterprise—and thus inappropriate for a Title I project that would advance a public purpose. By the early 1950s, O'Malley had decided on a parcel of land at the intersection of Atlantic and Flatbush Avenues near downtown Brooklyn, about two miles from Ebbets Field, as the site of his proposed new ballpark. The location was perfect for mass transit. The Brooklyn terminal of the Long Island Railroad was under the street, and nine subway lines stopped there. O'Malley planned to construct the stadium at his own expense, but he clearly would not be able to afford the cost of acquiring the land. Unlike Charles Ebbets, who had been able to buy up the parcels he needed without letting slip his purposes, O'Malley had already tipped his hand about his desire to locate the new Dodger stadium on the Atlantic-Flatbush properties. Only Robert Moses, through the use of Title I condemnation, could get him the land he needed at a price he could even remotely afford. There were perhaps ten men in New York City at the time with the financial resources to purchase the entire Atlantic-Flatbush property out of their own pockets, and O'Malley was not one of them. Even a bank would not have been willing to lend him the sum necessary to purchase the land. But from the beginning of their negotiations in 1953,

Moses was implacable: the stadium was a private project, not a public one, and there would be no Title I funding for it.

O'Malley's need for Moses's support put him in the unaccustomed position of a supplicant. For a man who prided himself on being the master of his own destiny, this was undoubtedly difficult. O'Malley controlled the Dodgers, but not the surrounding political environment, in which Moses stood preeminent. And because Moses disdained the idea that a privately owned ballpark constituted a public purpose and also disdained the civic value of baseball itself, the result was a quest for a new Dodger home in Brooklyn that at times seemed close enough to touch but was ultimately out of reach. "We tried for ten long years to acquire land, which we were going to pay for to build a stadium which we were going to pay for," O'Malley recalled ruefully years later, "all without success."[35]

Further complicating O'Malley's stadium plans was the inhospitable political culture of 1950s-era New York City. Beginning in the New Deal years of the Fiorello La Guardia mayoral administration, the city's public sector had expanded to become a driving force in the municipal economy. By the 1950s, New York had more government jobs than any other American city except Washington, D.C.[36] Along with confidence in the efficacy of public authority to govern and manage came ambivalence toward private enterprise and those who engaged in it.[37] Making matters worse for O'Malley was his application of business principles to the management of a baseball club that was perceived by its fans and by the media as constituting a public trust.

Romanticized notions of baseball as a pristine American sport notwithstanding, O'Malley's business-oriented approach to the game made sense. Indeed, it could be argued that it offered more benefits to Dodger supporters than one that was less profit-driven and more tied to emotion. Measured by results on the field, O'Malley delivered value for the fan dollar and outperformed the more popular baseball men who preceded him as Dodger president. Branch Rickey won two National League pennants during his time in Brooklyn (1942–50) and Larry MacPhail (1938–42)

one. O'Malley won four in only seven years at the helm in Brooklyn, adding the franchise's first world championship in 1955. His
understanding that the Dodgers had to be run as a business was a
major contribution to that success, as well as an acknowledgment
of financial and competitive reality. But Robert Moses, who invariably professed to represent the public against the interests of business and capital, could leverage economic antipathies dating back
to at least the New Deal era to deny O'Malley the Atlantic-Flatbush
site for his stadium. Moses's narrow understanding of the idea of a
public use or purpose ran parallel to that of the city's political culture. The fact that O'Malley stood to gain financially from a new
Brooklyn stadium loomed large enough to outweigh the public
benefits—taxes, jobs, entertainment, infrastructure—that could
accrue from it.

After Moses's Title I rebuff, O'Malley and New York city and
state officials tried another tack in 1956 with the creation of the
Brooklyn Sports Center Authority as an alternative means of
financing a new stadium. Approved by Governor Averell Harriman
and nominally supported by New York City mayor Robert Wagner and Brooklyn borough president John Cashmore, the authority would conduct an engineering and architectural study of the
Atlantic-Flatbush property, determine the cost and feasibility of
constructing a stadium there, and issue bonds in order to finance
it. But Moses hampered the work of the authority board and made
sure that it received minimal funding. He even influenced the
content of the engineering report, which estimated the cost of
land acquisition and stadium construction at $20 million and
annual bond interest at $2.5 million, both unaffordable.[38] Moses
further dampened enthusiasm by stating unequivocally that the
authority bonds were unsalable. As the city's most prominent
marketer of municipal bonds through his Title I and other building projects, Moses was considered the authoritative voice on the
subject. By the summer of 1957 the Sports Center Authority plan
had petered out.

Moses also shot down a separate proposal by the New York
City Corporation Counsel to condemn the Atlantic-Flatbush properties for the stadium as a slum area, employing his familiar lack-

of-public-purpose grounds. Moses's best offer to O'Malley was a municipally constructed stadium in the Flushing Meadows section of Queens near the site of the 1939 World's Fair, in which the Dodgers would be tenants. O'Malley visited the area and engaged in some preliminary niceties with Moses, but it was clear that he had no interest in a ballpark he would not own and which would not even be located in Brooklyn. If he had to leave Brooklyn, O'Malley averred, it would not matter if he was "five miles or 3000 miles" away.[39]

By 1957, the possibility of being three thousand miles away from Brooklyn was a very real one, thanks to the efforts of two politicians from Los Angeles, California, whose differing political allegiances did not stand in the way of a common vision for their city. Norris Poulson, a Republican former congressman who had been elected mayor in 1953, represented "Downtown," the city's power center of corporate, financial, media, retail, and real estate interests. Downtown leaders desired a major league baseball team both as a symbolic marker for Los Angeles's status as a growth-oriented, world-class metropolis and as a means of revitalizing downtown itself, which was run-down in areas and lacked the cultural and leisure resources of other notable American cities.

Rosalind Wyman, a liberal Democrat from the "Westside," a center for the city's entertainment, building and loan, construction, and sportswear industries, with a sizable Jewish population, had been elected to the City Council, also in 1953, at the age of twenty-two. Wyman was the youngest member in that body's history and its first woman in almost forty years. One of Wyman's campaign planks had been bringing major league baseball to Los Angeles. Once in office, she made this a top priority. Like Poulson, Wyman envisioned a civic infrastructure for Los Angeles that would complement and reinforce its post–World War II economic and demographic expansion. That Poulson and Wyman, a business Republican and a labor Democrat, could unite in the effort to attract a major league team to Los Angeles spoke to their common agenda of modernization and growth for a city that, in their view, required civic institutions that would match its power and influence. Another point of agreement between the two may also have been of significance: unlike Robert Moses, Wyman and Poulson were both baseball fans.

O'Malley's first contact with Los Angeles came in 1955, when Wyman attempted to arrange a meeting with the Dodger owner in New York. O'Malley, who was still hopeful he could reach an accommodation with Moses, told her he was happy in his home city. Wyman left without seeing him.[40] In October 1956, O'Malley and the Dodgers stopped off in Los Angeles on their way to visit Japan after the World Series. County supervisor Kenneth Hahn sought to interest O'Malley in a move to Los Angeles, but the Dodger owner instead held a press conference at which he reiterated his intention to remain in New York and expressed confidence in the progress of negotiations for a new Brooklyn stadium.[41] But by the next year, O'Malley was frustrated enough with the pace of those negotiations to agree to see a delegation of Los Angeles city officials during the Dodgers' 1957 spring training camp at Vero Beach, Florida. There O'Malley sketched out what it would take to get him to move west. He asked for what New York had thus far refused to offer: affordable land upon which to construct his own stadium.

O'Malley's acquisition in February 1957 of Los Angeles's Wrigley Field from the Chicago Cubs in a minor league affiliate trade gave him a local property that could be used as consideration for any land deal. It now became a race to the finish for both Los Angeles and New York, as O'Malley negotiated with both simultaneously. It was clear that the city offering the land O'Malley desired would win the Dodgers. O'Malley's heart was with New York. He had built his life and career in the city and had the native New Yorker's outsized pride in it. O'Malley was almost completely unfamiliar with Los Angeles except as a potential business market. But he would go with the first city that met his terms. In May 1957, he flew to Los Angeles for more discussions. During a helicopter ride over the city in search of possible stadium sites, O'Malley observed a large expanse of sparsely occupied land close to downtown. It was known as Chavez Ravine, and he decided almost immediately it was where he wanted to build his Los Angeles ballpark.

Los Angeles mayor Norris Poulson and *Los Angeles Examiner* sportswriter Bob Hunter survey Chavez Ravine for a proposed Dodger ballpark, March 13, 1957. University of Southern California, USC Digital Library, *Los Angeles Examiner* Photographs Collection.

O'Malley was not aware of the Ravine's history. Home to a tightly knit, traditional Mexican American community of some twelve hundred families, it had passed the first half of the twentieth century largely ignored by the rest of Los Angeles, despite its location about a mile from City Hall and the downtown area.[42] Its isolation ended in 1949, when it was designated as the site of a public housing project and all but a handful of its residents removed and dispersed. But after a Red scare–influenced campaign against the housing project as "socialistic," the newly inaugurated mayor, Poulson, canceled it in 1953, leaving the Ravine empty except for a small number of families who refused to leave. The city of Los Angeles acquired the property from the federal government in 1955. It had not decided on a use for the land when O'Malley flew over it in May 1957.

As the summer of 1957 proceeded, events began to rush to a conclusion. In June, O'Malley was called to testify before the U.S. House of Representatives Judiciary Committee's Antimonopoly Subcommittee, which was considering challenges to major league baseball's exemption from antitrust laws. Under sharp questioning from the committee chair, Representative Emanuel Celler of

Brooklyn, O'Malley refused to say whether his team would still be in New York in 1958, although he reemphasized his intention to build a new Brooklyn ballpark at his own expense. O'Malley raised Celler's ire when he expressed satisfaction at the Dodgers' financial success.[43] Hearing this violation of the sport's unwritten taboo against public references to baseball as a business, an angry Celler jeered at O'Malley: "I glory in your profits. . . . I hope you make twice as much next year."[44] The hearings ended with baseball's antitrust exemption intact but even more uncertainty about O'Malley's intentions.

It is probable that at this point O'Malley himself did not know. The chances were now greater that Los Angeles would offer him the deal he wanted. But if a way could be found around Moses and if the Atlantic-Flatbush land could made available at a price he could afford, he would stay in New York. His hometown was familiar territory. Los Angeles was terra incognita. To a man who wished to be in control of his surroundings, New York—if it came through—was his preferred option.

The New York option became more complicated on August 19, when the New York Giants announced they would play in San Francisco beginning in 1958. O'Malley's role in this decision has long been the subject of debate.[45] The Giants' stadium situation was even worse than that of the Dodgers. The Polo Grounds were antiquated, difficult to access by automobile, and located in a deteriorating section of Harlem in Upper Manhattan. Despite featuring Willie Mays, one of the most exciting players in baseball history, the Giants drew only 629,000 fans in 1956, ranking last in the National League.[46] Before the 1957 season, Giants owner Horace Stoneham told O'Malley that he was seriously considering moving his team to Minneapolis, where the Giants had a minor league affiliate. O'Malley urged Stoneham to reconsider and instead investigate a possible move to the West Coast, where the Giants-Dodgers rivalry might be rekindled in a new setting. This made obvious sense, and the flirtation of the two teams with San Francisco and Los Angeles proceeded on roughly parallel tracks in 1957. While O'Malley did not push Stoneham to San Francisco, he did offer advice and furnish governmental contacts that facilitated the consummation of the move. In contrast to Los Angeles, San Francisco agreed to construct a municipal stadium for the Giants to rent.

Stoneham's August 19 announcement did not guarantee that the Dodgers would also move. On May 28, the National League owners had passed a resolution granting the Dodgers and Giants permission to relocate to the West Coast if they gave notice by October 1 and if they moved together.[47] This meant that in the event O'Malley chose to remain in New York, the Giants' move to San Francisco would likely be nullified and the team presumably transferred to the more geographically accessible Minneapolis instead. But one way or the other, the Giants were leaving New York, and this fact would alter the circumstances under which O'Malley would make his own decision to stay or remain. If he stayed in New York, he would have a monopoly on National League baseball as the only team in town. If he departed, he could employ the already existing Los Angeles–San Francisco rivalry to pick up where he had left off in New York. As he pondered his future after August 19, O'Malley could reassure himself that he would have a degree of investment protection no matter what city he chose.

But which city? O'Malley had set his own internal deadline with the sale of Ebbets Field to developer Marvin Kratter in 1956; it would belong to Kratter beginning in 1958. In 1956, the Dodgers had played seven home games in Jersey City's Roosevelt Stadium, a not-so-subtle means of emphasizing Ebbets Field's inadequacies. O'Malley continued the practice during the 1957 season. The pressure was now clearly on New York.

In July 1957, Los Angeles appointed Harold McClellan, a local businessman and former undersecretary of commerce in the Eisenhower administration, as its chief stadium contract negotiator. O'Malley now could bargain with a single individual who possessed the authority to speak for Los Angeles. This arrangement offered an advantage over New York, where Moses held power but was effectively refusing to negotiate with O'Malley, leaving the task to an uncoordinated group of New York officials, including Mayor Wagner, Brooklyn borough president Cashmore, city comptroller

Lawrence Gerosa, and City Corporation counsel Peter Campbell Brown, among others.

By early September, McClellan's offer had taken shape. Los Angeles would exchange approximately 300 acres of Chavez Ravine land for Wrigley Field. The city already owned 185 acres of this land, and promised to use its best efforts to acquire the rest for transfer to the Dodgers. The city of Los Angeles would contribute $2 million for land excavation and grading, and Los Angeles County would allocate $2.74 million from its motor vehicle fund for stadium access roads. O'Malley would build a new stadium and construct a public recreation area on a portion of the Chavez Ravine land, both at his own expense. The Los Angeles County Board of Supervisors ratified the offer of access roads on September 17. The remainder of the deal would require approval by the Los Angeles City Council to become official. That body met on September 16 to consider it.

With New York seemingly out of options, a last-minute possibility emerged from an unlikely source. Nelson Rockefeller, the most well-known and politically ambitious of the dynastic family's heirs, was considering a run for the New York State governorship in 1958. Concerned about the possibility of the Dodgers leaving town and mindful of the benefits in publicity and goodwill he would enjoy if he saved the day, Rockefeller stepped forward on September 10 with a plan to buy the Atlantic-Flatbush property after the city condemned it and lease it to the Dodgers at no cost for twenty years, after which the team would buy it. The Dodgers would build a stadium on the site with their own funds.

The estimated condemnation price of the land was $8 million. Rockefeller offered $2 million toward it. Moses and members of the city's Board of Estimate, which was required to approve all municipal land use measures, criticized the plan, arguing that the $6 million loss New York would need to absorb on the transaction was unaffordable.[48] Rockefeller then sweetened his offer to $3 million, but O'Malley responded that the numbers did not add up for him. After financing the new stadium himself and paying real estate taxes on it for 20 years, he would not have enough money to buy the land from Rockefeller at the end of that period.

And without the land, he would essentially be what he had resolved not to be: a tenant. Rockefeller would have to further increase his bid on the Atlantic-Flatbush property to make the transaction work. When he did not do so, the deal sank, although the chance remained that the legendarily deep-pocketed candidate-to-be could resuscitate it with a richer offer. As things stood, however, the way was clear for Los Angeles to decide if it would give O'Malley what he needed. The last Dodger home game of the 1957 season was played at Ebbets Field on September 24 in a funereal atmosphere. While no official announcement had yet been made, it was obvious that the pendulum had swung toward Los Angeles.

2

WALTER O'MALLEY'S LOS ANGELES

But even so, O'Malley hesitated. As late as October 7, he was still not sure what he wanted to do. The Rockefeller proposal had smacked of grandstanding, the work of a famous heir with his eye on elective office. But it would have achieved O'Malley's primary goal of remaining in Brooklyn, and for the rest—owning his stadium, siting it at Atlantic-Flatbush, financing it—perhaps there were the seeds of a workable deal there. All it would take was more money, and Nelson Rockefeller certainly had plenty of that. With Stoneham and the Giants gone, the National League portion of the city was his alone if he so chose. Marvin Kratter would be happy to lease him Ebbets Field through 1960 while a new ballpark was constructed. O'Malley had received a reprieve of sorts on October 1, when the National League extended by two weeks its deadline for him to formally announce his intention to move. He now had exactly eight days to make up his mind.

On September 16, the Los Angeles City Council had met for a preliminary vote on the agreement that would transfer the land at Chavez Ravine to the Dodgers, in exchange for the Wrigley Field property O'Malley had acquired from the Chicago Cubs in February, and commit the use of municipal funds to upgrade roads in

Los Angeles city councilman John Holland speaks against the Dodger contract, September 30, 1957. University of Southern California, USC Digital Library, *Los Angeles Examiner* Photographs Collection. Photographer: Lou Mack.

the area. A contentious debate ensued. Councilman John Holland, a fiscal conservative who represented the equally parsimonious white-middle-class-homeowner-dominated Eagle Rock section, attacked the deal as a "giveaway." Citing the disparity in land values between the Chavez Ravine and Wrigley properties, he charged that O'Malley was receiving public assistance for a private undertaking. This position echoed that of Robert Moses in New York. Holland was outnumbered on the City Council by the Wyman-led pro-baseball faction, and the motion for preliminary approval of the agreement carried by a vote of 11 to 3. Holland himself voted aye as a strategic maneuver to ensure that another vote on the contract would occur.

On September 30 the agreement was brought before the council for final approval. Since it called for the spending of public monies, council rules required a unanimous vote for passage. When it failed to gain unanimity that day after more contentious debate—as well as a telephoned bomb threat—the deal was scheduled for one last vote on October 7. While approval would now require only a two-thirds vote of the fourteen council members (one, Edward Roybal, was out of the country), October 7 was Los Angeles's day of decision. Any chance of attracting the Dodgers hinged on ten yes votes. Five no's would kill the contract and keep the team in Brooklyn, at least for the time being. Holland's strategy on that day was a filibuster. He read a lengthy series of statements into the record in the hope of dragging the proceedings into adjournment. A no decision was effectively a decision to reject. Holland had three committed negative votes in addition to his own, so his side was one vote short. As he droned on, spectators arrayed on either side of the council gallery according to their positions on the contract cheered and heckled. The meeting, broadcast live on television, brought the city to a virtual standstill as the drama played out.

Although he did not see it in person, Walter O'Malley was of course following the council session with great interest. He was in Milwaukee on October 7, in attendance at County Stadium as the Braves played the Yankees in Game 5 of the World Series. There was much irony in this setting. The Milwaukee ballpark was one of the major reasons O'Malley was on the verge of moving the Dodgers. The deal the Braves had received to play in County Stadium in 1953 had made O'Malley fear for the future of his team and lent his quest for a new ballpark in Brooklyn much of its urgency. Now he sat in County Stadium watching the sum of his fears play out, as the young Braves, having bested his aging Dodger roster for the 1957 National League pennant, defeated the Yankees 1–0 to take a three-games-to-two lead in the World Series. Three days later, they would become world champions. If O'Malley mused about what had brought him to this day of reckoning, the scene on the field at County Stadium would remind him.

By the time the game ended, it was early afternoon in Los Angeles. O'Malley flew from Milwaukee back to New York while the council meeting continued. As it dragged into the evening hours, O'Malley arrived at his home in Amityville still unsure of his final destination. In Los Angeles a nervous Poulson pulled Wyman off the council chamber floor to confer in his office. Twelve of the fourteen votes were set, eight in favor of the contract and four opposed. Two wavered, including Karl Rundberg, whose support for the contract was particularly tenuous. O'Malley and the council now resembled romantic suitors, skittishly probing the other's intentions. Poulson and Wyman knew that the undecided council members would benefit from O'Malley's unequivocal declaration that he would formally accept the contract if it was approved. Poulson begged Wyman to call O'Malley to get this commitment. When they reached him in Amityville, she pressed him for a definitive answer.[1]

Even at this late hour, O'Malley could not offer it. He had already compromised his negotiating position by renouncing half of the oil and mineral rights at Chavez Ravine and promising to construct a public recreation area on a portion of the land and pay for its upkeep for twenty years. But there was more to his hesitation than a desire to drive a better bargain. Now that he was on the precipice, did he really want to jump? With the exception of his years at Culver Military Academy in Indiana and the University of Pennsylvania, he had never lived anywhere but New York. Despite his interactions with Los Angeles's public officials over the preceding two years, he was strikingly unfamiliar with the city. O'Malley had not set foot in Los Angeles until October 1956, and the total of his three trips to the city came to about ten days. He and Rosalind Wyman, with whom he was discussing the future of his professional and personal life, had never met in person.

Who were these Los Angeles politicians, with their expansive promises and glib beguilements? Did he really know them? Could they be trusted? What of John Holland, the contract's chief opponent on the City Council? How many other public officials also believed that the Dodger Stadium project failed to rise to the level of a public purpose? How many ordinary citizens shared their views? What was the political terrain in Los Angeles like? Was there a Robert Moses in the city, an unelected power broker who could crush his plans on a whim? O'Malley had promised to build the new stadium with his own money. He would clearly have to borrow to do so. Could he get financing? And where would he play in 1958? Wrigley Field was even smaller than Ebbets Field, and the Los Angeles Memorial Coliseum and Pasadena Rose Bowl were massive football stadiums. Inadequate as Ebbets Field might have been, he knew he could open the 1958 season there if he chose, just as he had in years past.

There was also the matter of New York itself. Did O'Malley really want to relinquish the most important city in the nation and his sport's largest market? A mayoral election loomed in a month. Every elected New York City official, including the City Council president, the controller, all five borough presidents, and the entire council, would face the voters on November 5. If O'Malley chose to make the inaction and disorganization of these officials a campaign issue, would enough voters pressure enough politicians worried about keeping their jobs to come up with an acceptable stadium deal? Did he wish to take a chance on this, going around Robert Moses directly to the people of New York? Wherever O'Malley looked, in fact, he was taking a chance. And as far as Los Angeles was concerned, he had run out of time.

On the telephone from Poulson's office, Wyman asked O'Malley what she could tell her fellow council members about his intentions. His reply captured the ambivalence that had marked his negotiations with both cities over the past two years. "You know, Mrs. Wyman," O'Malley said, "we're New Yorkers, and I believe in New York. I don't know if Major League Baseball will succeed in Los Angeles. I'm a New Yorker, and if I could get my deal in New York, I would stay."[2] But then, switching gears, he told Wyman that he thought Los Angeles was a good fit for him and his team.[3] O'Malley ended the conversation on a note of indecision: "I don't know if we will come."[4]

Some observers have interpreted O'Malley's backing and filling as evidence of his wiliness, of his ability to play one side in a negotiation against the other. But it is more likely that as he faced the most important decision of his professional life and peered into the unknown, he simply did not know what to do. Just as a straight line is the shortest distance between two points and the logical principle known as Occam's razor states that simpler explanations of phenomena should prevail over more complicated ones when they are of relatively equal probative weight, it may be best to allow O'Malley's words on October 7, 1957, to speak for themselves.

Over the course of the preceding ten years, he had made his goals clear: a privately constructed stadium built on affordable land, preferably located in Brooklyn. His agenda was no different on October 7, 1957, than it had been on October 7, 1947; only the means to his desired ends were unclear. This accounts for the speculation that has swirled around O'Malley's "true" motives.

It is tempting to reason backward from an outcome we already know, to trace what appears to be a road of inevitability leading toward it. Viewing O'Malley's actions in this way, one might argue that he had planned to move to Los Angeles all along, since we know that he eventually arrived there. But events and the emotions that drive them are much less determined than we believe. Life courses swing on hinges, contingent and uncertain. Walter O'Malley knew what he wanted but not how to get it. This could have led him down any number of paths, including one that circled back to New York, right up to the moment of his conversation with Rosalind Wyman on the evening of October 7, 1957. To argue otherwise reduces history to a series of certitudes at odds with the vagaries of circumstance and experience. Assuming that O'Malley had planned in secret to move to Los Angeles years in advance and that his negotiations with New York were thus a sham accords him substantially more influence over events and individuals than he possessed. If O'Malley's ambiguous exchange with Wyman proves anything, it is this.

After she rang off with O'Malley, a shaken Wyman went back to her office to collect herself. A few minutes later she returned to the council chamber, unsure of her strategy. She clearly did not have the commitment she had hoped for. On the floor, the debate went on. Holland, who would dearly have loved to hear Wyman's conversation with O'Malley, was still holding forth on the contract's "giveaway" features. As Holland spoke, Wyman wondered if he would ask an obvious question: had the Dodger owner stated unequivocally that he would move his team to Los Angeles if the contract was approved? If Holland asked, Wyman would be forced to admit that O'Malley had hesitated, and the entire deal could collapse. All it would take was one vote. But amazingly, neither Holland nor any of the contract's opponents thought to ask this question. It became lost in the fog of parliamentary battle, the swirl of statement and counterstatement, charge and countercharge that runs through legislative floor debates. To her immense relief, Wyman never had to answer it.[5] This unasked question is another example of the contingencies of human choice that dot history's landscape. Holland gave no explanation for his omission. It simply did not occur to him or any of his allies to ask. On such vagaries do events turn.

After hours more of debate that stretched into the Los Angeles evening, Wyman, still unsure of the final tally, called for the contract to be brought to a vote. She held her breath as the wavering Rundberg was called on. He voted aye. Two other previously undecided council members, Everett Burkhalter and Ransom Callicott, did the same. The final vote was 10 to 4. By the slimmest of margins, Los Angeles had its deal.

But did it have O'Malley? The city would have to wait one more day to find out. On the morning of October 8 the Dodger owner met with his fellow team stockholders in Brooklyn and formally approved the move west. At four o'clock that afternoon, Dodger publicity director Red Patterson walked into the World Series headquarters press room at New York's Waldorf-Astoria Hotel and passed reporters a single-sentence announcement that brought an end to Walter O'Malley's ten-year campaign for a new ballpark in his home town as well as his team's sixty-eight seasons in Brooklyn: "In view of the action of the Los Angeles City Council yesterday and in accordance with the resolution of the National League made October first, the stockholders and directors of the Brooklyn Baseball Club have today met and unanimously agreed that the necessary steps be taken to draft the Los Angeles territory."[6]

O'Malley had made up his mind at last. Almost a century earlier, in the midst of the Civil War, Abraham Lincoln had averred, referring to his emancipation policies, "I claim not to have controlled events, but confess plainly that events have controlled me."[7] The same could have been said of O'Malley. With a defined goal but a multitude of possible ways to reach it, he was only partially the

Mayor Norris Poulson celebrates City Council approval of the Dodger contract, October 7, 1957. University of Southern California, USC Digital Library, *Los Angeles Examiner* Photographs Collection. Photographer: Gray.

master of events. His time to come in Los Angeles would bear witness to the power of others over his plans and dreams.

In any event, it was done. The reaction in New York was largely resigned, although the city's sporting press was greatly incensed. Red Smith, the *Herald-Tribune* columnist who was the most respected sportswriter in the city, walked out in disgust as a bumbling statement by National League president Warren Giles was read following the distribution of Patterson's press release. Giles, an executive of limited imagination, incongruously sought to portray his league as "progressive" for permitting the move. "The transfer of the Dodgers and Giants," he averred magnanimously, "means that two more great American municipalities are to have major league baseball without denying another city of the privilege."[8] This was of course cold comfort to Dodger and Giant fans who would apparently now be expected to support the rival Yankees, an almost unthinkable proposition whatever Giles's fantasies may have been. The next day an angry Smith accused O'Malley in print of "operating like a dealer of three-card monte," who moved his team "in order to latch onto a big chunk of property near the heart of Los Angeles."[9] Dick Young of the *Daily News*, the Dodger beat writer with the largest following in the city and thus the most to lose from the team's departure, called O'Malley a "momentous manipulator" with "an acute case of greed" who would be departing for the West Coast "a rich man and a despised man."[10]

But Mayor Wagner, whose reelection bid faced a potential voter backlash for losing the Dodgers, was more sanguine. A methodical—some would say slow—decision maker, he simply announced his intention to form a committee to bring another National League team to New York.[11] Wagner was brief and businesslike, offering little hint of the tumult and controversy that had preceded the Dodgers' move. In time, the events surrounding the team's departure would give rise to a belief that the entire city was plunged into despair by the news. Certainly there was a sense of betrayal among Dodger fans and in the borough of Brooklyn generally. But it appeared that the journalists, many of whom had a professional stake in the matter, were angrier than the public at large.

What almost all New Yorkers seemed to share was an unwillingness to hold public officials accountable for the Dodgers' move. Robert Moses certainly had as much to do with the city's loss of the team as Walter O'Malley. But in 1957, Moses towered over New York like a colossus, almost impervious to criticism. He carefully cultivated the media, which, led by the *New York Times*, bathed him in adulation. Thanks to decades of positive and often fawning press coverage, Moses's reputation was that of New York's quintessential public servant, selfless and incorruptible. When Moses spoke, it was always with the voice of one immune to the temptations of self-interest. While in reality he pursued his interests vigorously and ruthlessly, much of Moses's maneuvering was conducted behind the scenes, hidden from his adoring public's view.

Moses also understood the city's political and economic culture and used it to his advantage in the Dodger controversy. Despite the fact that he dealt with the city's private sector virtually every day—real estate interests, construction firms, building subcontractors, financial institutions—Moses successfully portrayed himself as a steadfast champion of the public weal. He capitalized on the mistrust of self-interested businessmen that had taken hold in New York during the 1930s and 1940s as, for the first time in the city's history, a mayor (Fiorello La Guardia, in office 1934–45) employed the power of government on behalf of workers, consumers, and racially and ethnically marginalized groups to blunt the force of class injustice.

No American city featured a more powerful and influential left-wing politics during this time. New York was headquarters to the Communist Party of the United States of America, whose membership peaked at 85,000 in 1942, and which during the Popular Front period (1935–39) and World War II years established beachheads in New York's artistic, intellectual, labor, professional, and religious communities.[12] Socialism was a powerful force as well, with substantial constituencies in the city's Jewish and Italian communities. Socialist Party head Norman Thomas, who had received almost 900,000 votes in the 1932 presidential election, was prominent in New York City politics.[13] New York was also a major hub of the nation's labor movement. During the 1930s and 1940s it boasted more industrial jobs than any other American city and was, at least in the private sector, highly organized. The Amalgamated Clothing Workers of America, International Ladies' Garment Workers Union, International Brotherhood of Teamsters, International Longshoremen's Association, and skilled trade unions in the building and construction sectors all played major roles in New York City's economic and political life.

But there was more to this left-wing environment than institutional power and influence. A class-conscious labor culture had developed in the city during the La Guardia years, one deeply suspicious of business and its motives. In this culture, private enterprise was viewed not as a wealth creator but an exploiter.[14] One did not have to be a Marxist in Fiorello La Guardia's New York to regard capital with hostility. In no other American city, with the possible exception of Washington, D.C., was government accorded such respect and gratitude as the protector of the average citizen from the rapacious boss. The rise of government employment combined with that of the civil service examination system was creating both a permanent constituency and a powerful rationale for the public sector as an active and engaged force in the life of the city.

Thus developed a public culture to intersect with the culture of labor in New York. Robert Moses had been the beneficiary of both. He had cultivated the idea that the public sector he embodied could "get things done" in New York. He also embodied the argument that if freed from the profit-centered motives of the private sector, public-spirited administrators could work efficiently and effectively for the good of all. Businessmen wanted what was best for them. Moses wanted what was best for New York. Public culture, yoked to New York's class-conscious labor culture with its suspicion of businessmen and private enterprise, created a powerful civic impulse. During the Dodger stadium dispute it enabled Moses to caricature O'Malley as a self-interested "boss." It enabled Moses to present himself, in contrast, as the epitome of public-spirited moral rectitude. Moses's skill at self-definition, combined with the weight of New York's labor/public culture, almost preordained who the victor in his battle with O'Malley would be.

Wagner and other city officials need not have feared that New York's electorate would exact revenge for their failure to keep the Dodgers in Brooklyn. Less than a month after O'Malley announced his departure, Wagner was reelected overwhelmingly, besting his opponent by almost a million votes.[15] It would be the largest margin of victory of his three mayoral campaigns. Wagner won Brooklyn with 75 percent of the ballots.[16] Even Brooklyn borough president John Cashmore, who would have been the most logical scapegoat for losing the Dodgers, was reelected easily. Incumbents won three of the four remaining borough president races as well as the other two citywide elections for Council President and Comptroller. In a city of divided geographical and athletic allegiances, it may well have been that Brooklyn's case for a new stadium was no stronger than that of any other borough. It was in any event unlikely in the New York of the 1950s that Wagner or any other public official would suffer a popular backlash for standing up to a representative of business. As he took his leave of Robert Moses's city, O'Malley could only hope that his new home would prove more hospitable to private enterprise and the profit motive.

Early signs were mixed. O'Malley flew west with team officials in the Dodgers' Convair 440 on October 23, 1957, landing in Los Angeles around 6:00 P.M. local time. He was met by a happy crowd, a high school band, and UCLA cheerleaders. Also on hand were an ecstatic Rosalind Wyman—meeting O'Malley for the first time—and Los Angeles County supervisor Kenneth Hahn, both festooned with baseball caps. After disembarking and making a few remarks, O'Malley was served with process in a lawsuit filed by Los Angeles taxpayers to void the Dodger contract. Less than five minutes into his time in the city O'Malley was already a defendant in a legal action.

He also learned of the existence of an organization that would effectively plant land mines on the road to his new stadium, called the Citizens Committee to Save Chavez Ravine for the People. It had been formed immediately after the October 7 City Council vote approving the Dodger contract with the goal of overturning it. Its mechanism would be a referendum, a legacy of California Progressivism through which voters could set aside legislative acts. A little over 50,000 valid petition signatures would be required to place the question of the contract's validity on a referendum ballot for the following June, at which time the citizens of Los Angeles could override the City Council and void it.[17] The Citizens Committee surprised O'Malley, as did the existence of the referendum device itself. Familiar with the ins and outs of New York City's political world, O'Malley was accustomed to dealing with Tammany Hall bosses or power brokers such as Robert Moses who could deliver on their promises. The idea of a popular vote to overturn a deal he had negotiated with government officials came as a shock. Indeed, O'Malley later admitted he had never heard of the referendum procedure until he arrived in California.[18] He would need every bit of his political acumen to meet this unexpected challenge.

Los Angeles municipal politics in the late 1950s illustrated the law of unintended consequences, or perhaps the adage that no good deed goes unpunished. Its nonpartisan electoral system, a high-minded carryover from the Progressive era, was designed to protect against the party strife and bossism that plagued eastern and midwestern cities. This it may have done, but it also created a chaotic political landscape that defied both convention and conventional analysis. Los Angeles was divided not by political parties but by factions and cultures, even by moods. Downtown was ruled by an oligarchy of conservative Protestant businessmen. Most prominent among them were the Chandlers, owners of the city's dominant newspaper, the *Los Angeles Times*. By the time O'Malley arrived in Los Angeles, the Chandler family patriarch was Norman Chandler, who had succeeded his father, Harry, and grandfather Harrison Gray Otis as the newspaper's publisher and head of a dynasty with influence that extended into almost every aspect of the area's economic life.

Also situated downtown were banks and insurers, oil companies, real estate firms, the legal community, large retailers, and representatives of what by the late 1950s was one of Los Angeles's defining industries: aerospace. As a whole, Downtown was insular and old-line, a tightly knit club that controlled the Los Angeles economy and sought to enhance the city's standing and influence through commercial, financial, and cultural growth.

Los Angeles's other defining industry, of course, was film. But Hollywood in the 1950s was geographically, politically, and culturally distinct from Downtown, which considered it vulgar and déclassé. Situated northwest of the downtown business district, significantly Jewish, open in lifestyle, Hollywood may well have been an outsider's first impression of Los Angeles, but in the 1950s Downtown was where the city's center of gravity lay. Nonetheless, Hollywood and its geographic extension, the Westside, offered a more liberal counterweight to Downtown's business conservatism. What both areas shared was a civic ambition to acquire the trappings of major city status. This, of course, would include a major league baseball franchise and stadium; it was no coincidence that Rosalind Wyman's council district was based in the Westside. There were, however, elements in Hollywood that had reason to fear the arrival of the Dodgers. Studio heads knew of O'Malley's interest in pay television, and they worried about potential competition. They would prove less than supportive during the upcoming referendum campaign.

Arrayed against growth-oriented Downtown conservatives and Westside liberals was an awkward alliance. Los Angeles's leftist politics were rooted in its bitter class wars of the early twentieth century. In few other American cities were labor-capital relations more starkly antagonistic. And in no other American city did a single family represent capital more powerfully and completely. Harrison Gray Otis, a Civil War veteran and migrant from Ohio, had acquired an interest in the fledgling *Los Angeles Times* in 1882. He was soon controlling owner, and built the *Times* into the dominant media voice in the city.

By the turn of the twentieth century Otis had expanded his reach into the region's economic and civic life, buying holdings in real estate and ascending to kingmaker status in Los Angeles municipal politics. From the *Times*'s headquarters downtown at Broadway and First Street—known as "The Fortress"—Otis controlled the power levers of the city. A staunch Republican and free marketeer, Otis ran the *Times* as a stridently anti-labor vehicle. He vowed that his city would never go the way of union shop San Francisco. Along with a group of Downtown businessmen Otis formed the Merchants and Manufacturers Association (M&M), which employed a combination of payoffs, detectives, informants, and intimidation tactics to prevent organized labor from getting a foothold in Los Angeles. Nonetheless, an energetic union organizing campaign had launched by the early years of the twentieth century, buoyed by the growing Progressive movement as well as by a Socialist Party with its eyes on capturing the mayoralty in the Los Angeles municipal elections of 1911. Backed by the national

American Federation of Labor, the Los Angeles Central Labor Council sponsored a union shop drive in the city that featured a series of sometimes-violent strikes. By 1910, the Labor Council and Otis's M&M resembled opposing armies girding for battle.

Early on the morning of October 1, 1910, a huge explosion ripped through the *Los Angeles Times* building, destroying it and killing twenty-one. Through an accomplice, the crime was traced to John and James McNamara, two officials of the Bridge and Structural Iron Workers Union, which had been conducting a months-long strike in the city. They were arrested and charged, and a trial scheduled for December 1911. Just before the trial was scheduled to begin, the McNamara brothers pled guilty to planning the bombing. The association of labor leaders with violence was enough to affect the outcome of the election for Los Angeles mayor, which took place only days after the McNamaras entered their pleas. Job Harriman, the Socialist candidate who was part of the McNamaras' defense team and who had been given a good chance to win the election, instead lost to the *Times*-sponsored incumbent, ushering in a decades-long era of pro-business municipal government. The bombing also discredited the labor movement in Los Angeles, bringing Otis's open shop agenda to fruition. It would last until the 1940s.[19]

In 1913, the Los Angeles Aqueduct opened, bringing water from California's Owens Valley to the parched city. Otis and his son-in-law Harry Chandler had bought up real estate in the valley, which they sold to the city of Los Angeles at inflated prices. They then had a portion of the aqueduct's water supply diverted to the San Fernando Valley, northwest of downtown Los Angeles, where they already owned substantial amounts of land, increasing its value exponentially. The Chandler family now had an empire built on a newspaper with unrivaled circulation, a commanding political influence, and a vast acreage of real estate developments in the newly irrigated San Fernando Valley. Harrison Gray Otis died in 1917, succeeded by Harry Chandler as *Times* publisher and family head. Harry continued the newspaper's conservative and anti-union editorial policy and made the *Times* into the paper of record for the city's white Protestant masses—the midwesterners who had flooded into Los Angeles after World War I.[20]

But with the advent of the Great Depression, the political atmosphere of Los Angeles began to change. Submerged leftist impulses
emerged in the form of Pasadena-based novelist Upton Sinclair's
End Poverty in California movement, known as EPIC. With its
production-for-use-based plan to use revenues from increased taxes
on corporations, real estate, and high personal incomes to fund an
ambitious program of state-sponsored social services, EPIC pro-
pelled Sinclair to victory in California's 1934 Democratic guber-
natorial primary.

Although Harry Chandler, aided by Hollywood studio heads,
real estate, insurance and oil interests, and the ubiquitous M&M,
succeeded in defeating Sinclair in the general election utilizing hysterical anti-Red tactics, the EPIC movement revitalized liberalism
in Los Angeles and the Democratic Party on a statewide level.[21] In
the words of a late twentieth-century observer, EPIC was "the acorn
from which evolved the tree of whatever liberalism we have in California."[22] California turned from a four-to-one Republican registration advantage in 1932 to a roughly even split between the
parties three years later in the wake of the Sinclair campaign.[23]
Meanwhile, as journalist-historian David Halberstam wrote, the
Times, through Harry Chandler and after his death in 1944 his son
Norman, "*was* the Republican Party" in Southern California.[24]

By the 1940s and 1950s the labor movement, working through
the vehicle of the Democratic Party, had finally come of age in Los
Angeles. Yet the New Deal–inspired political legacy of the region
had a relatively weaker staying power than it did in Eastern cities
like New York. By the late 1950s, much of liberalism in Los Angeles had been converted from what historian Don Parson labeled
an anti-business "community modernism" to a "corporate modernism" that was generally acquiescent to growth-oriented and
nonredistributionist approaches to the city's political, economic,
and spatial development.[25] Given that the proposed Dodger Stadium project fit with this approach and indeed may have epitomized
it, O'Malley could hope for a workable level of support from
liberal Los Angeles.

But there had been a moment of possibility for the leftist impulse
in Los Angeles, and it had come in the immediate aftermath of

World War II, when a severe housing shortage affecting defense industry workers and returning veterans ignited a powerful public housing movement in the city. Supporters of the Housing Authority of the City of Los Angeles's (CHA) plan to construct public housing—most prominently in Chavez Ravine—included labor leaders, civic and religious groups, professionals, and left-leaning social democrats, all of whom wished to extend the reach of the New Deal. To them, public housing meant more than merely providing shelter. It symbolized state planning's potential to improve the material conditions of the poor and marginalized and to create a new model of urban civic engagement. Frank Wilkinson, a high-ranking CHA official, was one of the most prominent of the leftist public housing advocates, and his investigation by a Red-baiting California Senate Committee on Un-American Activities in 1952 and subsequent dismissal coincided with the defeat of public housing at the hands of Downtown interests and middle-class white homeowners who accused the program and its advocates of harboring socialist tendencies.[26]

Los Angeles's left/populist moment had essentially passed with the defeat of public housing in the early 1950s. But there were still enough leftists on Los Angeles's political landscape in 1957 to form a small but determined constituency in opposition to the city's contract with the Dodgers. Their rationale, given expression by the "public purpose" clause of the CHA's 1955 deed of the Chavez Ravine property to the city, was that public funds should not be expended for private gain.

Joining these leftist opponents of the Dodger contract were a group of unlikely allies, which included many of the same middle class white homeowners who had pilloried them as socialists only a few years earlier for their support of public housing. New Deal–influenced populists had hoped that the state would become the dominant force in the Los Angeles housing market, planning and building for the people. Instead, private developers such as Fritz Burns, whose standard-design detached homes sold by the thousands, captured that market. Burns and his colleagues were assisted by generous Federal Housing Authority mortgage guarantee policies that incentivized banks to lend, as well as the government's tolerance of redlining restrictions on minority home buying which kept the new developments virtually all-white. By the 1950s, the private sector controlled Los Angeles's housing supply. It, and not the state, decided where homes would be built, how they would be built, and who would live in them.

The men and women who lived in the homes that men such as Fritz Burns built, whether in the San Fernando Valley north and west of downtown, the tract developments near the Los Angeles International Airport and the aviation plants, or the small homes that dotted the Eagle Rock and Highland Park neighborhoods in the northeast part of the city, were the descendants of what the California historian Kevin Starr has called the "Folks."[27] During the first half of the twentieth century, hundreds of thousands of midwesterners had descended on Los Angeles from towns and farms, bringing the values of their places of origin with them. They and their children made Los Angeles the most Protestant large city in the United States as well as one of the most culturally rigid and economically conservative—another irony considering the city's national identification with Hollywood.

The Folks were quiet and conventional. They had come west for their modest portion of the American dream: a home of their own on land of their own. This foreshortened vision translated to an austere politics of limits on taxes, spending, and growth. To many of them the Dodger contract smacked of dangerous civic adventuring. John Holland, suspicious of the powerful and wealthy "interests," spoke for the Folks and jealously guarded their tax dollars. Here Los Angeles politics produced a coalition that drew from both the right and the left. Opposition to O'Malley's agreement with the city united populists of different ideological stripes. Both Holland's conservative Folks and the leftist veterans of the public housing wars viewed the Dodger contract as an example of unwarranted government largesse. In 1952, the votes of the Folks had doomed the public housing program in Los Angeles. A year later, they helped elect Mayor Norris Poulson, a man who regarded government-constructed housing as a form of socialism. Now Poulson was a driving force behind the Dodger contract, and those whom the Folks had derided as statists and enemies of the free enterprise system were their allies. John Holland and supporters of Frank Wilkinson were now comrades-in-arms.

The ambiguous position of Latinos in Los Angeles also contributed to the city's political vertigo. By the late 1950s, Latinos, primarily immigrants from Mexico and their descendants, constituted approximately 10 percent of the city's population.[28] Despite a concentrated residential base to the east of the Los Angeles River, they were significantly underrepresented at the elective level. Edward Roybal, the city's first Latino city council member since the 1880s, was the only one serving in that body in 1957. Latinos had a direct stake in the Dodger contract due to the location of the proposed stadium in Chavez Ravine.

The Ravine had been home to a Latino community for the better part of a century. Downtown's proximity vastly enhanced Chavez Ravine's business value. Before being selected as a public housing site in the late 1940s, the Ravine was a traditional and insular neighborhood of modest homes and dirt roads. Despite the tendency of government officials and urban planners to view it as a slum—much of its housing stock was classified as substandard— the Ravine was socially cohesive, with a vibrant ethnic and religious culture.[29] Its residents had opposed the planned public housing project, knowing that it signaled the end of their community. Once again, this made for an almost counterintuitive political alignment, as Democratic-leaning Latinos joined white middle-class Republican homeowners to fight public housing at Chavez Ravine, to the dismay of left/liberal New Deal populists and planners who believed that they were promoting the interests of the poor and marginalized.

Most Chavez Ravine residents succumbed to the pressure of eminent domain proceedings and vacated their homes, often after contentious negotiations over the value of their properties. This added an economic dimension to the Chavez Ravine controversy that would prove to be as consequential as that of ethnicity, race, and culture. Few Chavez Ravine property owners were completely satisfied with the valuation of their homes for condemnation purposes. But most felt they had no choice, and by 1952 almost all had accepted their checks and relocated—just as the public housing project itself was being canceled. A few families, however, refused to leave, and the land remained in limbo between 1952 and 1957. Despite the relatively small number of these squatters, the land had by the time of the Dodgers' move become a symbolic issue for the city's Latino population as a whole, a place where an endangered way of life would make a final stand. It would be Walter O'Malley's misfortune to find himself enmeshed in an ethno-cultural controversy with which he had no prior familiarity—yet another illustration of the intricacies and ironies of Los Angeles political culture in the 1950s.

The Dodger contract was on more solid ground in the city's African American community. In 1957, Los Angeles was one of the most racially segregated metropolitan areas in the United States. Blacks who had moved west during the World War II years to work in defense industry plants were crowded into the enclave of Watts, south of downtown. There they were denied the credit opportunities afforded white homebuyers by Federal Housing Authority mortgage programs, subjected to redlining that prevented them from crossing racially demarcated residential boundaries, and hounded by the notoriously overzealous police force of heavy-handed city police chief William Parker.

But the Los Angeles African American community, which grew from 8.7 percent to 13.5 percent of the city's population during the 1950s, was a potential source of support for O'Malley and the Dodger contract.[30] The council district encompassing the Watts neighborhood was represented by Gordon Hahn, who, like his brother, county supervisor Kenneth Hahn, was a leader in the campaign to bring the Dodgers west. There were also deeper reasons for African Americans to look favorably upon the Dodgers. The team was, of course, a pathbreaker in American civil rights history, having brought Jackie Robinson to the major leagues in 1947. The club subsequently signed a group of other high-profile black players, including Roy Campanella, Don Newcombe, and Jim Gilliam, which linked the Dodgers with the cause of racial progress. Jackie Robinson, moreover, was a Los Angeles–area native, prominent as a young athletic star at Pasadena Junior College and at UCLA, where he was a football All-American.

The Dodgers were, in fact, the major league organization most closely associated with the cause of civil rights. The team's Dodgertown spring training site in Vero Beach, Florida, had been constructed in the late 1940s in large measure to shield African American players from the Jim Crow practices of the surrounding area. Dodgertown was entirely self-contained. It was the only Florida spring training facility to provide working, eating, residential, and recreational accommodations on-site. Black and white Dodgers lived in a communal atmosphere, building a camaraderie that management hoped would pay dividends during the heat and pressure of pennant races. At Dodgertown's dining hall, according to general manager Buzzie Bavasi, players were required to take "the first seat available" regardless of race. "This has been done deliberately," explained Bavasi.[31] In the 1950s, black Dodgers were the only African American baseball players spared the humiliations of segregated public facilities in the Jim Crow South.[32] Dodgertown, in fact, may have been the largest single integrated venue of any kind in the state of Florida.[33]

The Dodger organization's racially progressive reputation preceded it in Los Angeles, and the city's African American community embraced the team as its own. Many in that community knew that the initial cohort of pioneering black Dodgers—Roy Campanella, Don Newcombe, and of course, Jackie Robinson—was about to be supplemented by a new group of African American players coming up through the Dodger organization. Among them were John Roseboro, a catcher viewed as the successor to Campanella; Tommy Davis, a Brooklynite who came west with the team and was its most prominent slugging prospect; and Willie Davis (no relation to Tommy), a product of Los Angeles's Roosevelt High School who would eventually take over for Duke Snider in center field. There was also Maury Wills, who had been bouncing around the Dodger minor league system since 1951 but was showing signs of the ability that would in time make him a record-setting base stealer and league most valuable player.

To the African American community of Los Angeles, the import of this group of players went well beyond the ball field. They were a source of collective pride in a city of redlined neighborhoods, hostile police, and foreshortened job opportunities. The young black Dodgers were frequently mentioned in the city's black newspapers, lauded as local celebrities but also charged with responsibility for "representing the race." The *Los Angeles Tribune* kept close watch on the number of African Americans in the Dodger farm system, praising it as "one of the outstanding organizations in developing Negro players for major league play."[34] The *Los Angeles Sentinel* chastised black Dodgers it believed were not living up to its standards of civic respectability, reminding players who had refused autographs to black youngsters that "some of you are the idols of little children because you represent an opportunity for them as Negroes" and asking, "Why do you let them down by your actions which sometimes seem ignorant and country?"[35]

By associating rudeness with the rural-infused traits of the Jim Crow South—subservience and ignorance—the *Sentinel* sought to articulate a more worldly and aspirational culture, one that connected to an image of African American Dodger players as worthy community exemplars. This in turn linked the African American population of Los Angeles to the Dodger organization and its quest for a new stadium. Stripped of the ethnocultural issues that embroiled the city's Latino population, the contract question devolved into a simpler one of baseball versus no baseball that would be much easier to answer.

A combination of Jackie Robinson–inspired civil rights loyalty, "black Dodger" pride, and the cultural politics of racial respectability thus forged a bond between the Los Angeles African American community and the Los Angeles Dodgers that would create both a solid constituency for the stadium battle at hand and a stable and loyal fan base in the years to come.

The Los Angeles labor movement was also a base of support for O'Malley. It had taken organized labor decades to gain a foothold in Los Angeles, which had remained an open shop city until the 1940s. By 1957, the local AFL-CIO was practicing what could be described as business unionism as opposed to that of a more militant, class-centered model rooted in the ideology and tactics of the New Deal. This meant viewing O'Malley's planned stadium primarily as a source of steady work for its members. Most Los Angeles unions had supported the public housing movement of the late 1940s and early 1950s, less for ideological reasons than for the opportunities it offered for construction industry employment. Now the city's labor leadership had lined up behind the pro-growth plans of the Downtown interests, notably the Chandlers, who had sought to thwart union organizing efforts throughout most of the twentieth century—yet another case of the city's politics creating unexpected alliances and outcomes. With the notable exception of Local 123 of the city's Furniture Workers and Upholsterers and Woodworkers Union, which was Latino-led and fearful of the destruction of the Chavez Ravine community, the Los Angeles labor movement backed the Dodger Stadium project as a potential jobs generator.[36] The imperatives of economic self-interest thus outweighed those of labor and class solidarity, and worked to O'Malley's benefit.

The Los Angeles media community, whose support would be crucial to the stadium project, was more divided. The city's large daily newspapers, led by the *Times*, but also including the *Mirror News* and the Hearst-owned *Herald and Express* and *Examiner*, were solidly behind the Dodger contract. The *Examiner*'s Vincent Flaherty had been one of the first to promote the Dodgers' move west. Sportswriters, not surprisingly, desired a major league baseball team to enhance their beats. But there was also good reason for management and nonsports staff to want the Dodgers in Los Angeles. The addition of the team would boost the prestige of the city, and by extension that of their own newspapers. By the late 1950s, Los Angeles was the third-largest city in the United States. That fact, however, may have surprised many Americans who viewed it as an enclave of film stars and beach habitués and not as a "real" city like New York or Chicago. Culture offered a city definition and identity. That O'Malley had come from New York, the epicenter of American culture, made the Dodgers even more attractive to Los Angeles and the newspapers that covered it. During the public debate over the Dodger contract, the city's major daily newspapers would prove to be among O'Malley's most reliable sources of support.

The same, however, could not be said of other sectors of the city's media. O'Malley's flirtation with forms of pay television had alarmed local station owners, who feared not only losing the ability to broadcast Dodger games in Los Angeles themselves (in 1957, all home and about twenty road games had been carried free in New York) but also potential competition from pay-TV companies, which could use the Dodgers to cut into over-the-air viewership. Television broadcasters were thus much more hostile to O'Malley and the contract than those connected with the daily newspapers.

Also hostile to O'Malley, albeit for different reasons, were the neighborhood newspapers that dotted the city's media landscape. The outlying neighborhoods were instinctively suspicious of Downtown, and the Dodger contract was exactly the type of big-money project that would arouse their ire. A particularly fertile ground for resistance was the San Fernando Valley, cut off geographically from the city's Downtown and Westside centers of influence. The Valley's populist-tinged resentments were ripe for stoking. The neighborhood's weekly newspapers claimed to speak for the Folks, who were excluded from the insiders club and the precincts of power. The Dodger contract would present an inviting target to a segment of the media that operated at ground level and defined its journalistic mission as afflicting the comfortable on behalf of the people.

Finally, there was the apparatus of Los Angeles municipal government itself, most of which was nominally in O'Malley's corner. He could count on Mayor Poulson, who had worked so diligently to bring the Dodgers west, as well as a majority of the City Council and Los Angeles County Board of Supervisors. But political power was diffuse in Los Angeles. Thanks to the city's Progressive-influenced political structure, there was no Robert Moses, able to ensure the success of a project with a nod of his head. The very existence of a referendum mechanism signaled that Los Angeles prized democracy over efficiency. Beyond the realm of elected officialdom, O'Malley would need to navigate bureaucracies in the Departments of Recreation and Parks, City Traffic Department, and Office of Zoning Administration, all of which operated as semi-independent entities. O'Malley would also have to negotiate with the Los Angeles Police Department and its formidable chief, William Parker, over its Police Academy property, which was located in Chavez Ravine. Parker was known for a near-fanatical devotion to protecting his turf and institutional prerogatives. He would be a difficult bargaining partner.

The power structure of Los Angeles, then, was diffuse and decentralized. In New York, O'Malley could maintain a mental list of the men who got things done—political bosses, public administrators, bankers, and builders. But there was no such list in Los Angeles. New York's road map of power was a familiar one. It was a harsh, demanding road that often ran uphill, but its mileposts were clearly defined. Not so in Los Angeles. There lines of power crossed and blurred. It was unclear where the true levers of authority lay. Ultimately the impending referendum would ensure that the people of Los Angeles and not a group of power brokers would determine O'Malley's entrepreneurial future. This, of course, was a democratic outcome with which few could disagree. But the degree of public control over what was largely a business transaction disconcerted O'Malley. He had staked his professional career on an unfamiliar city whose inner workings he did not fully understand, one with a confusing political, social, and economic topography where the line between friends and enemies blurred.

New York had been so much simpler. There were defined ethnic and racial groups—Italians, Jews, Irish, African Americans, and Puerto Ricans—with defined political and cultural positions. There was a Catholic-dominated political machine, Tammany Hall, still powerful despite its engagement in a well-publicized struggle for control of the city's Democratic Party apparatus against a growing reform movement. There was a power broker, Robert Moses, who essentially determined New York's built landscape. But thanks to the Protestant Folks, Los Angeles was much less defined by ethnic tribalism. It had no visible political machine and no official party affiliations. Where was the man, or at least the small group of men, with whom O'Malley could sit down to make the roadblocks to his stadium project disappear? Even Norman Chandler, the closest Los Angeles equivalent to a Moses-style power broker in Los Angeles, did not possess this kind of power. Los Angeles was unlike any-place Walter O'Malley had seen. It did not seem to follow rules he could understand. But if O'Malley wished to see his stadium built, he would need to take the measure of this confounding city and do it quickly.

3

FIGHTING THE
DODGER DEAL

Speaking to reporters on the Los Angeles International Airport tarmac on
October 23, O'Malley admitted he was unsure of where his team
would play its home games in 1958. Wrigley Field, which he still
owned, was a possibility, as was the Los Angeles Memorial Coliseum and the Rose Bowl. The latter two venues were football
stadiums and would require substantial reconfigurations to accommodate baseball's different field dimensions. Meanwhile, newly
minted Los Angeles Dodger fans were not waiting to learn where
their team would play before seeking to purchase their seats.
More than a thousand season ticket applications were distributed
within an hour of being made available on October 25.[1]

O'Malley was buoyed further by his reception at a "Welcome
Dodgers" lunch at the Staler Hotel three days later, where he received
a standing ovation from eleven hundred guests. Framed against a
banner reading "The Greatest Catch in Baseball," O'Malley promised "there will never be a time when mothers and fathers will
have the right to ask any of our officials, players or anyone else in
the Dodger organization to apologize for their conduct." As players Duke Snider, Gil Hodges, and Roy Campanella looked on from
the dais, O'Malley lauded the citizens of his new home: "You can

feel it at every turn—on the streets, in the cabs, all over the city. People, in welcoming us, make us feel they mean it and we want you to be proud of the day you decided to make the Dodgers the Los Angeles Dodgers."[2]

The banquet gave O'Malley the opportunity to mingle with such influentials as he could discern in the city—politicians, bankers, oil executives, developers, and media leaders. Certainly the toy baseballs tossed from the dais to the tables below were a nice touch. But O'Malley knew only a tiny fraction of the men he dined with that day. Even if he had been acquainted with everyone in the room, men such as Poulson, Chandler, and Burns could not by themselves deliver Los Angeles for O'Malley. The city was too much the unruly democracy for this. Already opposing forces— the Folks, who were not munching on free peanuts and Cracker Jack at the welcoming gala—were organizing against him. Indeed, they were ahead of him.

The taxpayer suit to void the Dodger contract that occasioned the subpoena served on O'Malley as he disembarked in Los Angeles had been filed by a local attorney named Julius Ruben in Superior Court on October 14, only seven days after the City Council voted to approve the Dodger agreement. While it argued generally that a public entity had no right to dispose of public property for anything other than a public purpose, the complaint relied more specifically on the language in the 1955 deed of Chavez Ravine land from the CHA to the city of Los Angeles after the demise of the public housing initiative there. The deed mandated that the transferred land be employed solely for a "public purpose" without defining what those words meant. Ruben contended that the deed barred use of the land for the benefit of any private business, including a baseball team.

Ruben took pains to point out that he did not oppose the Dodgers' move to Los Angeles. In what would become a familiar refrain from O'Malley's opponents, Ruben claimed to welcome the team. His quarrel was not with major league baseball but with the allocation of public resources to it. If the city wished to build a municipal stadium and O'Malley desired to rent it, Ruben would not stand in the way. But as long as the public purpose restriction remained in the CHA deed—and despite the city's promise to either have it removed or held harmless and of no effect, it was still there—it had to be enforced. Ruben, in fact, questioned whether it was legal to take the clause out of the deed under any circumstances. He wished to force a court adjudicating his case to specifically apply the words "public purpose" to the Dodger contract. Robert Moses had made this determination for O'Malley in New York, but of course, he was not a judge. Now the Dodger owner faced the prospect of a legally binding adjudication of the issue. All things being equal, O'Malley would have preferred to proceed with his stadium plans without this type of definitive resolution. Thanks to Ruben, he had no choice. And since Ruben's case would take months to be heard, O'Malley faced the prospect of further delays.

Julius Ruben was only one of O'Malley's problems that fall. On October 17, the Citizens Committee to Save Chavez Ravine for the People announced its presence with a news conference. Its chairman was C. A. Owen, the former president of the Apartment House Owners Association of Los Angeles County and a fierce advocate of limited government spending and low taxation. Five years earlier, Owen and the association had opposed public housing in Chavez Ravine, arguing that it was an unwarranted state intrusion into a traditionally private market sector and an assault on free enterprise principles. Now Owen was determined to protect the remaining residents of the Ravine, despite the fact that, having been served with eviction notices they had defied for years, they were no longer legal owners. He was also determined to prevent what he called "a stupendous gift of untold millions of dollars worth of public-owned land for the sole benefit of a baseball club."[3] Owen, like Ruben, claimed to support the Dodgers' move to Los Angeles, objecting only to the terms of the deal. The Citizens Committee would be the driving force behind the anti-contract referendum campaign, soliciting signatures on the petitions required to place it on the ballot from offices on La Brea Avenue and Sunset Boulevard.

The sources of the financing behind the Citizens Committee were not made public. Owen insisted he led a grassroots movement, and in some respects he was correct. He could point to substantial support among San Fernando Valley homeowners; in the Latino community, where sentiment ran high in favor of the Chavez Ravine squatters; and generally with white middle-class Angelenos suspicious of expensive government projects that seemed only to push property taxes higher. The Citizens Committee was, in fact, an interracial, cross-class alliance, something that was comparatively rare in the Los Angeles of the late 1950s. But there was another aspect to the Citizens Committee that Owen was less likely to celebrate publicly. Much of the committee's financial backing came from the Smith brothers, J. A. and C. Arnholt, of San Diego, where the latter owned the local Pacific Coast League baseball team. This team's fortunes would certainly suffer from the presence of the Dodgers in nearby Los Angeles.

The Smiths' obvious economic interest in defeating the Dodger contract made it imperative that their support for the Citizens Committee be obscured. The brothers were hardly representative of "the people" for which the committee claimed to speak. The Smiths accordingly remained in the background, much to O'Malley's frustration, as did another group of silent partners in the anti-contract campaign, movie studio heads, whose product might be forced into competition with major league baseball. With weak state oversight laws making it difficult to follow the money, the movie moguls' participation in the effort to defeat the Dodger contract was never more than an often-repeated rumor, but O'Malley was convinced they were quietly seeking to sabotage him. While it remained to be seen how many of "the people" the Citizens Committee would actually muster, the organization clearly possessed the resources to make a fight of it with Walter O'Malley.

Flanking Owen as he introduced the Citizens Committee was John Holland. This may have been the worst news of all for O'Malley. Holland was not a real estate man dabbling in politics like C. A. Owen. Holland was *in* politics. He had come within one vote of derailing the Dodger agreement in the City Council on October 7, and now he was more determined than ever to stop O'Malley from acquiring the Chavez Ravine property. "There are so many things wrong with this deal," Holland told reporters, "that my sense of duty and my oath of office . . . compel me to continue the fight to save this centrally-located land for the present and future citizens of Los Angeles." Holland demanded "public ownership" of the Ravine. He predicted that "if this wonderful area is preserved in city ownership that rentals therefrom to the city will far exceed any possible tax income if it is given to the Dodgers or into any other private ownership." Comparing Chavez Ravine to New York's Central Park in potential benefit to the city, Holland proposed that a civic auditorium, world trade center, and zoo be constructed on the site in addition to a ballpark.[4]

Holland's remarks seemed to run against his political grain. How could a businessman and conservative Republican advocate a publicly financed stadium project while opposing government assistance to a private entity? The answer lay in Holland's deep sense of fiscal prudence. Convinced that a municipal ballpark on which the Dodgers paid rent would produce revenues in excess of those generated by taxes from a team-owned property, he cast his lot with the option he believed would bring more dollars into the city's coffers. O'Malley certainly would have challenged Holland's mathematics, but in opposing the Dodger contract, the councilman was remaining true to his economic principles, convinced as he was that Los Angeles would save money in the long term through an up-front stadium investment.

By late October the community newspapers of the city, in keeping with their self-defined roles as gadflies for the Folks, were training their rhetorical fire at the Dodger agreement. The *Highland Park News-Herald and Journal*, which covered a neighborhood northeast of Chavez Ravine, was typical. Urging its readers to sign petitions to place the anti-contract referendum on the ballot, it excoriated "a deal so outrageous that this 'court of last resort' must be employed to restore sanity to the conduct of our city's business," and labeled it "the most appalling real estate transaction in the history of our city." It demanded a county grand jury or congressional investigation of a "gift to the Dodger baseball team" of "something between $10,000,000 and $15,000,000 of the people's money." Like Holland, Ruben, and the Citizens Committee, the *News-Herald* called for public ownership of the

Dodgers' new stadium, praising San Francisco's municipal arrangement as a model for Los Angeles to emulate, and also supported Holland's proposal for a complex of "public institutions" to be built in the Ravine. A photograph accompanying the *News-Herald* article showed Earle Baker, one of the four councilmen to vote against the stadium contract on October 7, as the ceremonial first signer of the referendum petition. Pictured with him was John Holland. Posted on the wall behind them was a poster reading "We Want the 'Bums' but Not the Bum Deal!"[5]

O'Malley opened a temporary office for the Dodgers in the Statler Hotel, located downtown at 930 Wilshire Boulevard, only about a mile and a half from Chavez Ravine. He also took a suite of rooms at the hotel to serve as his in-town residence. From the suite he could see his proposed stadium site, as well as the scattered homes of the remaining residents. He wondered if what he envisioned there would ever take shape. Certainly he had reason to question the wisdom of his move to Los Angeles. Poulson, Wyman, and the Hahns had assured him that the city was ripe for major league baseball and would welcome him with open arms. On the first point they had spoken the truth. The potential in the city of well over 2 million, which could boast only one other established major professional sports team, the National Football League's Rams, was enormous. But O'Malley now faced taxpayer lawsuits and a referendum campaign aimed at voiding his stadium deal, a hostile portion of the local media, significant opposition in the City Council, an anti-contract organization that ostensibly spoke for ordinary citizens, and a Latino community warily eyeing the fate of the homes in Chavez Ravine. As he stared out of his Statler suite window at the hilly, pockmarked landscape before him, O'Malley must have wondered why he had come to this city, so different from the one he knew best and so far from home.

A "fact sheet" distributed by the Citizens Committee on October 30 did little to improve O'Malley's disposition. It was designed to play on Los Angeles's rivalry with San Francisco, a city with a much more well-defined civic identity and one that according to the fact sheet had struck a much more advantageous deal with the newly arrived Giants. The Fact Sheet claimed that San Francisco was spending approximately $6 million to build its municipal stadium, about the same amount the city and county of Los Angeles would expend for road access and land acquisition under the terms of the Dodger contract.[6] It projected that San Francisco would realize some $600,000 per year from rent, $300,000 per year in parking revenues (which would go to the city and not the Giants), and $100,000 from stadium advertising revenues. In addition, the city of San Francisco could rent the stadium on non-baseball dates and keep all proceeds. The fact sheet predicted that thanks to this steady stream of revenue the San Francisco stadium would be fully paid off in twenty-five years, while the property tax income from a privately owned Dodger ballpark would take considerably longer to recoup Los Angeles's investment.[7]

The Citizens Committee also raised a series of innuendo-laden questions about the terms of the Dodger contract. The city had committed to obtaining more than a hundred acres of Chavez Ravine land that it did not already own and adding them to the stadium parcel. How much, the fact sheet asked, would this cost? In addition, the city had agreed to employ its best efforts to rezone the Ravine property to C-3 status, which permitted broadly defined commercial and/or residential use. Armed with this wide latitude, would O'Malley build a shopping center and high-rise apartments instead of a ballpark? The contract required the team to expend a sum "not to exceed" $500,000 on a public recreation area adjacent to the stadium. Did this mean the team could pay only $1 and still fulfill its obligation? The contract furthermore contained a severability clause allowing the document as a whole to remain in effect even if the team defaulted on its legal duty to pay for and maintain the public recreation area. Could O'Malley simply walk away from his responsibilities without penalty, keeping the rest of the Chavez Ravine property as if the promise had never been made?[8]

The fact sheet answered all of these questions in ways calculated to cast the Dodgers, the contract, and the city of Los Angeles in the worst possible light. Even while reiterating support for major league baseball in Los Angeles—"We welcome the Dodgers ... but NOT the 'deal'"—the Citizens Committee articulated the suspicions of the tax- and spending-averse white middle class of the city.[9] "Let's keep Chavez Ravine for the people!" was the group's egalitarian slogan.[10] The fact sheet protested the deeding of land "to be used for public purposes only" to "a privately owned ball club."[11] O'Malley's New York roots worked against him with the Citizens Committee members. In their view, the big businessman from the big city in league with the big people of Los Angeles was the beneficiary of a special arrangement on a special piece of city real estate, and average Folks were being asked to assume the costs of the deal. The Citizens Committee was formed to end this kind of business-as-usual in Los Angeles politics.[12]

On November 6, as the deadline for collecting referendum signatures neared, John Holland begged the Folks to mobilize against the Dodger contract. "Only the registered voters of our city," he warned, "can save the day. . . . You have just received your tax bills. They are higher—and they will be still higher! . . . You may lose forever a priceless asset which you now possess and which may save you and future citizens of our wonderful city untold millions and millions . . . in taxes."[13] Implicit in his call to arms was the idea that special interests were conspiring to divert the people's resources for the benefit of a privileged few. It was also clear that Holland considered O'Malley one of those privileged few.

But was this characterization a fair one? It was, of course, true that O'Malley was a businessman. He had left New York because it could not offer a hospitable environment in which to operate. O'Malley never apologized for his entrepreneurial sentiments or actions, and this had made him unpopular in a New York civic culture that viewed businessmen as little more than a source of tax revenue. He had hoped to find in Los Angeles a more welcoming atmosphere and at the very least a recognition that his baseball team was indeed a business, something that many in New York found difficult to accept. When he arrived in Los Angeles, O'Malley was only vaguely aware of the controversy over public housing in Chavez Ravine and of the impending eviction battle there. He was unacquainted with his new city's political terrain and had assumed that the public officials who courted him—particularly Poulson, Wyman, and Kenneth Hahn—represented the sentiments of the

broader community. He was unaware of the existence of the referendum mechanism. He had not anticipated the taxpayers' suits
that were filed against his contract with the city. O'Malley had few
ready sources of financing in Los Angeles. In order to obtain private funding for his stadium, he would have to negotiate in an
unfamiliar banking environment with potential lenders who did
not know him.

In many respects, then, O'Malley was not the "insider" the
opponents of the Dodger contract made him out to be. Had he
known more about Los Angeles and its sources of power, he might
well have been able to improve on a deal that required him to raise
at least $15 million to construct his own stadium. In reality, the
"inside deal" against which Holland, Ruben, and the Citizens
Committee railed was laden with risk for O'Malley. Chavez Ravine
could become an extraordinarily valuable property, but as of
November 1957 it was barren and unimproved, with land valued
at only $7,000 an acre.[14] It was conceivable that O'Malley could
be saddled with property whose topography made the construction of a first-class stadium impossible. A scenario could also be
imagined under which he would be forced to sell the Chavez
Ravine land in order to keep the stadium project afloat, which
would have negated the very purpose of his move to Los Angeles.
The Dodger deal, then, was hardly a no-risk, sweetheart arrangement born of a cozy relationship between O'Malley and city elites.
A stranger in strange surroundings, unfamiliar with local customs,
cultures, and rules, O'Malley was more of an outsider than his
opponents realized.

On November 14, an armored truck, accompanied by John
Holland, delivered petitions containing more than seventy thousand signatures in support of a referendum on the Dodger contract to the City Hall office of city clerk Walter Peterson, almost
double the number required.[15] It was clear that the measure was
headed for the ballot.[16] Publicly, O'Malley reacted to the news
with equanimity. "Anything worth having is worth fighting for,"
he said, professing to welcome the challenge.[17] Privately, he was
less sanguine. He wrote to Kenneth Hahn, "It might be a blue
moon before we start construction and that annoys me no end"[18]

In a letter to *Examiner* columnist Vincent Flaherty he called the petition drive "quite distressing."[19] O'Malley also told Flaherty that he believed the Citizens Committee had duped voters into signing the referendum petitions by falsely representing them as "pro-baseball."[20]

O'Malley was frustrated by the professions of contract opponents that they welcomed the Dodgers but not the Dodger deal. To him, this was disingenuous. O'Malley was determined not to renegotiate the contract under any circumstances, and with the referendum now a virtual certainty, he faced an existential struggle over his future in Los Angeles. For the moment, he decided to stay on the sidelines as the public argument over the contract played out, leaving it to his political allies to make his case to the voters. But he would discover this would not be enough and that he would need to intervene more directly in order to save his stadium.

The Los Angeles sports media sought to sway the city's sports fans toward the contract with strong rhetorical support. Part of this effort involved humanizing the Dodger owner, who had been portrayed by the New York media as a heartless manipulator. Los Angeles sportswriters painted a different picture. Recalling O'Malley's initial press conference upon his arrival at Los Angeles International Airport on October 23, *Times* sports editor Paul Zimmerman observed that the Dodger owner had "proved himself to be a far different person than the one we've been reading about recently in stories emanating from New York . . . Unless there has been a case of mistaken identity, this forthright and witty gentleman who stepped off the 'Los Angeles Dodgers' airplane must have undergone a complete metamorphosis during the half day it took him to fly from Gotham to our fair city."[21] Rube Samuelsen of the *Pasadena Star-News* described him as "a man who could give Dale Carnegie a run for it in demonstrating ways of winning friends and influencing people. His faculty of saying the right thing at the right time is innate."[22] The *Examiner*'s Melvin Durslag praised O'Malley's "pioneering quality in his shift to Los Angeles" and voiced the hope that his "faith in this city hasn't been misplaced."[23] Durslag mused that "some day they may name a place out here O'Malley Ravine."[24]

One of the most influential sportswriters in Los Angeles and arguably the best was Jim Murray, whose graceful, metaphor-laden columns set him apart from his less-inspired colleagues. Murray wrote for *Time* and *Sports Illustrated* magazines, and would join the *Los Angeles Times* in 1961. He understood that his career trajectory was closely linked to the Dodgers and that it was thus vitally important that the Chavez Ravine ballpark be built. In a November memorandum on the escalating stadium controversy, Murray argued that "a major league baseball team is meant to be a kind of national or even international promotion for the city. . . . The mere fact it wears the legend 'Los Angeles' on its uniforms and carries the dateline 'Los Angeles' on all wire stories . . . has a real hard commercial value to a city which depends on both tourism and population (and industrial) influx for its continued health and vitality."[25]

Murray worried, however, that Los Angeles was not up to the challenges of "major league" status:

> LA historically has been a hell-for-leather, take-a-chance city. Recklessness and the visionary approach have historically paid off for LA. But the city's new population comes largely from other, more cautious areas of the country where the work of the day is to watch out for your neighbor and treat him as a confidence man. The men who built the [Los Angeles] Coliseum, the Rose Bowl, the Ascot Raceway, the movie industry or even the eight-lane highways would welcome O'Malley with open arms or hearty backslaps. But these men, I am sometimes afraid, are in the minority in their open air playground now. Or at least, if the referendum succeeds at the polls . . . one will have to conclude that they are. I am satisfied in my own mind that will be a sad day for Los Angeles.[26]

Murray's clear-eyed understanding of the Dodger contract dispute as a battle between two competing visions of Los Angeles—that of an ambitious, growth-oriented city and a cautious, fiscally restrained one—would be reflected in the coming referendum campaign. More than a dispute over a ballpark, or even sports generally, it would play a major role in shaping the modern identity of the city of Los Angeles.

On December 1, city clerk Peterson certified enough valid signatures to place the issue of the validity of the Dodger contract on the municipal ballot as a referendum question. To save the expense of a special election, the vote was slated for the same day as the regularly scheduled state elections, June 3, 1958. It was designated as Proposition B, asking Los Angeles voters to decide if "the ordinance authorizing and approving the contract set forth therein between the City of Los Angeles and the Brooklyn National League Baseball Club, and authorizing the execution thereof, be adopted."[27] A yes vote would approve the contract and a no would reject it. Because the referendum would coincide with statewide primary elections for governor and the United States Senate, a substantial turnout was guaranteed. The opposing forces had six months of rhetorical argument and political maneuvering ahead of them.

The battle over the construction of Dodger Stadium in Chavez Ravine has been described as an argument between "core" and "periphery" over the direction and identity of modern Los Angeles.[28] There is much truth to this. Historian Michael Mott has correctly identified the stadium issue as a crucial moment in the "city-building process" and "the struggle for spatial meaning," dividing civic unifiers advocating "a coherent centralized metropolis" and those supporting land use for "the outlying districts as much as the downtown center."[29] But support for or opposition to the Dodger Stadium project was not a function of geography alone. Contract opponent Patrick McGee's council district was in the San Fernando Valley, but John Holland's was not. James Corman, a pro-contract councilman, resided in the Valley. Edward Roybal, who had absented himself from the October 7 contract vote and became a leading opponent of it, represented a largely Latino constituency in East Los Angeles nearer to downtown. J. A. Smith, the Citizens Committee's leading major financial donor, did not even live in Los Angeles. Opponents of the contract from the ranks of local television and radio news and theater owners were more closely associated with the core of the city than its periphery.

Positions on Proposition B reflected culture as much as location. At their heart were different understandings of civic identity. Did Los Angeles need a downtown similar to those in East Coast cities, a center of activity around which outlying areas revolved like planets around the sun? Or could a collection of satellite communities themselves constitute a viable urban structure? The debate over the Dodger contract thus represented a larger one over the nature of modern Los Angeles. The city's downtown in 1958 was a noir backwater that most affluent whites abandoned after the business day ended. Did it matter? To the civic unifiers at the major newspapers, oil companies, and real estate firms, it did. A new ballpark within a five-minute drive of the Civic Center would be a first step in creating a modern downtown that would resemble those in more established cities.

Downtowns in New York, Chicago, and San Francisco were more than office space for business and government. They were gathering places for recreation, entertainment, culture, and consumption, as well as residential hubs in their own right. They were also white. While they served people of color, they were not "for" them. Central core advocates viewed the nonwhite populations of the downtown Bunker Hill neighborhood and the nearby Boyle Heights area, not to mention Chavez Ravine itself, as a problem, an impediment to progress.[30] For years, plans to revitalize Los Angeles's downtown in a modern image had been floated without tangible impact.[31] But now a new Dodger Stadium could be the first step toward realizing this goal. If built, it could be followed by concert venues, museums, and upmarket housing developments. It would attract a white middle-class clientele that otherwise would flee to the periphery. With a vibrant, attractive core area, Los Angeles would at last become, in the words of historian John Findlay, a "legible city."[32]

But periphery advocates—who were not all from the periphery—countered that Los Angeles's decentered pattern of development served real communities, not imagined ones. The Chavez Ravine stadium project would not just divert population toward the core. It would divert resources as well. Patrick McGee argued that "it is the fundamental obligation of government to provide the necessities before you provide the luxuries," and with unpaved roads and uninstalled sewer lines endemic in his San Fernando Valley home district, he had a legitimate point.[33]

That many Angelenos identified more closely with their communities than with the city as a whole was not necessarily a disadvantage. Los Angeles might acquire a baseball team from New York, but it did not have to be New York. A decentralized city with relatively autonomous peripheries substituting for the core in constituent services that provided a host of personal connections between its citizens was a workable, sustainable urban model. Los Angeles, in fact, could conceivably have not one but many downtowns. But of course if power continued to flow toward the traditional downtown in the form of land contracts with private entities such as the Dodgers, peripheral areas would be choked off and marginalized. The Proposition B opponents represented an alternative vision of urban life that sought to reverse the centralizing tide threatening local identities and maintain what they viewed as an equitable balance between central core and peripheral communities in modern Los Angeles. The referendum election was thus freighted with significance beyond that of its immediate setting. Building or not building a Dodger ballpark in Chavez Ravine would determine the course of downtown Los Angeles and with it the nature, shape, and direction of the entire city and region.

The animating issue of the Proposition B campaign was whether targeted forms of government assistance to private corporations and business entities were appropriate or even moral. This question was considerably older than Proposition B. Its roots lay in disagreements between Alexander Hamilton and Thomas Jefferson during the early years of the Republic over government's proper role in encouraging industry and commerce. When Hamilton promoted and Jefferson opposed the federal assumption of state war debts and the establishment of a national bank, they were seeding the ground for an argument that would in various forms travel through national history.

Jacksonian Democrats and Whigs divided over the issue in the 1830s and 1840s, as Whig leader Henry Clay's American System sought to foster economic growth through government encouragement of internal improvements—roads, canals, and, in time, railroads. Whigs also supported a national bank as a source of financing and credit to developing American industries, only to see the Second Bank of the United States destroyed by Andrew Jackson, who opposed what he regarded as unwarranted privileges accorded the wealthy and well-connected. Public resources, Jackson believed, should be expended equally, without cronyism or favoritism.

This rejection of the idea of state capitalism, in which government largesse helps determine the outcomes of economic transactions, has been a durable and persistent impulse in American political culture, occupying both its left and right flanks. Elements appear in Populism, Progressivism, the New Right of the 1970s, and both the Tea Party and Occupy Wall Street movements of the early twenty-first century. The idea that business owners are receiving state-sponsored privileges is one that resonates across class, ideological, and party lines. This helps explain the nature of the anti-Dodger contract alliance. The populist-influenced belief that taxpayer resources were being unfairly distributed could animate a white homeowner from the San Fernando Valley as readily as a Latino Chavez Ravine evictee. It turned John Holland and Edward Roybal, whose racial, political, and geographic backgrounds and affiliations could not have been more different, into allies.

Proposition B's placement on the June 3 ballot did not come as a surprise to O'Malley. He decided his best response would be a focus not on the referendum but on his team's play on the field in 1958. The most important aspect of this would be the field on which they would actually play. As of December 1957, he had thousands of ticket applications but no way to fill them. His fellow National League owners were privately voicing concern over the location of the Dodgers' 1958 home field, as was league president Warren Giles.[34]

Each of the three possible venues O'Malley was considering had serious drawbacks. Wrigley Field held only 21,500 spectators, making it smaller than Ebbets Field.[35] It was also located in a poorly accessible residential neighborhood south of downtown with limited parking availability. The Los Angeles Memorial Coliseum was adjacent to the campus of the University of Southern California and in the city's Exposition Park. It could accommodate more than 100,000 football spectators and had adequate nearby parking areas. But it was a football and track facility that had never been envisioned as a baseball stadium. Shoehorning a diamond into the Coliseum's oval dimensions would produce an asymmetrical configuration in which either right or left field was unsettlingly short. In addition, its closely packed rows of plank seating hindered spectator access and vendor movement and forced even fans purchasing high-priced tickets onto uncomfortable bleacher-style benches.

O'Malley's third option, the Rose Bowl, was not even in the city of Los Angeles. Its Pasadena location raised the question of whether the Dodgers, if they played there, could be considered a "Los Angeles" team. Residents of the neighborhood surrounding the stadium were accustomed to the inconvenience of the Rose Bowl football game every New Year's Day but would be much less forbearing if faced with the traffic congestion that accompanied seventy-seven baseball home games. And of course, the Rose Bowl, like the Coliseum, was a football facility, albeit without the scheduling inconveniences posed by the presence of the latter's three existing tenants, the University of Southern California, UCLA, and the NFL Rams.

None of the venues, then, was optimal. But O'Malley needed to settle on one of them if he wanted to have a 1958 Dodger season, and in early December he began to negotiate in earnest. It became clear almost immediately that Wrigley Field would serve only as a fallback choice. O'Malley sought to obtain the best possible deal from the Coliseum or the Rose Bowl.

His discussions with the two proceeded simultaneously and almost ran afoul of each other. On December 12, O'Malley spoke

The Los Angeles Memorial Coliseum in 1957, configured for football. University of Southern California, USC Digital Library, *Los Angeles Examiner* Photographs Collection. Photographer: Sansone.

with officials of the Rose Bowl, which benefited from a north-south field configuration that would not force players to stare directly into the sun.[36] Meanwhile, the commissioners of the Coliseum, despite the presence of the sympathetic Kenneth Hahn, were driving a hard bargain. On December 16 the *Examiner*'s Vincent Flaherty reported that the commission was demanding O'Malley pay what would be the highest rent in baseball: 10 percent of the team's gross receipts plus all concessions revenues. Flaherty noted that the typical major league baseball rental averaged 7 percent of gross receipts, with the team and the municipal lessor customarily splitting concessions income. "The Coliseum Commission," he wrote, "should welcome the Dodgers and be proud of its chance to do something great for Los Angeles and all of Southern California."[37] The next day O'Malley flew to New York for the Christmas holidays, leaving his ally Hahn to attempt to coax a better Coliseum deal. O'Malley also announced that he would reconvene Rose Bowl negotiations upon his return.

In O'Malley's absence, the Coliseum Commission on December 20 voted down a deal that would have had the Dodgers guarantee $175,000 in annual rent and $350,000 for two seasons, with concessions income credited to the team. The arrangement would have made it possible for the team to avoid paying rent if concessions revenues were high enough. This was too generous for four of the commissioners, one of whom charged that allowing the Dodgers to play "rent-free" was tantamount to "giving away public money."[38] The commission vote on the plan was 4–4, with one absence; six positive votes were needed for adoption. Hahn protested that the city's income take under the deal would have been substantial enough to justify it, and, appropriating the rhetoric of the Dodger contract opponents, he maintained that "we owe that much to the taxpayers."[39] A number of the no voters on the commission claimed that O'Malley's negotiations with the Rose Bowl gave them reason to reject the plan. It appeared that the venues were getting in each other's way. In any case, a glum Hahn remarked, "today's vote blew up any hopes of the Dodgers playing in the Coliseum."[40]

On December 29, 1957, Walter O'Malley and his family took their final leave of New York and flew west into uncertainty. The Dodgers had no home field for the 1958 season. Their stadium contract was the subject of a public referendum and taxpayer lawsuits. Major segments of the city's population opposed the team's move to Chavez Ravine. O'Malley, with his suite of rooms at the downtown Statler Hotel, did not even have a permanent Los Angeles residence (he rented and later purchased a house on Lake Arrowhead, some seventy-five miles away, to which, schedule permitting, he commuted). O'Malley had often been criticized in New York for what was perceived as his calculating opportunism. Yet the challenges facing O'Malley in his adopted city were immense. Had he indeed schemed for years to take his team west, as some New Yorkers charged, he could hardly have planned less successfully. O'Malley's goal—a modern, privately owned stadium for his team—was clear. His preference for that stadium's location—Brooklyn—was also clear. His turn to Los Angeles had all the qualities of a fallback plan. As 1957 came to an end, O'Malley was adrift in Los Angeles, less the master of events and individuals than their captive.

On his return to the West Coast, O'Malley shifted his attention to the Rose Bowl. Before resuming negotiations, he attended the annual *Los Angeles Times* sports dinner, where his search for a home field became the object of comedian Bob Hope's humor. The Dodgers, Hope quipped, were now "the orphans of baseball," and would be playing "house to house."[41] Meanwhile, O'Malley's opponents continued on the attack, with Holland arguing in a letter to voters that Chavez Ravine was a potential "gold mine" and warning that "beneath this land may lie one of the greatest pools of oil in California."[42] Anti-Dodger-contract real estate developer Don Blaha claimed that the city of Los Angeles's share of stadium property taxes would amount to only $100,000 per year, low in comparison with San Francisco's annual $525,000 rental fee for Candlestick Park.[43]

In January 1958, another group, hailing from the anti-communist right, joined the campaign against the stadium deal. The Committee for Public Morality, consisting largely of white homeowners, circulated an apocalyptic flyer warning that the Dodger contract would "destroy forever that basic American right—*your right*—of a man to dispose of <u>his</u> property, hard-won and paid for by <u>his</u> efforts, as <u>he</u> sees fit."[44] It charged that contract proponents were "a totalitarian clique" aiming to "kick aside the Constitution" by permitting "a public body to seize private property for some pretended public purpose, and then *turn it to the private profit of third parties.*"[45] The Committee for Public Morality placed itself on the side of the evictees of Chavez Ravine, linking their plight to a more generalized assault by collectivist forces on American free enterprise:

> *Hundreds of families,* innocent and helpless, were driven from their homes where they had thought they were secure—*an entire community wiped out, soviet style,* on the excuse of socialized housing. The public . . . rejected the projects. But the unused land, instead of being returned to the former owners, for whatever future gain *they* might obtain . . . was transferred from the

Housing Authority to the city itself . . . *"to be used for public purposes only." Any attempt to divert this property to the private property of anyone* other than the original owners would be . . . *a theft from the local public—and treachery to the nation!* [46]

The entrance of the Committee for Public Morality into the stadium controversy symbolized the splintering of the coalition that had successfully opposed public housing in Chavez Ravine in the early 1950s. Then, Downtown interests led by the Chandlers had worked the Folks into an anti-socialist frenzy. The private sector and not the government, they had argued, should control the city's housing market. The private property rights of the Chavez Ravine homeowners, they had maintained, were sacrosanct and must be protected against an intrusive, confiscatory state. But now Downtown was backing a plan that would not only evict the remaining Chavez Ravine residents from their property but also offer public resources to an entrepreneur for a privately owned stadium there. To the members of the Committee for Public Morality, this was just another one of the forms socialism could take. Their erstwhile allies in the Downtown business community had abandoned the cause of free enterprise.

Embedded in the hysterical rhetoric of the Committee for Public Morality were legitimate policy questions worthy of the more cerebral and rational Robert Moses. What was the proper role of the public sector in facilitating private sector growth? At what point did government aid to businesses and businessmen shade into statism or at the very least crony capitalism? Downtown supporters of the Dodger contract sought to distinguish municipal assistance to a tax-revenue-generating corporation such as the Dodgers from state-built, -owned, and -operated housing. But to the Folks-dominated Committee for Public Morality, not to mention the Citizens Committee to Save Chavez Ravine for the People, they were much the same thing. In denying O'Malley the Atlantic/Flatbush land tract in Brooklyn, Robert Moses had applied his own restrictive interpretation to the words "public purpose." "The jig's up, Walter," Moses had reportedly said near the end of their negotiations, and by and large, the people of New York agreed.[47] Now Proposition B would decide what "public purpose" would mean in Los Angeles and how much the government could do for the Dodgers before it crossed the line into "socialism."

O'Malley attended the Rose Bowl football game between Ohio State and Oregon on January 1, 1958, in the company of his old World Series nemesis, Yankees manager Casey Stengel. Five days later he reopened negotiations to play baseball in the Bowl. Hovering over his discussions was a cryptic warning from National League president Warren Giles that playing in Pasadena, outside the city limits of Los Angeles, might open the territory to another franchise.[48] While it was doubtful that the cautious Giles, whose salary was paid by the owners, would have followed through on his warning, the issue complicated the Rose Bowl talks. Also giving O'Malley pause was the announcement of a petition drive aimed at placing a referendum blocking the Dodgers from using the Rose Bowl on the June 3 ballot, where it would join the already scheduled Proposition B.[49] A group of citizens took out an advertisement in a local newspaper to rally voter support for the drive.[50]

O'Malley was stymied. After a few more days of fruitless discussions with Pasadena city manager Don C. McMillan, he gave up on the Rose Bowl. On January 13 O'Malley and McMillan announced jointly that negotiations had failed, citing the $750,000 cost of converting the facility to baseball and the "damage" the work would do to the field.[51] Probably more determinative was O'Malley's fear of yet another legal and electoral morass to go with the one in which he was already enmeshed. In any event, he had now forfeited his only bargaining chip in negotiations with the Coliseum commissioners and was essentially at their mercy.

Seeking to put the best face on things, O'Malley drove directly from his announcement in Pasadena to Wrigley Field, which he introduced as the Dodgers' home for the 1958 season. "We've got to get tickets printed," he said, stating the obvious.[52] Then, offering more than he probably should have under the circumstances, O'Malley admitted to reporters that he was "not burning any bridges behind me" and that he was still interested in the Coliseum.[53] The day before, he had witnessed an event there for the first time. Fittingly, it was a football game.[54] The stadium's 100,000-plus capacity was more than four times that of Wrigley Field. There was no telling when the new Dodger stadium would be ready, and O'Malley required sufficient revenue to survive until then. The 1958 season was scheduled to begin in a little over three months. The impatient sports media was referring to Los Angeles as "the laughing stock of the nation."[55] Bob Hope was enjoying a comic field day, joking that the team would play in "Zsa Zsa Gabor's rumpus room."[56] O'Malley needed the Coliseum and he knew it.

The Coliseum was a logistical nightmare. The stadium was a massive oval with a set of peristiles at one end, below which were a foreshortened bank of seats. The Coliseum commissioners had originally demanded that home plate for a baseball configuration be located at this end, despite the fact that it would drastically reduce the number of prime home-plate-area seats and would force batters and spectators to stare into the late afternoon and early evening sun.[57] O'Malley sought a plan that placed home plate at the Coliseum's opposite, closed end and minimized the resulting cramped configurations. He wished to reduce the inconveniences to the stadium's football tenants from modifications to outer walls and the creation of spaces for dugouts, screens, and protective barriers. There would, however, be the issue of an unconscionably close left field fence, which would measure only about 250 feet down the line if the diamond was sited in the Coliseum's closed end.

O'Malley wrestled with these problems for weeks as negotiations for the use of the facility sputtered and stalled. Finally, during one of the many sleep-interrupted nights through which he suffered after moving to Los Angeles, the outline of a solution came to him. Home plate would be at the Coliseum's closed end. There would be a bare minimum of structural changes in that area—dugouts and a backstop screen would be added—to placate the stadium's three football tenants. There would be a forty-two-foot-high wire mesh fence running from the left-field foul pole to

O'Malley's "3 A.M. plan" for the baseball configuration of the Los
Angeles Coliseum, January 1958. University of Southern California,
USC Digital Library, *Los Angeles Examiner* Photographs Collection.
Photographer: Unknown.

left-center field. A shorter fence would cut down the vast dimensions in right field, although its 440-foot distance would be daunt-
ing, to say the least.[58] What became known as O'Malley's "3 A.M.
plan" did not solve all of the Coliseum's logistical problems, but it
did make it possible to play something resembling the game of
baseball there.

The remaining challenges were financial. O'Malley would
clearly need to improve on the deal the Coliseum commissioners
had rejected in December, under which he would have received
credit for concessions revenue against an annual rent of $175,000.
This he did. O'Malley agreed to pay a rent amounting to $300,000
a year, higher than that of the football lessees and the highest ever
for a major league baseball team, yet another reminder of the
advantages of private stadium ownership.[59] In addition, O'Malley
would remit to the Coliseum 10 percent of his gross receipts and
all concessions monies for nine home games early in the season.[60]
Beer sales were banned at Coliseum events and O'Malley would

lose this lucrative source of income. The Coliseum would also receive all parking revenues. O'Malley would be responsible for the cost of changing the field over to a baseball configuration and then back to football, as required by the other tenants. Since it was clear that the new Dodger stadium would not be ready until at least 1960, if then, the Coliseum lease would run for two years. In all, it would cost the Dodgers between $600,000 and $700,000 to play in the Los Angeles Coliseum in 1958. Presented with this advantageous deal, the Coliseum commissioners brushed aside their earlier doubts, as well as the lingering objections of USC, UCLA, and the Rams, and unanimously approved the Dodger lease on January 17, 1958.[61]

So O'Malley now had a stadium, although not one that he owned. He had paid more for it than he wished, but the huge capacity of the Coliseum offered the opportunity to recoup his investment and more. With this agreement O'Malley had a profit ceiling Ebbets Field could not match. There would be no need to gouge fans at the box office. On January 20, with lease in hand, O'Malley announced his ticket prices for 1958.[62] His $3.50 and $2.50 charges for box and reserved seats would remain unchanged for the next seventeen seasons. "We intend to take care of the little man," O'Malley said as he made his ticket price announcement, "because he is the one that keeps us going."[63] A massive stadium as well as the promise of a permanent Dodger ballpark projected to have almost twice the capacity of Ebbets Field allowed him to make his game affordable to average fans and their families while simultaneously wooing entertainment industry celebrities with special treatment and accommodations. Celebrities in turn would attract more everyday fans, as Dodger games grew into events having as much to do with entertainment as with the sport of baseball itself.

O'Malley's Coliseum deal, as expensive as it may have been, represented the first step toward transforming baseball into a commodity of mass leisure, a product comparable to a movie, television program, amusement park, or day at the beach. Traditionally, winning was all that mattered in the baseball business. Won-loss records were the sole measure of team success. But if the game

A Los Angeles Coliseum
worker prepares the
field for Dodger
baseball, January 22,
1958. University of
Southern California,
USC Digital Library,
Los Angeles Examiner
Photographs Collection.
Photographer: Lapp.

could be made to transcend the final score, if it could be transformed into an event providing an enjoyable experience largely
independent of victory or defeat, the opportunities to expand a
customer base were almost limitless. "Fans" cared only about winning games. "Customers" wanted to win, of course, but they also
wished to be entertained. An enjoyable ballpark experience could
outweigh the outcome of the game itself.

As he planned his team's 1958 season in the Coliseum, O'Malley
envisioned new possibilities for the marketing of his game. He
grasped a truth that had largely eluded his fellow owners. They
were all businessmen, of course. But they viewed the game and
only the game as their product. Los Angeles would give O'Malley
the chance to drastically reduce his business's win-loss risk by
changing its essential nature, making the final score only part of
the value his customers would receive for their money. He could
offer a day of excitement, fun, and adventure, even if the Dodgers
lost. Los Angeles would thus enable O'Malley to begin the business of baseball over again.[64] Brooklyn Dodger fans may well have
been unsurpassed in their passion for and knowledge of the game.

But more casual Los Angeles Dodger customers were far greater in number. Baseball purists might decry the practice of boosting attendance by selling Dodger games as "the thing to do" and "the place to be." But O'Malley knew that for every hard-core Dodger fan there were dozens of potential Dodger customers with families who could as easily choose to go to a ballgame as a movie if the cost of a ticket was comparable for each. Thanks to the vast Coliseum, he now had the space to accommodate all of them. Baseball could be both competition and entertainment. The Dodgers could be both a team and a brand. If he could invest his product with these qualities, O'Malley would see a lot of people—both fans and customers—in his seats. This would be his goal in Los Angeles.

One of the most important vehicles through which O'Malley would present his team to his new city, of course, would be electronic media. In New York, all home and twenty-odd road games a year had been carried on free television. His concerns about giving his product away on local airwaves were assuaged somewhat by the rights fees he received. During his final New York years O'Malley had begun to explore the possibilities for pay television with Skiatron, a fledgling cable broadcast company.[65]

Now that the Dodgers were on the West Coast, Skiatron was attempting to establish a base there, but its progress was slow. With prospects for pay television uncertain, O'Malley faced a dilemma. Should he continue to show games on free TV, as he had in New York? The Milwaukee Braves, whose operations he followed with great interest and no small amount of envy, blacked out all games. The Braves had outdrawn the Dodgers by more than 800,000 fans in 1956 and almost 1.2 million in 1957.[66] Presented with the opportunity to start over in Los Angeles, O'Malley decided on a different approach. On January 19, he announced that while every Dodger game would be broadcast on the radio, there would be none on free TV. He would partially relent later in 1958, when he agreed to televise the team's road games in San Francisco, reasoning that local broadcasts of contests with the Dodgers' traditional rivals would stimulate ticket sales.[67] But there O'Malley drew the line, departing from his New York strategy and embracing the business proposition that over-the-air television rights payments could not compensate for gate receipts lost when potential customers watched at home instead of coming to the ballpark.

Radio, however, was another story. O'Malley understood that in Vin Scully, he possessed not only one of the very best play-by-play announcers in the game but a peerless marketer for Dodger baseball in Los Angeles. Scully was a native New Yorker who had become a team broadcaster in 1950, only one year out of Fordham University. When Dodger lead announcer Red Barber left for the Yankees after the 1953 season, Scully took over as the primary voice of the team. A gifted storyteller with an unsurpassed ability to paint a word picture with his voice, Scully was perfect for baseball on the radio. By the time the Dodgers left Brooklyn he was as closely identified with the team as any of the players, a trusted source of news, insight, and entertainment. Indeed, to many fans, Scully *was* the Dodgers.

Scully came to Los Angeles at the urging of O'Malley, who would need him to connect the team with its new audience. Los Angeles, unlike New York, was a city built around the automobile, magnifying the importance of radio to drivers trapped on crowded freeways. With television coverage unavailable, Scully would carry the entire burden of publicizing the Dodgers over the airwaves. O'Malley was confident Scully would turn Los Angeles Dodger radio listeners into Los Angeles Dodger ticket buyers. Hearing Scully describe the game so vividly would make them want to see the real thing in person at the Coliseum. And even though O'Malley wished to stay out of the Proposition B battle if at all possible, Scully would attract yes votes without overt on-air campaigning. The friendly, humorous, and knowledgeable voice on the other side of the radio would be an unsurpassed source of goodwill for the team and by extension the Dodger stadium contract.

O'Malley made another broadcasting decision that would have major long-term ramifications for his team. Los Angeles's Latino population represented a huge potential market for the Dodgers. Baseball had deep roots in the Mexican American community, with neighborhood leagues serving both to cement social bonds and to showcase the talents of sandlot players.[68] O'Malley was also concerned about the ongoing effects of the looming Chavez Ravine eviction controversy. Although not responsible for its genesis—he had, of course, been in New York when the original notices to vacate went out—O'Malley knew he would be associated with the ultimate outcome of the dispute. He decided that Spanish-language broadcasts of Dodger games were essential to the success of his franchise in Los Angeles, and he instituted them for the 1958 season.

In 1959, O'Malley hired Jaime Jarrin, a local radio sports reporter and a native of Ecuador, to do play-by-play over station KWKW. Jarrin, a vivid wordsmith whose dramatic calls made him the most recognizable and beloved "Dodger" in the city's Latino neighborhoods, would become the Spanish-language counterpart to the English-speaking Scully. Like Scully, Jarrin's career in the team's broadcasting booth would span more than half a century. O'Malley was not oblivious to issues of racial justice, and while credit for signing Jackie Robinson in 1945 had gone almost exclusively to Branch Rickey, the hiring of Jaime Jarrin was O'Malley's idea alone. The origination of Spanish-language Dodger broadcasts not only made O'Malley a racial pioneer but also bound his team to the Latino community of Los Angeles. The developing crisis over the Chavez Ravine squatters would strain those bonds, but thanks in large part to Jarrin they never broke.

The quality of the team O'Malley would put on the field in Los Angeles suffered a severe blow in the early morning of January 28 when star Dodger catcher Roy Campanella's car skidded and crashed on an ice-slicked road in Glen Cove, Long Island, leaving him paralyzed below the neck. O'Malley had a friendly, almost paternal relationship with Campanella and had helped his player purchase the Harlem liquor store from which he was driving home when he was injured. O'Malley was in New York to finalize his purchase of the stock of a minority team owner and was deeply shaken by news of the accident. He traveled to Glen Cove to visit Campanella at his hospital bedside. The O'Malley family would keep the permanently paralyzed Campanella in the employ of the Dodgers as a coach and team ambassador until his death in 1993.

Campanella's loss further weakened a team that was already aging and in decline. The stable lineup that the Dodgers had fielded for the better part of a decade was coming apart. Longtime short-stop and captain Pee Wee Reese was thirty-nine. First baseman Gil Hodges was thirty-four, right fielder Carl Furillo was thirty-six, and both center fielder Duke Snider and starting pitcher Carl Erskine were thirty-one. Don Newcombe, ace of the Dodger staff and Cy Young Award winner as baseball's best pitcher in 1956, was in the midst of a precipitous alcohol-fueled and injury-plagued decline. Robinson had retired after refusing to accept a trade to the Giants after the 1956 season. Campanella himself was thirty-six at the time of his automobile crash. The team O'Malley planned to unveil in April 1958 would be the worst in his time as majority owner. With an uncertain mix of fading stars and untried young-sters, it was clear he would be unable to rely on the promise of a pennant race to lure fans.

Nor did he have an attractive home stadium. The Coliseum had plenty of seats, but its field layout was almost comically dispro-portioned. Many spectators would be so far from the action as to require the radio voice of Vin Scully to inform them of what was occurring on the diamond before their own eyes. In Brooklyn the game had sold itself. Los Angeles would be different. The novelty of the team would help, of course, but O'Malley knew that would not last for long. Without a winning team to sustain interest, he would have to work to make the Dodgers an attraction, an inte-gral part of the entertainment culture of the city. If the team became a lingua franca for its citizens, a way to measure them-selves as Angelenos, O'Malley would have a chance to succeed regardless of where the Dodgers finished in the standings. He would also have a chance to succeed on Proposition B. And even-tually he could build the stadium of his dreams, one that would merge the worlds of sports and entertainment so seamlessly that his millions of fans and customers would no longer distinguish between the two.

Meanwhile, the Proposition B campaign continued. The Los Angeles Chamber of Commerce, perhaps Downtown's quintessential institution, began circulating a flyer in late January that headlined "It's a good contract," arguing the merits of a privately constructed stadium that would remain on the municipal tax rolls and generate income for the city.[69] But clearly a coordinated approach was needed to counter the arguments of the Citizens Committee to Save Chavez Ravine for the People, not to mention the likes of the Committee for Public Morality.

It was also clear that O'Malley could not be associated personally with any pro-contract campaign, since he was now a lightning rod for the opposition. He could, however, nod discreetly toward contract supporters as they organized on his behalf. Assistance came in an unlikely form. Joe E. Brown, a sad-faced actor and comedian best known for his role in the classic movie comedy *Some Like It Hot* and a devoted baseball fan, announced the formation of the Taxpayers' Committee for "Yes on Baseball" to spearhead the pro-contract drive. While Brown was, of course, a representative of Hollywood, he understood the importance of Downtown to the new organization and moved to ally with it. Even the group's use of the word "taxpayers" in its name reflected Brown's savvy appreciation of the arguments being employed by contract opponents and his determination to counter them.

Los Angeles had a history of rejecting public outlays for projects that had the potential to increase taxes. Just three years earlier, in 1955, voters had rejected proposed bond issues for a municipally owned stadium, an expanded Los Angeles International Airport, and even additional sewer services. Since the heart of the Citizens Committee's campaign against the Dodger contract was its ostensible "giveaway" of tax revenues, Brown's group needed to position itself as taxpayer-friendly. If the contract could be shown to generate municipal income by keeping a privately constructed stadium on the property tax rolls and if that income could be shown to exceed the rental income on a publicly built ballpark, then the giveaway argument would evaporate. Further, if a stadium could be advertised as vastly increasing the value of the Chavez Ravine land—something even contract opponents conceded it would do—its fiscal attractiveness would also be enhanced. The Taxpayers' Committee's strategy was clear: emphasize the ways in which a privately owned ballpark was superior to the municipal stadium planned for San Francisco and for that matter every stadium built since 1923, when the New York Yankees had paid for Yankee Stadium with their own funds.

The numbers for public ballparks, however promising on paper, never seemed to add up in the real world. Cities such as Milwaukee, Baltimore, and Kansas City had financed stadiums primarily through bond issues. This public debt was to be retired, at least in theory, from annual payments of rent from the tenant ball club. But these payments, along with the cities' share of concessions, parking, and ticket revenue, were never enough to cover the bond obligations, turning the stadiums into money losers.[70] In addition, since special taxes or increases in existing levies were often employed to supplement the bond issues, the stadiums were viewed as unnecessary burdens by city residents who were not baseball fans and who resented paying for a facility they did not use. The taxpayer would thus be the target voter for both the Taxpayers' Committee for "Yes on Baseball" and its already existing competitor, the Citizens Committee to Save Chavez Ravine for the People. Specifically, it would be the white middle-class homeowning taxpayer who would be that target. Latinos and African Americans paid taxes too, of course, but the Folks held the key to power in the very white, very Protestant Los Angeles of 1958. The Citizens Committee would try to convince them that the Dodger contract would increase their tax burden. The Taxpayers' Committee would try to convince them it would not. Public or private: which option would cost the taxpayer the least? The Proposition B campaign would turn on the answer to this question.

The Taxpayers' Committee quickly assembled a powerful base of supporters. In addition to Chandler's *Times* and real estate and business interests, they included representatives of the aviation and aerospace sectors (Northrop Aircraft, Aerojet General, and Trans World, Western, and United Airlines); banking and insurance (Bank of America, Union Bank and Trust, and Equitable and Pacific Mutual Life Insurance); oil and automotive (Union Oil,

Signal Oil and Gas, and Firestone Tire and Rubber); retail (Bullock's Department Store); building (McNeill Construction); and manufacturing (General Electric). The Taxpayers' Committee also drew substantial support from organized labor. The California State Congress of Industrial Organizations, the Los Angeles County Central Labor Council, the Los Angeles Building Trades Council, and the American Federation of Labor's Central Labor Council all signed on, attracted by the employment possibilities offered by the construction of a new stadium. The Downtown Business Men's Association and Southern California Hotel Association added to the weight of the new organization, and Brown would use his contacts in the entertainment industry to attract an array of film, television, and music stars.[71]

Perhaps the most significant addition to the pro-contract team, however, was the public relations firm of Baus and Ross, which the Taxpayers' Committee brought in to run its campaign for Proposition B. The firm was a pioneer in political campaign management and in 1958 still something of a novelty. Certainly the Citizens Committee possessed nothing like it. Beginning in 1945, Herbert Baus and William Ross had applied the persuasive techniques of modern advertising—creating demand for a product or service—to political candidates and issues. Most of their clients were right of center. The firm had worked on the "anti" side of the referendum held in 1952 to decide the fate of the public housing program in Los Angeles and advised conservative Norris Poulson's successful campaign for the Los Angeles mayoralty the next year. Baus and Ross boasted a consistent record of electoral success—close to 90 percent, according to its promotional material.[72] It sprang into action on behalf of the Dodger contract, composing letters to editors of the major metropolitan newspapers in mid-February extolling the virtues of the contract and the money a privately financed stadium would save Los Angeles taxpayers.[73]

More problematic, however, was the question of the firm's relationship with O'Malley himself. The Dodger owner had announced his intention to stay out of the Proposition B campaign but had an obvious interest in Baus and Ross's success. While silent in public, O'Malley established quiet contacts with the firm, exchanging letters and memos on strategies and tactics with the partners, who attempted to guide him through Proposition B's public relations thicket.

On February 7, William Ross reported to O'Malley that "our campaign is off and running" and discussed what he considered his two most significant problems.[74] The first involved the oil and mineral rights to the Chavez Ravine land. O'Malley had already agreed to place his half share of potential oil revenues into a trust fund for the public recreation area called for by the stadium contract. But Ross feared that this would not be enough to satisfy the deal's critics. Oil, Ross wrote, was "a hot issue in Los Angeles," one that needed to be handled carefully. "Every time mention is made of oil rights," he warned, "people see another Houston," referring to the Texas city that was built on petroleum. "Our unanimous recommendation is that somehow or another you come up with a 'quit claim' to all control over oil money (if any)." This would put a stop to the "insinuations and innuendoes" that the Chavez Ravine transaction was merely a subterfuge to acquire valuable real estate.[75]

The other image problem O'Malley faced, according to Ross, concerned the nationally broadcast Game of the Week that CBS and NBC carried in areas without major league franchises. Los Angeles fans had become accustomed to seeing the Game of the Week, but now that the city had the Dodgers, who themselves would be blacking out most games, they stood to lose it. Ross urged O'Malley to at least permit Game of the Week telecasts when the Dodgers were on the road, again to assuage Proposition B voters.[76] While O'Malley was willing to surrender potential oil rights in the interest of public relations, he could not yield on the Game of the Week issue since baseball rules prohibited these telecasts in major league territories.[77] The issue of free television, however, was mitigated somewhat by the broad popularity of Vin Scully's radio descriptions.

If the pro-contract forces had one advantage over the deal's opponents during the Proposition B battle, it was Baus and Ross. The firm offered an innovative approach to what was simultaneously a political and public relations campaign. Baus and Ross employed direct mail to reach hundreds of thousands of Los Angeles households. It took advantage of electronic media to persuade voters. It formed speakers' bureaus to address area organizations whose support it was courting. Its messages were consistent and coordinated. The Citizens Committee relied on J. A. Smith's financing and a dedicated group of volunteers. It employed no advertising firm. It boasted few high-profile members. It may have been the model of grassroots organizing, but without a media-savvy, mass-persuasive approach similar to that of the Taxpayers' Committee, it was relegated to one-vote-at-a-time retail-style politics. As events would prove, however, not all Los Angeles voters were susceptible to the attractions of celebrity and spectacle.

As O'Malley struggled to assemble his operation in Los Angeles, his rivals in San Francisco could not resist sarcasm-laced comparisons between the two cities' preparations for major league baseball. "It hardly seems possible," the *San Francisco Chronicle* gloated in mid-January,

> that a deal in one city could be so clean and classy while a comparable one in another could get as fouled up as a boot camp fire drill. In San Francisco, the city that knows how, the Giants are in business, flourishing and making friends like sixty. In Los Angeles, the city that never has known how, chaos and frustration are roomies. . . . In San Francisco, civic government from its highest to its lowest level has done everything for the Giants except scrape the infield. Pride of possession and dedication to progress is an administrative fever. In Los Angeles . . . ugh![78]

To a large degree, this was true. While Giant owner Horace Stoneham was reaching an amicable agreement with San Francisco city leaders to rent cozy and picturesque Seals Stadium and watching work proceed on his team's future permanent home at municipally owned Candlestick Park, O'Malley was bogged down in taxpayer lawsuits and a referendum battle, not to mention contentious negotiations for temporary upkeep in a football stadium. O'Malley, in fact, found himself defending the entrepreneurial impulse itself in Los Angeles. Speaking at a meeting of the Coliseum Commission in January, he said:

> If it is the function of the government to get rich on private enterprise, then of course get the last dollar out of the Dodgers. If, on the other hand, it is the function to make a beautiful facility available for something that was effectively invited to come to this community, then I say, do it on a basis where we will make money, and you should want us to make money, because the money we make will make it possible for us to build the stadium we have contracted to build. And we can't do it if our earnings suddenly start falling off . . . because our bank credit will not be good . . . I don't know why it is in some cases I find that a person is subject to criticism for making money. We made the money and we kept the money and we did it because we were husbanding our earnings in order to be able to accumulate the money to pay for what we think will cost us $12,000,000 at Chavez Ravine. And we think Los Angeles will have the most beautiful baseball stadium in the world . . . And we want to build that.[79]

O'Malley concluded by telling the commissioners, "I always think it is refreshing when private enterprise [gets] into competition with the government."[80] Here, O'Malley was not arguing for free enterprise in its purest form. Rather, he was seeking a partnered arrangement in which government offered assistance to industries and entrepreneurial undertakings that promised to produce tangible public benefits such as jobs and tax revenues, or even less tangible ones such as those related to recreation and entertainment.

Contract opponents, however, did not believe it was the function of government to decide which private entities would succeed by weighting the scales of influence, power, and resources in their favor. They were suspicious of both big business and big government and especially to any perceived alliance between the two. An editorial in the *Hollywood Torch-Reporter*, a community newspaper, captured this sentiment:

In Chavez Ravine, "Giveaway" Poulson did not ask the taxpayers to vote on this deal—it was their money that was involved. . . . Mayor Poulson and 10 city councilmen voted for an unconstitutional ordinance giving away "public property" to "private enterprise." . . . In fact, they voted to give O'Malley land that is still occupied by several families in Chavez Ravine. Who has the right to give away "mortgage free" homes to out of state franchises? . . . Every trick imaginable has evidently been tried to fool taxpayers into thinking they are getting a "big deal" by giving away "public property" to the Dodgers Baseball Club.[81]

The contract, the newspaper charged, was riddled with "loopholes that can be filled in for O'Malley, without telling the taxpayers how they strangle them and benefit him."[82] Citizens Committee secretary Bessie Smith, in a letter to the *Torch-Reporter*, proceeded along similar skeptical lines, claiming that Poulson "overwhelmed the majority of the [city] council, [which] . . . turned deaf ears to the pleadings of hundreds of desperate people, asking [him] to save them from destruction of their beloved homes."[83] To Smith, the Chavez Ravine deal was symptomatic of a larger assault on private property in Los Angeles: "Chavez Ravine was the beginning of what is happening in LA today. Drive through our downtown section—Bunker Hill, Westlake Park, etc.—and you will see barren acres of destroyed property, [which] only a few months ago were private enterprise or private homes, now only empty lots of rubbish. Who get this property? . . . Will the insurance companies, oil companies, Hollywood Bowl, or perhaps another Eastern enterprise? . . . Better still, Russia . . . I understand how they respect [Poulson] for destroying private enterprise. God help the rest of you to wake up before it is too late."[84]

O'Malley had the support of the mayor, a majority of the City Council, and an alliance of business, civic, labor, and professional groups. But in the Citizens Committee and the readerships of community newspapers such as the *Torch-Reporter* as well as in Holland, McGee and their constituents, he faced a powerful populist impulse rooted in the city's white middle-class population. It combined an aversion to large-scale government initiatives with an equally intense desire to defeat the plans of the wealthy and powerful.

This explained how John Holland could oppose both public housing in Chavez Ravine (as a socialistic intrusion into the private market) and the Dodger Stadium contract (as a transfer of public resources to a private entrepreneur). It explained how Patrick McGee could praise the municipally financed stadium in San Francisco and advocate a similar arrangement in Los Angeles. It even explained why Bessie Smith, a white homeowner who had likely lost little sleep over the plight of Latinos in a neighborhood she quite possibly had never visited, would take up the cause of the Chavez Ravine evictees. All were expressing a populism of the Folks and their descendants, a white small property–owning middle class that defined "the people" in markedly self-referential terms. Like Los Angeles municipal politics itself, it traversed ideological and party lines, yoking the conservative's resentment of unchecked government power to the liberal's hostility to entrepreneurial ambition. Its perspective was conspiratorial, a natural complement to the traditional insecurities of the Folks.

Los Angeles had long been a city replete with inside dealing over water, land, housing, oil, transportation, the film industry, and even organized crime.[85] To those accustomed to such machinations and used to being excluded from them, the Dodger contract was in keeping with their darkest imaginings. To the Folks, the people, the ones who did not belong to the business groups, the real estate boards, the civic organizations, and the political classes, Proposition B represented the classic outsider's moment.

In late January, O'Malley accepted an offer from the widow of Dodgers minority owner John Smith to purchase her 25 percent interest in the team, giving him total control of the franchise and its direction in Los Angeles.[86] He now pondered the costs of building Dodger Stadium with his own or borrowed money in the event Proposition B passed. There had not been a ballpark constructed with private funds in the thirty-five years since Yankee Stadium opened in 1923. The cost of that undertaking had been $2.4 million. O'Malley's dream would be considerably more expensive, even accounting for inflation and increases in the cost of living.

O'Malley estimated the price of constructing Dodger Stadium itself at $12 million to $15 million. In addition, he had promised to build a public recreation area on the Chavez Ravine property for approximately $500,000, with maintenance costs over twenty years that would total $1 million. While the city had allocated $2 million toward land grading and filling, O'Malley could see that this would not be enough and that he would have to contribute a similar amount to this work. And while the city had promised to use its "best efforts" to acquire Chavez Ravine land parcels from individual owners, O'Malley knew that if these efforts were unsuccessful, he would have to step in and buy them himself at greatly inflated prices. Finally, since the Chavez Ravine land would increase substantially in value with the addition of a stadium, property taxes would rise correspondingly, to at least $300,000 per year and perhaps higher. Upkeep and maintenance would guarantee additional expenses in the future.

The costs associated with the stadium greatly exceeded team cash reserves, and it would be necessary to take on debt in order to move forward. But in a new and unfamiliar financial environment it was not at all clear where and from whom the money would come. The same arguments that Proposition B opponents leveled against the stadium—that it was poorly sited, that the land tract was unsuitable, that it would disrupt traffic patterns, even that it misallocated public funds—could easily be used by local banks as reasons to deny O'Malley funding. As spring training at Dodgertown in Vero Beach, Florida, approached, the Dodger owner's worries were not confined to an aging team lacking dependable pitching and a starting catcher. He faced political and financial challenges that threatened to derail his plans in Los Angeles in their entirety.

A thousand miles north of Vero Beach, Ebbets Field stood abandoned, with a solitary caretaker on duty to guard against vandals. Across the Hudson River in Jersey City, Roosevelt Stadium, where the Dodgers had played a portion of their home schedule in 1956 and 1957, also sat empty and unused. Back in Los Angeles, Wrigley Field, O'Malley's property as well, was without the Pacific Coast League Dodger farm team, which had transferred to Spokane, Washington, after its parent moved west. As O'Malley ruefully observed, he owned or paid rent on three ballparks and was not actually playing baseball in any of them.[87] He was also a tenant in a football stadium with a plan for a new stadium on land he did not yet own. Under the circumstances, O'Malley looked forward to the familiarities of Dodgertown—the communal dining, golf outings, and convivial St. Patrick's Day celebrations—as restoratives. But this year he would be denied even these pleasures. After breaking his anklebone during a hunting trip to Cuba and undergoing intestinal surgery in New York, O'Malley missed all of spring training.

The New York press corps, however, was in Vero Beach in full force and ill humor, filing stories complaining of second-class treatment, reporting on O'Malley's stadium travails with malicious delight, and even speculating on the possible return of the team to New York. The absence of the paralyzed Campanella also cast a shadow over training camp. While catching prospect John Roseboro was ready to assume a starting position and would be selected to play in the All-Star Game during the coming season, the popular and affable Campanella would be missed as much off the field as on. The team played its first game as the Los Angeles Dodgers on March 8, an exhibition against the Philadelphia Phillies. Their home opening game in the Los Angeles Coliseum was only forty-one days away.

4

THE REFERENDUM

Back in Los Angeles, the Proposition B battle ground on. The Taxpayers' Committee continued to blanket the city with Baus and Ross–produced literature, all the while claiming, in the words of Joe E. Brown, "the Dodgers are taking no part in this campaign. They are contributing neither money nor personnel, because they believe the referendum is an issue for the people to decide without outside interference."[1] The Dodgers' public forbearance may have been good political strategy, but it did not help the Taxpayers' Committee's bottom line. Sectors of the city's economy that would presumably benefit from a new stadium—hotels, restaurants, Hollywood, retail, downtown real estate—were initially slow to contribute. "More financial woes," Ross wrote to the Mayor's office in March, lamenting a "100% turndown" from the motion picture industry.[2] A dour Ross warned that his firm would "take no responsibility for the successful outcome of the campaign."[3]

Even accounting for these difficulties, however, the Taxpayers' Committee would outspend the Citizens Committee by a significant margin. Much of this spending was on Baus and Ross itself, which regarded "Yes on Proposition B" as the equivalent of a consumer product to be positioned, marketed, and sold. Only five years earlier, Rosalind Wyman had walked door to door during her successful run for a City Council seat, speaking with individual voters on their front steps and in their living rooms. Such tactics were quaint compared to Baus and Ross's sophisticated approach, as were those of the Citizens Committee, which ran virtually no newspaper, television, or radio advertisements during the Proposition B campaign.

But even if Baus and Ross could reach voters, could it convince them? In March, it was not at all clear that it could. A *Wall Street Journal* reporter covering the referendum found substantial anti-contract sentiment in a series of sidewalk interviews. "All levels of government are overspending as it is," said a Los Angeles dentist. "If there's one thing we don't need it's subsidized sports."[4] "It's a good deal all right," an insurance company employee remarked in a sarcastic reference to Baus and Ross's pro-contract slogan, "for the Dodgers."[5] He predicted that "the footprints of the movie stars outside Grauman's Chinese Theatre will draw more tourists than any baseball team," noting that "the city didn't give the theatre owner his front yard."[6] Out in the San Fernando Valley, an officer of the West Valley Property Owners' Protective Association, a small business group, complained, "If they're going to give this land to the Dodgers, they ought to go out and buy 300 acres for the [Los Angeles] Rams. . . . In fact, there doesn't even have to be a sports outfit. You might as well do it for General Motors; there's no difference."[7] The Citizens Committee's C. A. Owen boasted of his group's version of direct mail advertising, in which apartment house owners opposed to the contract would place flyers under their tenants' doors. "We want to put fear into those people at City Hall," he announced.[8]

J. A. Smith, who was responsible for most of what financing the Citizens Committee possessed, took direct aim at O'Malley and his motives. "That [Chavez Ravine] property is worth $25 million and I don't want it turned over to O'Malley for a goddam ballpark," he told *Sports Illustrated*. "I know what he's got in mind. He wants to put in motels and bars and restaurants along with baseball. Let's hear him say no."[9] Smith also demanded to know if O'Malley planned to leave Los Angeles if Proposition B was defeated.

O'Malley was concerned enough about this potential trap question to ask Baus and Ross for advice. If O'Malley's answer was yes, he would appear to be holding the city hostage to his stadium ambitions. If it was no, he was effectively inviting a renegotiation of the Chavez Ravine contract on less favorable terms. W. B. Ross counseled him to say neither, since "no matter what you say about staying here, [Smith] will use it against you. Put yourself in his position and you will see how he can put you in a very poor light."[10] Despite his misgivings, O'Malley went along with Ross's advice and refused to be drawn in.

Still, O'Malley was getting his message out through friendly media, including *Sports Illustrated*. In an interview with its reporter Robert Shaplen, O'Malley defended the stadium contract as an example of entrepreneurial initiative: "I think it's rather significant that in this era of socialism and government effort there is someone who wants to put up the first new ball park with his own funds since Yankee Stadium was built with baseball dollars in 1923. I think it's a rather refreshing idea at a time when everyone expects the taxpayer to take the rap."[11]

O'Malley also offered *Sports Illustrated* readers a glimpse into his plans to market the Dodgers as an entertainment experience centered around fan amenities. "We're way behind in baseball," he told Shaplen. "Race tracks are way ahead of us in imagination, planning, showmanship. Why, Santa Anita [racetrack] has only 25,000 grandstand seats, but it has room for 30,000 cars. Why should baseball fans be treated any less advantageously? Why shouldn't they have good restaurants and other services? Baseball is the same old show in dull, drab-green parks. Even the outdoor theatres are ahead of us."[12] Referring to Los Angeles fans, O'Malley said, "Folks will always come out in person if it's made convenient and pleasant for them. They'll come in buses from 100 miles away."[13] While O'Malley's faith in the willingness of Southern Californians to embrace public transportation may have been misplaced, he understood the role amenities had come to play in the spending decisions of entertainment customers.

Baseball had always marketed itself, to the extent it did so at all, by creating an almost mystical connection between fan and team. These loyalties gestated early and lasted a lifetime. "Give me the child until he is seven and I will give you the man," went the famous Jesuit maxim, and baseball team owners had always relied on a variant of it to nurture fan allegiances.[14] They were passed from fathers to sons at an early age and resembled the power of religion itself in intensity and longevity. But in Los Angeles, where a vast proportion of residents were originally from somewhere else, home team allegiances might prove less than Jesuitical. O'Malley thus understood that in his new city entertainment values would matter all the more.

O'Malley did not mention Disneyland to Shaplen, but he very well could have. Opened in 1955, it embodied everything the contemporary major league baseball park was not and all that O'Malley envisioned for Dodger Stadium. Disneyland was accessible by freeway and offered acres of parking. It was conveniently laid out, offering "guests" (as Walt Disney insisted on calling his customers) a seamless flow from parking lot to ticket window to entry gate to a "Main Street, USA" portal that established Disney's intended mood of small-town American nostalgia. This street funneled guests into a series of clean and safe attraction areas manned by efficient and unfailingly polite park staff. Prices were affordable, aimed at families and repeat visitors. O'Malley hoped his new stadium would reproduce these features in a baseball setting. Dodger Stadium would be the sport's version of Disneyland, a park for customers— for "guests"—and for families. No other owner had imagined the presentation of baseball in this way. The game would draw them in but the experience would bring them back. In time, every baseball franchise, major and minor league, would adopt O'Malley's vision. Game presentation managers and even departments would become as essential as uniforms, bats, and balls. Cleanliness, access, convenience, and safety would become ballpark watchwords. Team executives would pay as much attention to what occurred off the field as on it. Dodger Stadium would change the ways in which baseball, and sports generally, were viewed and consumed.

But first it had to be built, and in March 1958 that was by no means certain. *Sports Illustrated*'s Shaplen wrote that "if [O'Malley] occasionally has some private doubts, he acts like a man in complete control of the situation."[15] But even this reflexive optimist seemed to be flagging in spirit. Shaplen overheard Harold

McClellan, who had negotiated the Dodger contract on behalf of the city, tell the Dodger owner, "Everybody says fine things about the way you're handling yourself." Unimpressed, O'Malley replied, "That's nice but I'm not getting anywhere." "You will, you will," reassured McClellan. "I know this town." Then, out of O'Malley's earshot, he muttered, "I've never before been ashamed of my city, but I am now."[16]

The start of the regular season offered O'Malley a distraction of sorts from the stadium battle. On April 15, 1958, the Los Angeles Dodgers played their first regular-season game—fittingly, against the Giants, at Seals Stadium in San Francisco. Giant owner Horace Stoneham had boasted that he had never seriously considered Los Angeles as a possible new home for his team. "I prefer San Francisco," he claimed. "Why? Because it's a cosmopolitan city. Los Angeles is a 'transient city.' . . . San Franciscans are a different breed of people. They're business people, substantial, with more pride in their community. Los Angeles fans? . . . [T]hey go to an event to be seen or because it's the thing to do. They'll break their necks to get to a World Series, but how will they respond, day in, day out?"[17] Stoneham's characterizations of his new city were borne out on his team's opening day, as 100,000 San Franciscans lined the streets in welcome and sold out 22,900-seat-capacity Seals Stadium.[18] With O'Malley in attendance, the Giants won 8–0 behind pitcher Ruben Gomez, knocking out Dodger starter Don Drysdale in the fourth inning.

After splitting the next two games in San Francisco, the teams traveled down the coast for the opener in Los Angeles on April 18. The night before, Dodger ownership, staff, and players gathered for a Baseball Writers' Association welcome dinner at the downtown Biltmore Hotel along with twelve hundred guests. After master of ceremonies Art Linkletter joked that O'Malley was "building an ulcer-shaped swimming pool here" and singer Dinah Shore entertained, the Dodger owner addressed the gathering. "It's been a fascinating honeymoon here," he announced, choosing to express his sentiments regarding his team's relationship with Los Angeles through the metaphor of courtship and marriage. "Tomorrow, we hold open house in the Coliseum and on June 3 we hope to make it all legal."[19]

The next day, sunny and hot, the uniformed Dodger players gathered on the steps of Los Angeles City Hall to be officially greeted by the public officials most responsible for bringing them west, including Poulson, Wyman (who had just given birth to her first child), and Kenneth and Gordon Hahn. The players then piled into open-top convertibles for a motorcade through downtown Los Angeles. Reporters from New York newspapers, who had been dispatched to cover the event, sneered at what they described as a "perfunctory" parade that "sped through town in twenty minutes" amid "only a token smattering of confetti."[20] Photographs, however, show crowds deep on the sidewalks of Los Angeles's relatively compact business district, with some enthusiastic supporters milling in the streets.[21]

Driving south from downtown's "skyscrapers"—a word the *New York Times* story sarcastically placed in quotation marks—the players were deposited at their temporary home, the Los Angeles Coliseum, replete with a 251-foot left-field line topped by a forty-two-foot screen, a massive right field, and, perhaps most important, 78,672 customers.[22] They made up the largest regular-season crowd in major league baseball history.[23] It was more than three times larger than the opening day attendance at Ebbets Field in 1956, when the Dodgers hoisted their world championship pennant from the previous year.[24]

Taxpayers' Committee chairman Joe E. Brown presided over a pregame ceremony for an audience that included dozens of the brightest Hollywood stars and Proposition B supporters, with Jimmy Stewart, Bing Crosby, Gregory Peck, Jack Lemmon, Groucho Marx, and Edward G. Robinson, among others, on hand.[25] O'Malley had sent invitations to celebrities and politicians to serve as honorary Dodger coaches on opening day, placing them in special boxes adjacent to the field; his courtship of high-profile fans with prime seating accommodations would become a hallmark of Dodger operations.[26] Poulson threw out the first pitch as California governor Goodwin Knight, state attorney general and future governor

Edmund "Pat" Brown, San Francisco mayor George Christopher, and Jack Norworth, the lyricist for the baseball song classic "Take Me Out to the Ballgame," looked on.[27] The hospitalized Roy Campanella was honored as a schoolboy player stood in for him at a home plate tribute.

Carl Erskine, a veteran Brooklyn fan favorite who had so few connections in Los Angeles that he invited the only resident he knew—a transplanted friend from his Indiana hometown—to be his guest on opening day, was the Dodger starting pitcher.[28] His first pitch, broadcast by Scully on KMPC radio, was picked up by thousands of transistor radios in the Coliseum stands, a comment both on the poor sight lines in the vast stadium and the young broadcaster's descriptive skills, which enhanced what was occurring before the spectators' eyes. Erskine threw a strike to Giant third baseman Jim Davenport, then a brushback pitch toward his head. Davenport hit the next offering on a line off the centerfield fence. It bounced back so sharply that he was held to a single.[29] This set the tone for an afternoon of bizarre plays befitting the strange dimensions of the Dodgers' new field. The Giants suffered the indignities of two men on a base in the first inning, and Davenport missed third on his way home in the ninth, nullifying a run. A number of batted balls that would have been home runs in virtually any other major league ballpark instead hit the high left-field screen and bounced back into play, while normally catchable flies became homers. After more than three hours, a marathon game for 1950s-era baseball, the Dodgers prevailed 6–5, with Erskine getting the win.[30]

Though attendance diminished somewhat for the remaining two games in the series with the Giants, the totals—41,303 and 47,234—substantially exceeded those obtainable even from a sold-out Ebbets Field.[31] Over the succeeding seven weeks leading up to the June 3 referendum the team played poorly, posting a 17–26 record and falling into last place. The Giants, in contrast, led the National League in early June. The Dodgers even managed to embarrass themselves when games were not being played. On April 23, outfielder Duke Snider bet a teammate he could throw a ball out of the Coliseum and injured his arm attempting to do so.

He was fined by irate general manager Buzzie Bavasi.[32] But attendance figures, the numbers that mattered most after the standings
themselves, were stellar. Over their first twenty home dates, the
Dodgers drew 586,797 fans to the Coliseum, an average of over
29,000 per game. Total attendance for the Ebbets Field Dodgers
of 1957 was 1,028,258.[33] The transplanted team had attracted
more than half as many fans as had turned out in Brooklyn in
about a quarter as many games.

The 1958 Los Angeles Dodgers would go on to finish second
in National League attendance even as they ended the season on
the field in seventh place, twenty-one games behind the pennant-
winning Milwaukee Braves. O'Malley had taken in approximately
$4 million in ticket revenue.[34] The Dodgers' 1,845,566 customers,
the most in their history, compared favorably with the Braves'
1,971,101.[35] The team O'Malley had feared more than any other
was now on the way to being neutralized as a competitor. Its fan
base shrinking each year, hemmed in by the Chicago market to
the south, the Braves franchise would never again challenge the
Dodgers for revenue and young talent. In 1966, the team would
abandon Milwaukee altogether and move to Atlanta.

In his April 19 story on the Dodgers' home opener, Frank Finch of the
Los Angeles Times had referred to the team as "our guys."[36] This
bit of hometown boosterism captured the conundrum of Proposition B opponents as the referendum campaign headed into its final
weeks. How could they oppose the Dodger deal while professing
to support the Dodgers themselves? O'Malley had even been able
to use his team's poor performance early in the season as a subtle
argument for the stadium deal by blaming it on uncertainty over a
permanent home. "I think we have to recognize the fact that the
players have not been at ease," he said in May, "and I think that
after this election on June 3, when all of this dies down, one way or
the other, I think they will come through and play up to their capacity."[37] There was no denying that the Dodgers were immensely
popular in Los Angeles. and undoubtedly the Coliseum fans cheering on their new team could connect their desire for a better

on-field product with the idea of a modern stadium for "our guys." Even Holland, McGee, and Owen claimed to want the Dodgers in Los Angeles. But distinguishing between opposition to the Chavez Ravine contract and to the presence of the franchise itself was nearly impossible.

O'Malley, however, had a dilemma of his own. He needed a new ballpark in order to run an artistically and financially viable operation in Los Angeles. But he was making a significant profit in a converted football stadium. How could he say that he intended to stay in Los Angeles but had to have a new place to play without sounding as if he was threatening to leave in the event Proposition B failed? This too was a difficult distinction to sell to voters. Each side, then, was telling a story that was shaped and shaded to place the tellers in the best possible light. Holland and O'Malley and members of the Citizens Committee and Taxpayers' Committee avoided directly articulating the implications of their positions and actions, constrained by necessity from saying exactly what was on their minds. It would be up to the voters of Los Angeles to resolve the tensions between them.

On April 19, another taxpayer lawsuit was filed against the Chavez Ravine contract in Los Angeles County Superior Court, this one on behalf of Louis Kirshbaum, represented by Phill Silver, a notorious local gadfly attorney. His complaint alleged that the City Council had exceeded its authority in agreeing to the elimination of the public purpose clause from the deed that had transferred the Ravine land from the CHA to the city in 1955.[38] It also objected to the allegedly unequal exchange of Wrigley Field for the considerably more valuable Chavez Ravine property. Silver argued that this amounted to an illegal gift to a private entity that now had effective control over how public monies would be spent. On April 28, Silver obtained a temporary restraining order placing any enforcement of the contract terms in abeyance until a hearing on a preliminary injunction could be held in Superior Court in June. Thus, even assuming a victory for Proposition B at the polls, there would be no immediate progress on stadium construction.

Meanwhile, the contract opposition kept the pressure on. The Citizens Committee sought to cast suspicion on O'Malley's plans for the Chavez Ravine property. One of its flyers charged that since the Dodgers were attempting to have the Ravine zoned C-3, which permitted the broadest range of commercial use, it was possible that "bars, hotels, restaurants, amusement parks, apartment houses, stores, and shopping centers" could appear on land now worth "tens of millions of dollars!"[39] In his *Sports Illustrated* piece, Shaplen had observed that the Dodger contract was "involved with two things about which Los Angeles can wax highly emotional."[40] One was oil, around which a controversy over rights and use was swirling even though it was unclear what actually lay beneath the Chavez Ravine soil. The other was "the price and purpose of real estate."[41] The thought of O'Malley turning land he had acquired into a commercial empire ancillary to a ballpark was guaranteed to stoke already existing resentments and paranoia. The Dodgers' defense that the C-3 zoning classification was necessary because it permitted the construction of a fifty-thousand-seat stadium was much less dramatic and compelling than speculation over a possible "Dodgerland" or "Dodger Mall" at Chavez Ravine.

The contract opposition began to grow more confident. "It is just possible," editorialized the resolutely anti–Proposition B *Hollywood Torch-Reporter*, "that a combination of neighborhood throwaways, an honest and alert small daily newspaper, and a score of aroused television and radio commentators may prove to be more influential than the downtown interests who once thought they had City Hall in their pocket."[42] In May, public opinion seemed to be shifting the opposition's way. An internal poll conducted by Baus and Ross had indicated a solid yes margin everywhere but in the San Fernando Valley, but now the contest was tightening significantly.[43] A *Herald and Express* poll even found a slight plurality for no, 42.7 percent to 40.2 percent.[44]

It was now clear that O'Malley's public reticence on the subject of the contract would need to change and a more aggressive strategy adopted. The strategy would have two components. The first was O'Malley's testimony at hearings conducted on the Chavez Ravine contract by the California State Assembly's Interim Committee on Government Efficiency and Economy on May 15 and 16. The other involved having National League president Warren Giles state publicly that the June 3 referendum would decide whether the Dodgers would remain in Los Angeles. Both would help turn the tide of the election.

On May 15, the Assembly hearings began in Los Angeles's downtown State Building with a blow to O'Malley. Karl Rundberg, one of the city council members who had voted in favor of the Dodger contract the previous October, announced that he had changed his mind.[45] Rundberg claimed that he had been misled as to the contract's implications, which he now viewed as full of loopholes and opportunities for private enrichment at public expense. His objections mirrored those of his new allies Holland and McGee. The stadium project, claimed Rundberg, did not constitute a public purpose. It was an unwarranted gift from taxpayers of land that was far more valuable than the Wrigley Field property offered in exchange. O'Malley, Rundberg insisted, could renege on his promise to fund the recreation area called for in the contract and still be in technical compliance with it. The Dodger owner's real goal, he now thought, was not erecting a baseball stadium but acquiring valuable real estate for commercial purposes. "I have been told there is no money available for landslide problems in my district," Rundberg announced, reflecting the view that the Dodger deal siphoned off funds better spent on local needs.[46]

While Rundberg's change of heart did not retroactively invalidate the City Council vote to approve the Chavez Ravine contract, it did call into question the pact's legitimacy, since it had passed by only one vote. Now Rundberg was disavowing his yes vote. Moreover, Edward Roybal, who had been absent when the October 7, 1957, vote was taken, was also opposing the Dodger contract. It was clear that if the contract had been on the council agenda on May 15, 1958, it would have been rejected.

It was in this atmosphere that O'Malley presented his testimony to the Assembly committee. Expanding on a theme he had sounded previously, he sought to link his team's lackluster play to the uncertainty over a permanent home, thus turning a negative into a positive. Subtly he raised the issue of whether the Dodgers would remain in Los Angeles if the contract were invalidated. His players, O'Malley insisted, "don't know to this day whether they are going to stay here or not."[47] With the Coliseum clearly unsuitable as a permanent venue, he was clear that "the future of the franchise is dependent on a new Major League Baseball park being built with a traditional playing field of proper Major League dimensions. The Dodgers want to stay in Los Angeles and build such a park."[48] O'Malley did not directly address the implications of not being permitted to build a new stadium in Chavez Ravine, but he did not have to. He could leave the legislators and the voters to their own conclusions.

O'Malley also made a case for the advantages of the private model of stadium development. "We were advised," he testified, "that Los Angeles was not prepared to build a stadium for us on tax-exempt property. This fitted in with my own thinking. It so happens that for ten years I have been old-fashioned enough to believe that a ball club should build its own stadium on its own land and that the stadium and land should be subject to normal taxes."[49] He promised that "in beauty, landscaping, maintenance, and comfort, it will be absolutely the finest baseball park in the nation."[50] He went on to detail the Dodgers' free ticket programs, which offered free admission during the 1958 season to 600,000 youth along with 100,000 adult chaperones, plus 100,000 service members and 20,000 disabled and senior citizens. This, O'Malley told the committee, amounted to a contribution of approximately $1 million to the Los Angeles community wholly apart from the public recreation center he had already contracted to construct and maintain on the Chavez Ravine property. The team would further support the youth of the city by sponsoring free baseball instruction clinics on a regular basis.[51]

O'Malley's testimony was powerful and effective. He highlighted the attractions of a privately built, property-tax-paying ballpark that would offer fans state-of-the-art amenities. He emphasized the Dodgers' commitment to the area's youth as well as to those who had served and were in need. And he raised obliquely the possibility that without a voter-approved stadium deal the team might leave Los Angeles. In contrast to the image presented by contract opponents of a self-interested businessman, O'Malley appeared reasonable and public-spirited. The hearings were not televised but they were covered extensively in the city's daily newspapers, all of which were editorially sympathetic to the Chavez Ravine deal.

O'Malley was supported by Poulson, city attorney Roger Arnebergh, chief contract negotiator Harold McClellan, and other sympathetic witnesses. Poulson framed his advocacy of the stadium project in terms of his responsibility to "all of Los Angeles."[52] He described contract opponents as "people from outlying communities [who] are apparently afraid that this is going to bring in some business downtown that they are not going to participate in."[53] Poulson predicted that the Dodgers would leave if the contract failed at the polls: "I'm sure they will and we'll be the laughingstock of the United States."[54] In his testimony, Arnebergh expressed surprise that O'Malley had consented to a private construction deal in the first place: "As far as I can see, under this agreement, Mr. O'Malley is taking a lot of risks that I wouldn't take if I were he."[55]

McClellan emphasized that he had represented the city's interests and not O'Malley's when he negotiated the contract and asserted that "from a balance sheet approach, I am convinced this is a sound and fair deal for the city. . . . [T]remendous indirect benefits . . . will flow to the city such as the hundreds of thousands of dollars the Dodgers will pay in taxes and the millions of dollars that will be spent in Los Angeles by Dodger fans."[56] Comparing the Los Angeles and San Francisco stadium deals, he said: "It boils down to whether you want the city to go into business or whether you sell property to private enterprise. We stand to collect $350,000 a year in tax money from land on which we now receive practically nothing."[57] An officer of the Downtown Business Men's Association underscored McClellan's point, citing a survey showing that almost half of Dodger ticket buyers came from outside the city and estimating that these visitors spent an average of $10 per day in Los Angeles.[58] This meant that $2.5 million had already flowed into the municipal economy as a result of the Dodgers' presence. He also praised the contract as "a vastly important one between private enterprise and the citizens of Los Angeles" which would stimulate "prosperity and unprecedented expansion."[59]

There was even a witness brought in from Milwaukee. Ray Weisbrod, the executive vice president of that city's Association of Commerce, testified to the economic benefits of major league baseball, brushing off the issue of O'Malley's potential enrichment with the remark that "to our businessmen [it] is not how much money do the Braves make in Milwaukee, but how much money does Milwaukee make as a result of the Braves."[60]

The audience for the hearings was divided between contract supporters and opponents, who cheered or booed witnesses in a display reminiscent of the scene at the City Council meeting the previous October when the deal had been approved. A Chavez Ravine resident, Mrs. Glen Walters, rushed the speaker's stand, exclaiming, "I own the oil rights in Chavez Ravine! The city is trying to steal them from us!" She was ejected.[61] Her photograph was featured prominently in the major newspapers in a veiled bit of editorializing on the contract opposition's lack of emotional stability.

McGee, Roybal, and other critics of the deal did their best to rebut the contract proponents' arguments without appearing to be wishing the Dodgers out of Los Angeles altogether. McGee charged that Wrigley Field was "nothing more than a white elephant. The Dodgers don't want it. They just threw it into the deal to make it look like a good deal."[62] The Giants' arrangement with the city of San Francisco, he averred, was "a million times better" than what the Los Angeles City Council had approved.[63] In an exchange with committee member Lester McMillan, McGee insisted that the Dodger contract exceeded the city's legal authority. "Do you mean to say," asked McMillan, "the City Attorney recommended an illegal contract?" McGee responded bluntly: "Yes, sir, I do."[64] When McMillan remarked, "There have been some very trenchant indictments made here about our public officials. We have a very good mayor and city council," McGee parried him deftly: "Yes, sir, but a poor contract."[65]

Roybal insisted he wanted the Dodgers to remain in Los Angeles, but that he also wanted a contract that "makes sense." McMillan pressed him to go further, asking, "Are you saying that there is a conspiracy existing between the mayor and the City Council to sell out to the Dodgers?"[66] Roybal, representing a constituency that was divided over the contract's merits, replied carefully: "We're not here to make accusations. We were over-anxious in the deal and we're paying dearly for it."[67]

McGee and C. A. Owen, who also testified against the contract, were put on the defensive by questions about the sources of the Citizens Committee's funding. Wyman, clearly referring to J. A. Smith, urged the Assembly committee "to ferret out the shadowy opposition, which is so anxious to run the risk of losing what has taken so long to gain."[68] Owen and McGee disavowed rumors that Smith was the power behind the anti-contract campaign. But the very act of minimizing the influence of this out-of-town business-man on an issue that should have been of concern only to Los Angeles residents diminished Owen and McGee's position. If Wal-ter O'Malley was an interloper from another city, than what was J. A. Smith?

The Assembly hearings exposed the weaknesses of the contract opposition while permitting the yes forces to cast their arguments in the best possible light. McGee, Roybal, and Owen claimed to want the Dodgers in Los Angeles, but not under the terms agreed to by the City Council. However, renegotiating the contract, even if it was possible—and O'Malley was adamant that it was not—would risk driving the team away. The city already looked, as Poulson put it, like a "laughingstock," dithering while its rival San Francisco forged ahead. During the hearings the contract oppo-nents were unable to articulate a realistic alternative plan for a sta-dium in Los Angeles.[69] The contract, even with its flaws, created facts on the ground that trapped its critics.

In contrast, O'Malley and his allies were able to use the hearings to present a concrete vision of the Dodgers' future in Los Angeles. A state-of-the-art ballpark, constructed at private expense. A property-tax-generating location adjacent to freeways and downtown. A rec-reation area for public use, built and maintained by the Dodgers. A steady stream of baseball-related spending and revenue that would foster economic growth in the city and surrounding area. The permanent enshrinement of Los Angeles as a major league city with national and international stature. And finally, a threat, under-stated by O'Malley and articulated more explicitly by Poulson, that the Dodgers would move elsewhere if Proposition B failed. Overall, the contract proponents had given the electorate a clear idea of what a yes vote on June 3 would produce. The opponents had articulated no such vision. O'Malley emerged from the Assembly proceedings in a better position than he had entered them.

In the days following the hearings, O'Malley pressed the momentum from what had become his strongest argument—that he might be forced to move his team unless the contract passed—in the second element of his more active role in the Proposition B campaign. In May, Baus and Ross sent a memorandum to the Dodger owner suggesting that National League president Warren Giles announce from his Cincinnati headquarters that the Chavez Ravine contract could not be renegotiated under any circumstances and that the Dodgers would only be permitted to play in a temporary stadium for two years, that is, through 1959. Giles would emphasize that the National League and not the Dodgers had the final say in matters relating to franchise moves, since a three-quarters vote of teams was required.[70] He would end with a warning that the vote on Proposition B would determine the future home of the Dodgers. Baus and Ross advised O'Malley to follow Giles's announcement with a statement of his own in which, after repeating his reluctance to become actively involved in the Proposition B campaign, he declared, "In view of Mr. Giles' remarks in Cincinnati, it is apparent that an unfavorable vote might leave me with no alternative but to seek a home for the Dodgers elsewhere."[71]

While there is no direct evidence that O'Malley agreed to this plan of action, nor proof that he even responded to the memorandum, actual events unfolded roughly as Baus and Ross had suggested.[72] Giles spoke to reporters on May 22. The Proposition B referendum, he asserted, "will be an expression by the people of Los Angeles as to whether they want major league baseball." Giles was clear as to the consequences of a no vote: "If [it] indicates we are not welcome, it will be my personal recommendation to our league that we take immediate steps to study ways and means of relocating the franchise in another city."[73] Poulson immediately supported Giles. The National League president, he said, had "laid it right on the line."[74] The battle over the Dodger contract was really about "whether we want to be classed as a big league throughout the United States or whether we want to be classed as bush leaguers . . . We have a very, very good [stadium] proposition. I think it is better than the one in San Francisco because it's a free enterprise situation. After Walter O'Malley spends his $12,000,000, it's up to him to make good."[75]

Predictably, the contract opponents responded to Giles with outrage. McGee thundered that Giles's threat was "an insult to the intelligence of the people of Los Angeles. If that is the type of what this city and our people can expect from the National League, I, for one, don't want them at all."[76] Rundberg echoed his council colleague: "If this is the kind of statement we can expect from the National League, the Dodgers can go home."[77] Holland viewed Giles's words as an expression of "the last desperate threat of a frightened group of greedy men. If the people of Los Angeles bow to this threat, it will be to the everlasting shame of our city."[78] These agitated responses allowed O'Malley to appear reasonable and public-spirited when he made his own statement. Giles and the anti-contract councilmen had staked out the extreme positions, with the former threatening to move the Dodgers and the latter seemingly willing to allow him to do so.

O'Malley could now occupy the middle ground. "The National League does have the right to move the franchise," he said in a press release, "[but] I shall fight any such attempt with all my strength. The players and our staff want to stay in Los Angeles. We like the location, the weather, the fans, and the attendance records. We plan to be in Los Angeles permanently."[79] O'Malley cast the contract dispute in terms the average citizen would understand. It was simply a matter of honoring one's word. "We have kept every promise we have made and we know the city and county will do likewise," he stated, and was emphatic that "there is neither the time or the willingness on either side to renegotiate what is already a fair contract."[80] If O'Malley and not the contract critics had demanded a renegotiation, "can you imagine the uproar these same critics would raise?"[81] In a radio interview earlier in May, O'Malley had remarked pointedly that "they used to say that out in the West a handshake was as good as a written contract, but we came out here not only [under] a handshake and look in the eye but a written contract as well. What kind of people would they be to repudiate that?"[82] Now, in a deft bit of table turning, O'Malley, an easterner, was asking westerners to keep their word.

O'Malley's press release also sought to put to rest the idea, circulated by the contract opposition, that he coveted Chavez Ravine either for what might lie beneath it or for its commercial use. "We are baseball folks," he promised Los Angeles fans, "not oil operators or real estate promoters."[83] O'Malley was thus able to reap the rewards of a threat to leave Los Angeles that Giles made for him and that Holland, McGee, and Rundberg appeared to be encouraging. O'Malley could present a yes vote on June 3 as the only sure way to save major league baseball in Los Angeles. In reality, as the contract opponents had charged, O'Malley was determined to remain in his new city. The fan response, despite an uncomfortable football stadium with terrible sight lines, had been overwhelming. Profit margins had been remarkable. Even Poulson, who publicly portended Armageddon if the referendum failed, privately doubted that O'Malley would actually leave. In his memoirs, Poulson admitted initiating what he termed a "scare campaign" aimed largely at lower-class voters, warning that the city would lose the Dodgers if Proposition B were defeated.[84]

There was also nowhere else for O'Malley to go. Some New York City newspapers were keeping alive the idea that his troubles in Los Angeles might force the Dodgers back to Brooklyn.[85] But O'Malley had closed that door. Nothing had changed on the stadium front since October 1957 save for plans for a municipal facility at Flushing Meadows that he had already rejected. There was also, of course, the matter of personal pride. It would be embarrassing to return to New York in the wake of failure on the West Coast. While there were other cities clamoring for major league baseball, none was comparable to Los Angeles in population or influence. O'Malley was essentially trapped where he was, a hostage to the Proposition B referendum. But by making what appeared to be a credible threat to do what he had no realistic intention of doing he played a disadvantageous hand masterfully. The contract opponents—Holland, McGee, Owen, and Smith—were reduced to the role of speculators, predicting a future that might or might not come to pass. O'Malley maintained that he intended to stay in Los Angles but that the Coliseum was inadequate for his team's needs. What did this mean? Increasingly frustrated and shrill, the critics of the Dodger deal were unable to offer a definitive answer. In the absence of one, they were allowing O'Malley to outflank them.

On May 24, a poll commissioned by Los Angeles congressman Joe Holt showed a slight lead for the "No on Proposition B" side, 44.7 percent to 43.3 percent.[86] Two days later, however, another survey commissioned by O'Malley attorneys O'Melveny and Myers indicated a shift of votes in favor of the contract. Here, 43 percent of the sample said they would vote yes and 31 percent no, with a comparatively large undecided cohort of 27 percent, indicating that the final outcome was still in doubt.[87] In an effort to predict how this substantial group who had not yet made up their minds would eventually vote, the pollsters projected that two-thirds of undecideds would vote no, on the assumption that unanswered questions about the contract would translate more heavily into negative votes on election day. This narrowed the final yes margin in the survey to only 2 percentage points, 51 percent to 49 percent.[88]

A breakdown of the poll results revealed more men than women supporting the contract (58 percent versus 49 percent) and slightly more support among respondents who were over fifty years old (53 percent) compared to those in their twenties (48 percent).[89] Voters in Central Los Angeles, which included the largely African American Watts neighborhood, favored the contract by 55 percent to 45 percent.[90] West Los Angeles, within which Rosalind Wyman's council district lay, backed it by 52 percent to 48 percent.[91] The San Fernando Valley was opposed by 53 percent to 47 percent.[92] The campaign thus entered its final week with both the yes and no forces showing strength in their base areas and the contract enjoying a narrow overall lead. The race was still too close to call.

Momentum, however, was moving in O'Malley's direction, which may have prompted Holland and McGee to make moves of their own. In May 1957, as he visited Los Angeles to negotiate the possible transfer of his team, O'Malley had written "vetoed in toto" on a press release prepared by city attorney Roger Arnebergh that discussed contract terms and referred specifically to the "Brooklyn Dodgers." Holland unearthed the release, which had not been issued officially, and made it public, charging on the council floor that its existence proved the "participation in the intimate operation of our city and county government by a resident of Brooklyn while visiting Los Angeles to seek concessions from the city."[93] Holland sought to give credence to the worst innuendos about O'Malley: that he was an out-of-town political boss who had manipulated weak-willed public officials such as Poulson, Wyman, and even the respected Arnebergh into an advantageous deal at the expense of the taxpayers of Los Angeles.[94]

Indeed, on its face the release made it appear that O'Malley was effectively running Los Angeles city government. Why else would a document that he had "vetoed in toto" have been hidden from public view until Holland publicized it? The truth, however, was considerably less dramatic. O'Malley explained that he had "vetoed" the release because "the Dodger ownership [in May 1957] was not ready to give up efforts being made in New York to keep the franchise there. The proposed press release mentioned the Brooklyn Dodgers by name and that was not acceptable to me for the above reason."[95] O'Malley had merely sought negotiating cover in case new possibilities arose for a ballpark in Brooklyn. He pointed out that he had not objected when the city issued a replacement press release on May 6, 1957, that contained no specific mention of the Brooklyn Dodgers. "This is a red herring," he complained, "and an old one."[96] Arnebergh backed O'Malley's version of events and termed Holland's charges "ridiculous."[97]

Tempers on the City Council floor were now at a boiling point. Wyman, along with contract supporters John Gibson and James Corman, walked out in protest after Holland made his "vetoed in toto" accusations.[98] On another occasion, when the valuation of Wrigley Field came before the council, Rundberg scoffed at its assessment of $2.25 million, claiming that Chavez Ravine was worth $18 million. "What's that got to do with Wrigley Field?" retorted Wyman. Rundberg snapped, "I'm sick and tired of you needling me every time I discuss the Dodger deal." After Wyman's ally James Corman rose to tell Rundberg to stick to the Wrigley Field valuation, McGee interjected, "Why don't you sit down and be polite?" The council session then adjourned in what a reporter described as a "general tiff."[99]

McGee also attempted to derail the contract with an alternative proposal of his own, which he unveiled on May 28. Why, he asked, did O'Malley need 315 acres for a stadium that would actually occupy only about sixty of them? The city should let the Dodgers keep Wrigley Field and sell them the sixty Chavez Ravine acres at the same price it had paid, retaining the rest of the land for a municipal parking facility.[100] Those revenues would then flow into public coffers and not O'Malley's pockets. McGee also dismissed the possibility of the team's departure in the wake of a no vote on June 3 as "so much eyewash in the light of O'Malley's strong declaration that he will fight to keep the Dodgers in Los Angeles."[101] O'Malley was making too much money to seriously contemplate leaving, said McGee, quoting Oliver Kuechle, a sportswriter for the *Milwaukee Journal*, who, referring to the Dodger owner, asked sarcastically, "Does a hungry dog walk away from a juicy bone?"[102] McGee argued that since "the Dodgers will remain in Los Angeles whatever happens June 3," the contract was ripe for renegotiation.[103] The councilman also claimed that O'Malley could veto any National League attempt to move the team if he wished to do so.[104] McGee took exception when Corman asked him if J. A. Smith had signed off on his plan, and the councilmen glared angrily at each other across the chamber floor.[105]

O'Malley himself offered a strong response to McGee's proposal. He flatly contradicted McGee's assertion that the Dodgers could unilaterally block a league-imposed transfer, characterizing the councilman's argument as "misleading" and "typical of the tactics of the opponents of Proposition B."[106] National League bylaws, O'Malley noted, could force a team to move with six out of eight votes, meaning that he and Giants owner Horace Stoneham would still need one additional franchise to agree to keep the Dodgers where they were.[107] McGee's plan had virtually no chance of adoption and only made the already existing divisions in the council sharper and bolder. McGee's eye, however, was not on his legislative colleagues but on the referendum voters. By raising the idea that there was an alternative to the contract as originally negotiated and driving home the point that the "juicy bone" of the Los Angeles market was irresistible to O'Malley, he was able to aid the "No on Proposition B" forces at a fraction of the cost of Baus and Ross to the Taxpayers' Committee.

The final days before the Proposition B vote were a frenzy of charges, countercharges, public posturing, and Hollywood-style hoopla. Rundberg floated a scheme for a stadium on an old movie lot in the San Fernando Valley, which O'Malley immediately dismissed.[108] The Taxpayers' Committee inundated the city with pamphlets, flyers, and advertisements. Playing the class issue, it alleged that one of the leading foes of the contract was "a prominent horse-fancier who has proposed that Chavez Ravine be the site for a glamorous arena to show blue-ribbon horses."[109]

Sympathetic sportswriters whose beats would stand to benefit from a new Dodger Stadium pitched in. Melvin Durslag, the influential columnist for the *Examiner*, wrote that cities "are getting their brains knocked out" on municipal stadiums.[110] San Francisco, he claimed, was anticipating losses of $400,000 a year on its investment in Candlestick Park and staggering under the weight of operations and maintenance costs and bond repayments. He accused contract opponents of being "phonies," since "if in their hearts they want major league baseball, they know they must give the Dodgers the land, or build them a park at public expense. They don't want to do either. It is financially impossible for the Dodgers to put up maybe $12,000,000 for a stadium—and buy the land too. The city must make a fair contribution for value received. So these great friends of baseball who begrudge real estate to the Dodgers can take their counterfeit friendships elsewhere. This is a matter for hard realists. Either we give them the land, or we build them a stadium, or we let them leave town."[111]

The Taxpayers' Committee, working both sides of the class divide, obtained testimonials from the Los Angeles Chamber of Commerce as well as the city's Building and Construction Trades Council, which envisioned "employment for hundreds of construction workers and a large and permanent payroll . . . built around the baseball operation into the future."[112] Baus and Ross also pitched the advantages of pass-along taxes to "you businessmen" in a "fact sheet": "The revenue from the Dodgers is a voluntary form of taxation which you do not have to pay. . . . Our Dodgers will pay more in taxes than other teams pay in rent. The taxes paid by the Dodgers and their financial commitment itself, are going to be taxes you and I won't have to pay—unless we want to! The fans will pay it—gladly!"[113]

Baus and Ross's most significant contribution to the "Yes on Proposition B" campaign in its last days was right out of show business press agentry. The Dodgers would end a lengthy road trip on Sunday, June 1, with a game against the Chicago Cubs, then fly back to Los Angeles in the evening. What if Dodgers fans came to Los Angeles International Airport en masse to greet them? It would serve not only as a gesture of support for the struggling players but also as a tacit endorsement of Proposition B. And if there were television cameras present to broadcast the scene, the visuals would be powerful and dramatic, coming only two days before the election. Accordingly, Joe E. Brown and the Taxpayers' Committee spread the word: "Let's all get out to the airport and let the players know we appreciate what they are bringing to our city. . . . Two things will restore [the team's] confidence—a big turnout at the homecoming and a big turnout at the polls Tuesday to vote 'Yes on Baseball.' "[114]

Brown's gambit was yet another illustration of Baus and Ross's sophisticated approach to political media and mass persuasion. The Citizens Committee staged individual events—Holland's speeches on the council floor, a McGee press release, Owen's testimony at a hearing. But choreographed by Baus and Ross, the Taxpayers' Committee produced mass events—meetings of targeted supporters' groups, market-saturating advertisements, and rallies that leveraged their product brand, which of course was the Dodger team itself.

There was one event that could surpass even a televised airport demonstration in impact and reach: a special "Yes on Proposition B" television program airing in conjunction with the Dodgers' airport arrival on June 1. O'Malley and the management of KTTV-TV planned "Dodgerthon," a five-hour televised testimonial to the stadium project that would ensure the pro-contract message would dominate the airwaves in the final hours of the campaign. Simultaneously Baus and Ross and the Taxpayers' Committee purchased a flood of radio spots they knew the Citizens Committee could not match.[115] The electronic media, so essential to success in Los Angeles, would serve the cause of the Dodgers.

The final preelection editorials of the daily metropolitan newspapers all favored the Dodgers. The *Mirror News* described the Proposition B vote as "a matter of basic integrity. Do we keep our word on a legitimate contract? The opposition has contrived a synthetic indictment of the terms of the agreement, from whatever vague motives. Actually, the city benefits greatly from the plan. . . . Tax revenues from Chavez Ravine are now $6000 a year. The Dodgers will pay $350,000 a year in taxes when the stadium is built."[116] The *Examiner* charged that "the opposition's reckless wrenching of the facts has confused the issue in many ways. . . . The 50,000 seat ballpark planned for the Ravine will be built with some $10,000,000 to $12,000,000 of Dodger dollars—not tax dollars. And who has spoken out against Proposition B? A few individuals who fear their narrow, personal interests might be in some way harmed. But not one representative civic organization."[117]

It fell to the *Times*, the city's dominant newspaper, to make the argument for the proposed stadium as a symbol of civic purpose and the foundation of a new Los Angeles. "Do you, a citizen-voter," it asked, "want Los Angeles to be a great city, with common interests and the civic unity which gives a great city character; or are you content to let it continue its degeneration into a geographical bundle of self-centered sections each fighting with the others for the lion's share of the revenues and improvements that belong to all?"[118] It asked for a yes vote on June 3 to "help to restore the communion of citizens in Los Angeles that has been dissolving so alarmingly."[119]

The editorial views of the Downtown newspapers reflected a significant degree of self-reference. It was true that a broad consensus of civic groups, labor unions, political elites, major media, the entertainment industry, and the business community supported the contract. But taken together they did not constitute "Los Angeles," whatever Norman Chandler, Norris Poulson, and Joe E. Brown may have believed. Interests of their own, not surprisingly, shaped their understandings of what constituted "common interests" and a "communion of citizens."

A nearby stadium built on city-owned land at private expense would certainly benefit downtown Los Angeles. It would raise real estate values and stimulate economic activity. It would give Los Angeles an important cultural asset. But was this enough? Did it confuse Norman Chandler's interests—and Norris Poulson's, and Joe E. Brown's—with those of the city as a whole? Were the concerns of the residents of the San Fernando Valley, some of whom lacked paved streets and sewer lines in their neighborhoods, any less valid? What about the middle-class homeowners, the Folks, who worried about fiscal responsibility? Or the Mexican Americans who mourned the destruction of a Chavez Ravine community that had sheltered and sustained generations? Couldn't they also claim to represent the well-being of the city as a whole? Weren't they also "Los Angeles"? Could there be true civic unity without them? Or were the attractions of a new home team playing in a new stadium enough to connect all Angelenos?

In late May, a contract opponent wrote to Rundberg arguing that "to subsidize a baseball organization that is a business living off the prosperity that has been created by constructive industry . . . adds nothing but glamour. Glamour is a good thing for people who are in that business, but not a good thing to be subsidized by the taxpayer."[120] June 3 would decide what part of Los Angeles would speak for all of Los Angeles.

The five-hour "Dodgerthon" was broadcast live on KTTV on Sunday, June 3. This last appeal to the voters of Los Angeles featured a list of Hollywood celebrities that read like a who's who of the industry—Jerry

Dodgerthon, June 1, 1958. Left to right: Jeff Chandler, Danny Thomas, Walter O'Malley, and William Frawley. University of Southern California, USC Digital Library, *Los Angeles Examiner* Photographs Collection. Photographer: Rustan, Gray, Otto.

Lewis, Groucho Marx, Dean Martin, Debbie Reynolds, Jack Benny, and Ronald Reagan, along with Yankees manager and Los Angeles area resident Casey Stengel, among others. Retired Dodger star Jackie Robinson, an invaluable asset in the city's African American community, contributed a taped endorsement of the stadium deal.[121] Halfway across the country in Chicago, the Dodgers faced off against the Cubs in the last game of a road trip that had begun on May 14 and had seen them win only seven out of sixteen games.[122] This would be the last Dodger contest before the polls opened on June 3. In view of the Taxpayers' Committee's invitation for fans to greet the team when it arrived home during the time Dodgerthon would be on the air, this was clearly a game the Dodgers needed to win. Stan Williams, a young, hard-throwing right-hander who had never started a major league game, was Manager Walter Alston's choice to pitch what had the feel of a September pennant race contest.

On the morning of Dodgerthon Ronald Reagan had received a telegram from the Citizens Committee criticizing him for agreeing to appear on the program and "endorsing giveaway of 315 acres Chavez Ravine city property and spending of millions of tax dollars developing it for private ball club . . . [and] selfish interests promoting this real estate deal."[123] An incensed Reagan went on the air and blasted the committee, characterizing their anti-contract position paper as "one of the most dishonest documents I've ever read in my life." He told the television audience, "I have always believed there are two sides to every question, but in this case they are the good side and the bad side. Chavez Ravine has been sitting there in the heart of Los Angeles for years and nothing was done with it. Now that a baseball team is to have it, it's worth a lot of money, we are told. Sure, Walter O'Malley got a good deal when he was offered Chavez Ravine as a site for his ballpark. Any deal to be good, must be fair to both sides, not to one."[124]

Beneath Reagan's angry rhetoric was an important substantive issue. Assuming the city made money on the Chavez Ravine deal but Walter O'Malley made money as well, was it still a good contract for the people of Los Angeles? Or did the fact that O'Malley stood to realize substantial revenue at a new stadium delegitimize the Dodger deal? Reagan and other supporters of the contract chose to emphasize O'Malley's risks, opponents his rewards. O'Malley always emphasized the benefits his team would bring to the local community. New York had effectively rejected that argument; there the focus was almost obsessively on O'Malley's profits.

There were many in Los Angeles with the same perspective. Dodgerthon was aimed at them. In addition to entertainment celebrities, the telethon brought in businessmen, unionists, religious officials, journalists, politicians, and Asian, black, and Latino community spokesmen to convince skeptical voters that a privately owned Dodger Stadium was a civic consensus builder backed by a consensus of Angelenos. Consensus, of course, lies in the beholder's eye, and opponents of the contract viewed Dodgerthon participants merely as self-interested parties. The cost of the telethon alone exceeded the amount spent by the Citizens Committee during the entire Proposition B campaign.[125] To the volunteers and door-to-door canvassers of that organization, Dodgerthon was yet another instance of influential Angelenos employing that influence to impose their will on the city, all the while claiming to represent its "common interests."

But whether the Citizens Committee or the Taxpayers' Committee better represented "Los Angeles" may have been beside the point. That was what the election was for. It was clear that the two committees harbored different visions of the city's future. One was that of a localized city of decentralized neighborhoods built around the provision of basic services. The other envisaged a national city with a vibrant central core built around business, entertainment, and culture. Dodgerthon's Los Angeles was an ambitious, outward-looking city, eager for status and influence. It looked to men like O'Malley to realize its dreams. The diorama of a new Dodger Stadium displayed prominently during the telethon was the physical embodiment of those dreams.[126]

Dodger Stadium would be the most important civic structure erected in the city since the Los Angeles Aqueduct in 1913. Then, water had made the continued growth and development of the city possible. Now, Dodger Stadium could give modern Los Angeles a profile commensurate with its demographic, economic, and cultural power. It would be an icon for what Los Angeles had become. Major league baseball in an aging converted football facility would not do. Only the finest new stadium in the United States would rise to the moment. Dodgerthon sought to convince the people of Los Angeles that Dodger Stadium would project what they already knew about their city to the nation and world. In that respect, they needed Dodger Stadium as much as their grandparents needed water.

On June 1 in Chicago, Stan Williams, the untried right-hander, pitched an unexpected shutout and beat the Cubs, 1–0. As Dodgerthon continued, the team plane headed home. By the time it touched down at Los Angeles International at 9:45 P.M. local time, a crowd of 7,500 had braved half-hour traffic delays to gather beside the runway.[127] Dodgerthon shifted its live broadcast to the scene at the airport as Scully interviewed players on the tarmac.

Back at the KTTV studio, O'Malley answered questions submitted by fans, assuring them he had no plans to leave. "We have to stay here for thirty years to get our money back at least," he quipped.[128] The fortuitous win over the Cubs and the televised airport rally ended Dodgerthon on a triumphant note. In its last hours, extra telephone operators had to be brought in to handle a crush of calls—overwhelmingly supportive—to the station switchboard.[129]

An estimated audience of 1.8 million viewed the broadcast.[130] It had unquestionably given the "Yes on Baseball" forces momentum heading into the Proposition B campaign's final forty-eight hours. The opposition, save for an appearance by Holland, McGee, and Smith in a June 2 Proposition B forum broadcast by KCOP-TV in which they shared time with O'Malley, Wyman, and Poulson, was virtually shut out of the airwaves during these last days.[131] Dodgerthon, a five-hour advertisement for the Dodger contract, went essentially unrebutted.

Even so, the vote on June 3 was close. Turnout was heavy, boosted by Democratic and Republican primary elections for governor and senator. Two-thirds of the eligible electorate, the largest in the city's history for a non-presidential election, went to the polls.[132] With approximately 10 percent of precincts reporting, yes held a 3,425-vote lead, about 52 percent to 48 percent.[133] That margin would narrow slightly as the count proceeded over the next day and a half, falling to 51.7 percent to 48.3 percent with the tally one-quarter complete, but it never disappeared.[134] In the evening, O'Malley followed the returns from the Coliseum, where the Dodgers were playing the Cincinnati Reds. A man familiar with the vicissitudes of electoral politics from his days in New York, he refused to claim victory despite his early lead. "I well remember," he told the *Herald and Express*, "Charles Evans Hughes going to bed [on the night of the presidential election of 1916] thinking he had won and waking up to find he had lost. . . . [T]his thing isn't won yet."[135] Taking note of the Reds' 8–3 victory, O'Malley remarked, "The only one sure of winning tonight was Cincinnati."[136]

By late in the afternoon of the fourth, however, it was clear that "Yes on Baseball" and the Dodgers had prevailed. O'Malley issued a victory statement: "We certainly appreciate the support of those who voted 'Yes' on Proposition 'B,' and we will be zealous in our efforts to gain the support of those who voted 'No.' . . . It is our sincere desire to . . . begin work on the new stadium as soon as possible."[137] Despite his outward calm, the referendum campaign had exhausted him. A *Long Beach Press-Telegram* reporter who was with O'Malley as the outcome became clear on the afternoon of June 4 described him as "obviously close to the breaking point." The Dodger owner "sank into a chair in the Statler Hotel, and sighed in an almost imperceptible voice, 'I sincerely hope this is it. If anyone, even the Good Lord himself, had told me nine months ago of what the Dodgers would go through in this move to California, I would not have believed it. I still can't believe I'm not dreaming. This is the most confusing move West since someone opened the Oregon Trail.' "[138]

O'Malley had good reason to be emotionally wrung out. The final count was 351,683 to 325,898, an uncomfortably close margin of just 25,785 votes.[139] "We nearly won!" exclaimed McGee, stating the obvious.[140] Indeed, the absentee vote, counted in mid-May, offered a snapshot of the state of the race before the Assembly hearings, Giles's threat to move the team, and Dodgerthon: 4,174 no, 3,299 yes.[141] It was possible that had the election been held just three weeks earlier, Proposition B would have lost.

But O'Malley had squeaked through. And it had been the Mexican American and African American voters who gave him his margin of victory. Yes had won by more than ten thousand votes in the Eighth Council District, which covered the largely African American South Central section and included Watts.[142] Edward Roybal's heavily Latino Ninth District defied its anti-contract representative and provided a yes margin of almost thirteen thousand votes, the largest of any council district.[143]

The 23,500 extra yes votes these two districts generated offset the four San Fernando Valley districts (First, Second, Third, and Seventh), which voted no by a combined margin of 15,579.[144] The only other districts decided by more than five thousand votes were

John Holland's Fourteenth (the Eagle Rock area, bordering Pasadena north of downtown), which went against the contract by 5,824, and the yes-voting downtown (6,250 votes) and West Central (8,487) areas.[145] In the referendum's aftermath, anti-contract leaders regretted not pursuing the black vote more vigorously. Ridgely Cummings, whose Civic Center News Agency had been a consistent anti-contract voice, admitted that while the committee "may have had some Negro member . . . on the key groups which decided policy and strategy I failed to notice them." Somewhat condescendingly, he argued that African Americans who believed they were voting "against juvenile delinquency (and for baseball)" had "endorsed a contract which they didn't understand."[146] However Proposition B opponents wished to interpret it, the strong black support for the stadium project was a product of the Dodgers' residual goodwill in the local African American community as the organization that had brought Jackie Robinson—himself a local hero—to the major leagues.

But the strong level of Latino support for the Dodger contract was harder to explain. Roybal was deeply respected in the Los Angeles Latino community as a pioneering public official and an effective advocate for the remaining residents of Chavez Ravine. He was a vocal critic of the contract, which he viewed as bad for both the city and his own constituency. How could that constituency have rejected him? It was clear that the construction of Dodger Stadium under the terms of the contract meant the eviction of the remaining Chavez Ravine residents and the destruction of the last vestiges of their community.

Why did the heavily Latino Ninth Council District vote yes on Proposition B by more than two to one?[147] The support of the city's leading Spanish-language newspaper, *La Opinión*, which editorialized in favor of the stadium project, certainly influenced the result.[148] But perhaps the pull of baseball, a deeply ingrained cultural signifier in the Mexican American community of Los Angeles, was too powerful to resist. That the Dodgers came to Chavez Ravine at the expense of marginalized Latinos would not be forgotten. Indeed, the Chicano movement of the 1960s in Los Angeles has been linked to the dislocation of the Ravine's population.[149] Yet the fact of the pro-stadium vote in the Latino community remains. It serves as a reminder of the complexities of the Mexican American experience in modern Los Angeles. Blood ties explain many things but not all things. In the Proposition B referendum a substantial majority of the city's Latino voters chose Dodger Stadium over Chavez Ravine. This choice was by no means an endorsement of the impending removals at the Ravine. But in this instance the imperatives of entertainment and leisure overcame those of ethnicity and culture. The last reckoning in Chavez Ravine, however, was yet to come.

Blurred emotions and motivations extended into the Ravine itself. In the aftermath of the Proposition B vote, the *Mirror News* sent a reporter to gather reactions from the remaining residents. One couple, Mr. and Mrs. Francis Scott, whose house sat on what would be the new stadium's home plate area, had voted in favor of Proposition B. "We think it'll be good for the city and good for us too. Somebody's going to pay a darn good price to get us out of here now."[150] The Scotts had been previously offered $9,000 for their property but were now hoping for at least $20,000. Another resident expressed similar sentiments. "I'm ready to sell just as soon as O'Malley makes the right offer," said Harry Hansen. "The city offered me $6000 for my place a few months ago. I laughed at them. . . . Now I'm sitting on my porch waiting to hear from O'Malley and the Dodgers."[151]

But Frank De Leon, the owner of the last remaining grocery in Chavez Ravine and a resident of forty-five years' standing, had voted no. De Leon's granddaughter Lisa Villa lived across the street. "I've lived here all my life," she told the newspaper. "I love it here. It's like being out in the country. But I'm moving away anyway. I knew the place was bound to change."[152] A neighbor, Joe Carranza, expressed mixed emotions: "I guess it will help property values and people will start selling out. But a lot of us will always be bitter. We just didn't want to move."[153] Nearby, Catalina Contreras spoke of her father Ramon, a cabinetmaker who had lived in Chavez Ravine for thirty years. "He's turned down offers in the past," she said. "He'll never sell."[154]

The *Mirror News* story illustrated the moral ambiguities of the Dodger contract issue even in the Ravine itself. For some, the life they had built over the years was everything and was not for sale at any price. Others, even as they grieved the loss of their community, were willing to engage in the bargaining customary to everyday real estate transactions. And there were those for whom nothing existed but commerce. While almost everyone wanted the Dodgers in Los Angeles, not everyone wanted them in the Ravine itself. The claims of culture and capitalism intersected in Chavez Ravine as they did elsewhere, forming tangled motivational webs. With the referendum campaign concluded, some Raviners prepared to negotiate, others to depart, and still others to resist.

The results of the Proposition B referendum, like many election results in Los Angeles, defied conventional political logic. As the *Los Angeles Metropolitan Area Newsletter* observed, "The baseball deal won victory through a strange political coalition. Its leaders were the openly Republican four metropolitan newspapers, downtown business groups and taxpayer organizations. Yet the voting for the Dodgers came in the heavily Democratic, low income areas where Negro and Mexican balloting was solid for 'Yes on Baseball.' Meanwhile the normally Republican suburban areas, like San Fernando Valley and Pacific Palisades either rejected the contract or approved it by a hair-breadth."[155] A vision of civic unity, economic growth, and downtown development—not to mention individual financial advantage—motivated business, professional, and media supporters of the contract. Many of these were nominal Republicans who found common ground with minority-group Democrats on this issue. The constituencies coalesced around the idea of government assistance to private enterprise for a public purpose.

The concept of state-aided capitalist development was rooted in the Hamiltonian politics of the Early Republic period and passed through the American System of Henry Clay's Whig Party and the free labor Republicanism of the mid-nineteenth century. While both Progressive and free market principles challenged state-aided capitalism in the Republican party of the twentieth century, the idea of the state as promoter of private gain for the public good still retained potency and influence. By the 1950s, when O'Malley proposed to build his own stadium on land acquired with government assistance, it was a central tenet of business Republicanism.

The Proposition B referendum allowed business Republicans to join with black and Latino Angelenos, to whom a new home for the Dodgers held its own attractions, as well as with working-class voters, who viewed the contract in terms of potential employment opportunities. In addition, liberal Democrats and Westsiders desired economic growth and cultural status commensurate with Los Angeles's position as the soon-to-be third-largest city in the nation. They were willing to accept government assistance to a private entrepreneur in the service of what they believed to be a civic enterprise. Animating the yes voters as well was a belief in the crucial role of the downtown core in defining the city's identity and a determination to use a developed urban center to counter the forces of spatial dispersal with which Los Angeles was so prominently and negatively associated. To them, Dodger Stadium meant more than major league baseball for downtown. It would begin the process of recasting Los Angeles as a national and world city.

But Holland, McGee, and the many no voters in the San Fernando Valley and neighborhoods such as Holland's Eagle Rock and nearby Silver Lake did not share this vision. They represented a form of taxpayer Republicanism, which sought to minimize the fiscal burdens on the middle-class property owners who were their core constituency. This flinty-eyed determination to protect taxpayer interests through budgetary prudence was in keeping with the cautious sensibilities of the small-property-owning Folks, with their Midwest-rooted culture of circumspection and thrift. A newly arrived O'Malley ran up against this culture in 1957 amid the flurry of ballot petition signatures that signaled the start of the Proposition B campaign, and he would struggle against its political undertow as he sought to build Dodger Stadium. Taxpayer Republicanism did not dominate Los Angeles completely—Fletcher Bowron, the city's mayor from 1938 to 1953, was a New Deal–oriented liberal, and Poulson, his successor, was a prototypical business Republican—but it was potent enough to influence every major municipal policy issue, as Holland, McGee, and the Citizens Committee illustrated so vividly. Their criticism of the Dodger contract was in keeping with the low-tax impulse that motivated the Los Angeles of the Folks and the neighborhoods.

Yet even taxpayer Republicanism in Los Angeles was not blindly hostile to government-sponsored initiatives. Its disagreements with business Republicanism concerned wasteful allocations of tax resources and not public spending per se. Holland and McGee supported the idea of a municipally constructed stadium because they believed it would cost taxpayers less—or, conversely, generate more revenue for Los Angeles—than a privately built ballpark on valuable public property deeded to the Dodgers. If the public sector could perform a function more efficiently and economically than government-assisted private enterprise, they would support it. Indeed, for Holland and McGee it was as much a matter of dollars as ideology. They argued that the city of San Francisco would realize more income from the rental of its municipally owned stadium than would the city of Los Angeles from a privately owned ballpark.

In many respects, the disagreements between taxpayer and business Republicans in Los Angeles revolved around accounting. Poulson, and Norman Chandler for that matter, believed that a public investment in the Dodgers through a favorable land contract would produce financial rewards for the city. Holland and McGee believed they would not. On June 3, Poulson and Chandler won the first round of this argument by a narrow margin. But Holland, McGee, and other Los Angeles taxpayer Republicans would not concede defeat. Their battle to stop Dodger Stadium from being built was far from over.

The contract opponents also continued their battle against what they believed the Dodger deal symbolized: the encroaching power of Downtown at the expense of the city's outer neighborhoods and communities.[156] Downtowners and Westsiders might lampoon Valley residents as unsophisticated and culturally myopic, but thanks to Los Angeles's decentralized pattern of development there were more than enough of them to profoundly influence the debate over the future of the city.[157] The close outcome of the Proposition B vote had underscored the power of the periphery in

Los Angeles. Even in victory, Poulson had stirred a hornet's nest in the precincts outside the city center. For Holland and McGee, the issue went beyond that of whether to build a ballpark downtown or even how to ensure that their districts received basic resources— sidewalks, roads, school buildings, and sanitation services. It went to the issue of the identity of the city. What was "Los Angeles"? Holland and McGee thought they knew. Their Los Angeles was local, not national. It was a neighborhood city, not a downtown one. The struggle between taxpayer and business Republicanism in Los Angeles would thus be for the aspirations and dreams of an entire city.

5

IN THE COURTS

O'Malley had only two days to savor his Proposition B victory before the battlefront shifted to the courts. On Friday, June 6, Superior Court judge Kenneth Newell issued a preliminary injunction blocking the execution of the contract that the voters had just approved. The Ruben and Kirshbaum cases, which had been consolidated, were set down for a pretrial hearing on June 17 before another Superior Court judge, Arnold Praeger, with a nonjury bench trial to follow.

In the interim, O'Malley sought to remove the issue of oil rights, which he knew could only hurt the Dodgers' case, from the litigation. On June 13 he sent a letter to Poulson relinquishing those rights in full to the city. Originally the team had received a half interest, with its share to be placed in a trust fund for youth programs.[1] While no oil had been located under the Chavez Ravine soil, criticism nonetheless mounted. Now O'Malley washed his hands of a public relations embarrassment as well as a potential legal obstacle at trial.

The Dodger owner was justified in his concern about the dangers the contract faced. The combined resources of the city attorney's office and Dodger counsel O'Melveny and Myers, one of Los Angeles's most prestigious law firms, outweighed those of their adversaries. But Julius Ruben, a local lawyer who was representing

himself, and Phill Silver, representing Louis Kirshbaum, were formidable in their own right. Both were known as taxpayer advocates and champions of the little guy. Both bitterly opposed the
Chavez Ravine contract on philosophical grounds and were thus
more tenacious than attorneys working merely for fees. And Silver
was a notorious publicity hound whose clients included celebrities and on occasion local mobsters. O'Malley could expect no
quarter from him.

The case against the Dodger contract contained six essential
points. Ruben and Silver contended that the City Council had
exceeded its powers by making what amounted to a gift of public
property for the private use of the team.[2] They also objected to the
city's promise to acquire additional Chavez Ravine properties to
transfer to the team as a similar abuse of power. They attacked the
city's allocation of $2 million for land preparation at the stadium
site, claiming it gave the Dodgers undue control over the selection
of public streets to be closed in order to make space for the ballpark.[3] They asserted that the contract's provision for the Dodgers
to spend a sum "not to exceed" $500,000 to build and maintain a
public recreation area on a portion of the Chavez Ravine property
was fraudulent because the expenditure of only one dollar would
constitute technical compliance. They averred that the city's agreement to obtain a waiver of the "public purpose" clause in the 1955
deed transferring the Chavez Ravine land from the CHA to the city
of Los Angeles was beyond the agency's power and thus illegal.[4]

Finally, they posed the litigation's central question: did a privately owned Dodger Stadium serve a public purpose? Robert
Moses had answered no, which was why Walter O'Malley was in
Los Angeles in June 1958. Ruben and Silver answered no as well.
For years politicians, journalists, bureaucrats, businessmen, and
team executives on both coasts had debated the issue of the public benefit of a new Dodger ballpark. A court had never addressed
it. Now one would.[5]

During the pretrial conference, Ruben and Silver made a concession they would later regret. The relative values of the Chavez
Ravine and Wrigley Field properties that were to be exchanged
under the terms of the Dodger deal had already been the subject

of controversy. Holland, McGee, and other contract opponents claimed that the Ravine land was actually worth much more than the city's official valuation of $2,289,204 and Wrigley much less than its assigned $2,250,000.[6] A judicial finding of inadequate consideration—a grossly unequal trade—could void the entire contract. But Ruben and Silver stipulated that property values would not be made an issue in the upcoming trial under the rubric of a more general stipulation that the parties would litigate questions of law and not fact.[7] This would preclude the admission of evidence relating to appraisals of the two properties not only at trial but also on any subsequent appeals.

Ruben's reasons for agreeing to this stipulation are unclear. It is possible that he was confident enough on questions of law, especially those relating to the public purpose issue, that he was willing to concede the complicated property argument in the interests of a clean case. Unlike O'Melveny and Myers and even the city attorney's office, Ruben and Silver's resources were limited, and they may not have been able to afford a drawn-out proceeding. In any event, the issue of whether the city had given up a lot for a little in the Dodger deal was, as far as the law was concerned, off the table.

The trial began in Los Angeles County Superior Court on June 20 with a touch of farce. Silver called Poulson to the witness stand intending to examine him on his attempt to induce the CHA to eliminate the "public purpose" clause from the 1955 Chavez Ravine deed. But the mayor was able to answer only one question in his two hours on the stand, as city lawyers lodged objection after objection to Silver's meandering and argumentative line of inquiry.[8] Finally, Judge Praeger ordered the mayor to answer the question of whether he had attempted to "extinguish" the public purpose provision. Poulson offered a tentative "I presume I would have to say 'yes.'"[9] He had in fact written to the CHA on June 11, 1957, requesting the agency's assistance in getting a stadium built in Chavez Ravine, which meant revising or excising the requirement that the land be used for a public purpose.[10]

Here Poulson and the city were working both sides of the street, asserting that a new Dodger Stadium did in fact serve a public

purpose while at the same time attempting to have the public purpose clause removed from the CHA deed. Silver argued that the
stadium did not qualify as a public purpose and that neither Poulson nor the CHA had the right to initiate changes in the deed language.[11] As these were legal questions and not factual ones, Praeger
could rule on them. He cut off the remainder of Silver's questions
on the issue as immaterial.[12]

The city began its case on June 23. Judge Praeger's questions
and remarks from the bench did not bode well for the contract's
future. He queried assistant city attorney Bourke Jones on the public recreation area clause, seemingly adopting Ruben's argument
that it permitted the Dodgers to spend only a token amount while
technically complying with its provisions.[13] What legal recourse
would the city have, asked Praeger, if the team chose to scrimp on
recreation area expenditures?[14] Jones's response—that if the Dodgers and the city could not agree on a mutually acceptable money
amount, a court of equity would adjudicate—did not appear to satisfy the judge.[15] Praeger also was dissatisfied with Jones's argument
that the fact that the Dodgers would derive substantial private benefit from the contract was not relevant to the public purpose question and that if there was an established public gain it did not
matter how much money the team made.[16] Ruben zeroed in on
the Dodgers as a profit-making entity: "The question is whether the
contract is a gift of public property under the law. The whole
question hinges on whether the ball club is a private or public
purpose."[17]

The next day, Praeger continued his skeptical line of inquiry, challenging Dodger attorney Pierce Works to justify the contract provision requiring the city to vacate public streets at the team's behest
for stadium construction. Wasn't this, the judge asked, clearly for
the benefit of a private entity? Works attempted to answer as Jones
had, stressing the incidental nature of the ball club's benefit compared to the more substantial advantages accruing to the city and
its residents from the new stadium.[18]

Works also tried to counter Ruben's assertion that the Dodgers
would control the choice of streets to be closed, stressing that the

city would first identify those that were no longer needed.[19] Praeger still seemed unimpressed, comparing the street-closing clause in the Dodger contract to a recently invalidated one vacating a street for the benefit of a local business.[20] He also suggested that he believed the clause was an illegal delegation of public authority to a private entity and in essence a grant of legislative power.[21] The team's control over the recreation area, which under the contract would remain public property for twenty years, appeared vulnerable under the same logic.[22] Although the Dodgers and the city won a tactical victory when Praeger, citing the pretrial stipulation, held that evidence on the relative values of the Chavez Ravine and Wrigley Field properties was inadmissible, the judge was clearly troubled by the contract as a whole and its implications.[23] The trial ended on June 25 with Praeger promising a ruling in seven to ten days.[24]

Trying to remain optimistic, O'Malley pushed ahead with his plans for the stadium. He had a long-standing professional relationship with the architect and engineer Emil Praeger (no relation to Judge Arnold Praeger), whose firm, Praeger, Kavanagh and Waterbury, had built Holman Stadium at the Dodgertown spring training site in Vero Beach, Florida. There Emil Praeger had pioneered an innovative approach to ballpark construction. Traditionally, baseball stadiums had situated playing fields at ground level and built upward, creating steeply vertical structures with decks supported by pillars that often blocked spectator views. Fans entering from city sidewalks were faced with long climbs to their seats. But Praeger's Holman Stadium rejected this long-standing architectural form. He scooped out tons of dirt to create an amphitheater effect, offering spectators a short walk down to their seats. The stadium contained no poles and no obstructed sightlines.

Although Holman Stadium's capacity of 5,000 was only a fraction of what was projected for Dodger Stadium, O'Malley envisioned it as a model for what he would build at Chavez Ravine. The Ravine's hilly terrain, with all the challenges it presented, offered the opportunity to create the first baseball stadium in a modernist form. Like Holman Stadium, it would be pillar-free and feature a lower grandstand that would place entering ticketholders as close to their seats as possible. But Dodger Stadium as O'Malley planned it would also employ Chavez Ravine's hills to go Holman Stadium one better. It would feature parking lots on levels corresponding to fans' ticket locations, enabling them to walk directly from their cars to their seats with a minimum of climbing. This would negate the topographical disadvantages of the Ravine.

Dodger Stadium would be a ballpark built for Los Angeles, a city centered on the automobile, in which convenience and accessibility were paramount virtues. Los Angeles was a reflection of a new postwar America with similar characteristics. It may not have mattered to diehard Brooklyn Dodger fans that they had to negotiate the steep ramps and high stairs of Ebbets Field and sit behind poles or under overhanging roofs that blocked their view of the field, but O'Malley knew it would matter to his customers in Los Angeles. Emil Praeger, he believed, would build a stadium for what mattered to his new fans.

In late June, O'Malley wrote to Praeger discussing Chavez Ravine traffic patterns and freeway access, a clear indication that the New York–based architect would get the stadium commission.[25] The Dodger owner also began to plan the details of the stadium Praeger would build. In another June memo, O'Malley wrote of his plans to attract fans to the stadium even on "off" days.[26] Year-round revenue generators would include a Dodger team store and stadium tram tours with "loudspeaker[s] like Disneyland."[27] He also wished to adopt the Disneyland parking system, which offered guests receipts on which to note the locations of their cars. The new stadium would feature a variety of restaurants, with offerings ranging from casual to elegant, to suit fans' tastes. The eateries would offer views of the field along with fountains and a "cathedral of trees" beyond the stands.[28]

Dodger Stadium thus would not merely occupy its physical setting but also become an organic part of it. Sunken into the hills of Chavez Ravine with the San Gabriel Mountains rising in one direction and the downtown skyline in the other, the stadium would create an environment as powerful in its own right as anything occurring on the diamond. It would be a ballpark built not just to house a team but also to embody an atmosphere. While there were obvious differences between a theme park such as Disneyland and a ballpark, most notably the latter's elements of team competition and unpredictable outcomes, O'Malley planned Dodger Stadium as an entertainment attraction. Like Disneyland, it would be a place to leave the outside world behind, to become lost in the moment, and to feel wonder and joy.[29] Like Disneyland, it would house dreams.

But would such a stadium ever be built? On July 14, Judge Praeger, in a sweeping decision, held the Dodger contract invalid. His opinion was effectively an endorsement of the arguments Ruben and Silver had made at trial. Praeger ruled that a privately owned stadium did not fulfill a public purpose and that the deed conveying the Chavez Ravine property to the city could not be altered to benefit the Dodgers. Thus the proposed transfer by the city of public land to a private entity was illegal, as was the promised use of public funds to purchase other Chavez Ravine properties for conveyance to the team.[30] "There is nothing in the City Charter," wrote Praeger, "that in any wise indicates that [it can] use public funds for the purchase of property for the purpose of selling it to a private person or private corporation for the operation of a private business for private profit."[31] The judge saw no difference between purchasing land for a revenue-generating baseball team and "acquir[ing] property for the purpose of selling it for use for a private bowling alley, a private golf course, a steel mill, a hotel, or any other private purpose."[32]

Praeger also struck down the city's agreement to close streets in Chavez Ravine and to spend $2 million on roads at the Dodgers' behest as an impermissible delegation of discretion from the City Council to the ball club. "A City Council," he wrote, "has no right or power to give to a private organization carte blanche with respect to the spending of public money."[33] He rejected the city's argument that the Ravine property was no longer needed by the people of Los Angeles and could thus be offered to the Dodgers, reasoning that if a recreation area was to be built there, the land still had value. Praeger also ruled that if the additional land the council promised to obtain for the team was "no longer required for the use of the city, then it is an abuse of discretion and an illegal expenditure of public funds to continue with the process of acquiring lands for which the city, as such, has no public use, solely for the purpose of conveying it to a private corporation for private use."[34] Praeger even invalidated the contract provision relating to Chavez Ravine oil rights despite the fact that the Dodgers had waived them on the eve of trial. In sum, ruled Praeger, "this is an illegal delegation of the duty of the City Council, an abdication of its public trust, and a manifest gross abuse of discretion."[35]

O'Malley sought to put the best face on a potentially fatal setback. "I am perhaps a stubborn man," he told the press. "But we were offered the Chavez Ravine site, accepted it and came out with the intention of building a park on it. We are not abandoning the program. . . . Early settlers found the Overland Trail to the West long and arduous. We have the same faith they had. We fully expect all difficulties to be resolved within the law. The building of your modern baseball stadium is unfortunately further delayed but I believe it is worth the fight."[36]

Contract opponents, of course, were ecstatic. Ruben, who had represented himself in the case as a complaining taxpayer, praised Praeger as "an able and conscientious judge" who had ruled correctly "that public money and public property should be used for the benefit of the public and not for the benefit of a private corporation."[37] A valuable location such as Chavez Ravine that was situated within walking distance of downtown, Ruben stated, "should be used for a greater public purpose than for ball games on only 77 days of the year."[38] Holland said he was "gratified beyond measure," and pronounced somewhat disingenuously that the way was now clear for a renegotiation of the contract on a more taxpayer-friendly basis. He proposed that a public facility be built in the vicinity of the Coliseum.[39] Ridgely Cummings of the Civic Center News Agency celebrated a victory over "the downtown newspapers and certain narrow thinking sportswriters and announcers who selfishly and irresponsibly promoted this illegal contract."[40]

The Citizens Committee's Owen expressed similar sentiments: "The Judge's ruling confirms what thinking people of this city who have opposed the Dodger contract all along have continually said . . . that the contract is illegal and a preposterous document. This decision should be cause for serious reflection by those prominent businessmen and attorneys who apparently without reading or studying the contract allowed their names to be used to promote it."[41] Mocking Downtown interests such as the Los Angeles Chamber of Commerce for misleading its members, Owen praised the city's neighborhoods, where in the San Fernando Valley the local chambers of commerce had vehemently opposed the contract on behalf of "many thousands of small homeowners" and their "tax dollars." He savored what he considered a victory of the people over the interests.[42]

The image of the Dodgers as connected to sources of influence and power, which critics of the Chavez Ravine deal emphasized in so many of their public statements, continued to resonate even in the team's former home, where famed cartoonist Willard Mullin of the *New York World-Telegram and Sun* published a drawing of the famous Brooklyn Bum standing behind O'Malley and whispering, "Ain't there no fine print, Walter, where yez c'n read between th' lines?"[43] Indeed, in the immediate aftermath of the Praeger decision the Dodger attorneys were already planning legal strategies aimed at securing a reversal by a higher court. An internal memorandum produced by O'Melveny and Myers was optimistic. It argued that Praeger's rulings on land acquisition, street closings, the recreation area, and the public purpose question were all vulnerable on appeal.[44]

The Dodgers' chances of overturning Praeger were also enhanced by a legal blunder committed by the overeager Silver, who in typically aggressive fashion had brought suit to prevent official certification of the Proposition B referendum results on the grounds that they had been superseded by the July 14 decision. In Silver's defense, there was some historical precedent to justify his action. In 1951, the Los Angeles City Council had sought to cancel its contract with the federal government to construct public housing at Chavez Ravine and other locations in the city. A referendum was scheduled

on the issue, and in June 1952 voters terminated the housing contract, or so they thought. Having previously ruled that the public
housing contract could not be canceled via referendum and that
the election would thus be of no effect, the California Supreme
Court invalidated its results.[45] Silver believed he could use Praeger's decision to similarly negate the Proposition B vote.

But while Silver's action appeared to rest on logic—if the Dodger
contract was in fact illegal, it would appear that a referendum could
not validate it and thus it could not be certified—it was nonetheless
a blunder. It permitted the Dodgers and the city to bypass the inter-
mediate California appeals courts and instead proceed directly
to the California Supreme Court, substantially shortening a time-
consuming process. The procedural device through which they
would move was called a writ of prohibition. Granting the writ
would prevent Silver's suit from being tried on the ground that a
court could not prevent a legislature or administrative agency from
performing an act required by law, in this instance certifying the
result of the Proposition B election.[46] Applying for a writ of prohibition gave the state Supreme Court the opportunity to rule not
only on this procedural question but also, if it so chose, on the
merits of the appeal itself. Silver's strategic error, along with his and
Ruben's stipulation excluding property value evidence at trial,
would bear heavily on the fate of the legal challenges to the construction of Dodger Stadium. They would illustrate that in law as in
life, procedure matters as much as substance, and sometimes more.

The day before Judge Praeger's decision, the San Francisco Board of
Supervisors by an 8-to-2 vote approved the final piece of enabling
bond issue legislation for the new municipally owned stadium
that the Giants would occupy as tenants.[47] The contrast to Los
Angeles could not have been starker. Once again, San Francisco was
moving ahead while its rival to the south lagged behind. O'Malley
lamented the state of affairs in an August speech to members of the
Los Angeles Rotary Club. "I am keenly disappointed that work on
the stadium hasn't already begun," he told them. "I had hoped to get

a bulldozer up in the Ravine last month to begin shoving a pile of dirt around, even if it was simply pushing the same pile back and forth. We want to build our dream stadium—the best of any in the world and the first one to be built with private funds since 1923."[48] He complimented Los Angeles fans as constituting "the finest sports-minded public in the United States."[49] As O'Malley was making this speech, a City Hall observer was describing the relationship between team and town as "the courtship of a lunatic ballclub and a lunatic city."[50]

Until the Kirshbaum/Ruben cases were finally adjudicated, that courtship was on the slow burner. O'Malley could press ahead on his efforts to market the Dodgers in the Coliseum. But while matters were still being resolved on the Dodger Stadium issue, he was swimming upstream. On some fronts he was actually going backward. In September, the Los Angeles County Board of Supervisors, anticipating a long delay in construction as the Kirshbaum/Ruben litigation wound its way through the courts, reassigned funds it had originally approved for stadium access highways to other projects, a clear vote of no confidence in the Dodgers' chances of obtaining a reversal.[51] The month of September and the 1958 baseball season ended with the team in seventh place, the Praeger decision still in effect, and the road to Chavez Ravine seemingly blocked.

If the 1958 season did not end well on the field, it had a happier resolution on the team balance sheet. Home attendance totaled 1,845,556, an increase of more than 800,000 from the team's last year in Brooklyn.[52] The $288,181 total cost of renting the Coliseum was almost completely offset by concessions revenues of $268,101.[53] Income from sales of souvenirs and novelties, all of which the Dodgers kept, put O'Malley squarely in the black even before ticket sales were added in. Despite lost television monies— the team had broadcast only seven road games in 1958, in contrast to the close to one hundred that went out over the free airwaves the year before in Brooklyn—the season had been an extremely lucrative one. The team's profit after taxes was estimated at $650,000.[54]

Assuming the new stadium could be built, there was much more to come. O'Malley planned to leverage the gate successes of 1958 with an aggressive campaign of promotion and marketing coordinated by Dodger public relations director Arthur "Red" Patterson. In late September, Patterson outlined the team's strategy in a memorandum to O'Malley.[55] He argued that personal contacts with players were central to building fan loyalty. In Brooklyn the Dodger players had lived alongside the fans in the borough's close-knit neighborhoods and were visible in the community. But Los Angeles featured a more privatized residential environment that secluded players behind fences, walls, and gates as well as a decentralized geography that scattered them throughout the metropolitan area.

Patterson proposed to compensate for this disadvantage with an organized series of player appearances at workplaces, connecting the team directly to its potential customers. He noted by way of example that Douglas Aircraft had its own director of recreation for the company's eighteen thousand employees, a man who could serve as a conduit to a vast market of potential ticket buyers.[56] Patterson maintained that visits to Douglas and other "industrial plants" would offer the Dodgers a wide degree of coverage for a relatively small investment of time and money. He also planned to send Dodger scouting director Al Campanis to a different Los Angeles–area high school each week during the off-season to speak with students, thus helping to create "the Dodger fans of the future."[57] "Thanks to the question-and-answer program which I have tacked on to most of the appearances I've made this year," Patterson informed O'Malley, "I have an excellent cross-section of what the fans are thinking about, what their complaints are. . . . Truly, these are wonderful fans. . . . They're out to have a good time, and we should do everything possible to make sure they do."[58] Patterson also proposed an organized ticket-selling program aimed at "service groups" such as the Kiwanis Club and the League of Women Voters, which were more active and visible in Los Angeles than in New York, as a means of reaching the casual customer.[59]

Patterson made no little plans. "I'm convinced," he concluded, "that our organization, as NOW constituted, can become the outstanding sports enterprise in Los Angeles. In the right park, with good parking facilities and a team in the race all the way, we are going some year to draw 3,000,000 fans. That, and not 2,000,000, should be our goal."[60]

The Dodgers clearly intended to promote the team and connect it to its fans in new ways. In 1958, many major league baseball franchises barely marketed themselves at all. Teams relied on traditional allegiances and habits to maintain their fan bases. Clubs that had been in one city for generations were embedded organically in the civic fabric. Loyalties were passed from parents to children almost reflexively, offering team owners a built-in level of support and sparing them the task of seeking out new sources of ticket income.

But this of course applied only to teams that remained in "their" city. Those that relocated, including the Dodgers, faced a new set of challenges once the novelty of a transplanted team wore off. If the shift was to a city such as Los Angeles, which also was filled with transplants from other parts of the country, these challenges were magnified. As the June 3 referendum results showed, Angelenos loved baseball and coveted major league status. But many of them would be going to the Coliseum and perhaps eventually to Dodger Stadium to cheer the St. Louis Cardinals, Chicago Cubs, or Cincinnati Reds. These were the teams they and their parents had grown up with. O'Malley would need to turn them into Dodger fans who would not require the presence of their old teams as an inducement to come out to the ball park. In a city of transients and migrants searching for community, O'Malley understood that it would be the intimate links to the Dodgers that mattered most.

Vin Scully, whom many listeners regarded as a personal friend, was of course among the most important of those links. The Dodger marketing operation, built around personal contact with Dodger players, was another. The team would later add a formal speakers' bureau that coordinated player appearances at clubs, businesses, schools, churches, civic groups, and trade associations.

In Brooklyn, fans often saw players in their neighborhoods. In Los Angeles, a very different city, the team brought the players to them. Tradition is the glue that ties a baseball team to its fans. But in a new city bereft of tradition, O'Malley was able to establish the Dodgers as a central civic institution almost immediately. While novelty played an obvious role in the initial success of the franchise, the sustained and focused marketing program initiated by O'Malley cemented the bond between the Dodgers and the individual fan, ensuring that the Los Angeles Dodgers would build in a handful of years what had taken decades for more established teams.

The Dodgers' 1958 season in the Coliseum, which ended with a home loss to the Chicago Cubs on September 27, would be remembered as one of the strangest in baseball history. The proximity of the left-field screen benefited average right-handed hitters. But left-handed-hitting Duke Snider, a future Hall of Famer, was hamstrung by the gargantuan dimensions of right field and hit a mere six Coliseum homers. Pitchers, especially left-handers who could expect to face opposing lineups loaded with right-handed batters, had nightmares about the close-in fence and often felt beaten before their games even began. Criticism of the quality of play on the Coliseum field was rampant.

Spectators also suffered. The football-style configuration of the Coliseum, with a bowl of stands sloping back and up a single deck, produced distant sightlines. Views down the long right-field line were especially poor. The stadium offered no protection from the heat and sun, and fans attending day games were routinely parched and broiled. Ubiquitous transistor radios in the stands carrying Vin Scully's vivid game descriptions to far-flung spectators made games at the Coliseum seem almost recreated, with fans appearing to pay more attention to the Dodger broadcaster than to what was occurring before their eyes. Many observers, especially in New York, ridiculed Los Angeles fans' penchant for listening to Scully while they attended games, but given the distances between seat and playing field, their need for his guidance was understandable. The thirsty Coliseum spectators were also deprived of a traditional ballpark staple, beer, under the terms of the stadium's ban on alcohol sales.

In all, the 1958 season was a unique one for both players and fans. Whether it produced quality baseball was open to question. Certainly the numerous critics of what had occurred on the field and in the stands did not think so. The season also could not be judged a success if measured solely by winning percentage. But despite his difficulties in the Coliseum, O'Malley had been able to establish the Dodgers as a Los Angeles brand, with the attendance and revenue figures to prove it. Certainly this was a businessman's measure of success. And if the preceding years had proven anything at all, it was that baseball was very much a business.

As the 1958 season came to a close, Coliseum general manager W. H. Nichols wrote to O'Malley: "I know there were a lot of things [that] happened that you would not want to happen in a ball park, however you have to realize that we are a public agency and a lot of things happen that we would prefer not to have. I wish you the best of everything in 1959."[61] O'Malley hoped that 1959 would be his final year in the Coliseum. Even if he put the best possible face on things, the Coliseum was not a true home and not a place in which he could realize his dreams, both financial and aesthetic. But, facing a sweepingly adverse court decision and an uncertain future in Los Angeles, he had to admit the possibility that the Coliseum would be his residence, if not his home, for considerably longer than he wished.

Meanwhile, the legal maneuverings continued. Dodger counsel O'Melveny and Myers and Los Angeles city attorney Roger Arnebergh agreed on a strategy that was based on applying for a writ of prohibition in order to bring the Ruben/Kirshbaum appeal directly and immediately before the state Supreme Court, with the hope that the justices would decide to combine a procedural ruling with one on the substance of Praeger's decision.[62] Praeger had aided the writ-of-prohibition gambit himself, albeit unintentionally, when shortly after his ruling he enjoined the certification of the referendum results until Silver's suit to invalidate them could be heard.[63] This made an application for a writ of prohibition the next logical step.

On October 15 the state Supreme Court issued a temporary order halting the referendum decertification and scheduling a hearing on the application for a writ of prohibition.[64] On that day, Chief Justice Phil Gibson intimated that he favored taking up the entire case along with the writ-of-prohibition question, since Praeger's decision had not involved questions of fact. Gibson asked Silver to submit a brief containing the factual issues that remained in the case. When Silver was unable to do so to the Court's satisfaction, the stage was set for a full adjudication.[65] Thanks in large part to Silver's overreaching on the referendum certification issue and his and Ruben's decision to stipulate away a potentially powerful issue of fact relating to the relative values of the Chavez Ravine and Wrigley Field properties, the Dodgers now had a second chance in the court system.

The team's lawyers challenged Praeger's decision head-on. The appellate brief produced by O'Melveny and Myers took issue with each of his holdings. The centerpiece of their argument was one the Dodgers had been making in one form or another for a decade: a privately constructed baseball stadium built on land acquired from a municipality or state agency could fulfill a public purpose.[66] The proper way to analyze the contract, they maintained, was through "the various benefits to be derived by the City from the transaction as a whole," and not solely on the basis of how much money the Dodgers would make.[67]

The City Council had determined that it no longer needed the Chavez Ravine land and that increasing its property tax value with a stadium would aid municipal finances, as would the sales and income tax revenues the new ballpark would generate. The council had also decided that it would benefit the city if the Dodgers built the stadium at their own expense, as opposed to incurring substantial cost and debt on a public structure. A public recreation area at Chavez Ravine, such as the one the Dodgers had agreed to create, was also in the city's interest as a means of combating juvenile delinquency.[68] Wrigley Field, which the city would acquire as part of the bargain with the Dodgers, would provide additional help in this regard.[69] The presence of major league baseball in Los Angeles, which the new stadium would ensure, would increase the number of jobs in the city. The assignment by the Dodgers of all Chavez Ravine oil rights to the city was yet another derived benefit, albeit a contingent one.[70] Taken in aggregate, the Dodgers' lawyers argued, there were clear "overall benefits to the City" in the contract and a manifest "public purpose."[71]

The brief prepared by O'Melveny and Myers also took aim at Praeger's other holdings. The city's contractual promise to improve the Chavez Ravine property in a manner "to be designated by the ballclub" was not the unlawful delegation of legislative power to the team that Praeger had ruled it to be.[72] The City Council could have simply paid the $2 million it had set aside for land preparation directly to the team, thus ceding all control over its disposition. Instead, it retained some degree of oversight of the condition of the Ravine land.[73] It was also customary, the lawyers argued, for land transfer contracts to require the seller (in this case the city) to "place the property to be conveyed in condition satisfactory to the vendee (the team) prior to the passage of title."[74] Affirming Praeger's decision could potentially jeopardize every transaction involving the sale of city land to a private party.[75]

The Dodgers also challenged Praeger's ruling that they would impermissibly control the selection of Chavez Ravine streets to be vacated for stadium construction. The contract stated that "the existing public streets [in the stadium area] which would no longer be needed for present and future street purposes will be vacated and the City shall, upon demand of ball club, commence proceedings to vacate such streets and deliver any title which may remain in the City without further consideration."[76] Praeger had construed this language to mean that the Dodgers and not the city would decide which streets should be closed off. But the team averred that this power of choice originated with the city government and would be exercised before the Dodgers would formally request that a particular street be vacated. "The City has not bargained away its charter duty," the team maintained.[77]

Furthermore, the Dodgers argued that Praeger had erred when he ruled that the City Council could not make a finding that a recreation area was needed at Chavez Ravine while simultaneously holding that the land on which the stadium would be built was no longer needed by the city.[78] The Dodgers claimed the two findings were severable and thus not contradictory and that the recreation area provision was a contract within a contract.[79] They maintained that the City Council had the discretion to determine that the Chavez Ravine property was not needed and to then determine that a recreation facility was needed, siting it on a portion of that land. The city would keep title to the facility for twenty years while the Dodgers kept it up at team expense. This was an additional benefit to the city, providing a form of security for the team's performance of the entire contract.[80]

The Dodgers asserted that the City Council was also acting within its lawful powers when it promised to acquire and convey to the team additional Chavez Ravine land. The city's charter permitted the council to "buy . . . or sell anything useful or convenient in connection with the exercise of the city's rights and powers."[81] Since the relative property values of the Ravine and Wrigley Field had been stipulated out of the litigation and the adequacy of consideration in the contract was thus not at issue, the Dodgers argued that the City Council was within its discretion in agreeing to transfer additional acreage to the team.[82] Finally, the Dodgers' brief claimed that Praeger should have ruled that the issue of oil rights was a moot point since the team had assigned them to the city immediately before the trial.[83]

The Dodgers' attorneys had thus employed the application for a writ of prohibition as a means of obtaining an expedited and definitive ruling on the substance of Praeger's decision from the state's highest court. Now, however, they had to wait. O'Malley left for a six-week African hunting trip in October, after informing the media he had no plans to build his new stadium anywhere but in Chavez Ravine.[84] His attorneys had told him that they believed the chances of obtaining a reversal were good, so the Dodger owner left for Africa with a clear conscience.

But O'Malley was not in control of events, as he customarily wished to be. During the summer, O'Malley had visited Los Angeles's Olvera Street, the birthplace of the city. Wandering among its shops and stalls, he had his handwriting analyzed. The report he received, while hardly scientific in the accepted sense, nonetheless captured O'Malley's personality and outlook remarkably well. "You have always been independent . . . rather than follow another's footsteps," it stated. "Having to take orders from someone else is something you wish to avoid. You prefer to think as an individual, to work and express your opinions independently."[85]

From the moment he acquired a share of the Dodgers in 1944, control of his surroundings had been of paramount importance to O'Malley. While he had served and collaborated with others, including George McLaughlin, Branch Rickey, and John Smith, he was much more comfortable keeping his own counsel and wished to run the Dodgers by himself. His desire to chart his own destiny led him to reject Robert Moses's offer of a municipal stadium—what O'Malley dismissed as a "political ballpark"—in New York.[86] It drew him to Los Angeles, a city he barely knew. And it explained why he clung so tenaciously to his dream of building his own stadium in Chavez Ravine. But now, having won narrowly at the polls, his fate was still in the hands of others. An African safari would offer some respite and distance, but upon his return to Los Angeles in late November O'Malley would have reason to reflect on how, despite years of effort, he had no more control over the arc of his career than did the average appellant awaiting the ruling of a higher court.

And if the state Supreme Court affirmed Praeger's decision, what would O'Malley do? His options were circumscribed. There was no realistic possibility of leaving Los Angeles; the gate receipts and fan support of his first year in the city had seen to that. He could attempt to renegotiate the contract, but on more disadvantageous terms, possibly including the payment of substantial monies up front and an agreement to share parking and other stadium revenues with the city.

No alternative site within Los Angeles proper was free from serious drawbacks. Wrigley Field was just as it had been when the Dodgers arrived in the city: tiny, antiquated, almost devoid of parking facilities, and hard to reach. A new stadium in the Coliseum area was conceivable, but there were land acquisition issues that promised to be as trying as those at Chavez Ravine, since the neighborhood was an amalgam of public and private owners, with the presence of the nearby University of Southern California presenting an additional complication.

In a 1955 referendum, Los Angeles voters had rejected a municipally constructed park, which O'Malley had never found an attractive alternative in any case. Pursuing one, even assuming he wished
to do so, would require O'Malley to work closely with Holland,
McGee, and other Chavez Ravine critics who had become political
enemies and could not be relied upon to protect his interests. While
a number of suburban Los Angeles towns had expressed interest in
serving as a backup site for a new Dodger ballpark, none of them
could offer the central location that would ensure access to the
maximum possible number of area fans. And New York? By late
1958, O'Malley's old city was a chimera, past history for a man
whose gaze was invariably fixed on what lay before him. The
Dodger owner thus faced a host of unappetizing choices in the
event of an adverse Supreme Court ruling. O'Malley might still get
a stadium, but not the one he wanted where he wanted it and with
the control he desired. Walter O'Malley had struggled throughout
his life to be the master of his fate. Now it was out of his hands.
Other men would decide it.

Thanksgiving and Christmas of 1958 passed without a decision
from the court. O'Malley and the Dodger organization prepared for
another season in the Coliseum, the last on their lease but, it was
now clear, not their last spent playing there. The Coliseum Commission had driven a hard bargain on the initial rental agreement. Now
that he essentially had nowhere else to go, O'Malley could only
imagine the terms he would be offered. And not a spade of dirt had
been moved at Chavez Ravine, where a handful of residents hung
on, a confrontation in the making. It was a holiday season filled
with uncertainty. O'Malley's Olvera Street handwriting analyst
had written: "To keep the other fellow guessing as to what you
will do next, you enjoy."[87] But now O'Malley was the one reduced
to guessing, a most uncomfortable position for a man of his vision
and outlook.

On January 13, 1959, the California Supreme Court spoke. In a 7–0
decision, it granted the writ of prohibition, allowing the Proposition B referendum results to be officially certified. More impor-

tant, as the Dodgers had hoped, it ruled on the validity of the contract itself. The court unanimously upheld the City Council ordinance on which the Dodger Stadium contract was based, and overturned Praeger's decision blocking its enforcement.

Just as Praeger's ruling had adopted most of Ruben and Silver's contentions, Chief Justice Phil Gibson, writing for the Supreme Court, employed the arguments of the Dodgers and the city to support his reasoning. After a decade's worth of legal and policy debate over the question of whether a privately constructed baseball stadium fulfilled a public purpose, Gibson weighed in. "In considering whether the contract made by the city has a proper purpose," he wrote, "we must view the contract as a whole, and the fact that some of the provisions may be of benefit only to the baseball club is immaterial, provided the city receives benefits which serve legitimate public purposes."[88] Gibson found these public purposes in the transfer of the Wrigley Field property to the city and the construction of the recreation area at Chavez Ravine.[89] With these established to his satisfaction, Gibson did not find it necessary to reach the issue of indirect public benefits such as tax revenue, job creation, and positive publicity.[90]

Through this holding, Gibson ensured that Los Angeles would do what Robert Moses and New York would not. In determining what was and was not a public purpose, New York officials had concentrated on what the private entity—the Dodgers—would receive, rather than on public advantage. Gibson reversed this perspective. Once he decided the city of Los Angeles would realize benefits from the agreement, his inquiry essentially ended. That Walter O'Malley might also realize benefits may have mattered to Robert Moses but not to Gibson. By reconciling substantial private gain with public good, the California Supreme Court both settled a legal question and gave expression to a culture of entrepreneurship and risk that had drawn O'Malley to Los Angeles in the first place. It was true, of course, that the issue of the relative worth of the properties exchanged in the Dodger contract had been stipulated out of the case and Gibson thus did not need to rule on it. But the court's approach to the public purpose issue was certainly more encouraging to private enterprise than the more limited view taken in New York. It was as if the burden of proof had shifted. In New York, O'Malley had had to show that his benefits would not substantially outweigh those of the city in any stadium deal. The fact that he would profit significantly was enough by itself to tip the scales against a finding that a public purpose existed.

O'Malley's burden was considerably lighter in Los Angeles. To Chief Justice Gibson, it did not matter that O'Malley stood to make a great deal of money on the stadium deal. As long as he could show that the city of Los Angeles would receive something tangible in return for Chavez Ravine, in this instance Wrigley Field and the recreation area, a finding of public purpose was still appropriate. Under this more generous legal standard, entrepreneurs like O'Malley could count on assistance from government and greater freedom of action generally in achieving their goals. Gibson's decision reflected the outlook of business Republicanism, in which the state's role was to facilitate enterprise whenever possible and regulate only when necessary, and in which public-private collaborations such as the Chavez Ravine contract were viewed not as giveaways but as economic stimuli beneficial to the entire region. In New York, a privately owned Dodger Stadium was not considered a public purpose. In Los Angeles, in the opinion of Chief Justice Gibson, it was. O'Malley's vision had carried the day.

The remainder of the Supreme Court decision was an almost point-by-point refutation of Praeger's ruling. It held that neither the city's agreement to improve the Chavez Ravine land to the satisfaction of the team nor its commitment to vacate streets needed for the stadium were unwarranted delegations of legislative power.[91] Gibson found that the city retained sufficient control of the land preparation process simply by retaining the $2 million it had allocated for this project.[92] Similarly, since the initial determination that the public no longer needed a particular street was made by the city, it had not ceded its authority over closings to the Dodgers. Gibson upheld both the City Council's finding that the Chavez Ravine land was no longer required by the city and that a recreation area *was* required and could be sited at the Ravine.[93] He also ruled that the city could lawfully agree to purchase additional land in Chavez Ravine for transfer to the Dodgers as part of the agreement. Since the contract itself was valid as fulfilling a public purpose, acquisition of property that "enables the City to enter into a bargain which it deems advantageous" was by extension a public purpose as well.[94]

The effort by the city to obtain the removal of the public purpose clause from the 1955 CHA deed of the Ravine property, which had so exercised Phill Silver during the Praeger trial, was held to be legal and proper, as was the city's plan to indemnify the CHA for any future legal liability resulting from such a removal.[95] Even the oil rights issue went the Dodgers' way, with Gibson ruling that the team's formal waiver had taken it out of the case.[96]

O'Malley's victory was a testament both to good lawyering— O'Melveny and Myers had poured a huge amount of time and money into the appeal—and to Silver and Ruben's tactical mistakes. But it also testified to the ways in which California's political culture differed from that of New York City. The California Supreme Court had ruled unanimously that private profit was not the measure of public gain. The court had construed the discretionary power of a legislative body broadly, permitting it to interpret "public purpose" in a way that could confer substantial private advantage. It had also given legal sanction to the idea that the state could partner with business in the interests of both, and more specifically that entrepreneurial gain sponsored and abetted by the state meant gain for all and was thus public in intent and effect. Government promoting favored enterprises, picking winners and losers: this is what Holland, McGee, and Owen had opposed. These men represented a political impulse with lineage tracing back to the Age of Jackson and even to Jeffersonianism. But in this instance the Hamiltonians had won. The California Supreme Court had ruled that the state could do more than seek to create an economic climate that benefited business generally. It could also assist specific businesses that in the view of government officials promoted a public purpose. And sports entertainment, the court had held, was such a public purpose. Robert Moses would have disagreed strenuously, but of course he was back in New York.

O'Malley had come to Los Angeles to work in an environment in which profit seeking was not equated with profiteering. There were segments of the population and elements of the political culture of the Los Angeles region opposed to government-business partnerships such as the Dodger Stadium project and especially sensitive to what they considered evidence of giveaways. But by January 1959, O'Malley's state-aided entrepreneurial vision had come out on top in close contests in both the electoral and legal arenas. He had won two victories that would not have been possible in New York. Only time would tell if he would ever build his stadium in Chavez Ravine. But both the voters and the courts had justified his decision to move to Los Angeles.

While Silver and Ruben made the obligatory noises about continuing the fight up to the United States Supreme Court, the Gibson decision essentially ended their hopes of stopping the stadium project through the legal system. Since the decision was technically on the application for a writ of prohibition, Ruben and Silver appealed formally to the California Supreme Court, which on April 21 unanimously sustained its ruling.[97] In somewhat circular reasoning, it held that any public purpose requirement for the Chavez Ravine land applied only as long as the city owned it, and now that it did not, the Dodgers were free to use it as they would any piece of private property.[98] The court denied Ruben and Silver's petition for rehearing on May 20, after which Silver petitioned the United States Supreme Court to hear his appeal. Its refusal to accept the case for review on October 19, 1959, brought the Dodger Stadium litigation to an end, leaving the January California Supreme Court decision as the definitive legal word on the validity of the contract.

While Gibson's decision was a legal ruling and not a policy statement, it did reflect what had become a powerful economic idea in the city of Los Angeles: if government determined that entrepreneurial success was in the public interest, it should commit its resources to that success. O'Malley believed sincerely that what was good for the Dodgers was good for Los Angeles and that no tension existed between the two. Others, of course, were not so sure. But it was clear at least that O'Malley had gotten what he wanted from the California Supreme Court. He had permission to build his stadium. He was now free in ways he never had been in New York. He had control over his surroundings, or so he now thought. As he would discover, however, electoral and legal victories were crucial but not definitive. O'Malley's greatest challenge, a residue of past wounds and unresolved grievances at Chavez Ravine itself, was yet to come.

6

WHOSE LAND?

O'Malley rejoiced in the immediate aftermath of the Gibson decision. With what turned out to be misplaced optimism, he announced that construction of Dodger Stadium would commence immediately and would be complete by opening day 1960.[1] He promised "the finest stadium any sports fan ever has entered."[2] Poulson was equally ecstatic: "One World Series in Los Angeles, and every cent that Los Angeles has invested in this project will be repaid many times over. Progress must not be stopped in Los Angeles."[3]

Still, the mayor and city officials hedged their bets somewhat, since the Silver lawsuit would not be officially disposed of until the United States Supreme Court ruled on whether it would accept an appeal. Pending this event, which would not occur until October 1959, the Dodgers would be required to reimburse the city for monies spent on land grading despite the city's original promise to provide $2 million for this purpose.[4] The team would be out-of-pocket for these sums as an insurance policy of sorts against a reversal of the Gibson decision. But this too was a small price to pay, in O'Malley's view, if the stadium project could finally get under way. The city also discontinued its efforts to negotiate prices for twelve small Chavez Ravine land parcels it had condemned, forcing the Dodgers themselves to step in and bargain for them piecemeal. The central location of the parcels—they all were part of the planned stadium property—combined with the workings of the market promised to cost O'Malley a great deal of money.[5]

There were other land parcels required by the team for which the city was more helpful. It purchased a tract co-owned by Fritz Burns, the area's leading real estate developer, for $120,000, and deeded it to the Dodgers.[6] The state legislature also approved the sale of thirty-four Chavez Ravine acres to the city for transfer to the Dodgers, in the face of harsh criticism from anti-contract lawmakers and their allies. Owen demanded, with more than a touch of irony, that a public purpose clause be inserted in the deed from the state to the city; he was well aware of the fate of the similar provision in the 1955 CHA deed to the city conveying the Chavez Ravine land.[7]

A Los Angeles real estate agent appeared before the State Assembly committee considering the land sale and offered to buy it for twice what the city would be paying. "No governmental authority can afford to lose control of this land," he argued. "I think the mayor of Los Angeles is out of his mind."[8] A San Jose Republican assemblyman charged that the legislation would perpetuate "the greatest giveaway of public property to a private group in the history of California."[9] Assemblyman John "Bud" Collier, whose Eagle Rock district was roughly coterminous with that of Councilman John Holland, demanded an investigation of the land deal. "When we transfer land," he told the committee, "I want the state to get value received."[10] Collier announced that he would introduce a bill making it impossible for a private entity to receive land sold by the State of California to a locality.[11] Despite this opposition, however, the bill authorizing the state-city-Dodgers transaction passed the legislature, with the argument that Los Angeles no longer needed this portion of Chavez Ravine winning out in the end.

The Dodgers now owned most but not all of the land required for the stadium. The team still lacked parcels owned by the Los Angeles Board of Education and the Archdiocese of Los Angeles. Most important, it did not have about a dozen pieces of property scattered around the Ravine area that if not acquired would create a series of privately held islands on Dodger Stadium land.[12] A determinedly obstinate landowner might conceivably demand the same commercial zoning that the stadium would receive and, as a community newspaper gleefully speculated, open a hot dog stand in the middle of its parking lot.[13] Under these circumstances, owning almost but not quite all of Chavez Ravine would be tantamount to owning nothing at all.

The news that the individual property owners had banded together as a group for bargaining purposes was especially ominous for O'Malley. A half century earlier, Charles Ebbets, O'Malley's predecessor as Dodger owner, had secretly bought up the individually held parcels on which he intended to build his new Brooklyn ballpark, fearing a ruinous price war if his plans leaked out. During O'Malley's negotiations for a new stadium in Brooklyn, Robert Moses had facetiously suggested that O'Malley acquire the necessary plots of land at Atlantic and Flatbush Avenues on his own, knowing full well the expense would be prohibitive. Now O'Malley was facing the scenario he and Charles Ebbets had dreaded: organized landowners, with full knowledge of his need for their parcels, ready to squeeze every possible penny from him. The courts had given him the go-ahead. The state and city had offered him assistance. But ultimately O'Malley would be on his own with these property owners. He would simply be a businessman seeking to make a deal, this time with the market as his enemy.

Uncertainty over land acquisition also complicated O'Malley's efforts to obtain bank financing, which began in earnest early in 1959. Without clear title to the entire Chavez Ravine property, banks would be less likely to commit funds to a project whose successful completion was by no means assured. O'Malley identified four established Los Angeles banks—Security First, Bank of America, California Bank, and Citizens National Bank—as possible lending partners.[14] By 1959, O'Malley was a well-known figure on the Los Angeles sports scene as well as in city politics, but in the tight world of municipal financial institutions he was still an outsider from New York without local connections. The project for which he sought financing was unique in that there was no way to measure it against similar undertakings.

The potential lenders were thus cautious. Bank of America officials asked O'Malley for audit reports, financial forecasts, stadium cost estimates, other funding sources, and architectural plans, without making any commitment of their own.[15] Dodger assistant treasurer E. J. Burns wrote to O'Malley in January, evaluating the prospects for success at each of the four target banks and making follow-up recommendations.[16] He described Security First as having shown the most interest thus far and suggested scheduling lunches with key bank executives to sell the stadium project. Burns scrambled to locate contacts at the banks, an indication of O'Malley's relatively low recognition level in the city's lending community. Burns admitted that they had yet to "'size up' the men with whom we will be dealing."[17]

O'Malley left for Dodger spring training in mid-February, asking lenders that negotiations get "real serious" after his return for the start of the regular season in April. He received no promises in return.[18] Indeed, a Bank of America official warned O'Malley that after he obtained clear title to the Chavez Ravine land—itself no sure bet given the number of parcels still outstanding—he should neither commence work on stadium construction nor accept delivery of building materials until a lender's lien was recorded, so it could take priority over all other obligations.[19] The official told O'Malley that secondary liens would not be acceptable to his institution and would not be the basis for financing.[20] It was clear that the process of arranging stadium loans would be arduous.

Arguments over the Chavez Ravine project continued even in the wake of the January California Supreme Court decision. Now, in fact, another dispute was developing over a separate downtown project that was similar to Dodger Stadium in its goal of central core revitalization. Bunker Hill was an area of tenements, rooming houses, and aging homes adjacent to the Los Angeles business district, the *Times* building, and municipal offices. Downtown leaders viewed it as an eyesore and an embarrassment. To its residents, a working- and lower-class mix of races and ethnicities rarely found elsewhere in the city, Bunker Hill provided inexpensive housing close to places of employment. But with City Hall, courthouses, and the administrative agencies of the ambitiously named Civic Center almost cheek-by-jowl to the "blight" of Bunker Hill, political and business elites considered the neighborhood ripe for demolition and redevelopment. Under the auspices of the Community Redevelopment Agency (CRA), a plan was developed to raze most of the structures on Bunker Hill and replace them with modern office buildings, upscale residential towers, and cultural institutions.

Many of the same elements of the coalitions that had supported and opposed the Dodger Stadium project lined up in similar positions on the Bunker Hill redevelopment issue. Bunker Hill was, to be sure, an undertaking more in line with the goals and mechanisms of Title I of the Federal Housing Act of 1949 than was Dodger Stadium. There is little doubt that Robert Moses, had he resided in Los Angeles, would have approved of it. The CRA was a municipal agency that would funnel federal and city monies to purchase and clear properties through eminent domain procedures and then sell them at below-market rates to private developers— exactly what O'Malley had sought unsuccessfully in New York. Financing would come through the sale of tax-exempt municipal bonds with payment guaranteed by the federal government, thus creating an investment opportunity that was almost risk-free. Displaced Bunker Hill residents would be relocated by the city at federal expense.

But this arrangement, advantageous as it was to them, did not completely satisfy private developers in the Los Angeles area. If Fritz Burns, the city's largest and most influential home builder, had his way, the government would have left redevelopment in the city to him, his colleagues, and the private market.[21] Burns had helped lead the movement against public housing in Chavez Ravine in the early 1950s. That campaign had been notable for its crude portrayals of public housing as socialistic and its Red-baiting of City Housing Authority officials.[22] But along with McCarthyism, the anti-public housing crusade articulated serious policy arguments. Burns believed that government should leave as small a footprint as possible on the American housing market and that private owners, builders, and lenders left largely to their own devices could fulfill most of the nation's housing needs.

There was of course a good deal of irony and even hypocrisy in this position. The federal government was already in the national housing market, and not just in the public housing sector. Federal Housing Authority (FHA) mortgage guarantees, in addition to the subsidies and tax concessions of Title I of the Federal Housing Act itself, subsidized private developers such as Burns, who assumed little or no risk on their investments. In fact, each of the four major constituents of the American housing industry—landowners, developers, builders, and lenders—was receiving substantial government assistance by the 1950s, as were homebuyers themselves. Even Fritz Burns, who often combined the functions of landowner, developer, and builder in an example of vertical integration that John D. Rockefeller might well have envied, would have been out of business without them. But while Burns was willing to accept public assistance in his own enterprises, he insisted that the private sector should be the main engine of the American housing industry. Government's role, he argued, should be that of a facilitator, not a producer.

It was thus not surprising that Burns's initial reaction to the Bunker Hill redevelopment plan was skeptical. He offered an alternative plan of his own, which would employ private financing, free enterprise, and market forces to rebuild the area. Burns's advocacy group, ACTION (American Council to Improve Our Neighborhoods), founded by the National Association of Home Builders, promised to solve the nation's housing problems without resort to direct government intervention. Burns proposed that he and other private sector real estate entrepreneurs buy substandard Bunker Hill properties and rehabilitate them, constructing attractive, livable homes in their place. "This is not a pork barrel deal seeking government support," he wrote. "Rather it is American free enterprise working for the good of the national economy."[23] ACTION's version of Bunker Hill redevelopment would be "financed entirely by private investors. It is a truly free enterprise operation."[24]

Burns even attempted to attract Edward Roybal, a liberal Democrat not customarily sympathetic to market-centered arguments and who championed the preservation of traditional working-class neighborhoods like Bunker Hill. Burns told Roybal that the proposed government-sponsored CRA project would gut the entire

Bunker Hill community, destroying good housing along with bad. He sought to convince the councilman that ACTION could successfully rehabilitate the area on a piece-by-piece basis, "tearing down old buildings and [constructing] new ones . . . at no expense to the taxpayer."[25] Bunker Hill would retain a portion of its original population since only substandard dwellings would be razed, and the area would remain primarily residential.

But Roybal was suspicious of the claims of private real estate interests. He viewed them as Trojan horses through which the forces of capital would put to rout working- and lower-class Bunker Hill residents. Roybal's goal was affordable housing that would allow those residents to stay where they were. This would require direct government intervention as a housing provider. But by the late 1950s public housing was essentially dead in Los Angeles as an alternative to the private market. Since Roybal also opposed the CRA's Bunker Hill project as an unwarranted subsidy to the real estate industry and downtown corporate interests, he was boxed in, forced to oppose Bunker Hill redevelopment without a viable alternative plan other than opposition and delay.

With his ACTION plan for Bunker Hill essentially stillborn, Burns moved to his version of plan B. This involved acceptance of government assistance to the private homebuilding industry, all the while seeking to maintain as much independence as possible. Whether this constituted hypocrisy or simple business pragmatism lay in the eye of the beholder.

Like the Dodger Stadium project, Bunker Hill redevelopment presented three broad alternatives for planning and financing. The first, which relied exclusively on the private market, was economically unfeasible—even Burns did not possess the necessary capital to buy up property unaided—and anathema to liberals and public housing advocates. The public approach, involving direct state intervention in the form of public housing and municipally constructed stadiums, had been opposed by business elites and rejected by Los Angeles voters. This left a third way, in which government supported private enterprise but did not replace it. At Chavez Ravine, this meant making public land available to O'Malley at an affordable cost so he could build a stadium that would serve the people of Los Angeles. At Bunker Hill, it would mean utilizing federal housing policy and specifically the provisions of Title I of the Federal Housing Act of 1949 to offer land to private developers and builders at below-market prices for offices and residences that would also advance a public purpose.

But which people and which public? Certainly the evicted people of Chavez Ravine and Bunker Hill had their own ideas about what constituted a public purpose. Both projects embodied the tensions inherent in the idea of the public good in urban life, as well as illustrating the tendency of human beings to equate what is good for them with what is good for all. Supporters of the Dodger Stadium and Bunker Hill projects, such as Norris Poulson and Norman Chandler, believed that a revitalized downtown would reap benefits for all of Los Angeles. Left unstated were their own financial and political interests in these projects. Opponents including John Holland and the remaining residents of Chavez Ravine and Bunker Hill claimed to speak for the "real" Los Angeles but did not wish to cede resources or their homes to a new downtown to which they felt little or no connection. Somewhere on the border between the interests of proponents and opponents of the Chavez Ravine and Bunker Hill projects lay those of all Angelenos. But no one could say for certain where they were.

This, of course, did not prevent each side from professing to speak for all. The *Mirror News*, in an editorial hailing the state Supreme Court's decision upholding the Dodger contract, linked the stadium and Bunker Hill undertakings as essential for the good of the entire city. It took to task "a small group of suburban oppositionists who selfishly seek to block any improvements which benefit 'downtown.' These narrow jealousies cannot impede, for very long, the progress of the whole community. The fair-minded everywhere among us recognize that downtown is only an interdependent part of what has become a vast metropolitan complex. A healthy 'core area' is necessary to the health of the various suburban communities. One segment of this metropolitan community cannot prosper at the expense of another. We're all in this together."[26] The *Mirror News* pressed for the CRA-sponsored redevelopment at Bunker Hill, which it likened to Chavez Ravine as "a weatherbeaten, unproductive slum," in order to promote "progress and the general welfare" and to meet the "need of the whole community."[27]

Speaking in opposition, C. A. Owen asked, "Why must the city involve itself in a [Bunker Hill] program . . . which involves visible and invisible costs to the taxpayer when so many unresolved problems already confront the community? For the benefit of the few, this venture involves subsidization of development by the city when in truth the area will develop with very nice structures built without subsidization if the city will just get off the backs of the affected property owners."[28] The Apartment House Owners Association of Los Angeles County, which had also opposed the Chavez Ravine contract, charged that the Bunker Hill redevelopment would be "for the benefit of downtown merchants only, to the detriment of all other areas of the city, without regard to the economic consequences of owners in other sections of the city."[29] Roybal also criticized the Bunker Hill plan on the same grounds as he had the Dodger Stadium deal—as an unwarranted transfer of private property by the city to powerful business interests.[30] When the Bunker Hill measure came before the City Council in February 1959, Roybal joined John Holland in casting the only nay votes as it passed.

The council's approval of the CRA mechanism as a third-way approach to redevelopment set downtown Los Angeles on a new path, albeit one that would be decades in the making. Both the Chavez Ravine and Bunker Hill projects would shift resources toward Los Angeles's core and away from areas represented by Edward Roybal and John Holland. The partnership of such different men with such different political constituencies in opposition to these models of downtown redevelopment would at first glance appear paradoxical. A Republican fiscal conservative from a district of white homeowners would seem to have little in common with a Latino councilman with a public sector orientation and a heavily Democratic base. But the two men shared the suspicion held by those on the margins of power for those connected more directly to it.

One could certainly make a strong case that Holland's white supporters were considerably closer to the Downtown centers of political, economic, and social influence than were Roybal's East

A woman stands outside her Bunker Hill home, July 24, 1961. University of Southern California, USC Digital Library, *Los Angeles Examiner* Photographs Collection. Photographer: Unknown.

Side voters. But both sets of constituents felt they were on the periphery: the Eagle Rock whites who believed the city was run by well-connected Downtown capitalists, and the East Los Angeles Latinos whose racial, ethnic, and religious marginalization in a white- and Protestant-dominated city was driven home every day. Both subscribed to the idea that the "interests" were victimizing weaker people: racial minorities, small property owners, the poor, and the middle class. Under the circumstances, a white conservative Republican and a Latino liberal Democrat might well find common ground in a neighborhood-centered vision of Los Angeles that was the antithesis of the central-core-oriented plans of Poulson, Chandler, and Wyman. The more power flowing downtown, whether in the form of a new ballpark or a revitalized Bunker Hill of office towers, luxury housing, and cultural institutions, the fewer resources available to Holland's and Roybal's people.

Advocates for downtown development argued that it was not a zero-sum proposition, that benefits would travel outward to the periphery, and that the entire community—all of Los Angeles—would thereby grow and prosper. But those who represented that periphery, including Holland and Roybal, viewed the Dodger Stadium and Bunker Hill projects precisely in those zero-sum terms. The benefit multipliers for Poulson were cultural prestige and major league status, which did not always lend themselves to precise empirical measurement. Holland and Roybal measured with greater exactitude. Every tax dollar spent on Dodger Stadium or Bunker Hill was one their constituents did not receive.

Holland and Roybal believed their communities and not the soulless buildings that made up downtown represented the real Los Angeles. The true life of the city was situated in neighborhoods like theirs. Poulson, Chandler, and Wyman may have assumed that without a central core that rivaled those of New York, Chicago, or San Francisco, Los Angeles could not hope to be a national or international city, but to Holland and Roybal this was beside the point. Their people, the real people of Los Angeles, needed services. They needed schools, roads, sanitation, and security, and not, as a Bunker Hill residents' group charged, "mansions and gaming rooms for the rich."[31] The costs associated with a glittering downtown would mean fewer of those services for their communities. This neighborhood-oriented vision of Los Angeles would continue at odds with that of downtown development. It would thus clash with Walter O'Malley as he tried to get his stadium built. The next ground of battle, in fact, would be the ground of Chavez Ravine itself, as the remnants of what may have been Los Angeles's quintessential neighborhood fought to survive.

On March 9, 1959, the City of Los Angeles sent letters to the approximately twenty remaining households in Chavez Ravine ordering them to vacate their properties in thirty days so that preliminary grading and leveling work for Dodger Stadium could begin.[32] The California Supreme Court decision in January had given city officials enough confidence to move ahead, although the Dodgers would still be required to indemnify them against monies spent in the event of a reversal on appeal.[33] Poulson hoped that the departure of the last families from the Ravine would be the final act of a municipal drama that had been playing out for almost a decade.

The drama's roots lay in the severe housing shortage Los Angeles had faced in the aftermath of the Second World War. Returning veterans competed for scarce shelter with the defense workers who had poured into the city after Pearl Harbor and who themselves had stretched the limits of available housing stock. By 1946 Los Angeles seemed on the verge of bursting at the seams, and a powerful impetus had formed in support of public housing as a solution to its space constraints. The New Deal–era Housing Act of 1937 had established a national public housing program, but it had been poorly funded during the war years. The end of the conflict and its accompanying population overflow imparted a new urgency to the idea that the solution to the nation's housing needs lay with government.

The postwar public housing impulse in Los Angeles proceeded from a variety of motives. New Deal liberals, led by Mayor Fletcher Bowron, were attracted by its potential for social transformation. Public housing programs could employ an array of state-sponsored services to uplift residents, fostering a spirit of cooperation and, although this was rarely stated explicitly, political loyalty to the national Democratic Party. Leftists welcomed public housing's contribution to social democracy. Los Angeles city officials, including the city council members who would vote to authorize public housing construction, coveted the federal funds that would flow into their districts. Labor unions envisioned job opportunities for their members. Religious and civic groups hoped to eradicate slums. Veterans' organizations sought homes for returning soldiers. Angelenos and their families, with rents rising and residential housing at a premium, simply wanted places to live.

In 1946, spurred by the expanding housing demand, the City of Los Angeles Planning Commission began a study of local "blighted areas."[34] Almost immediately, it zeroed in on Chavez Ravine, a hilly area hidden in plain sight less than a mile from downtown. The Chavez Ravine community had grown alongside the city's Elysian Park, which traced its roots back to 1781 and a grant of land to the newly established pueblo of Los Angeles from King Carlos III of Spain.[35] The land had come into the possession of a local landowner and entrepreneur named Julian Chavez shortly before the Mexican-American War of 1846–48. Chavez became a local grandee and gave the area its name.

By the early decades of the twentieth century, Chavez Ravine was home to a tightly knit, working-class Mexican American population living in relative isolation from the rest of Los Angeles. Except for basic municipal services, the surrounding city rarely intruded into the lives of neighborhood residents. In 1913 a local attorney and entrepreneur named Marshall Stimson bought up plots of land in the Ravine and sold home sites to some 250 families. They built a community based on mutuality and tradition.[36] Few retail businesses existed there. Frank De Leon's small grocery store was for many years the only source of outside products. Many residents maintained their own food gardens. Some kept chickens and other farm animals. "Here," said De Leon, "we are happy in living our own lives our own way."[37]

In 1923, Manuel and Abrana Arechiga moved to homes at 1767 and 1771 Malvina Street in Chavez Ravine, where they raised their children, including daughters Aurora and Victoria and son John, and lived with their extended family. The Chavez Ravine community grew around them, an enclave unto itself in the very heart of Los Angeles. Plans for the Ravine emanated intermittently from City Hall, including its use as the site of a World's Fair that was waylaid by the outbreak of World War II, but none came to fruition. Chavez Ravine in 1945 was seemingly locked in time, a place of traditional work, family, and religious practices where, in the words of one observer, "more of life happened outside their homes, in public."[38]

With the advent of the post–World War II housing shortage, however, it was almost inevitable that the Ravine would draw the attention of city officials and urban planners. A low-density area adjacent to downtown, it could potentially offer housing relief to an over-crowded metropolitan area. In its "blighted areas" study, the City of Los Angeles Planning Commission cited Chavez Ravine for "improper use of land, poor street patterns, a high proportion of substandard housing, poor sanitation, juvenile delinquency, and the presence of tuberculosis."[39]

But to its residents, imbued with a powerful sense of place and surrounded by the familiar and the beloved, the Ravine was a true home.[40] One Raviner, responding to the charge that the area was a "slum," said: "We did not know we lived in slums. We thought of slums as narrow, crowded, airless places with houses jammed one atop another, with people packed in like sardines in a can. Here we have room for our children to play and there has always been light and air and space. I know nothing of slums. I only know this has been my home and it was my father's home.... Here is where I live. Here. In Chavez Ravine."[41] Marshall Stimson, who had sold most of the Ravine home sites, expressed similar sentiments. "I resent this talk of slum clearance," he complained. "These humble homes are not the finest but the same health standards do not apply where there is plenty of free air as compared with crowded tenements downtown."[42]

Nevertheless, the demand for public housing was too powerful and the residents of Chavez Ravine too powerless to resist it. The Federal Housing Act of 1949, in addition to its provision for subsidized private sector urban renewal, offered funds for the creation of public housing. This attracted Los Angeles officials pressured by constituents without affordable places to live. In August 1949, the City Council unanimously approved the construction of some 10,000 public housing units in Los Angeles under the auspices of the CHA.[43] Of those, 3,360 would be built at Chavez Ravine.

The CHA entered into a contract with the federal government whereby the latter would finance property acquisition, land clearance, resident relocation, and construction. Modernist architects Richard Neutra and Robert Alexander were engaged to design what would be known as Elysian Park Heights, a complex of 163 low-rise buildings and twenty-four 13-story apartment towers that they envisioned, perhaps overoptimistically, as combining the Ravine's traditional bonds of kinship and friendship with up-to-date amenities and conveniences. Neutra was confident the project would "bring this rejuvenated community the benefits of transportation, shopping, and cultural facilities."[44]

In July 1950, the residents of Chavez Ravine received form letters from the CHA that read: "This ... is to inform you that a public housing development will be built on this location for families of low income.... You will be visited by representatives of the Housing Authority who will . . . inspect your house in order to estimate its value."[45] The letters promised, "Later you will have the first chance to move back into the new Elyisan Heights development."[46]

Most Raviners had limited access to sources of political power and few connections through which to fight for their community. They did, however, discover allies in unexpected places. By 1950, a backlash against public housing in Los Angeles was building in sectors not usually associated with Chavez Ravine or with Latinos generally. Real estate, banking, and construction interests, fearful of the potential of public housing to harm them financially, launched an attack on it as a form of socialism. They were joined by Downtown businesses, notably the *Los Angeles Times*, and allied politicians, including an ambitious congressman named Norris Poulson. In these early Red Scare years it was not difficult to arouse the resentments of the Folks, the white middle-class small property owners represented by the likes of John Holland. They added numerical weight to the anti-public-housing impulse.

The local real estate industry sponsored a group, Citizens Against Socialist Housing (CASH), which promoted a market-based approach to the city's housing needs. It labeled public housing as the opening wedge of totalitarianism. CASH organized successfully on the grassroots level with thousands of rank-and-file members who began to bring pressure on the City Council to cancel its public housing contract with the CHA. The Small Property Owners Association, another anti-public-housing group, sent representatives into Chavez Ravine to stoke opposition to the contract and promote free enterprise principles.[47] "Public housing," charged John Holland, "follows the communist pattern. These are the people who are trying to wreck America. Those who have been warning us that liberty is in grave danger in this country are right."[48] Fellow councilman Harold Henry, adopting a description frequently employed by CASH, denounced public housing as "collectivist."[49]

Even as plans for the Chavez Ravine project moved forward, with residents either selling their homes to the CHA or going through condemnation proceedings if a price could not be agreed on, forces were in motion to bring it to a halt. Raviners had thus discovered a new source of support in people who had paid little attention to them in the past and who were often disdainful and condescending when they did. Norman Chandler, Fritz Burns, John Holland, and their constituencies rarely ventured to the East Side of Los Angeles, yet there they were, fighting for the rights of small property owners at Chavez Ravine and championing individual rights against the encroachments of the "collectivist" state. In the fervor of the anti-public-housing movement, the Raviners were transformed into independent and self-reliant symbols of the American way. Considerations of race, ethnicity, and social class fell before the imperatives of anti-statism for Chandler, Burns, and the white middle-class members of CASH, who under most other circumstances would have regarded the Raviners as outsiders and interlopers.

But in yet another irony, while its opponents were able to defeat public housing at Chavez Ravine, they were not able to act in time to save Chavez Ravine itself. Throughout 1951, even as the pressure on the City Council to cancel the public housing contract grew, the CHA proceeded with its buyouts and condemnations, totaling more than seven hundred in all.[50] By December of that year, when the anti-public-housing forces were able to prevail on the council to terminate the CHA contract by a vote of 8 to 7, most Raviners were going or already gone. Except for Holland, who viewed Ravine residents as homeowners similar to his own constituents in Eagle Rock, reaction to the demise of the Chavez Ravine community among public housing opponents was muted. Their goal was to defeat public housing in Los Angeles, not necessarily to preserve Chavez Ravine.

In any event, the public housing impulse had crested by the time of the council's vote. The rapidly growing Red Scare, which demonized public housing as the work of socialists and collectivists, was a major reason for this. There was, however, more at work than anti-communist hysterics. By 1951, the housing shortage in Los Angeles had begun to ease as private sector builders such as Fritz Burns moved into the residential market vacuum. They constructed acres of detached homes for returning veterans, aerospace industry workers, newly minted GI Bill college graduates, and recent arrivals from the East and Midwest. These new white homeowners were the beneficiaries of federally guaranteed low-interest mortgages and racially exclusionary building and zoning practices. Given a choice between living in apartments and living in single-family houses, they chose the latter.

The homes they chose, as architectural historian Dana Cuff notes, were a far cry from the modernist dreams of Richard Neutra and Robert Alexander, who had planned the Chavez Ravine public housing development. The Case Study homes of the California Modernist movement featured open floor plans that made liberal uses of glass to connect to the natural environment. But while architectural critics praised the Case Study homes effusively, actual buyers flocked to purchase the more prosaic offerings of Burns and other mainstream developers. Burns's prototypes, the Postwar House and House of Tomorrow, were formulaic and architecturally undistinguished. But they were loaded with amenities—refrigerators, dishwashers, kitchen cooking islands, patios—and they sparked a buying frenzy. Potential customers lined up to view Burns's models. Some even paid admission to get in.[51] As Cuff observes, "Architecture was not important for the contractor-designed house; features were."[52]

The impulse toward individual ownership, pent up during the Depression and war years, now burst to the surface. "In my wife's and my family," Cuff quotes one new home buyer, "we were the first ones to own a home—my parents and her parents rented. We thought we were in heaven when we got our house. . . . They built a few multiples out here, but they weren't too popular. Everyone wanted their own home."[53]

Burns and his colleagues in the home development industry were marketers as much as builders. They played to the hopes and fears of their buyers. "Burns, the consummate salesman," Cuff writes, "knew his customers' desires: No flat roofs and no blacks allowed. Institutionalized aesthetics as surely as public housing's modernism symbolized socialism."[54]

By the early 1950s, with privately built, individually owned, and racially segregated homes within reach of hundreds of thousands of white buyers, demand for public housing crested. Whites increasingly associated it with racial minorities and those who had failed in American life. Modernists, social planners, and liberals envisaged public housing as framing what Cuff termed a "single coherent approach to civic betterment"[55] in which the state assumed responsibility for "social reform, sanitation, community, family life, and healthy living."[56] The residents of the vanishing Chavez Ravine embraced a more traditional but no less communal culture, in which networks of family, friendship, and kinship were paramount. However, Fritz Burns's newly minted white homeowners rejected both modernist and traditionalist cultural forms, adopting instead a privatized, nuclear-family-based model grounded on notions of self-reliance, individualism, physical space, and personal distance. It privileged ownership over renting, outlying areas over the urban core, single-family over multifamily houses, and racial and class homogeneity over diversity and heterogeneity.

Of course, white homebuyers who prided themselves on independence and self-sufficiency were themselves reliant on the state for financing, without which their dreams of property ownership would have come to naught. So, for that matter, were Burns and his fellow developers. There may have been, however, a distinction between taking state direction and planning and merely taking state money. Burns and his buyers wanted government support to spend independently without the entanglements of state planning. Public housing opponents in the business and real estate communities and among rank-and-file homeowners drew a sharp philosophical distinction between state-built, "socialist" housing and individually owned "American" homes. They sought to link the latter with ideals of freedom and free enterprise, which they saw as the essence of national culture. They were less interested in cooperative or traditional models of social organization than in the pursuit of individual material dreams on their own terms. In perhaps the nation's most atomized city, they possessed an atomized view of culture. Such a view, especially with the area's housing shortage abating, doomed the public housing impulse. By 1953 the private market had won the housing war in Los Angeles.

While the anti-public-housing movement was driven by practical and philosophical motives, it expressed itself publicly largely through Red-baiting. The California State Senate Un-American Activities Committee launched an investigation of subversives within the CHA that focused primarily on Frank Wilkinson, the body's head of public relations and a leading public housing advocate. Wilkinson was a unifying figure for the public housing coalition, which included religious, veterans, and civic groups, elements of the labor movement, the local chapter of the NAACP, and, most notably, Fletcher Bowron, the mayor of Los Angeles.

Bowron was a reformer who had assumed office in 1938 after the recall of his corrupt and disgraced predecessor, Frank Shaw. He had cleaned up City Hall and had been as close to a New Dealer as the region produced. Bowron allied with labor, confronted downtown business interests, and promoted government-sponsored initiatives such as public housing, from which he refused to back away even in the face of the assaults mounted by CASH, the *Times*, and the real estate industry. In 1952, another public housing opponent, police chief William Parker, issued a report purporting to show that the rate of juvenile delinquency was higher in public housing than in areas classified as "slums."[57] When Wilkinson questioned the report's findings, the autocratic Parker denounced Wilkinson to Bowron as a communist. Bowron did not take immediate action against his ally on the public housing issue, but when Wilkinson refused to answer questions regarding his associations and activities before the California Un-American Activities Committee, he was fired by the CHA. Wilkinson would later spend nine months in prison, a martyr not only to a local version of McCarthyism but also, in the minds of his supporters, to the crusade against public housing in Los Angeles.[58]

In August 1951, Congress passed the Cain Law, barring federal funding of public housing projects that had been rejected by local governing authorities. By canceling the city's contract with the CHA in December of that year, the Los Angeles City Council called this law into play. But the CHA sued in state court to reverse the council's action and reinstate the public housing contract. In the meantime, the council placed the question of the contract's validity on the ballot as a referendum question, scheduled for June 3, 1952. In April 1952 the California Supreme Court ruled that the council had exceeded its powers in canceling the contract and that it remained in force. The referendum would thus not be binding.

What appeared on the surface to be a victory for public housing was, however, illusory. The referendum was held as scheduled, and on June 3 Los Angeles voters expressed their disapproval, rejecting the public housing contract by some 120,000 votes out of 636,000 cast, a margin of almost 60 percent to 40 percent.[59] Advisory as it may have been—and the United States Supreme Court upheld the validity of the contract in October 1952—the referendum result was a clear sign of what was to come. Urged on by Downtown business leaders, Congressman Norris Poulson entered the race for mayor against Bowron, promising to make the June 1953 election a true referendum on public housing. Bowron had tied his political fate to the public housing issue. He could not abandon it even had he wished to. After a campaign that was defined almost entirely by Poulson's attacks on "socialistic" public housing, Bowron went down to defeat on May 26, 1953. Poulson's victory margin of approximately 35,000 votes was considerably smaller than that of the contract referendum the previous year, but it was enough to doom the public housing program in Los Angeles.[60]

Once in office, Poulson negotiated a compromise with the CHA whereby work on the nine housing projects already under construction would be completed but no new projects would commence. Elysian Park Heights, for which most Ravine residents had been evicted but on which a shovel had yet to be turned, was thus a dead letter. Later in 1953 California senator William Knowland and Vice President Richard Nixon, a native of the Los Angeles area, brokered legislation in Congress that permitted the sale of the Chavez Ravine property by the CHA to the city of Los Angeles. The federal government would absorb the difference between the monies already spent on the project—which included land purchases, resident relocation costs, and engineering, architectural, and administrative expenses—and the sale price agreed upon with the city.[61] Under the terms of Poulson's arrangement, the CHA was permitted to abandon more than half of the planned but yet unbuilt public housing units in the city, 5,700 out of some 10,000.[62]

The Ravine now lay desolate and almost empty. About two-thirds of the residents served with notices to vacate in 1950 had agreed with the CHA and the city attorney's office on a sale price and left their homes to municipal bulldozers.[63] Others had refused the CHA's terms and gone through formal condemnation proceedings. In these an independent appraiser set a value for the property at issue. This in turn was subject to court review.[64] Even as the Chavez Ravine project moved toward extinction in 1951 and 1952, families moved out and condemnation cases proceeded. Beneath the surface of the workings of the condemnation protocol was a punitive device awaiting property owners with the temerity to force the institution of formal condemnation suits. The independent appraisal value of a home after condemnation was often less than the CHA's offer during negotiations, and the reviewing court could reduce this amount even further.

The Arechiga family had ignored the original eviction notice it had received in 1951, effectively forcing it into the formal condemnation process. After an appraiser set the value of their property at $17,500, a Superior Court judge reduced the amount to $10,050. The Arechigas refused to accept payment and remained in their homes. The city obtained a judgment officially evicting them in 1953 that the Arechigas challenged in court. By that year the Chavez Ravine project was virtually dead, as the newly inaugurated Poulson negotiated its demise. The Arechigas, by then among the few remaining Ravine occupants, argued that the termination of the project made the condemnation process moot and rendered their evictions illegal. While their case wound through the courts, the family maintained they still were the rightful owners of their homes and attempted to pay taxes on them. The city refused to accept these monies. City officials, while now claiming the Arechigas were tenants, did not attempt to collect rent on their properties.[65]

Meanwhile, a check for $10,050, representing the court-ordered condemnation price on the Arechiga property, sat unclaimed in a municipal escrow account. It was a classic stalemate, with the city arguing that the Arechigas had no right to remain on the land but making no move to physically remove them and the Arechigas continuing to claim full ownership but avoiding overtly provocative words or actions that would attract attention and force the city's hand.

The motivations behind the family's battle with the authorities were also mixed. Certainly the price they had been offered played a major role, but they were also driven by a powerful attachment to their home and way of life. The observation of photographer Don Normark, whose late 1940s images of Chavez Ravine captured the community in its last days, that those "who defied the eviction notices were impelled in part by a determination to get what they considered a fair price for their property, and in part by a deep reluctance to abandon the neighborhoods that had so long been theirs," aptly testifies to the difficulties in untangling the threads of historical causality and motive.[66]

Where "principle" ended and "principal" began for the Arechigas is, of course, impossible to know with certainty. We might not have known even if the court had confirmed the original appraisal price of $17,500. Would the Arechigas have simply taken the money and departed like so many of their neighbors? Later, amid the swirl of events surrounding their forcible evictions in May 1959, family members would assert that they would never accept less for their property than the $17,500 it was worth. But the ties of community, family, and tradition were such that the Arechigas might not have left their homes for any price. Chavez Ravine was where they wished to be.

After the demise of the Elysian Heights Village project, Poulson pondered alternative uses for the property—a zoo, a convention center, an expansion of the nearby police academy—but none materialized. Chavez Ravine's crevassed, gullied terrain made most plans to build in it impractical. Finally on September 27, 1955, the City of Los Angeles reached an agreement with the CHA to purchase the Chavez Ravine land for $1,279,203. This represented a loss of approximately $4,300,000 for the CHA, which, using federal government funds, had already expended $5,562,239 on it. The deal was thus a taxpayer-financed discount for the city.[67] The deed of transfer prohibited residential construction on the Chavez Ravine property for twenty years. It also restricted the uses of the property to those connected to a "public purpose."[68] This clause would be at the heart of the dispute over Dodger Stadium that began three years later.

But the "public purpose" issue had already emerged even before the official transfer of the Chavez Ravine property to the city, and it did so in a manner that would eventually make Poulson's support of the stadium deal appear hypocritical. In 1954, Mrs. Glen Walters, the owner of condemned Ravine property, wrote to Poulson asking if she could repurchase her home from the CHA in view of the public housing project's cancelation. The mayor replied that this would not be possible because "no portion of the land acquired for a public purpose can be resold for a private purpose."[69]

Manuel and Abrana Arechiga received a response similar to that sent to Mrs. Walters in 1957 when their appeal of the adverse ruling on their suit to set aside the condemnation of their property was decided. The Arechigas also had argued that the cancelation of the Elysian Heights Village development meant that the justification for seizing their homes no longer existed. But the California District Court of Appeal ruled that "when the judgment in the condemnation case became final the Arechigas were divested of all interest in the property, regardless of the purpose for which it might later be used."[70] Except for an order of eviction in the wake of this ruling that the Arechigas successfully resisted, enlisting Edward Roybal to induce sheriff's deputies to withdraw for the time being, city officials made no overt move to remove the family from their homes.[71] Stasis thus prevailed until the California Supreme Court decision of January 1959 validating the Dodger contract revived the machinery of enforcement.

When the notices to vacate went out on March 9, 1959, the Arechigas had occupied the land—whether legally, as they asserted, or as squatters, in the view of city officials—for almost eight years after the original condemnation notice. They clearly did not intend to leave quietly. The family picketed the Dodgers' April 14 season-opening ceremony on the steps of City Hall, carrying signs that read "We Are Being Forced Out So the Dodgers Can Move In" and "LA: The City That Loves to Give Away Our Homes."[72] Mrs. Glen Walters put her arm around Manuel Arechiga and told reporters, "This man is 72 years old. He has worked every day of his life. And what does he get? You take away his home." Walters shouted, "Thieves! Bandits!" at Poulson and the assembled Dodgers. "Go see Holland and McGee," the mayor jeered. A Dodger player laughed at Walters, who called him a "pipsqueak" as a plainclothes policeman moved her off the City Hall steps.[73]

By now Phill Silver was representing the Arechigas, and he lost no time in accusing city officials of malfeasance. Silver claimed that the city had been aware as early as 1953, as the condemnation action against the family proceeded, that the Elysian Heights Village project would not be constructed. Indeed, Silver charged, city leaders had known that the law permitting the cancelation of unbuilt public housing and the sale of the Chavez Ravine land to the city was about to be passed. There was thus no reason to evict the Arechigas then or now.[74] Silver, to whom evidence of collusion among municipal officials was like catnip, argued that dishonest "insiders" had worked against his clients to take their homes and destroy their community. Silver viewed the Arechigas as the quintessential "little people" whom he had spent his career defending against the "big people" downtown. With his instinct for publicity and self-promotion, Silver would also ensure that the Arechigas remained in the public eye as their story unfolded.

As the clock ticked down to the scheduled eviction date of May 8 (the original thirty-day order of March 9 had been extended for one month), Edward Roybal emerged as a possible mediator of the dispute. Roybal was in a conflicted position politically. He had made one of the first attempts to lure the Dodgers to Los Angeles. In September 1955, Rosalind Wyman had written to O'Malley asking him to meet with her and Roybal in New York to discuss a possible move west. O'Malley had replied that he was busy with World Series plans and would not be available; Wyman and Roybal visited New York but did not see O'Malley.[75] Along with many of his constituents in the heavily Mexican American East Side council district, Roybal had supported the idea of a new stadium for the Dodgers in the Coliseum area.

But like his constituents, Roybal was ambivalent when Chavez Ravine emerged as the actual stadium site. He had been absent, possibly by design, for the City Council's October 7, 1957, vote on the stadium contract. Roybal had then opposed the contract during the Proposition B referendum campaign. After its passage he resolved to cushion the blow of eviction for the Arechigas as much as possible while also preserving his political credibility within his own constituency, where anger over the destruction of the Chavez Ravine neighborhood blurred with pride and interest in the Dodgers. O'Malley had made outreach to the city's Latino community a priority with his groundbreaking Spanish-language broadcasts, and the team's growing popularity there placed the Dodger Stadium project and the pending Arechiga removals into sharp relief. Roybal had helped negotiate a delay of the family's scheduled evictions in August 1957 but knew they were now inevitable.[76]

Roybal thus sought to finesse the political and social issues that loomed before him. In an April City Council meeting he supported a plan under which the Arechigas would be permitted to remain on their property until the final disposition of the appeal of the January state Supreme Court decision upholding the Dodger contract, which Phill Silver was seeking to take to the United States Supreme Court.[77] This would give the family at least six more months, since the high court's new term would not begin until October 1959. Holland also argued for this delay: "It means a great deal to them to be able to live in their own homes, where they have been living for 30-odd years and which in some cases they still own."[78] But Wyman, out of patience after years of delay, disagreed: "It's about time these people began looking for a home. They haven't paid taxes and they haven't paid rent."[79] The council voted down the extension plan, narrowing Roybal's range of options as the May 8 deadline approached. He would need to show that he sympathized with the family even as the legal process ran its course.

But he also could not allow the matter to spin out of control. Roybal believed in order and the rule of law. A liberal but not a radical, he had climbed the political ladder in the city methodically, starting his career as a local health educator and becoming twentieth-century Los Angeles's first Mexican American council member in 1949. In 1954 Roybal had lost a bid for lieutenant governor, and in 1958 he was defeated by a handful of votes for a seat on the Los Angeles County Board of Supervisors. A future congressman, Roybal was sensitive to his position as one of the only elected Latino public officials in the region and aware of the need to maintain friendships and alliances with fellow liberals on the City Council. Rosalind Wyman, Gordon Hahn, and James Corman, all of whom enthusiastically supported the Dodger Stadium contract, were allied with Roybal on a host of other issues relating to race, labor, crime, and government services. Roybal's challenge would be to preserve these ties while continuing to protest the removal of the Arechigas, but not in a manner that would give the Latino community false hope that the family would be permitted to remain.

Much would depend on the manner in which the Arechigas departed Chavez Ravine. Roybal wanted the family to be permitted to take their leave in an atmosphere of dignity and respect. But he also knew that the authorities would not countenance any further delay and that one way or another the Arechigas would be leaving on May 8. The balance would be a delicate one.

Just how delicate it would be was underscored on April 29 when the *Mirror News* published a letter from Victoria Angustain, Manuel and Abrana's daughter, in which she attacked both the condemnation process and the idea that they no longer owned their land. "We were offered $11,500 [*sic*]," she wrote, "but just because we wouldn't accept that the judge lowered the price. . . . It's just as if somebody wants to buy the shoes that you are wearing and you don't want to sell them. . . . What right have they to give our land away?"[80]

Two days before the scheduled evictions, Manuel Arechiga wrote to the *Mirror News*: "I wasn't born in Chavez Ravine but I have lived there thirty-six years and raised my five children there. Back in 1923 when I bought this land . . . we lived in tents without gas, electricity, or toilet facilities. But I bought the land and paid for it."[81] He maintained, "I haven't anything against the Dodgers, but if they want my land let them pay a reasonable price for it, not take it away. I am 72, and cannot buy a house for the price they offer me, and stay out of debt. I have two houses and three lots and they offer me $10,050."[82] Left unmentioned was a fact that by this late date may have been decisive in determining the price the Arechigas would receive for their property: it lay within the planned recreation area, just outside the borders of what would become Dodger Stadium. This made the Arechiga property less valuable, and there was little financial incentive to increase the city's offer. In any case, with both sides locked into positions they had held for the better part of a decade, it was clear that the dispute's endgame would take place on May 8.

Another game, however, occupied O'Malley's attention the night before the scheduled evictions. On May 7 the Dodgers played an exhibition contest against the New York Yankees at the Coliseum as a tribute to Roy Campanella, the star catcher who had been paralyzed in an automobile accident in January 1958. Campanella had never been able to play as a Los Angeles Dodger, but the crowd of 93,103, a record in major league baseball at the time, gave him a hero's welcome. Before the bottom of the fifth inning former Dodger shortstop and captain Pee Wee Reese pushed the wheelchair-bound Campanella onto the field. Vin Scully, broadcasting the game on the radio, asked Coliseum fans listening in the stands to say a prayer for "Campy" and to light a match in his honor.[83] The stadium immediately exploded with light, simultaneously a tribute to the fallen player and a testament to Scully's reach and influence. Campanella received half the game's proceeds—the other half went to a Yankee-designated charity—to assist with his mounting medical expenses.[84]

As the "Campy" game was being played, city officials prepared for the evictions scheduled for the next day. O'Malley would not be present for them and was not their sponsor. Indeed, when the original eviction notices were served he was in Brooklyn, three thousand miles away. But of course he and his team would be associated with them. The removals of the Arechiga family would affect not only the relationship between the Dodgers and the Los Angeles Latino community but also serve as raw material for a legend that inspired the Chicano movement in the 1960s and beyond.[85]

7

THE ARECHIGA
DISPOSSESSIONS

The manner in which the evictions were carried out certainly influenced the ways in which they were interpreted, as did the nature of the media coverage accorded them. On the morning of Friday, May 8, Los Angeles County sheriff's deputies arrived to find the Arechigas barricaded inside their two homes. The deputies broke down their doors as bulldozers idled outside.

Also waiting outside was the city's news media corps. In addition to the usual newspapermen, there were reporters and cameramen from every local television station, ready to broadcast what they saw live. One of the deputies spoke to the family in Spanish, seeking to negotiate a peaceful resolution, but the Arechigas were adamant.[1] Abrana shouted in Spanish, "Why don't they play ball in Poulson's backyard—not in ours!"[2] Other family members bitterly criticized Wyman, who along with Poulson had been the most vocal eviction proponent over the preceding weeks.[3]

The Arechigas were then forced to leave, some more forcefully than others. As deputies moved furniture and dodged barking dogs and scampering chickens, Aurora Vargas, one of the Arechiga daughters, was carried bodily down the steps of her home with her head hitting the floorboards. The struggle lasted about ten minutes. Another daughter, Victoria Angustain, was also removed by force.[4]

After the Arechigas were out on the street, their furniture was piled into moving vans and water, telephone, and electrical lines were cut. Bulldozers quickly moved in and demolished the two Arechiga homes as television news broadcast the scene live. A crying Abrana threw a stone at them.[5] She pointed across the street and said, "We will stay here."[6] Nearby, another home occupied by Alice Martin and Ruth Rayford, two elderly women, was also cleared and demolished after deputies smashed in the door to gain entry.[7] Television captured Rayford swinging her cane at the authorities.[8]

That evening the Arechiga family pitched tents on a vacant lot across from the site of their bulldozed homes. Their purpose was to offer a physical manifestation of protest that could be seen and absorbed by passers-by and the media. They also offered the implication that they had nowhere else to go. Mike Angustain, Victoria's husband, told a reporter, "We don't know where we're going to sleep tonight."[9]

At hearings before the City Council on Monday, May 11, Arechiga family members contended they did not want charity, but again implied they were cash-strapped and homeless.[10] They accepted donations of food while living across from their former homes as well as the donation of a trailer provided by a sympathetic recreational vehicle dealer who had seen their tents. Did they do so because they were truly in need or to dramatize and underscore their refusal to give up their homes and way of life? The distinction is not insignificant. Different sets of motivations propel the Arechigas on different historical trajectories. One puts them on a course to inspire the Chicano movement with their principled defense of community and culture. The other leads elsewhere, to the understandable and human impulse toward self-protection and personal gain. But their intentions remain difficult to fathom. In the end, their supporters and critics each saw in them what they wished to see. Whether they were Chicano heroes or

The Arechiga family sits outside their home after the evictions of May 8, 1959. From left: Lucile Arechiga, Aurora Arechiga, Ivy Angustain, Victoria Angustain (holding son Ira), Ida Angustain, Manuel Arechiga. University of Southern California, USC Digital Library, *Los Angeles Examiner* Photographs Collection. Photographer: Miller.

system manipulators, the Arechigas divided Los Angeles along lines that paralleled those of the Dodger Stadium issue itself.

The disturbing television coverage of the evictions initially produced sympathy for the Arechigas and put stadium supporters on the defensive. John Holland, who was on the scene of the evictions, said, "You would think that you were in Russia. You cannot believe that what is happening here could happen in the United States." He described the events as "needless, sadistic cruelty."[11] Roybal, who had visited the Arechigas in their tents on the evening of May 8, charged that their treatment was "the type of action that occurred during the Spanish Inquisition and Hitler's Germany."[12] Attempting to balance respect for both the law and the Arechigas, he stated: "The eviction in itself is legal, but the manner in which it was carried out certainly was not. Someone stands to answer for violating the individual rights of these people."[13]

Commentary on the evictions in the electronic media was scathing. "With pained expressions on their faces," editorialized radio station KFWB on May 9,

> the reluctant dispossessed of Chavez Ravine came out of their hastily constructed tents to greet a new morning. But the horror of yesterday can't leave them. With an army of sheriff's deputies who had forcibly thrown them out of their dwellings so that O'Malley's baseball park can be built. They were forced to sit on the curb . . . and watch the bulldozers come up over the hill and reduce their homes to rubble. The children cried, the women wept and fought . . . The last eleven were coerced or bodily dragged out of their homes. One woman cried as she saw the house of her birth and dwelling place for 29 years crumble in front of the huge bulldozers. . . . The people were dispossessed so that Walter O'Malley's Dodgers can have the most modern baseball temple in the world constructed at that site. After the cries of pain are long since passed there will be a new shout: 'Popcorn' and 'Play Ball.' It's called civic progress—and the price? Possibly human rights, but certainly human dignity. That Ravine is costing Los Angeles more than money."[14]

The editorial concluded by comparing the CHA's offer to find the Arechigas space in public housing "to the one we made the American Indian many years ago."[15]

KTLA-TV was equally indignant. Its on-site reporter, Pat Michaels, emphasized the power disparity between the evictees and the forces arrayed against them. "The deputies," he lamented, "had the badges, the guns, and the brawn."[16]

The leading opponent of the Dodger contract among the city's "community" newspapers, the *Highland Park News-Herald and Journal*, thundered in an editorial titled "Government by Bulldozers" that the Arechigas and their supporters "cannot believe that now that the land is for private interests they should be forced to give up the homes they have lived in."[17] It expressed amazement that the family was "literally and physically hurled from their homes—simply because those people, American citizens, believed they had rights."[18]

The response from the public was also highly critical of the evictions and sympathetic to the Arechigas. Letters poured into Roybal's office from outraged citizens. "Who are these people," asked Joseph Babando of Wilshire Boulevard, "who have gone arrogantly, with every show of legality, into the business of uprooting social units and reorganizing the city's terrain? Do they really know what they are doing? I doubt it."[19] Alice Ingersoll, a resident of the Hyde Park neighborhood, southwest of downtown, wrote: "What a scene and to be on TV . . . We all sat there speechless. Free America. Something like this makes you wonder."[20] William Hagan protested the "invocation of 'the law' and 'legal process' to justify the violation of the most elementary human rights" and attacked Poulson as "undoubtedly a creature of big business [who] cannot be expected to have any sympathy with the problems of such little people as the residents of Chavez Ravine."[21]

Edgar Poe of Jefferson Park, west of downtown, signed his letter to Roybal as "just another angry and frightened property owner." He feared he would share the fate of the Arechigas, with his land condemned, its appraised value reduced by court order, and the property transferred to another private party. "Honorable businessmen," he wrote, "have acquired their property through the relatively meritorious method offered by the free enterprise system." If what had happened to the Arechigas had happened to him, he concluded, he "would be sorely tempted to raise a gun against this government."[22]

Frank Wright, another Roybal correspondent, stated flatly: "The people of Mexican descent are being treated worse than the colored! If this keeps up, the Mexican people will all have to ask to enter a restaurant or a public place like the coloreds are in the South."[23] "If you condemn private property for private enterprise," asked Una Urhelburt, "why not do it for Santa Anita Racetrack?"[24] H. Ratcliff wrote, "I was always led to believe that a man's home was his castle and that he had a right to protect it if necessary."[25] Even out-of-towners who had watched television news footage were outraged. New Yorker Meyer Jacoby called the evictions "the worst thing I have ever expected to see in our free country."[26]

These responses were those of whites throughout the Los Angeles metropolitan area. They showed that the shared interests of private property holders in the city could transcend racial and class lines. White Angelenos who may have viewed the Arechigas as part of an alien cultural universe could nonetheless identify with them as fellow landowners. What had occurred in the Ravine on May 8 could happen to them as well. The Arechiga evictions unleashed white middle-class anger at city elites, an impulse that was powerful enough to overcome racial divisions. In the moment, the Arechigas were associated with an American culture of individualism and opportunity with which white Angelenos identified. The right to hold property securely, safely, and free from outside interference had brought together elements of the white middle class (through Holland) and the nonwhite lower class (through Roybal) in ways that threatened those at the top of the city's power structure.

That moment continued at the City Council hearing of Monday, May 11. The Arechiga family made compelling witnesses. They were surrounded by supporters, some displaying signs reading, "We Refuse to Be Cheated Out of Our Land!," "Families in Chavez Ravine Ask Only for a Fair Price for their Property," and "Wyman Where Is Your Heart?"[27] Victoria Angustain presented the council with a petition protesting the evictions; it contained more than a thousand signatures, all obtained within the preceding seventy-two hours.[28] Roybal described the destruction of the homes as "one of the most inhumane acts of the century," a "Roman festival."[29] He asserted, "The people of Chavez Ravine are not protesting the law, but the way it was enforced—the ruthlessness."[30] John Arechiga, Manuel and Abrana's son, shouted at Rosalind Wyman as the crowd booed.[31] According to news reports, Wyman had requested police protection, citing threats to her personal safety.[32]

City attorney Roger Arnebergh attempted to explain the procedure by which property was condemned in Los Angeles and give the history of the dispute with the Arechiga family amid a cascade of boos and catcalls. Victoria Angustain rushed at him and was restrained by officers.[33] A shaken Arnebergh later charged, "Such

City councilman Edward Roybal speaks at City Council hearing on Arechiga evictions, May 11, 1959. University of Southern California, USC Digital Library, *Los Angeles Examiner* Photographs Collection. Photographer: Snow.

an incident is a breakdown in our constitutional form of government, and could result in anarchy."[34]

Poulson had refused to attend the council proceedings, snapping, "I won't go in there and listen to those crackpots."[35] Councilman Karl Rundberg, who had initially voted for the Dodger contract but then turned sharply against it, threatened to have the mayor subpoenaed and returned from Santa Barbara, where he was delivering a speech. Poulson instead raced back to Los Angeles in the afternoon.

The Arechigas publicly spurned CHA commissioner Howard Holtzendorff's offer of alternative housing in a public development elsewhere in the city. They maintained that they wanted not charity but only the opportunity to live independently on their Chavez Ravine property, remarks certain to resonate with white middle-class homeowners harboring their own fears of confiscation. Throughout the day, City Council president John Gibson repeatedly and unsuccessfully warned cheering Arechiga supporters to be silent.[36]

The May 11 council hearings were a triumph for the Arechigas. They had made their case emotionally and dramatically and put their opponents on the defensive. They had shaped the narrative of the evictions to elicit support from the widest possible section of the city's population. If any narrative could induce white middle-class Angelenos to make common cause with Raviners as aggrieved landholders, it was this one. No homeowner was immune to the argument that a lifetime's worth of work and savings could be lost on the basis of a government official's decision to reward someone who had better connections.

O'Malley and the Dodgers were also targets. O'Malley had sought to keep a low profile during the eviction process, not commenting in the media and concentrating on preparations for the Campanella tribute game. Dodger personnel played no direct role in carrying out the evictions. The land condemnations had been upheld in the courts, as had the Dodgers' acquisition of the land itself. Even Roybal did not claim that O'Malley had taken Chavez Ravine or the Arechiga property in an illegal manner. But O'Malley and the Dodgers would be associated with the televised images of the forcible removals, with Arechiga family members being carried down flights of stairs and bulldozers leveling cherished homes that had stood for generations. O'Malley had not personally destroyed the Chavez Ravine community. That process had been set in motion long before he paid his first visit to the area in May 1957. Nonetheless, as the beneficiaries of the evictions, O'Malley and his ball club would henceforth be viewed by many in the city's Latino population as the agents of the Ravine's destruction.

The city of Los Angeles, not the Los Angeles Dodgers, destroyed Chavez Ravine. But the passage of time often clouds perceptions of cause and effect and compresses chronologies of events. It is easier and simpler to say "the Dodgers evicted the Arechigas in May 1959" than "the Arechiga property was condemned by the city in 1951 for public housing that was never built and the family finally evicted in 1959 after the land had been transferred by the city to the Los Angeles Dodgers for use as the site of a new ballpark." O'Malley and the Dodgers have gone through history as the engineers of the Arechigas' eviction. This is unfair, as are imputations of anti-Latino prejudice directed at the Dodger owner. O'Malley's was a businessman's mind. He viewed Mexican Americans as potential customers, not as a hostile constituency. There is no evidence that he harbored special prejudices against them, and he certainly did not set out to evict the Arechigas from Chavez Ravine based on their ethnic identity. But simple myths often endure longer than complex truths.

Then on May 13, the Arechiga story took a new turn. That day, the *Mirror News* published an article revealing that the family, far from being homeless, actually owned seven other homes in the city of Los Angeles, one within walking distance of the tents they now occupied.[37] The other metropolitan dailies quickly joined in with their own reporting, increasing the number of other homes to eleven. "Evictees Own Homes in L.A.," headlined the *Herald and Express*.[38] "Eleven Other Homes to Go To, but Chavez Ravine Family Elects to Stay Here!" read a photograph caption to the accompanying story, showing the family's tent encampment.[39] The story listed the Arechiga homes. One was owned by Manuel and Abrana jointly, another solely by Abrana. Others were registered to their daughter Victoria Angustain and her husband, Mike.[40] Two were owned by Aurora Vargas, another Arechiga daughter. A third daughter, Celia Molano, was also listed as having title to a house. The next day it was reported that John Arechiga was the owner of three other houses.[41] Some of the homes were rented out, providing an income stream to the family. Others were vacant. The combined value of the homes was estimated at over $75,000.[42]

The Arechigas initially sought to minimize these revelations, arguing that they were irrelevant to the real issue in their dispute with the city, which was their right to remain on their own property in Chavez Ravine. Interviewed by the *Herald and Express* outside her tent, Victoria Angustain said, "The other property we own isn't important."[43] She pointed to the site of her demolished home: "This is important." She continued, "This is my parents' fight. They are fighting to protect their property rights in the Ravine. Their house [elsewhere] has nothing to do with this. The homes owned by my brother, sisters, and myself have nothing to do with my parents and their eviction."[44] The next day, she asked, "What's all the fuss about? We never denied owning any property. No one asked us if we did, and when we were asked about it we admitted it."[45] She revealed, "We offered our parents one of our places to live in but they refused. They feel their fight is right here in Chavez Ravine and won't leave."[46] Abrana Arechiga told the *Examiner*, "Money is no object—I'm too old for money anyway. I want to stay here the rest of my life with the dogs and the chickens. . . . If they take me out of here, they're going to have to take me out of here dead."[47] Victoria added: "What she really wants is to get the land back."[48]

Roybal, Holland, and Rundberg also attempted to lessen the impact of the story and limit its damage to the Arechigas. "It is proper for them to fight for their land," Roybal told the City Council. "They said they don't want charity. They only want justice."[49] He also argued, "The fact that the family and in-laws of the elder Arechigas have homes is not pertinent. Certainly the homes of my relatives do not belong to me."[50] The real issue, Roybal maintained, was not how many homes the family owned but whether the property rights of average Americans would be respected:

> It is not morally or legally right for a governmental agency to condemn private land, take it away from the property owner through eminent domain proceedings, then turn around and give it to a private person . . . or corporation for private gain. This, I believe, is a gross misuse of eminent domain, and some legislation with teeth in it must be enacted soon to prevent future occurrences of this kind. If this practice continues, the City of Los Angeles could approach anyone in the city and condemn the land, say for a park (public purpose); then several months later sell it to a supermarket chain (private enterprise) for private gain. That is what is happening in Chavez Ravine.[51]

Holland also sprang to the Arechigas' defense. "I am going to demand a full and complete investigation," he thundered.

Let's find out if the Arechigas did receive due process of the law. Let's find out who did order this secret and ruthless raid that evicted them. Let's find out who was behind the seizure of their property which the city is not taking for a public use but for a private ballpark. . . . The fact that some members of the family own other properties does not soften the harshness with which they were evicted. It is not charity the Arechigas are demanding, it is justice and humaneness. They may own other property, but their home was in Chavez Ravine and they are defending their home.[52]

Rundberg echoed Holland and Roybal. "I don't care if those people owned half of Los Angeles," he told the *Examiner*. "The way their private property was confiscated through the guise of public use only to be turned over to a private corporation is a miscarriage of justice and a flagrant violation of the Constitution of the United States."[53]

But these voices were overwhelmed by a wave of criticism and outrage from contract supporters who now sensed an opportunity to regain the moral high ground and shift the direction of the Arechiga narrative. They struck back with a vengeance. A furious, sarcastic Poulson charged: "For almost a week the Arechiga family has been described as destitute, as dispossessed unfortunates. The family was not destitute. It owns more property than most residents of Los Angeles. . . . The Arechiga family is a victim of its own eagerness to extract from the taxpayers more than it was granted by valid court decisions. The family used its own children as pawns, to gain sympathy. It is now perfectly plain that the family needs no sympathy. It was obviously, plainly, publicly, and shamelessly flaunting the law."[54]

Poulson took aim at Holland, Roybal, and his other City Council adversaries, reveling in the turning of the ethical tables: "Not one of these men, these bleeding hearts, made the slightest effort to find out the true need of the Arechigas or their true resources, but they did jump recklessly into the fight against due process of law, against the American heritage, which we all hold so dear.

I am sworn to uphold the law. And I will do so, no matter how disgusting and personally vindictive the opponents of the law become."[55] He told the *Mirror News*, "You keep seeing the same faces speaking on things like Bunker Hill, the Dodgers contract, and now the Arechigas. They are selfish and against undertakings to benefit the downtown area." Poulson closed with a shot at the "ham actors" in television news who publicized the Arechigas' plight.[56]

Poulson's City Council ally Ransom Callicott introduced a resolution on May 13 stating that in view of "the reprehensible manner in which duly constituted government and government officials were mocked and held up to the public scorn and criticism, there is reason to suspect that there was an ulterior motive behind the spotlighting of the eviction, or the family was ill-advised by persons or groups lacking respect for government and encouraged to continue to defy the accepted American tradition of law and order."[57] Callicott also demanded a city investigation of the Arechigas.[58]

Council president John Gibson, another Poulson supporter, linked the *Mirror News* revelations to the battle over the Dodger Stadium deal itself: "It appears that someone put this family up to stay on the land that the city owns and I wouldn't be surprised if this wasn't the work of obstructionists who have so steadfastly used every means to delay building a baseball stadium at Chavez Ravine. . . . There are certain agitators who have a fetish for brewing trouble."[59]

The daily newspapers also employed the Arechigas' ownership of other properties as an opportunity to advance the stadium project. The *Times* led the way with a scathing May 15 editorial that questioned the integrity of Dodger contract opponents:

When you look at the incident in perspective, its implications become more and more disturbing. They go far beyond the stage-managed resistance of the Arechiga family to a proper court order. You must face the fact that elected officials, sworn to uphold the law, actively condoned defiance of the law in the courts. . . . Every shabby tear-jerking trick in the book was employed to create a wholly false impression of the wicked driving the meek out into the cruel world with a blacksnake whip. . . . The backstage managers of this melodrama showed no conscience about hoodwinking the local public and dragging the city's good name in the mud across the country via TV. This was cold-blooded trickery. The anti-Dodger crowd knew that the Arechigas were under court order to move years before the Dodgers considered coming here from Brooklyn. . . . We face a very serious situation in Los Angeles if a well-financed group, for whatever devious reasons, can flout the will of the majority of the people's elected representatives on City Council and obstruct the orderly process of law. . . . No proper function of the city can be performed if rule-or-ruin fanatics can roadblock progress for any reason that occurs to a warped mind."[60]

The *Times* thus leveraged a dispute over an eviction into a wider attack on opponents of the stadium project itself and more broadly on those who questioned the idea of downtown development. The denunciation of the Arechigas' other properties was a means of discrediting both them and their allies, including Roybal, Holland, and Owen, who also stood in the way of civic improvements such as Dodger Stadium and Bunker Hill. The *Times* linked support for the Arechigas with opposition to progress in Los Angeles and with parochial self-interest at the expense of the common good. The existence of the eleven Arechiga homes allowed the *Times* to change the terms of argument, from whether forcibly transferring property between one private owner and another was legal to whether Los Angeles would be a city with influence and prestige commensurate with its size. Phrased in this manner, the argument was almost impossible to lose.

The other metropolitan dailies followed the *Times*'s lead, with the *Examiner* reiterating its support for the stadium project and lambasting its "shabby" opponents.[61] The Arechiga home ownership revelations, it editorialized, "burned away much of the oratorical underbrush that has sprung up around this incident. Those leading the fight in the Council to defy the legal eviction order are the very ones who, with respect to the Dodger agreement, set themselves above a majority of the Council, a vote of the electorate, the

State Legislature, the Governor and two unanimous rulings by the State Supreme Court."[62] The *Mirror News* decried "powerful connivers who have spent large sums to keep the Dodgers out of this site."[63]

Sports columnists sympathetic to the stadium deal also used the furor to lash out at the project's opponents. The *Examiner*'s Vincent Flaherty noted pointedly that the Ravine "had been a civic eyesore for years—a little lost dump of a wilderness . . . shunned by a growing community. Nobody wanted it. . . . But when the Dodgers came to town, overnight Chavez Ravine became important! Then and only then, it seemed a few people did have long-standing schemes for the area for personal gain or self-aggrandizement, or both."[64] Flaherty mocked the Arechigas, putting quotation marks around the word "destitute" when referring to them and denouncing their hypocrisy. "During the whole drawn out and unsavory business," he wrote, "the Dodgers, through no fault of their own, have been made the fall guys."[65]

Melvin Durslag, also of the *Examiner*, observed acidly that "as a general rule, you will find that individuals who make a flamboyant display of acting in behalf of the taxpayer are usually acting in behalf of themselves."[66] In a thinly disguised reference to Holland, he wrote: "A political argument of any kind usually boils down to a hollering contest in which the guy who shouts the loudest winds up winning. Those favoring the Dodgers were noticeably handicapped. They had as their weapons only facts and cool logic. Try to stand on a street corner with these items and win a debate from someone who is screaming, 'They're taking land away from the taxpayers! Stop thief!' "[67]

The media reports of the Arechigas' other homes swung public opinion sharply against the family. In the process, opponents of the stadium project lost credibility through their association with this issue. Almost overnight the response to the evictions of the Arechigas went from "a disgrace to the city of Los Angeles" (May 12, the day before the *Mirror News* story appeared) to "what a jerk you [Roybal] turned out to be, defending people who like to make a sucker out of you and Holland. This will teach you not to stand in the way of progress" (May 13).[68]

After the story broke, angry citizens, some motivated by racial animus, attacked the Arechigas and the public officials allied with them. "As far as what was paid to the Arechigas for their property," wrote Mrs. Mary Cummings of Hollywood, "it seems to have been much *more* than it was worth and when you add to that the rent they would have had to pay all these years had they moved when they were first supposed to, *they* owe the city a debt of gratitude, the city owes them nothing."[69] Mrs. Lee Bell asserted that "the Arechigas have gotten a lot better deal than the rest of us," since the family had not paid rent or taxes since 1951; "I wonder would their homeland have put up with this."[70] Mrs. John Galvin of Pacoima sniffed, "We were evicted to make room for the airport and have friends who were evicted for the freeway. It didn't take any of us six years to get out."[71]

Others directed their ire at the Arechigas' supporters, particularly Roybal. "How much *money* did those red Mexicans give you?" asked Mrs. L. Brown of the councilman. "If you attend a baseball game I hope you are hit in the head with a bat."[72] She contrasted the behavior of the Arechigas with that of "loyal white people."[73] S. J. Anderson of South Gate was even more blunt with Roybal: "You are a clown. When you make your stand on the issue of Chavez Ravine, make sure you collect the back rent and back taxes that the citizens of Los Angeles County have been cheated out of by the flaunting of the law by this Arechiga family."[74] Al Hill wrote to Roybal: "If you are correctly quoted in saying that said eviction of this very, very, very wealthy family was comparable to 'Hitler's tactics' or the 'Spanish Inquisition,' millions of Los Angeles citizens think that you are ignorantly supporting the Communists, and their brain-washed dupes."[75] And Edward Breslin taunted the Arechigas, calling them "the poor family that only owns 13 [sic] homes," and telling Roybal to "move into that tent with your lovely friends." "Walter O'Malley," he informed the councilman, was "a real man, not a bum like you."[76]

Although pro-Arechiga sentiment did not evaporate entirely—Erma Dutton of the Westlake area, near downtown, wrote Poulson, "It does not change the situation to learn that the Arechigas . . . own property. . . . [T]hey have said they remain on their land for a principle"—the revelation about the Arechigas' other houses effected a decisive shift in public attitudes toward the family.[77] If Poulson and Wyman were on the defensive before May 13, now Roybal and Holland were. When it was also revealed that Alice Martin, one of the other evictees, had an address book with the names and telephone numbers of C. A. Owen, J. A. Smith, and others connected with the Citizens Committee and that Martin had been "working with John Holland" to make a public show of resistance against the sheriff's deputies on May 8, it reinforced the connection between the Dodger contract opponents and the "eleven houses."[78] Sympathy for the Arechigas in Los Angeles's white community melted away.

The diminishing support for the Arechigas also spoke to the ephemeral nature of the television coverage of the evictions. Most who took exception to the handling of the removals had seen them on television. The dramatic and emotional on-the-spot reportage and subsequent editorializing had clearly shaped public perception of the events of May 8. The evictions were a visual story, perfect for a media form reliant on images. But after the original Arechiga coverage, the opportunity for compelling visuals diminished and Los Angeles television news moved on in search of other stories. In doing so, it effectively ceded the field to the daily newspapers, which favored the Dodger contract editorially and had publicized the "eleven houses" revelations in the first place. With shrinking television coverage, an embarrassing disclosure, and a lingering atmosphere of racial distrust, even whites who had defended the Arechigas were ready to move on.

But the Latino community of Los Angeles was not ready to move on. For its citizens, the Arechiga evictions symbolized a destroyed culture and life. Where many whites saw civic improvement and advancement, Latinos saw deception and inhumanity. *Examiner* columnist Vincent Flaherty, writing in favor of the Dodger contract, had dismissed Chavez Ravine as "a dumping place for trash and tin cans."[79] Clearly the Ravine did not resemble white middle-class sections of Los Angeles. Certainly it lacked the accoutrements of modern living available in those sections. Many white Angelenos argued that transforming Chavez Ravine into a venue for a stadium or even a public housing project was a necessary accommodation to modern urban life. But "progress," however it is defined, has its human costs. "With all the studies I see about what people need to grow up healthy, what psychologists say, that's what we had. I have beautiful memories of our childhood," recalled one Raviner.[80]

The loss of Chavez Ravine rippled through Latino Los Angeles, leaving an anguished and bitter legacy. Historian Eric Avila argues that "the Arechiga evictions widened the growing racial gulf in postwar Los Angeles and set the urban stage for the late-'60s explosion of the Chicano movement" and that they epitomized a racialized approach to urban renewal that aroused simmering resentments in other sensitive areas such as education, policing, and housing.[81] Today a mural painted by Chicano artist Judith Baca at the Tujunga Wash in the San Fernando Valley depicts Dodger Stadium wrecking Chavez Ravine.[82] "There's people who won't even step into Dodger Stadium," observed the son of a Ravine evictee on the ballpark's fiftieth anniversary in 2012. "They're still bitter."[83]

This bitterness is misdirected. It would make nearly as much sense to refuse all dealings with the Los Angeles municipal government for its role in the destruction of the Chavez Ravine community or to use a mural to depict city officials tearing down homes and evicting residents. But it has been the Dodgers and not the city government that have been most closely linked in historical memory with the Arechigas and with the visual images of May 8, 1959.[84] It is, after all, a ballpark and not a public housing project that now occupies the Chavez Ravine site.

But the attraction of the Dodger franchise itself to so many in the Los Angeles Latino community, one that has only deepened over time, means that the evictions cannot be viewed solely through the lenses of corporate greed and racism. Latinos may well constitute the Dodgers' most loyal and reliable base of fans since the team's move to California. Former Ravine resident Lou Santillan, who for many years arranged gatherings of his former neighbors at Chavez Ravine, never forgave the Dodgers, but his son told the Los Angeles Times in 2012, "I had no anger or frustration against them. I love the Dodgers. Growing up in LA, that's our team, you know."[85] John Arechiga's granddaughter recalled that while he would not attend Dodger games, he would listen to them on the radio.[86] Perhaps it is possible to feel love for the Dodgers as well as grief for Chavez Ravine. The Latino community of Los Angeles experiences both. It is tempting to view them in contradictory terms. But it is better to acknowledge the complexities of human emotion, where love and grief can occupy the same corners of the heart.

For Manuel and Abrana Arechiga, however, there was no such complexity. They would never accept what had happened to them. On May 14, the day after the revelation of the family's other property holdings, Edward Roybal met with Manuel and Abrana and after a ninety-minute conversation in Spanish convinced them to leave their encampment across from the demolished homes on the condition that their legal rights would be preserved.[87] The compromise came just in time. Defiant to the last, Abrana had ripped up a trespassing notice from the Board of Public Works as she stood before reporters the day before.[88]

Roybal too needed a satisfactory resolution of a situation that was politically dangerous for him. The "eleven houses" disclosure had embarrassed him, and he now needed to get the Arechigas to depart with the dignity they had been denied during the chaotic May 8 dispossessions. Roybal had worked within the confines of the law for years seeking to keep the Arechigas on their property. He knew he could now go no further without himself becoming an accessory to illegal activity. Yet he could not appear to accede to the removals or he would lose credibility with his political constituency. A departure under protest was not a perfect solution, but it did accomplish what Roybal knew was inevitable without further violence and without appearing to acquiesce in the end of the Chavez Ravine.

Manuel and Abrana Arechiga left the Ravine on the evening of May 18.[89] Represented by Phill Silver, they continued to fight the seizure of their land in court and refused to collect the condemnation check for $10,050 that waited for them in the Superior Court clerk's office. After suffering more appeals court defeats, the Arechigas finally accepted the condemnation check under protest in 1962.[90]

Manuel and Abrana moved a few miles to the east, to a house from which they could see the light towers of Dodger Stadium in the distance at night.[91] Manuel died in 1971. A *Los Angeles Times* story that year described Abrana as living on social security and, in her words, "my tears." She told the newspaper that the most important event during her time in the city "was what they did to me . . . That was the biggest and worst thing of all."[92] Abrana died a few months later at the age of seventy-five.[93] An epitaph for her lost community, one that she undoubtedly would have endorsed, came years later from an aging evictee standing near the site of his Chavez Ravine home, looking back almost a half century: "It wasn't Brentwood or Beverly Hills, but we were happy people here in this neighborhood. A lot of fond memories here. Now, it looks like a ghost town or a mining town. But beautiful, right? Beautiful."[94]

8

PRIVATE GAIN, PUBLIC GOOD?

THE BUSINESS OF BASEBALL IN LOS ANGELES

On June 3, 1959, exactly one year after the Proposition B referendum election, the Dodgers and the city of Los Angeles finally executed the formal contract authorized by the City Council ordinance of October 7, 1957, but which had since been lost in legal and political limbo. With Mayor Poulson out of town, council president John Gibson signed for the city. "Anything worth having," he observed, "is worth waiting for."[1]

The final contract was essentially the same as the one contained in the ordinance. It continued to require the city to convey 185 Chavez Ravine acres to the Dodgers and employ "its best efforts to acquire, at a reasonable cost, and convey additional land, to make a total of 300 acres, more or less."[2] The city also promised to use its best efforts to have the public purpose clause in the 1955

CHA deed of the Ravine property "eliminated or modified so as to permit the use contemplated by the ball club."[3] In an acknowledgment of the public purpose issue's importance and contentiousness, the parties agreed the contract would be "of no further force or effect" if the clause was not removed.[4] The city's outlay of $2 million for land preparation and the county's expenditure of $2.7 million for access roads remained in effect. The city promised to bring proceedings to rezone the Ravine property to C-3, which would allow a stadium with a capacity of over fifty thousand to be built, and to obtain a conditional use permit for the ballpark.[5] The Dodgers promised to construct a stadium of not less than fifty thousand seats at their own expense. In a form of collateral for the completion of the stadium, the Dodgers would also build a recreation area for public use on forty acres of Chavez Ravine property and maintain it for twenty years, after which the land would revert to the team.[6] The Dodgers conveyed all Chavez Ravine mineral rights to the city.

It had taken more than a year and a half, but O'Malley had received what he moved to Los Angeles for: the opportunity to build his own stadium on his own land on his own terms. Coming on the heels of the controversy over the Arechiga evictions, O'Malley was exultant. Yet he was also aware of the damage done to his reputation and to that of his organization from the televised images of May 8. In the months following the contract signing, he reminded Angelenos of the advantages of the agreement and the ways in which his stadium deal contrasted favorably with those of other cities. He reiterated that Dodger Stadium would be the first major league ballpark constructed with private funds since Yankee Stadium almost four decades earlier. "We are trying to get back to proprietorship instead of the trend toward socialism," he announced, in language calculated to resonate with many of the white middle-class homeowners who had voted against Proposition B.[7] O'Malley also told a civic club audience that "if it's greed that we want to build a ball park where people can park their cars, where people my age don't have to walk up 200 feet to their seats, then I guess we're all greedy."[8]

A substantial segment of the population, however, was still unconvinced and determined to carry on the fight against the stadium project. Certainly Holland, Roybal, and McGee would continue rearguard action. Their media vehicles would be the anti-contract community newspapers, prominently the *Highland Park News-Herald and Journal.* It made the case against the Dodger deal in a June 7 editorial. Why, it asked rhetorically, would it continue to oppose the Dodgers? "Because of the belief that some very basic American issues are involved, both legal and moral."[9] One of the most important of those issues, it argued,

> involves the freedom of private ownership of property . . . the power of government to condemn land and take it away from one set of private individuals and convey it to other interests for personal gain. The opponents to this contract . . . believe that if this can be done then the very basis of American democracy (the privilege of a citizen to own land that is really his) has been violated and the concept of the American Constitution and the Bill of Rights has been breached. Another basic American issue is whether government can function for the private gain of an individual. Can government spend taxpayer money for the exclusive benefit of designated individuals? These are constitutional issues which must be resolved.[10]

The *News-Herald* cited the example of the Dodger agreement's most powerful and committed proponent, the *Los Angeles Times,* which in the 1930s had fought successfully for a higher condemnation price on its downtown property. "In this case," the *News-Herald* observed, "the Arechigas may be taking their cue from the *Times,* who proved that property owners do have rights." Opponents of the Chavez Ravine contract, it concluded, "fight on because they do not like deals such as this to be made behind their backs in the darkness of closed conference rooms."[11]

Neither the Arechiga evictions, the "eleven houses" revelations, the Proposition B campaign, nor even the Ruben/Kirshbaum suits had definitively settled the policy question of whether it was legitimate for government to transfer property from one private owner to another and offer active assistance to one private citizen but not to another. Did "public benefit," as defined by government officials, cure all ills? What the *St. Louis Post-Dispatch* aptly described as "the first local real estate dispute to achieve national prominence" placed these questions squarely on the table for all of Los Angeles.[12]

In June 1959, it was not yet clear how Los Angeles would answer them. The city and county were offering the Dodgers a potentially lucrative land swap at Chavez Ravine. O'Malley stood to make money if his stadium was built. But he would have to build the stadium with his own money. The benefits to the city, in property and income taxes, increased employment, business stimulus, entertainment value, and major league status and prestige, were substantial. Under these circumstances, did it matter that O'Malley had received treatment denied to other entrepreneurs and stood to realize substantial personal gain? John Holland, Edward Roybal, and readers of community newspapers such as the *News-Herald* believed it did. Norris Poulson, Rosalind Wyman, and Norman Chandler of the *Los Angeles Times* believed it did not.

That Holland and Poulson were conservative Republicans and Roybal and Wyman liberal Democrats testified to the tangled and paradoxical qualities of these questions as well as to deeper ones relating to the meaning of equality itself in American history and culture. If ordinary Angelenos received some form of benefit from Dodger Stadium, whether in jobs, taxes, civic pride, or fun at the ballpark, all the while enabling O'Malley to profit, were these the indicia of inequality? Or was American equality the freedom to become unequal? How equal did Angelenos truly wish to be? The battle over Dodger Stadium crystallized this American dilemma in a local setting.

Walter O'Malley was a businessman, not a political philosopher. He desired to build a ballpark, not commence a debate over the civic culture of Los Angeles. But sometimes history alights in unexpected places. O'Malley's quest for a new stadium in Chavez Ravine had become the setting for arguments over the shape of the modern city—the relationships between private and public forms of power, the limits of property rights, the role of government in economic development and the contours of an equal society—that would transcend their immediate circumstances and work their way into the political and cultural bloodstream of Los Angeles. With the official signing of the Dodger Stadium contract O'Malley had won only one such argument. Others were yet to come.

On July 20, Mayor Poulson announced that the CHA, at the request of the City of Los Angeles, had removed the public purpose provision from its 1955 Chavez Ravine deed of transfer and would receive a hold harmless agreement from both the city and the Dodgers indemnifying it from any resulting liability.[13] It was approved by the City Council, but only after Holland recommended ominously that "each Council member consult his own personal attorney before voting for this blank check agreement."[14]

The elimination of the public purpose clause meant that, pending the United States Supreme Court's disposition of the Ruben and Kirshbaum appeals, the issue would no longer be a legal one. It would, however, continue in its political and moral dimensions for a divided city. As it stood, O'Malley would no longer need to defend the public utility of Dodger Stadium in a court of law. But another problem now loomed. The city had contracted only to pay a "reasonable price" for land it would acquire for the Dodgers at Chavez Ravine, and a group of affected property owners had banded together to obtain as much money as they could. Knowing that any attempt to condemn these properties would unleash a firestorm of criticism from the anti-contract forces, city attorney Arnebergh essentially threw up his hands and informed O'Malley that since reasonable terms of sale based on market value could not be arranged, the Dodgers were now on their own to negotiate with the owners and their representatives.[15] "If the present owners refuse to sell at this market price, and if the Dodgers need the land for their stadium or parking facilities," Arnebergh announced, "they will simply have to buy the land themselves."[16]

O'Malley now faced the prospect of paying far above market rates, or even assessed values, for property he had to have. Two of the homes, ironically, were located within a block of the Arechigas' former Malvina Street residences. In addition, work on the contract O'Malley had signed with Vinnell Constructors to grade the land at the stadium site could not begin until these holdout properties were acquired, putting even more pressure on him to resolve the situation quickly.[17] Reluctantly he began negotiations with the attorney for the twelve property owners, G. G. Baumen.[18]

O'Malley's initial offers were substantially in excess of the relevant appraised land values. He bid $75,000, for example, on the Francis Scott property that had been appraised at $9,000, and $50,000 for land owned by Harry Hansen appraised at $7,500.[19] Baumen rejected them out of hand. Knowing full well that stadium construction could not begin until the parcels were acquired and that consequently he was in the right place at the right time, he envisioned a windfall for his clients. Talks sputtered over what Dodger officials considered outrageous demands. But O'Malley knew that the best he could hope for was to chip them down a bit over time. He would not be as fortunate as Charles Ebbets. Few had known Ebbets's intentions as he quietly acquired the land parcels for his new Brooklyn stadium in 1911. In 1959, the entire city of Los Angeles knew what O'Malley had in mind. That public knowledge would cost him a great deal of money.

In the meantime, O'Malley addressed the touchy issue of rezoning the Chavez Ravine property for commercial use. This dry-sounding administrative issue unleashed the fury of the stadium opponents. O'Malley needed the rezoning to commercial use for more than bureaucratic reasons. His potential bank lenders had made it clear that their financing was contingent on obtaining that designation for the stadium property, because otherwise they could not be sure of recouping their investment in the event of foreclosure.[20] Their loan conditions blurred the motives behind O'Malley's insistence on unrestricted commercial or C-3 zoning for as much of the Chavez Ravine property as possible. Was he merely seeking to accommodate the banks or attempting to preserve the option to make non-baseball-related use of the land in the form of restaurants, stores, and hotels?

The contract opposition, not surprisingly, assumed the worst. In testimony at the City Planning Commission's mid-July hearings on rezoning, Citizens Committee chair C. A. Owen predicted that commercial zoning for the Dodger Stadium property would destroy the Coliseum as a venue, turning it into "a desert" and costing the city hundreds of thousands of dollars in lost revenues.[21] He insisted that the commission limit its commercial zoning designations to the stadium and the parking area that would surround it, that is, only what was absolutely necessary. Owen was suspicious of O'Malley's intentions for the remainder of the acreage if given free rein. Nevertheless, the Planning Commission recommended that the entire Ravine property be rezoned commercial. The anti-contract community newspaper *Wilshire Press* editorialized that this decision "added several million dollars to the value of the Chavez Ravine land for its new owners," amounting to inappropriate government assistance.[22] "It now seems likely," it complained, that the [Dodgers] . . . will have no investment whatever in the enterprise, but will wind up as sole owners of land and baseball establishment, plus considerable commercial property later to be developed or sold off."[23]

The zoning issue now shifted to the City Council, which would confirm or modify the action of the City Planning Commission. At the council hearings in August the opposition was again out in full force. Art Snyder, an aide to John Holland who was also head of the Small Property Owners League, argued that access roads to the stadium were not adequate to accommodate the traffic flow.[24] Owen, joined by Lincoln Freeman, president of the Apartment House Owners Association of Los Angeles County, argued that the blanket zoning designation was yet another unwarranted gift to O'Malley, enabling him to construct a private empire in Chavez Ravine at taxpayer expense.[25] Phyllis Seldon, who described herself as an "average voter," claimed that Proposition B had been approved only through a "misrepresentation of the contract" by its moneyed proponents.[26] Another average citizen, Evelyn Harris, asked the council members rhetorically if they were sure the Dodgers would use their new stadium for more than a year or two, or indeed if they would remain in Los Angeles at all.[27] An eagerly responding Holland averred that there were no such assurances. Joined by Harold Henry, Holland charged that O'Malley intended to build hotels on the commercially zoned land outside the stadium parking lot perimeter. The council postponed a final decision while it awaited a tract map to be produced by the Dodgers indicating their intended use of the land.

When the map was submitted in October it caused a furor on the council. It seemed to confirm the suspicions of Holland, Owen, and the contract opponents. The map contained drawings of restaurants, ice cream parlors, concession buildings, a car wash, and a service station.[28] Even council members who had supported the Dodger contract through its many travails were sharply critical. One called the map "unconscionable" and said it "could be another Farmer's Market or a shopping center. Just a loose designation of buildings for concession purposes could mean anything."[29] Another stadium supporter described the map as resembling a carnival midway.[30] L. E. Timberlake, who had provided a reliable pro-Dodger vote on the council from the moment the team came to Los Angeles, said the sketched map "looked like something kindergarten kids had stuck bits of paper on."[31] Even Ransom Callicott, another staunch contract supporter and a director of the pro-Dodger Downtown Business Men's Association, opposed the tract map in his position as chair of the council's Planning Committee.[32]

The contract opposition, for its part, was almost apoplectic. Holland demanded an end to the Dodgers' "ungodly and preferential treatment."[33] He claimed that downtown businessmen now feared that O'Malley intended to establish "a potential center for metropolitan Los Angeles" to compete with them.[34] Councilman Harold Henry announced that he would vote only for ten acres of commercial zoning, comprising the stadium itself and whatever space was necessary for parking.[35]

Even the normally friendly Los Angeles daily newspapers turned against O'Malley on this issue. The *Herald and Express* wrote: "We want once more to warn our Los Angeles City Councilmen and Zoning Commissioner that they must play fair with the taxpayers of Los Angeles in the proposed rezoning of the 300 acres of Chavez Ravine."[36] While it did not oppose the City Planning Commission's "commercial" designation for the 180 acres that made up the stadium and parking area, it objected strongly to similar treatment of the 120 surrounding acres. "This," it editorialized, "would allow Mr. Walter O'Malley to lease the land or construct facilities for all sorts of purposes, including cafes and cocktail bars, shopping centers, apartment houses and fun or amusement zones."[37] Even the *New York Times* speculated that the "Dodger Dynamo," as it sarcastically referred to O'Malley, "could be plotting a downtown Disneyland."[38]

After the *Herald and Express* criticized the Dodgers' tract map, it received letters of support from its readers for its position. "The taxpayers are getting a raw deal and I'm sick and tired of higher taxes each year and these giveaways," wrote one.[39] Another praised the newspaper: "I am glad that at least one Los Angeles metropolitan newspaper . . . has finally come to the aid of the taxpayers on the Chavez Ravine deal."[40] A third, while asserting "we are all for the Dodgers," asked, "But why does the city give so much to O'Malley? He will be very rich some day. I think we could spend our tax money for a better cause than for too much sports."[41] Yet another claimed that "the whole [Dodger] deal shows very clearly how it was all preplanned irrespective of the rights of property owners, taxpayers, or others. . . . If Mr. O'Malley wanted to have Los Angeles taxpayers 100 per cent back of him, he would have purchased his land as any businessman does."[42]

The question of how much government assistance was appropriate for a private business entity continued to hang unresolved over the Dodger Stadium project even in the aftermath of the successful conclusion—for the Dodgers, at least—of the Proposition B vote, the taxpayers' lawsuits, and the Arechiga removals. The angry reaction even by stadium supporters to a proposed tract map that allowed for the possibility of retail enterprises not directly connected to the business of baseball, including, according to one report, a "Hawaiian luau layout," illustrated the ongoing power of these issues and their knife's-edge qualities.[43] O'Malley had won at the polls, in the courts, and in the case of the Arechigas in public discourse, but with scant room to spare. It would take very little to turn allies into opponents. It would require only the perception of a line crossed between public good and private gain. When during the Proposition B campaign O'Malley had averred, "We are baseball folks—not oil operators or real estate promoters," he was implying that while economics had driven his move to Los Angeles, there had also been a motive that transcended balance sheets.[44] Baseball was both a business and a calling. Dodger Stadium would express both impulses. But a ring of restaurants, stores, and retail establishments around the ballpark perimeter would convert the Dodgers into just another moneymaking venture as well as a direct competitor with similar businesses located downtown.

Almost immediately the Dodger owner realized that he had made a mistake. He announced he would revise the tract map and resubmit a new one to the council. But he paired this carrot with a stick. Just as he had during the referendum campaign, O'Malley employed a threat to move his team to shift public opinion in his favor. This time, in fact, he was much more explicit about his intentions. Speaking at a council zoning hearing on November 5, he warned: "If these constant delays occur our location in Los Angeles may become untenable and we may accept offers to move somewhere else. If you attempt to rewrite this contract, which I do not believe you can do, I will not be able to finance the Dodger project in Chavez Ravine."[45] O'Malley reiterated that his potential lenders in the city's banking community were counting on commercial zoning and would not cooperate without it. "While these delays are going on," O'Malley lamented, "I must pay taxes on Wrigley Field. . . . I ask you to adopt the zoning ordinance so that we can start building our ball park."[46]

At the same time, he sounded a more conciliatory note. Responding to the City Council's concerns, he took responsibility for the flawed tract map and promised a revised plan that would feature a "dignified" use of the property.[47] "The baseball stadium," O'Malley announced, "will be set in a tastefully landscaped park and, of course, will be completely without any shoddy atmosphere or commercialism. This is what we have pledged and have always intended to build."[48]

In early November the team submitted a revised tract map that eliminated the retail ring around the stadium exterior. O'Malley presented it "with a deep sense of civic responsibility in mind, supported by the greatest investment anyone ever made in sports," and with a promise that "it is inconceivable that we would do anything shabby, overly commercial, or beyond the intention of our obligation and the dignity of the situation."[49] The team scaled back its zoning request from C-3—the most permissive classification—to a mix of more restrictive commercial categories.[50]

But O'Malley coupled this with an oblique statement about his former city's interest in luring the Dodgers back to New York that was certain to rattle city officials. "I am sure it is no secret," he told reporters, "that we have been approached by New York people over quite a period of time. Other than that I have nothing else to say on the matter."[51] This implied threat, of course, might have been impossible to carry out. Despite an increase of approximately $2.5 million in the expected cost of Dodger Stadium since he arrived in October 1957—a result of the Proposition B referendum, the taxpayer lawsuits, and additional labor and materials expenses—Los Angeles had already given O'Malley much and promised much more in the future.[52] Whether the council members realized it or not, had the Dodgers actually left Los Angeles there would have been a scrum of other teams jockeying to occupy the nation's third-largest market. But even so, these teams were not the Dodgers, and as O'Malley well knew, the mere intimation that the team would leave could be counted on to shift the dynamic in his direction.

In the end, the combination of the carrot of less ambitiously commercial stadium building plans and the stick of relocation rumors carried the day for the Dodgers. On November 5, after a four-hour meeting, the City Council approved the revised Dodger Stadium tract map. The stadium area itself plus the parking area, totaling 192 acres, received a "commercial use" designation.[53] There were nine yes votes, one more than required. Holland, McGee, Roybal and Henry voted no. They were joined by Ransom Callicott and L. E. Timberlake, Dodger contract supporters who nonetheless believed the grant of commercial zoning status to the team was overgenerous.[54] While the team would still need to apply for a separate conditional use permit for the land in order to construct a stadium exceeding three thousand seats, O'Malley had won another round.

Once again, though, it had been close and sharply contested. Even Dodger allies such as Callicott and Timberlake, not to mention stalwarts such as Wyman and Gibson, had become skittish at the thought of O'Malley following through on the original tract map. As long as the Dodger Stadium project appeared to meld private gain with a public purpose and as long as the team owner seemed to be an entrepreneur with a public spirit, they would support the contract and the stadium. But that a tract plan containing food and novelty retailing could elicit so much anger and criticism from virtually all quarters showed that the region's business culture was not completely open-ended. Los Angeles was a suspicious city filled with Folks acutely sensitive to what they considered "insider games." O'Malley would need to be careful not to arouse them. There was a line in their perceptual landscape dividing public good and private gain. If he gave even the appearance of crossing it, he would pay a high price.

On July 20 an essential precondition to the stadium contract was placed on the road to fulfillment when Poulson asked the City Council to authorize the signing of a hold harmless agreement indemnifying the CHA for executing a quitclaim eliminating the public purpose clause from the 1955 deed of the Chavez Ravine property to the city.[55] The CHA had executed the quitclaim on April 22 and it was now in escrow awaiting agreements from both the city and the Dodgers to indemnify it against any damages it might suffer as a result of waiving the public purpose requirement.[56] Since the Dodger Stadium contract itself was contingent upon the elimination of the clause—it had been agreed that the contract would be "of no further force and effect" without it—this was essential to the future of the project.[57] It would now be up to the council to approve the hold harmless agreement as well as for the Dodgers to execute one of their own.

Opposition coalesced in the usual places. Holland, McGee, and Henry succeeded in delaying Council action on the agreement.[58]

When it finally came before the council in early 1960, Holland pilloried the hold harmless clause as an "unlimited guarantee" that could result in substantial taxpayer liability.[59] Referring back to the circumstances surrounding the city's purchase of the land in 1955, Holland complained that the federal government had in effect offered a "big subsidy" to the Dodgers since it had sold the land to the city for some $4.5 million less than it had originally paid for it.[60] "The tendency on the part of the government [is] to fool the people and to fool each other," asserted the ever-suspicious Holland. "Personally, I think this is what happened here."[61] McGee again claimed that O'Malley intended to construct private residences on the property, and Harold Henry predicted that "hotels" would soon rise in Chavez Ravine.[62] The council vote pitted those who believed O'Malley was in the baseball business against those who believed he was in the real estate business. In February 1960, by a vote of 10 to 5, the City Council accepted the CHA's quitclaim deed after approving the required hold harmless agreement.[63]

The majority of the council had thus come down on the side of the baseball business. Holland, McGee, Henry, Roybal, and Rundberg, the five no votes, held out to the end. But the public purpose clause in the CHA deed was gone and the major contractual impediment to the construction of Dodger Stadium removed.[64] With most of the stadium acreage now zoned for commercial use, the ten yes voters on the council were showing their confidence in O'Malley's baseball business as a form of public business. But to the five dissenters the Dodgers were just another business with no special claim on taxpayer assistance.

These two understandings of the relationship between public and private power in Los Angeles were, of course, not diametrically opposed. Holland, for example, believed that the state had a general role in promoting business development in the city. He did, however, object to the government officials selecting a specific business for what he considered special treatment. Generally reluctant to spend taxpayer money, he was especially averse to spend it on improving a favored entrepreneur's bottom line. Wyman, perhaps O'Malley's most loyal supporter, was a liberal and not a socialist. She believed that O'Malley would ultimately have to rise or fall on his own, as would any businessman. Even she had objected to the Dodgers' original tract map as "too commercial" and unbefitting an enterprise that was ostensibly fulfilling a public function. But Wyman believed in the state as an engine of privately generated economic growth, which meant assistance to some and not to others. The positions of Holland and Wyman thus overlapped to a degree, though they clashed on the specific issue of government support for Dodger Stadium. Holland could not abide the use of taxpayer resources to enhance a businessman's bottom line. Wyman could not countenance denying government aid to a businessman acting in the public interest. Their views crashed together like waves, then moved apart, awaiting their next confrontation over the next stadium-related issue.

More contention awaited O'Malley when he attempted to negotiate a new lease for the Coliseum in 1960. He had originally expected to be in his new stadium by that year and consequently had paid relatively little attention to the provision in his original lease calling for the Dodgers to pay the same rent as the Coliseum's other tenants after 1959. This would amount to 10 percent of gross gate receipts and all concessions and parking monies, potentially a great deal more than the flat $200,000 per year plus 10 percent of gate receipts and concessions for nine designated games the team paid in 1958 and 1959.[65] Now that this unanticipated moment was at hand, O'Malley attempted to obtain an adjustment for 1960.[66] He had paid a total of $289,000 to the Coliseum in 1958, and the amount for the 1959 regular season would be just over $300,000.[67] Under the contract terms as agreed to, this amount could more than double in 1960. If it did, it would be more than any other major league team had ever paid in stadium rent.

But pushback against O'Malley was strong from all quarters. The Coliseum Commission was intent on obtaining more revenue from the Dodgers in order to pay off bond debt on the Los Angeles Sports Arena, an adjacent indoor facility that would house the city's new National Basketball Association franchise, the relocated Minneapolis Lakers. Apart from these dollars-and-cents considerations, the issue of favorable treatment of the Dodgers also surfaced. Phill Silver spoke for many when he charged that any lease adjustment "would be a gift of public funds."[68] The *Highland Park News-Herald and Journal* argued that it was already unfair to allow O'Malley to keep profits on concessions in 1958 and 1959 for all but nine games per season, permitting him to cover his $200,000 rent from these monies alone.[69] It warned that things would need to be different in 1960.

Other community newspapers agreed. A *Gardena Valley News* columnist wrote that he was "pretty well convinced . . . that this sharp city fellow from Brooklyn is going to take us unsophisticated Westerners for everything but our smog before he gets through."[70] "WE GAVE [O'Malley] $13 million worth of land in Chavez Ravine," exclaimed the *Beverly Hills Reporter*. "Does he want an equal amount around the Miracle Mile or just Downtown Los Angeles?"[71] As the negotiations for the 1960 Coliseum lease proceeded, the newspaper warned that both O'Malley and city officials "had better bear in mind that the taxpayers and voters will be watching their decision with great interest. This newspaper speaks for a great number who are tired of GIVING to the Dodgers."[72]

Even public officials normally sympathetic to the Dodgers weighed in against offering the team any special dispensations. Kenneth Hahn, one of O'Malley's most important allies, led the County Board of Supervisors in opposing a rent cut. County counsel Harold Kennedy advised his counterpart, city attorney Roger Arnebergh, that the provision for 10 percent of gross receipts and all concessions monies in 1960 had been part of the Coliseum Commission's consideration for entering into the original lease contract with O'Malley in 1958.[73] Kennedy noted that this was the standard rental for all Coliseum tenants and that any special terms granted the Dodgers would constitute an "abuse of discretion."[74]

Exacerbating the controversy over the team's 1960 Coliseum lease terms was a stroke of on-the-field good fortune. The 1959 Dodgers bore little resemblance to the bumbling seventh-place finishers of the year before. They featured a greatly improved pitching staff and added new position players to their veteran core.

By 1959, in fact, the three players who would define the Dodgers of the 1960s were in place. Don Drysdale, a six-foot-six right-handed pitcher, had grown up in Van Nuys, in the San Fernando Valley. He had signed with the Brooklyn Dodgers and pitched for them in 1956 and 1957 before returning home when the team moved to Los Angeles. Drysdale would help the Dodgers win four National League pennants and three World Series championships. He would win the Cy Young Award as the league's best pitcher in 1962 and be an eight-time All-Star. Blond and handsome, a stylish dresser, Drysdale was perfect for a city that thrived on glamour and celebrity. He appeared as a guest star on numerous television programs in the 1960s, making his face one of the most recognizable in Los Angeles. Drysdale was as much celebrity as athlete, and his cool, sleek style seemed to mirror that of his city.

Maury Wills, a shortstop originally from Washington, D.C., was twenty-six years old when he joined the Dodgers during the 1959 season, after an eight-year-long climb up the team's minor league ladder. One of the franchise's "new" black Dodgers, Wills quickly distinguished himself as a base stealer of extraordinary talents. Wills was one of the rare players with the ability to alter the momentum of a baseball game single-handedly, intimidating and distracting pitchers every time he got on base. In 1962 Wills broke Ty Cobb's long-standing season stolen base record with 104, a mark that would itself stand for another twelve years. His prowess on the base paths and in the field—he was a two-time Gold Glove designee— won Wills the 1962 National League Most Valuable Player award. That year he was also selected as Most Valuable Player in the All-Star Game. Wills led the National League in stolen bases every season between 1960 and 1965. Like Drysdale, Wills took advantage of opportunities in the entertainment field, playing the banjo professionally and appearing on the *Tonight*, Merv Griffin, and Mike Douglas shows. A hero in the Los Angeles black community, Wills also epitomized the dynamism of the Dodgers—a team that lacked consistent power hitting and relied on speed and defense to win games—to the entire city.

Finally, there was left-handed pitcher Sandy Koufax, the most intriguing Los Angeles Dodger of all. Koufax had an unlikely background for a baseball star. A product of a middle-class Jewish Brooklyn family with no discernable athletic pedigree, he grew up on neighborhood sandlots and was a freshman basketball player at the University of Cincinnati when he signed a bonus contract with the Brooklyn Dodgers in 1954. Koufax quickly developed a reputation as a hard thrower who could not always find the plate with his high-velocity pitches. His development was agonizingly slow. Koufax would tantalize with a stellar performance one outing and follow it with a walk-clotted debacle the next. An introspective, quiet young man who seemed to care little for the trappings of fame, Koufax even pondered quitting baseball in 1960. But a serendipitous piece of advice from a catcher during spring training the next year—to take a little off his pitches—changed the trajectory of his career. Koufax soon became the dominant pitcher in baseball. Between 1962 and his premature retirement after the 1966 season due to arm injuries, he won three Cy Young Awards as the National League's best pitcher; was the league's Most Valuable Player in 1963; was a two-time World Series Most Valuable Player; led the National League in earned run average five times and in strikeouts four times; and threw four no-hitters, including a perfect game in 1965.

Koufax's ambivalence about celebrity only stoked its fires. In a city filled with stars, he may have been the biggest of all. Very few Angelenos were identifiable only by their first names, but one did not have to be a baseball fan to know who "Sandy" was. Koufax burnished his reputation among Jewish fans by refusing to pitch the first game of the 1965 World Series because it fell on the High Holiday of Yom Kippur. In Koufax, the Dodgers had the ideal combination of on-field excellence and marketing power. Home attendance spiked when he pitched, and the three World Series to which he led the Dodgers poured extra money into team coffers. But Koufax's value to the team went beyond gate receipts and World Series revenues. The modest and universally respected left-hander with the once-in-a-lifetime talent was the perfect public face for a franchise striving to attract families and children. There may have been one immutable truth in a divided Los Angeles during the 1960s: everybody loved Sandy.

These, then, were the three players who would constitute the core of the on-field Los Angeles Dodgers and personify the Dodger

City councilwoman Rosalind Wyman presents Dodger pitcher Sandy Koufax with an inscribed box of baseballs from his no-hit game against the New York Mets on June 30, 1962. *Los Angeles Herald-Examiner* Collection/Los Angeles Public Library. Photographer: Unknown.

brand—an all-American native son, an African American, and a Brooklyn-raised Jew. They would be integral to O'Malley's plan to transform the Dodgers from a niche team in New York—the people's team—to everyone's team in Los Angeles. As O'Malley knew, a niche team made good copy, but everyone's team made money. Unlike the Brooklyn Dodgers, the Los Angeles Dodgers would realize their full marketing potential, selling themselves to the entire city. Thanks to Drysdale, Wills, and Koufax, the Dodgers became a civic touchstone in Los Angeles, enjoying status similar to that of the symphony orchestra or public library. O'Malley and his players did their work so well that by the time the competing Los Angeles Angels came to town in 1961, it was too late. The city already belonged to the Dodgers.

The Dodgers stayed close to the Milwaukee Braves and San Francisco Giants throughout the summer of 1959, and then surged in

September. A road sweep over the Giants pushed them into first place on the twentieth with five games to play. From there the Dodgers and Braves jockeyed for the pennant. On the morning of the regular season's final day, the two teams were tied for the lead. When both teams won, the stage was set for a best-of-three playoff. The Dodgers won the first game in Milwaukee 3–2 behind rookie reliever Larry Sherry's shutout work, and the series moved to Los Angeles. There the Dodgers came back from a three-run ninth-inning deficit to tie the Braves at 5–5. They won the National League pennant in the twelfth inning on a throwing error, sending the city of Los Angeles into a joyous frenzy.

For perhaps the first time since the team moved from Brooklyn, all Angelenos, even opponents of the stadium project, were united in support of "our" Dodgers. It can be argued that the team truly became the city's own the moment Milwaukee shortstop Felix Mantilla's throw skipped past first baseman Frank Torre, allowing the Dodgers' Gil Hodges to score the game's pennant-winning run from second base. Car horns honked on freeways and workers cheered in offices. Citizens celebrated spontaneously outside their homes, possibly meeting their neighbors for the first time. As the team traveled to Chicago to begin the World Series against the White Sox, city leaders exulted. "This team has done a wonderful thing for itself and for the entire community," said councilman Earle Baker. "They've unified Los Angeles in thinking as nothing else could have done."[75] His colleague Charles Navarro expressed similar sentiments: "It's amazing; people who never thought of baseball, have been following the Dodgers. . . . [T]his is the greatest morale booster we've had in years."[76] Navarro described the pennant as "a release to people of all walks."[77]

The civic celebration continued when the Dodgers returned to Los Angeles for their World Series home games. After splitting the first two games in Chicago, the team played games three, four, and five in the Coliseum before gargantuan crowds. All surpassed 90,000, and the fifth game's attendance of 92,706 was a World Series record.[78] The World Series attracted an estimated 25,000 visitors to the Los Angeles area and pumped some $3 million into the city's economy.[79] The Dodgers won two out of three games in the Coliseum and finished off the White Sox in Chicago 9–3 to clinch an unlikely world championship.

After a raucous victory party in a Chicago hotel marked by the singing of "Happy Birthday" to O'Malley, who turned fifty-six at midnight on October 9, the Dodgers flew home. A crowd of five thousand greeted them at the airport.[80] O'Malley was quoted as saying, "Brooklyn fans are born, Los Angeles fans are made."[81] If that was indeed the case, then the 1959 World Series–winning Dodgers made Los Angeles a city of deeply loyal fans. New teams are always a novelty, and O'Malley's promotional and marketing efforts were already working their charms, but the unexpected 1959 world championship may have been the most important single factor in creating the emotional bond between team and fan that would be stronger than many marriages. The Dodgers and the people of Los Angeles now had a romantic attachment that would weather the years.

But business is business, however strong the adulation for on-field exploits. The World Series surprised the Coliseum commissioners as much as the rest of the city, but less pleasantly so. They discovered that no provision had been made in the original 1958 stadium rental agreement for the payment of any monies by the Dodgers during postseason games. Perhaps the commissioners had considered the possibility of a National League pennant too remote to address in the contract. It is doubtful that this was anything more than an honest oversight, the kind that are endemic to business negotiations in which the parties concentrate on likely contingencies at the expense of less likely ones. O'Malley himself had assumed that the Dodgers would not be playing in the Coliseum after 1959 and had thus accepted the more onerous 1960 rental terms he was now attempting to modify.

Nevertheless, the news that the team had played in the Coliseum rent-free and kept all ticket and concession income during the World Series elicited a stinging public reaction. Community newspapers decried the financial windfall O'Malley received for the home World Series games, especially Game 5, since the commissioner's office requirement that team owners share revenues with the players applied only to Games 1 through 4.[82] Even the usually supportive daily metropolitan newspapers referred pointedly to

O'Malley's World Series profits, which one estimated at $1.8 million.[83] Anti-Dodger public officials cited the contract omission as yet another example of the team's preferential treatment. *Examiner* sports columnist Melvin Durslag, observing the contretemps, wrote that "the hardest thing to find in Los Angeles is an individual shedding tears over O'Malley's money problems" as he attempted to renegotiate the 1960 Coliseum lease.[84]

The Dodgers' pennant drive and World Series victory were thus mixed blessings. They cemented the team-city relationship and made the idea of a new ballpark to house the new champions more acceptable; the *Times* savaged the "effrontery" of those who continued to argue "that the movement to supply the Dodgers with a decent playing yard was against the public interest."[85] In the short term, however, the victories made it more difficult for O'Malley to obtain a reduction in his 1960 rent. Surely a world champion franchise could afford to pay what the other Coliseum tenants— USC, UCLA, and the Rams—were paying.

In these circumstances O'Malley was fighting an uphill battle. The best he could do, under the new lease agreement announced in October and finalized in January 1960, was to have the Coliseum Commission share the expenses of various improvements to the stadium infrastructure.[86] O'Malley's landlords would pay half the cost of the new running track encircling the field, a third of the bill for turf grading and resodding, and the cost of all repairs on dugouts, fences, lights, the drainage system, and the press box.[87] But the Coliseum Commission would go no further. The Dodgers would pay the standard terms of 10 percent of gross gate receipts and all concessions and parking revenues in 1960, and, if need be, in 1961 and 1962. While the arrangement for sharing the infrastructure bill meant that the Dodgers would not be paying the $800,000 that the Coliseum commissioners had envisioned when negotiations began, the new deal would cost the team at least $500,000 to use the Coliseum in 1960. It would result in nearly $1 million in extra costs over those in the 1958 and 1959 seasons, due to the increases in gross revenue and concessions payments plus the team's share of stadium improvement expenses. This would amount to the highest stadium rent in baseball history.[88]

The heated bargaining over the 1960 lease terms was yet another illustration of the fine line O'Malley walked in his relationship with the city of Los Angeles. On one hand, he was the public-spirited entrepreneur who had delivered both an iconic baseball franchise and a world championship. On the other, he was a businessman already realizing substantial profits from his team's operation. How much assistance from the citizens and taxpayers of Los Angeles did he merit? O'Malley had won a referendum, prevailed in the courts, and attracted millions of fans to the Coliseum. But the controversies over zoning, rent renegotiation, and the Arechigas had shown that there also existed a spirit of hostility to the accumulation of wealth that ran through Los Angeles civic culture. When the *Examiner's* Melvin Durslag, a reliable Dodger ally and advocate, wrote in reference to the Coliseum that, "irrespective of how much money O'Malley has made—this is merely his good fortune—no stadium is worth such an absurd rental fee," he was expressing a minority viewpoint.[89]

The desire for major league baseball and the resentment of an entrepreneur's profits—two impulses that existed simultaneously and were indeed dependent on each other—further blurred the boundaries O'Malley sought to negotiate in Los Angeles. They also exemplified the ambivalent position entrepreneurial capitalism occupied in the life of the city and region. The political culture of Los Angeles was not that of New York, where the Dodger owner was the subject of caricature as a "greedy" businessman. But beneath the surface of the civic rapture that greeted the Dodgers' on-field success was an undercurrent of resentment by the Folks against the better-off. Phill Silver had built a career representing the "people" against the "interests" in Los Angeles, and while he was not always successful, he drew from a deep well of public sympathy in his war against the "insiders." O'Malley did not always feel like such an insider in his adopted city—often with good reason—but that did not prevent those who opposed the Dodger Stadium project from perceiving him as such. The Dodger owner had now secured the Coliseum for 1960 and beyond, but with it he received yet another lesson on the limits on the culture of entrepreneurship in an environment more hospitable to his dreams than New

York's. Even in Los Angeles, there were lines that could not be crossed.

One line O'Malley was willing to take a chance on crossing involved breaking ground on Dodger Stadium before he was absolutely certain his contract with the city would be upheld in the courts. Phill Silver's appeal was still pending before the United States Supreme Court on September 17, 1959, but O'Malley was confident enough it would be rejected—and a month later it would be—to stage a ceremony at Chavez Ravine to mark the official start of construction. O'Malley invited city officials (council president John Gibson responded, "I would be happy to bring my own shovel but I wore it out shoveling the 'bull' of the opposition out of the City Council chambers") as well as the general public to the groundbreaking.[90] A crowd of some five thousand watched as five bulldozers raced over the Chavez Ravine hills and began moving dirt.[91] Dodger players took their positions on a mock diamond, offering onlookers a rough vision of the future in a new ballpark. Small boxes were distributed to collect samples of "You Were There" dirt.[92] In what stadium opponents read as an omen, a large traffic jam developed as cars crept up the narrow road that led to the site of the groundbreaking.[93]

But O'Malley had made his symbolic point, underscored by the Supreme Court's mid-October refusal to accept Silver's appeal. By then the Dodgers were world champions, capping the best month the Dodger owner had experienced since he came to Los Angeles. The city had also opened bids for the land-grading contract at Chavez Ravine, the first practical step toward actually building the stadium.[94] It had pledged $2 million for this purpose; any additional expenses would be the responsibility of the Dodgers. After the land was leveled, the concrete that would serve as the stadium foundation would be poured and the structure itself, a combination of concrete and steel, erected.[95]

The city awarded the grading contract to Vinnell Constructors of Alhambra, California, whose bid had come in lowest among the eleven submitted and almost 10 percent under the estimate produced by the city's own Board of Public Works.[96] This was the Dodgers' first contact with Vinnell and its contractor-in-charge, Jack Yount, but it would not be the last. Yount had a long resume in Southern California. He was regarded as a master of concrete construction and had built some of the region's freeways.[97] Yount was a no-nonsense man who had the reputation of getting things done on budget and on time. He realized that the grading contract was an audition of sorts for a bigger job, that of building the stadium itself. This would represent a departure from the smart money, since most observers expected O'Malley to award the stadium contract to Del E. Webb Construction Company, one of the largest and most prominent names in the industry. Del Webb was also the co-owner of the New York Yankees and thus one of O'Malley's colleagues. But Webb had his own eye on the Los Angeles territory, thinking he might bring a possible American League expansion franchise there, and so O'Malley viewed him as a potential rival. The door was thus open for others, and Vinnell and Yount seized the inside track through their performance on the land-grading contract.

While the September 17 groundbreaking was primarily for show, serious work commenced thereafter and proceeded through the rest of 1959 and on into 1960. The $2 million allocated by the city for land preparation was not sufficient to cover the cost of the work, since more earth had to be removed than originally anticipated. The Dodgers were forced to pay an additional $1.4 million in order to complete it.[98] But O'Malley was impressed enough with Vinnell's efficiency that in March 1960 he invited the company to bid on the contract for the stadium, even giving the company an exclusive two-week window to submit acceptable terms.[99] Edging out Del Webb, Vinnell won the contract and the opportunity to build the Dodgers' new home.[100]

But construction could not begin until the Dodgers had acquired all of the necessary Chavez Ravine acreage, and there were still parcels outstanding. After the controversy surrounding the Arechiga removals, the city did not dare use eminent domain to gain title to these outlier properties. O'Malley was on his own. The owners had banded together for negotiating purposes and held all the cards. G. G. Baumen, their attorney and representative, demanded a total of $950,000 for the combined properties, a sum almost double their appraised value.[101] There were twelve parcels in all. Nine were located on land designated for the contractually mandated recreation area.[102] The other three, belonging to Harry Hansen, Francis Scott, and grocery store owner Frank De Leon, were located within the area planned for the stadium itself.[103] Weaker and stronger claims were thus combined into a single bargaining entity, driving up the purchase price for all.[104]

O'Malley was able to jawbone the final numbers down a bit, since the astronomical asking prices had become public knowledge, but there was still an aspect of farce to the final purchase amounts.[105] The three parcels located on the grounds of the future stadium cost O'Malley a total of $310,000. The Scott property, appraised at $9,000, sold for $150,000. Hanson received $60,000 for land appraised at $7,500. De Leon's store, appraised at $14,500, fetched $100,000.[106] In all, the twelve parcels sold for $494,000, almost six times their combined appraised values.[107] But as of February 1960 the Dodgers at last owned the land necessary to construct their stadium.[108]

Additional obstacles remained. More than the specifics of the stadium project had motivated the contract opponents. They were concerned with the relationship between government and business in Los Angeles and the ways in which taxpayer resources were employed in that relationship. Even Roybal agreed that business activity, generally speaking, advanced the public good. Holland, himself a former small businessman, also believed in commerce and entrepreneurial activity. The Citizens Committee's C. A. Owen headed a group filled with small-scale property owners. It was not the idea of capitalism itself that they objected to, nor the idea of a stadium for the Dodgers per se. It was the idea of a private stadium abetted with public aid offered to some and not to others that aroused their ire. If O'Malley wished to build a ballpark with his own resources, they had no objection. Indeed, that was what entrepreneurial capitalism was about—O'Malley's risk, O'Malley's reward. But the reduction of that risk through preferential governmental assistance was unacceptable to them. It contravened the principle of free competition, what Woodrow Wilson had called "a free field and no favor," that lay at the heart of market capitalism.[109]

Roybal, Holland, Owen, and Phill Silver may have disagreed on issues related to race, housing, and policing, but they were united in the belief that Los Angeles was in the hands of the well-connected. Their vision of Los Angeles was a city of smallholders, neighborhoods, and everyday dreams. There was no room in this vision for a man like O'Malley and for a stadium facilitated in this manner. O'Malley needed to stand or fall on his own, the way other businessmen—at least those that Holland, Roybal, Owen, and Silver admired—did.

There was, of course, a strong element of unreality and even self-delusion to this view. Most if not all of those Holland, Roybal, and Owen claimed to speak for had benefited from state-sponsored assistance at one time or another. No one made it entirely alone. But this image of self-reliance and independence, a powerful one in American culture generally, worked its influence on the stadium opponents. It would remain the expression of the resentments of the city's marginalized of all races even as the ballpark began to rise from the hills and gullies of Chavez Ravine. Soon it would find a voice in mayoral politics in the form of a populist outsider who viewed Downtown as the enemy and would challenge it successfully.

Meanwhile, arguments over the stadium continued into 1960. Early that year, as Candlestick Park, the new home of the Giants, neared completion, San Francisco mayor George Christopher taunted his rival city. He predicted that Dodger Stadium would not be ready "until at least five years after [the Dodgers] arrived," meaning after the 1962 season had ended.[110] The Dodgers may have been world champions on the field, but if Christopher was correct, they faced three more seasons in a football arena. Once again, San Francisco appeared organized and efficient, Los Angeles chaotic and blundering.[111]

Contract opponents in the City Council adopted a new strategy when Rundberg proposed a municipal tax on ticket sales, taking a cue from New York, which had imposed such a levy in 1954, to O'Malley's chagrin.[112] In a testy February exchange with city attorney Arnebergh, who claimed that the Dodgers were "losing a lot of money by delay due to increased construction costs," Rundberg snapped, "So far it's our money being lost," referring to taxpayer funds. "The city's losing money every day in taxes," Arnebergh persisted, citing the property tax revenues that a completed stadium would generate. Rundberg would have none of it: "Don't give me that. I can't even get a ticket tax on [the Dodgers], because of the Mayor's commitment."[113] Rundberg charged that Poulson had promised O'Malley there would be no citywide tax on sports admissions as there was in New York.[114] Rundberg wanted a ticket levy to lessen the tax burden on small property owners. These, and not large-scale entrepreneurs like O'Malley, were his main constituency.

But Poulson's deal with O'Malley won the day and Rundberg's measure failed in the council. A frustrated Rundberg called Poulson "a vicious man." Roybal joined in, labeling the mayor "a dictator."[115] Acrimony and finger-pointing followed. Poulson accused Holland and his allies Roybal, McGee, and Henry of "promoting spite lawsuits" to stop the stadium project.[116] "We were only trying to prevent our city from selling its Manhattan Island for $24," retorted Holland.[117] Henry snapped that it was "unfortunate that important people have to spend money to go to court to prevent the chief executive [referring to Poulson] from giving away their land and money."[118] An infuriated Poulson blasted the "obstructionists" who opposed the stadium, the Bunker Hill project, and even the city zoo planned for another section of Chavez Ravine. "Their chief charge about the Dodger contract," he pronounced, "is that we are 'giving away' Chavez Ravine. I say that they are intellectual liars. You can't give away city property."[119]

By the spring of 1960, as land grading continued at Chavez Ravine and with stadium construction soon to begin, it was apparent that Holland and his allies were not going to be able to stop the project. Yet they would not let the issue go. They still engaged stadium supporters like Poulson in debates over past contracts, referendums, zoning, and land acquisitions. More than the stadium itself was at stake for them. The power dynamics of the city seemed to be working against them. The "big" people were using the government to promote their own projects. They had to be stopped. This hostility to the powerful evoked Jacksonian democracy in its resentment of privilege and influence.

O'Malley, along with Poulson and Wyman, saw things differently. The Dodger owner viewed his stadium as a civic project, beneficial both to him personally and to the community at large. O'Malley believed as well that he was uniquely positioned to build this civic asset, as he possessed the vision, the experience, the expertise, and the capital. This did not mean O'Malley understood himself as part of an elite. He was simply a businessman who wished to build a ballpark. But there were certain men whose dreams translated into great projects with lasting value. They got things done. These men deserved cooperation and assistance from the government. That they could be considered insiders did not matter as long as they produced benefits: goods, services, technology, jobs, tax revenue, or entertainment.

A half century earlier, the Chicago architect and city planner Daniel Burnham had famously proclaimed: "Make no little plans; they have no magic to stir men's blood."[120] O'Malley's plans for Dodger Stadium were in keeping with these sentiments. But he would require state assistance in order to realize them. Most makers of "no little plans" in America had required it as well. O'Malley and his allies maintained that such assistance was evidence not of cronyism or inside dealing but of a healthy and vigorous public life. Innovation, energy, risk—these should be rewarded, not resented or envied. Those who embodied them would create wealth not just for themselves but also for the civic community as a whole. To O'Malley this idea was obvious and unassailable.

By early 1960 his frustration with those who did not see it his way, especially on the City Council, had reached a boiling point. "For the past two years, " he complained in a letter to August Busch Jr., owner of the St. Louis Cardinals, "every matter of civic importance that has come up has been sabotaged and delayed by an organized minority of elected officials. . . . Thus far they have been almost successful in blocking the proposed new zoo which the public voted for in a referendum, the proposed new Dodger Stadium and youth recreation center which was also supported by the public in a referendum and the Supreme Court of the State of California and the United States Supreme Court, and the Bunker Hill Civic Center improvement program. These are just three examples of cases where every legal strategy possible has been employed to defeat the will of the public and the policy of the [Poulson] administration."[121]

In a March 1960 letter to Frank Schroth, the former owner of the *Brooklyn Eagle* and an old friend, O'Malley warned that the "final political battles" were at hand and that "this time, it must be victory or defeat." He lamented, "We do not have strong political figures who can get things accomplished. We have procrastinators, and I am sorry to say, saboteurs. Economic waste in local government and as it affects the taxpayers in their efforts to accomplish something is absolutely shocking."[122] O'Malley could easily have substituted the word "me" for "the taxpayers" in his last sentence. In his mind, he was besieged by those who restricted themselves to "little plans." O'Malley was seeking to build something in Los Angeles. John Holland and his like, men of more limited vision and ambition, were not. Who had a stronger claim on the resources of the state, those who built or those who obstructed? To O'Malley, as well as Poulson and Wyman, the answer was clear.

By 1960 O'Malley was more willing to intervene directly in the campaigns of candidates for political office to advance his interests. In March, Patrick McGee announced that he would run for Los Angeles county supervisor. In a memo to O'Malley Dodger executive Dick Walsh was blunt: "McGee is our enemy."[123] The Dodger organization would seek to defeat him, and indeed McGee lost his race. As Poulson himself pondered running for a third term as mayor in 1961, supporters and opponents of the Dodger deal would be scrutinized yet again, this time by the municipal electorate.

The choices faced by the voters, while rooted in the specifics of the stadium controversy, would also extend beyond them to bear on more general issues of identity and the kind of city they wished Los Angeles to be. By 1960 Angelenos had the Dodgers and the prospect of a stadium near downtown that promised to change the relationship between city center and periphery. There was more change on the horizon in the form of the Bunker Hill project and a proposed downtown Music Center, a West Coast version of New York's Lincoln Center. But did the new stadium presage the ascendency of a new downtown over outlying areas that had heretofore maintained semiautonomous identities? In which direction would municipal resources flow? Further, what would be the relationship between business and the state in the modern city? How much assistance could the latter offer, and under what circumstances?

Complicating these issues was their cross-partisan and cross-ideological nature. Liberal Democrats such as Wyman and councilman and future congressman James Corman backed the stadium contract as part of their larger vision of government-directed economic development, a form of corporatism in which the state facilitated and coordinated business activity and labor relations. They viewed Dodger Stadium as an example of a community-centered project worthy of government resources. The fact that most local unions also backed it solidified their resolve.

But other liberal Democrats, including Edward Roybal, reached entirely different conclusions. For them, the protection of minority and impoverished communities in Chavez Ravine and Bunker Hill took precedence over projects that were promoted as serving the public good but which actually benefited the wealthy and well-connected. A generalized suspicion of large-scale capitalism drove them to oppose what other liberals such as Wyman and Corman supported. Roybal and his anti-Dodger contract allies did not wish to manage business so much as confront and control it.

Conservative public officials were divided as well. Poulson and other business Republicans were not corporatists, but they did believe in the state's role in fostering economic development in order to create wealth for the greater community. For them the land exchange that brought O'Malley Chavez Ravine was a relatively small price to pay for the jobs, tax revenues, and entertainment-related spending that Dodger Stadium would generate. They backed the Bunker Hill project employing similar logic.

But Holland, McGee, Owen, and other taxpayer Republicans wished to separate government and business as much as possible and allow the market and not the state to determine entrepreneurial success or failure. The taxpayer resources offered O'Malley were by definition denied to other entrepreneurs, tilting the field of competition toward large-scale capitalists who, with their already existing advantages of scale and structure, hardly merited state assistance. The Los Angeles of taxpayer Republicans was a city of small businesses treated evenhandedly by the state. It provided basic services but chose no favorites.

Thus, liberals and conservatives, Democrats and Republicans divided internally over both the specific issue of the Dodger contract and the more general one of the parameters of the political and economic culture of Los Angeles. In this modern city, would business be managed, as Wyman advocated, or controlled, as Roybal wished? Would certain businesses, especially large-scale ones that were job and tax generators, receive government support, as Poulson desired, or kept at arm's length, as Holland envisioned?

It may well have been the nominal nonpartisanship governing Los Angeles electoral politics that made it so difficult to reconcile these conflicting approaches to the city's direction and identity. In a classic instance of unanticipated consequences, what seemed on paper to be a way to banish pernicious party politics from municipal government instead rendered them more chaotic and opaque. Liberal and conservative supporters and opponents of the stadium based their positions on different rationales. Wyman's managerial liberalism and Poulson's business Republicanism led to similar conclusions on the merits of the Dodger contract, but via separate routes, as did Roybal's class-based liberalism and Holland's taxpayer Republicanism. The upcoming 1961 mayoral and council elections would serve as referenda on all of these competing visions for Los Angeles. They would produce a new leader whose rise was as unexpected as were his policies once in office.

9

BUILDING THE DODGER
STADIUM EXPERIENCE

By April 1960, O'Malley was confident enough about the stadium's future to engage a construction company to build it. Vinnell Constructors, which had done the grading work, was the somewhat surprising choice; even Vinnell personnel had considered Del Webb's company the front-runner. But O'Malley and chief architect Emil Praeger knew what they wanted. They envisioned a concrete-centered stadium, not a steel-based structure that constantly required repainting.[1] Vinnell specialized in concrete projects, including many of the highways that crisscrossed the Los Angeles metropolitan area.

O'Malley and Praeger also wanted as much control over the work as possible, which meant keeping subcontractors to a minimum. While Webb was known for liberal use of "subs," Vinnell did the bulk of its work in-house.[2] Vinnell had already performed well as the grader for the project, and Jack Yount, the company's vice president, was a known quantity. O'Malley and Praeger were comfortable with him overseeing the ballpark's construction as the contractor in charge. On April 11, O'Malley wrote to Yount accepting Vinnell's bid to build Dodger Stadium.[3] It was agreed that the total cost of all work would be less than $4,400,000, with

Vinnell keeping 25 percent of the underage. Vinnell promised to keep subcontracting to a minimum and to use its own personnel whenever feasible. Union labor would be employed and materials American-sourced. Vinnell would complete the project within nineteen months of its start date.[4]

But when would it start? O'Malley was comfortable having only a memorandum of understanding with Vinnell and not a formal contract, and in fact stipulated that the agreement could be canceled if the stadium's political and legal roadblocks were not removed by July 11, 1960.[5] There were still hurdles to be surmounted before actual work could begin. A final plot map would need to be approved by the City Council, the deeds to the Chavez Ravine property and Wrigley Field exchanged, and the promised county monies for access roads disbursed.[6]

Meanwhile, as if to underscore the contrasts between the rival cities, Candlestick Park opened in San Francisco on April 12. *Examiner* cartoonist Karl Hubenthal published a drawing of Giant owner Horace Stoneham enjoying the Easter season with an egg labeled "Candlestick Park" while O'Malley held a broken egg with the phrases "empty promises" and "red tape" visible on the pieces.[7] At the time, San Francisco billed itself as "the city that knows how," an ironic commentary on its neighbor to the south as it lurched awkwardly toward its own stadium.[8]

More bad news for O'Malley came in the form of a prediction by S. S. "Sam" Taylor, Los Angeles's traffic czar, that massive tie-ups lasting between one and two hours each would occur entering and exiting the Dodger Stadium parking lots before and after each game.[9] This warning prompted the banks with which O'Malley was negotiating for financing to become, in his words, "greatly alarmed."[10] He told Emil Praeger that his potential lenders said, "We do not want to finance a fried egg at Chavez Ravine if there is no way to get through to eat it."[11] A nervous O'Malley wrote to a friend: "The banks will pretty much be in control of the situation due to the heavy amount of financing needed."[12] Dodger Stadium was also an undertaking with enough unique qualities to offer potential lenders little in the way of prior track records. Would providing financing for a large-scale, privately owned sports facility pay off? Would the banks get their money out? The pessimistic traffic forecasts added to the lenders' sense of caution toward this novel and seemingly risky venture.

O'Malley's investment in pay television was also coming apart. The Dodger owner had negotiated with Skiatron, a fledgling cable television company, to explore the logistics of carrying his team's games. But by April 1960, Skiatron was virtually defunct. It owed hundreds of thousands of dollars to its creditors including the Dodgers, it had no discernable assets, and the sale of its worthless stock had been suspended by the Securities and Exchange Commission. It was clear O'Malley's dream of cable television baseball broadcasts was dead for the time being.[13]

Adding to O'Malley's long-range concerns was Poulson's announcement in early May that he would not seek a third term in the 1961 mayoral election. Few had been stronger advocates for the Dodgers' move and the construction of the stadium. The field for Poulson's job as of May 1960 was wide open. With the city still divided on the stadium question and on downtown redevelopment generally, there was no telling where events would lead. Poulson accordingly warned O'Malley "not to drag [your] feet on projects involving the city," as he did not anticipate being on the political scene long enough to help him complete the stadium.[14]

The thought of City Hall sans Poulson could not have been comforting to O'Malley, who faced the prospect of confrontations with Holland and Roybal without the cover the mayor had offered. He now had even more incentive to push the stadium project through as rapidly as possible. The next step was the tentative plot map that would detail the stadium location, recreation area, parking lots, and interior roads on the property. If approved, the Dodgers would apply for a conditional use permit for the ballpark. O'Malley did not repeat his mistake of the year before, when he submitted a tract map that contained plans for stores, restaurants, and other commercial enterprises. Leery of Holland, who was ready to pounce, O'Malley restricted his plot plan to the essentials—the stadium itself, parking lots, internal roads, and the recreation area.[15]

Still, when the map was submitted to the City Planning Commission in May, the opposition was ready with objections. Owen testified against it in his capacity as Citizens Committee president, as did representatives of the Small Property Owners League, the Federation of San Fernando Valley property owners, and the Property Protectors Federation.[16] They claimed that the map failed to include the exact location of the stadium, omitted interior roads, and made no provision for rights-of-way on any freeways that might be constructed to provide access to the stadium in the future.[17] They also took exception to the manner in which streets would be vacated to make way for the stadium, resurrecting the issue of undue Dodger influence over the process that had animated the taxpayer lawsuits.[18] What had become known in the local media as the council's "Fearless Five"—Holland, McGee, Roybal, Rundberg, and Henry—joined in the objections, drawing criticism in turn from an increasingly impatient Poulson.[19]

The Planning Commission approved the map on May 5 and it was sent to the City Council for final action.[20] There it drew more opposition. A small property owner, H. Douglas Brown, in testimony before the council, asked "if there is one set of ordinances which governs ordinary subdividers and another set of laws for Mr. O'Malley."[21] Arthur Snyder, Holland's staffer, appeared as a witness against the map. He claimed that the roads inside the stadium property that O'Malley intended to build would cause delays and accidents, and he warned that inattention to public transportation services to the site would prove costly.[22] Council president and O'Malley ally John Gibson asked Snyder sarcastically if he was appearing on behalf of the property owner groups he claimed to speak for or for his boss, John Holland, and accused him of "unethical practices."[23] In a jab at Holland, Gibson told Snyder, "If you were my field deputy, I'd fire you."[24]

Owen again testified, repeating his objections to the map's omissions and arguing that the public had been misinformed about the stadium project from the beginning.[25] Holland attempted to affect the outcome of the plot map vote by moving that the report of the council's Police, Fire, and Traffic Committee, on which he, McGee, and Rundberg served and which had warned of huge traffic tie-ups at the new stadium, accompany the map as submitted to the full council.[26] Holland picked up the support of the pro-Dodger-contract Ransom Callicott to add to that of his Fearless Five but fell short of the majority of eight council votes required to pass his motion.[27]

The five also objected to the Dodgers' plan to have all interior roads within the stadium property owned by the team.[28] O'Malley insisted that public streets running through the areas around the ballpark would lead to vehicular chaos and argued that since he would construct the interior roads at his expense it was proper he should own them.[29] But Holland, with his eye constantly on the public purse strings, regarded the entire project as a gift to O'Malley from the taxpayers of Los Angeles. O'Malley also agreed to pay for public roads on the stadium's exterior that provided access to the nearby Los Angeles Police Academy as well as the Naval Armory and Elysian Park.[30] Holland countered that since these roads replaced others that were vacated for stadium construction, the Dodger owner was only returning to the people of the city what he had previously taken from them.

It was a classic instance of incompatible personalities viewing the same circumstances in incompatible ways. O'Malley could not understand how his plan to build a stadium that would generate economic activity, job growth, and tax revenue in Los Angeles could be received with anything less than gratitude and support. Holland could not understand how a stadium project that diverted public resources to a private entrepreneur could be received with anything less than suspicion and criticism. O'Malley believed that a businessman who created wealth for his community merited assistance from that community. Holland believed that no businessman merited assistance from the community that other businessmen did not also receive.

On May 25, O'Malley won his point in the City Council when it approved his plot map by a vote of 11 to 4.[31] Holland fought to the bitter end, initiating a three-and-a-half-hour debate that did not change the outcome. Even so, approval was made contingent on the team fulfilling a series of conditions that included provisions for street realignments, water mains, drainage, and lighting.[32] The Dodgers would also need to obtain a conditional use permit to allow the construction of a fifty-thousand-seat stadium

Excavation of land at Chavez Ravine for future Dodger Stadium,
June 15, 1960. University of Southern California, USC Digital Library,
Los Angeles Examiner Photographs Collection. Photographer: Unknown.

in an area zoned for venues with no more than three thousand
seats.[33] In addition, it was clear that the city's $2 million allocation
for land grading would not be sufficient to cover the costs of the
work and that the team would have to pay the overage, which
would eventually total $1.4 million.[34]

O'Malley still faced the issue of financing. While zoning changes,
tract maps, and conditional use permits were preconditions for
bank loans, they did not in themselves guarantee them. By June
1960, O'Malley was deeply concerned. It was possible that
he could succeed in surmounting all political, legal, and administrative obstacles to building his ballpark, yet fail to raise enough
money to do so. Unlike other owners in cities that had recently
welcomed new major league baseball franchises—San Francisco,
Milwaukee, Baltimore, and Kansas City—O'Malley could not
count on local government to assist him with a municipally financed
stadium. He had already received all the help he was going to get
from the city of Los Angeles in the form of land and funds for
grading and access roads. He needed at least $8 million. No

money meant no Dodger Stadium. With the banks still hesitating, O'Malley would have to look elsewhere.

He found a solution to his financing challenges in an unexpected place: an oil company. For years, Union Oil, one of the most established energy concerns in the area and one whose gas stations were a fixture on the metropolitan landscape, had been looking for a way to break into sports advertising. Reese Taylor, its president, was a Downtown insider, part of a small group with access to the levers of local power. *Life* magazine pictured him standing beside the *Times*'s Norman Chandler and other business leaders in a portrait of civic power published in their June 20, 1960 issue. Taylor had recently lost a battle for control of Santa Anita Park, a prominent Los Angeles horse-racing venue, and was now hoping that the Dodgers and their new stadium would provide an entrée to the city's sports scene.[35]

Taylor approached O'Malley at a low moment for the Dodger owner. The four banks with which he was negotiating—Security First, Bank of America, California Bank, and Citizens National Bank—were demanding an interest rate of 6 percent on any funds advanced, plus commitment and bond fees of 0.5 percent. An interest charge higher than 5.5 percent, O'Malley warned in a letter to his son, Peter, and wife, Kay, "could be financially fatal."[36]

But Taylor stepped in with a novel proposal. Through the sale of Dodger broadcast and advertising rights, Union Oil could act as a bank, loaning the team money against the payment of those rights. O'Malley agreed to make Union Oil the exclusive signage advertiser in the new stadium and allow it to operate a service station in the parking lot. The oil company would pay $9 million in rights fees through 1970, and the Dodgers would repay Union's loan of $8 million, plus interest at 5 percent (later revised downward to 3.3 percent), also through 1970. This would result in a virtual wash of funds coming in and going out. Repayment of principal and interest would not commence until the end of 1963, when the stadium would presumably be operational and generating revenue. The Dodgers would save more than $1.5 million in interest payments compared to what the banks were offering.[37] A relieved O'Malley called Taylor a "life saver."[38] Union cut its first check to the Dodgers under the deal on September 15.[39] O'Malley was in debt, but he now had the financing to get the stadium built. And if he could get it built, he would not be in debt for long.

Moreover, it was the Dodgers, a private entity, that was now in debt, not the city of Los Angeles. San Francisco might have already gotten its ballpark up and running, but the municipality now had to recoup its outlay on it. There would be a bond issue to pay off through rental income, parking fees, and other stadium revenues, plus increased taxes.[40] As with other city-owned ballparks, it would be a long, slow, expensive process. The costs of Candlestick Park were not paid off until 1993, much later than projected.[41]

In Los Angeles, O'Malley stood to make millions from Dodger Stadium. Los Angeles, once the stadium was constructed, stood to save millions. O'Malley's model of total private financing of the stadium structure has never again been attempted due to the almost prohibitive costs involved. But it is fair to say that most municipalities would prefer this model to the expensive mix of tax levies and bond debt that is now a standard element in contemporary sports arena financing. At any given time some American city is wrestling with the issue of how much public money can and should be paid out to construct a modern stadium that will either keep an existing team in town or attract a new one. By taking on debt himself, O'Malley relieved Los Angeles of this expensive choice. Once he received the deed to the Chavez Ravine land, the risk was all his.

The exchange of deeds, Wrigley Field to the city of Los Angeles and Chavez Ravine to the Dodgers, would indeed be the next step. Both deeds had been placed in escrow pending other administrative approvals, and the City Council was ready to consider them in early July. Community newspapers immediately began drumming up opposition. The *Wilshire Press* blasted the terms of the deed exchange, claiming that it left taxpayers "on the hook" for debts accrued by the Dodgers if the team defaulted on its contractual obligations, most notably by failing to finish the stadium itself, and the city was thus forced to retake the Chavez Ravine land.[42] It also revived the issue of comparative property valuations, arguing that Chavez Ravine had been grossly underpriced and that aging and isolated Wrigley Field was overvalued.[43] "Maybe it's time we come up with a new City Council, a new city attorney, [and] a new mayor," it editorialized, "before the old ones hang a price tag on our birthright itself."[44] The Civic Center News Agency, another dogged opponent of the Dodger contract, also charged that the team would not be paying taxes on the Chavez Ravine properties located in the projected recreation area that the team had purchased on its own and that the people of Los Angeles would thus be financing them.[45] Both outlets urged the City Council to reject the escrow agreement.

The Fearless Five did their part when the issue came up for a vote on July 1. As usual, Holland led the way. "The rush is on," he remarked sarcastically, "so Mr. O'Malley can get a loan on the Ravine to pay off for Wrigley Field and give it to us."[46] As he had during the referendum campaign two years earlier, Roybal described the Dodger deal as "the worst contract this city has ever had. Students of government in the future will wonder what has happened here. This will go down in history as the biggest gift of real estate a municipality has ever made to a private individual."[47] As Roybal finished, McGee added, "Amen."[48] Henry, generally the most reserved of the Fearless Five, said: "When I learned what was involved here, I couldn't conscientiously go for it. It violates the principles of good government. I felt so keenly that this was wrong that I've been consistent in opposing it. This is an unwarranted gift of public money and lands."[49] When Rundberg called the land transaction "a deal," contract supporter John Gibson protested his imputation of dishonesty. "I couldn't give a snap of my fingers," Rundberg shot back. "I hope some day the real facts of this deal come to light and the guilty parties are punished. This is not kosher or legitimate. If the true man-hours of city employees on this project were added up it would amount to some more millions of dollars."[50] Holland upped the rhetorical ante on Gibson, referring to the Dodger contract as not just a "deal" but a "stinking rotten deal."[51]

But McGee was realistic. "We consummate here today by our votes," he told his colleagues, "what the City Council agreed to do three years ago. There has been great delay, not the fault of the minority five on this Council, for we just haven't got the votes."[52]

Just before the escrow release vote, pro-contract councilman Gordon Hahn interjected a note of caution and uncertainty: "Some of you have a feeling some deal was made. I hope time will prove you wrong."[53] Then, offering a glimpse of the doubt lurking beneath the surface of even the contract's strongest boosters, he admitted, "There may be a small chance you're right."[54]

Then it was time to vote. As expected, it was 10 to 5, with the Fearless Five united in opposition. With the escrow agreement approved, the City Council relinquished control of the Dodger transaction. The anti-contract community newspaper *Wilshire Press* described the Fearless Five as speaking "resignedly, as if standing at the grave of a loved one, mourning the final loss of the last remaining large parcel of publicly-owned land near Civic Center, land needed for public purposes if Los Angeles is to take its place properly among other great metropolises."[55] On August 16 the deeds to Wrigley Field and Chavez Ravine were exchanged. Three days later, when their deed was formally recorded, the Dodgers became the official owners of the Ravine property.[56]

It had taken almost three years to reach this milestone, and it was a clear victory for O'Malley personally. But was it also a victory for the vision of a vitalized downtown that animated Poulson, Wyman, Chandler, and other stadium supporters among the city's political and economic classes? That was less clear. Defeated in the City Council, opponents of the Dodger deal fought on. To them, O'Malley's long-delayed acquisition of the Chavez Ravine land symbolized their city's wrong turn. It also symbolized to them the conflation of private gain with public good. Why should the city's downtown, headquarters to the corporate elite, siphon resources from outlying neighborhoods that needed roads, schools, sewer lines, and other essential infrastructure? Baseball was a luxury, not a necessity. The vote on the escrow agreements resolved these questions in the City Council but not in the city's political culture at large. There the battle continued, with the stadium serving as a prominent and divisive surrogate.

The issue of taxes began to bubble to the surface of Los Angeles's political dialogue in 1960. That year the city cut the property tax rate by 1½ cents as a consequence of overall economic growth and the resulting expansion in municipal revenues.[57] But taxes as a whole rose in the city because real estate holdings were now assessed by the county at higher values. At the same time the council increased the financial pressure on the city by approving a record-high budget and awarding raises to half of the municipal workforce.[58]

Taxes were thus in play as the 1961 mayoral election approached. There were a number of new or increased levies on the table in the council in 1960, including a proposed automobile tax that would affect a wide cross section of the population. The ticket admissions tax that Rundberg had previously attempted to push through the council was now back before it. A proposed city income tax measure that would probably raise the most revenue was also on the docket. There was even a measure for increasing the fees for rubbish collection, which was aimed squarely at the middle-class homeowning constituency in peripheral areas such as the San Fernando Valley, home to Folks whose interests were represented by C. A. Owen, Patrick McGee, and, although his council district lay elsewhere, John Holland.[59] The Dodger Stadium battle would continue in other forms and on other fronts, moving from Chavez Ravine to the electoral landscape of the city as a whole.

In early August, city zoning administrator Huber Smutz approved a conditional use permit for Dodger Stadium. Smutz had promised to "work out conditions and controls that will eliminate the major concerns" of the adjoining Ravine property owners.[60] Those would include requirements that the Dodgers pay for all roads within the stadium property; bear responsibility for street reconstructions, utility relocations, and traffic control; share parking with the zoo, which was planned for another section of Chavez Ravine; provide a shield against automobile lights for neighboring homes; control the use of stadium lighting and sound systems; and limit the number of non-baseball-related events at the stadium to no more than four per month.[61]

The Dodgers' application had omitted the recreation area acreage, which would not be subject to taxation.[62] Phill Silver objected, claiming the team would be receiving "a gift of public funds." Smutz countered that the land was tax-exempt because it remained city property. Why, then, Silver asked, would the Dodgers be using the acreage for "private commercial parking"? Team assistant general manager Dick Walsh responded by defending the Dodgers' occasional use of the recreation area for overflow parking as appropriate under the circumstances. The team might not have official title to the property, he argued, but they had committed to pay for its acquisition and upkeep and they should derive some benefit in return for that investment.[63]

Silver's charges spoke yet again to the divide between those who viewed the Dodger deal as a form of crony capitalism and those who viewed it as an example of the legitimate use of state power to stimulate economic growth. For the first group, every concession granted the Dodgers, including in this instance the right to use recreation area land for parking on busy stadium days, was illegitimate. For the latter group, reasonable governmental accommodations to the needs of a taxpaying and job-creating entity were legitimate and proper. Dodger Stadium continued to serve as a cockpit for broader arguments over Los Angeles's identity and future as the 1961 elections approached.

In a public ceremony at the team's Statler Hotel offices on August 25, O'Malley signed the contract with Vinnell Constructors to build Dodger Stadium.[64] As he had been on the land-grading project, Jack Yount would be in charge as construction chief. Work would start in earnest after Labor Day. In accordance with O'Malley's wishes, the stadium would employ concrete as its primary building material.[65] Vinnell would erect a casting yard on site, where some twenty-five thousand blocks of concrete would be fabricated and assembled to form the stadium's grandstand.[66] "Some of the refinements may not be ready," O'Malley admitted, "but we will have all the comforts and conveniences, including roads and parking, ready for the fans on opening day 1962."[67]

As important as the hiring of Jack Yount as construction coordinator was the almost simultaneous promotion of Dick Walsh to the position of Dodger vice president for stadium operations.[68] As

Walter O'Malley smiles as construction at Dodger Stadium gets under way. Photo by Peter O'Malley, courtesy of walteromalley.com.

assistant general manager, Walsh had advised O'Malley during the referendum campaign, the taxpayer litigation, and the Arechiga controversy, and had acquired a well-deserved reputation for efficiency and attention to detail. Now he would be the Dodger owner's point man for the construction of the stadium itself. Walsh, Praeger, and Yount set out to realize O'Malley's vision for the ballpark that had been held in abeyance for almost three years. "Don't ever doubt that Walter is a showman," Walsh told reporters. "Walter knows that baseball today demands more than three outfield walls and a covered stand. Chavez Ravine will have every innovation known to baseball—and a few known only to Walter."[69]

O'Malley's planned innovations would make Dodger Stadium the nation's first truly modern ballpark. It would contain no poles and no obstructed views. It would eliminate long climbs to seats by sinking the field so that fans entered closer to their destinations. Its parking would be leveled to further reduce fan inconvenience. The scoreboard would feature more space for electronic messages than any other in the major leagues. The seats would be substantially wider than those in older parks like Ebbets Field and offer more legroom. Aisles and interior corridors would also be increased in width. There would be more concession stands than in any existing stadium, distributed across its four seating levels (six including the club and dugout box areas), which would also be the most in baseball. As a baseball-only facility—Candlestick Park, in contrast, was convertible to football use—it would provide close-in views of the playing field. Every seat would be turned in the direction of the diamond. It would contain a stadium club with a well-appointed restaurant from which game action could be observed, open to season ticket holders at an extra charge.

The planned club was in keeping with O'Malley's conception of the stadium as an entertainment venue. He wanted to win on the field, of course; that was a given. But as Walsh had noted, O'Malley also viewed a ballpark as more than just a place to watch a game. What if the Dodgers lost a ballgame? If his business model were based only on "three outfield walls and a covered stand," the fan's day would be ruined. But this would not occur at Dodger Stadium as O'Malley envisioned it. His ballpark would host group days, giveaway days, and even camera days, on which fans could take posed player photographs. Ushers, vendors, security guards, parking lot attendants, and other stadium personnel would be trained in the manner of Disneyland to treat fans/guests with courtesy, consideration, and respect. There would be a multitude of attractive food options, ranging from the upper-end stadium club to middle-range snack bars to high-quality standard concession fare that would include a signature hot dog. While ticket prices would be kept low to attract families and groom the Dodger fans of the future, there would also be special provisions for entertainment stars and VIPs to be seen in the front rows as well as opportunities for conspicuous display by the well-heeled in the form of field-level boxes and stadium club memberships.

These plans also reflected O'Malley's desire to make Dodger Stadium a class-inclusive venue. Celebrities and elites, folks and families—there would be a place for all of them in his new ballpark. It was, of course, highly unlikely that a small business owner from the San Fernando Valley or a Mexican American family from

East Los Angeles would be seated next to Cary Grant or Norris Poulson, but a sense of openness and possibility would drive attendance at the new stadium. O'Malley was a businessman who wished to sell his product to as many customers as possible. That meant making every segment of the Los Angeles area's population comfortable in his ballpark, from field level to upper deck.

Latinos and women were would be special priorities. Baseball was enormously popular in Los Angeles's Mexican American community, and the Dodgers' Spanish-language broadcasts and media outreach were designed to create fans and customers.[70] The stadium would also be a place where female fans, a growing component of the team's base, would feel comfortable. O'Malley's plans for low-ticket prices and a family-oriented atmosphere in the ballpark were directed in large measure toward them.

The Dodger owner also planned female-specific discount and giveaway days, took handbags into consideration in seating design, asked that paint chips be removed from newly painted seats so as not to mar dresses, and even spent time on the details of the stadium ladies' rooms to ensure comfort and convenience.[71] Ballparks had historically been masculine, working-class venues. Ebbets Field, with its raucous, hard-nosed atmosphere, certainly fit that description. But O'Malley, who had become concerned about the dearth of families at Brooklyn Dodger games, resolved to soften the edges of his new stadium. Outreach to women and families was not social activism so much as marketing, aimed at attracting the largest possible number of spectators. But O'Malley's plans would nonetheless have the effect of broadening the class and gender reach of his franchise in Los Angeles, opening it to groups who in the past might have been reluctant to enter a major league ballpark.

In designing Dodger Stadium to be class- and gender-inclusive, O'Malley positioned himself to make money, certainly more than if he had been content to keep his ticket buyer base within more traditional boundaries. But he also would succeed in making his ballpark a unique civic unifier, positioning Dodger Stadium as a place of inclusion where Angelenos came together with a common purpose. It would be, in fact, one of the few public venues of any kind in the city that crossed lines of class, gender, and race and gathered the city as it was in a single space. By seeking to tap every possible customer market, O'Malley would create a civic institution that united a diverse population. It is a comment on the fractured civic life of Los Angeles that it would require a baseball team and a ballpark to address this need. But few baseball teams and ballparks served as such powerful cultural reference points for an entire metropolitan area. Dodger Stadium would ground a civic community whose members would disagree about many things, but not about the Dodgers.

Even before the outer walls of the stadium began to rise, O'Malley received a welcome revenue infusion in the form of a tenant. In December 1960 the American League awarded an expansion franchise to Los Angeles. Christened the Angels, the new team would play the 1961 season at Wrigley Field and then move into Dodger Stadium for its scheduled opening in April 1962. While the Dodgers would miss out on rental income for Wrigley Field in 1961, since they no longer owned it, they would profit from the Angels' time in Dodger Stadium as the facility's second team from 1962 on. The Angels agreed to pay their new landlords $200,000 per year, plus all parking and half of concessions revenues.[72] Never a serious rival to the Dodgers for the city's affections, they would move to their own stadium in suburban Orange County in 1966.

As 1960 came to an end, plans for another downtown enhancement—this one actually located downtown—moved forward. For decades, the city had lacked an indoor performing arts venue commensurate with its growing cultural prominence. The construction of Lincoln Center in New York beginning in 1959 put even more pressure on Los Angeles to match its cross-coast rival. The impulse for cultural renewal coincided with one for downtown renewal generally, in the forms of the Dodger Stadium and Bunker Hill projects and even that of the zoo planned for another section of Chavez Ravine.[73] A music and drama center could raise Los Angeles's fine-arts profile as well as the prestige of its central core. By late 1960 Dorothy Chandler, wife of *Times* publisher Norman Chandler, had led a successful public-private campaign to break ground on such a center, with the cost to be shared by the county and individual donors. Chandler was able to bring together

Downtown and Westside interests in her fund-raising effort, in itself an impressive feat of civic unification given the long-standing ethnocultural divisions between the two.[74]

Like Dodger Stadium, the proposed Music Center attracted support from both the Republican, Protestant Downtown corporate-financial establishment and the Democratic, socially liberal Westside of business, professional, and entertainment leaders. Located within the Bunker Hill redevelopment area, the Music Center would symbolize the revitalization of the city center that was so important to Poulson, Wyman, and Chandler. But to others, including Holland, Roybal, and Owen, the project was yet another example of over-reaching by moneyed interests and elites at the expense of those on the economic and geographic margins. It would be a bauble, a distraction from the everyday needs of their neighborhoods and constituencies. Streets and schools, spending and taxes—these took precedence over an extravagant concert hall for the well-to-do. The election year of 1961 would be very much about taxes, both their amount and their allocation. Dodger Stadium, symbol of a vision for Los Angeles that was sharply contested, would also be an issue even as it began to rise in Chavez Ravine. The argument over downtown Los Angeles—what it would look like, what would occupy it, who would own it, and what relation it would bear to the rest of the city—continued the argument over Dodger Stadium, repeating in many ways the referendum battle of 1958.

Also at issue was Norris Poulson's legacy as mayor. He had staked his administration on a reanimated downtown, and even though he had announced his intention not to run for a third term, the election would still center on the implications of his decisions, including bringing the Dodgers to Los Angeles and making Chavez Ravine available to them. Walter O'Malley and the team he owned would thus play a major role in determining the trajectory and identity of the city of Los Angeles. Dodger Stadium was now more than a baseball venue. It had come to represent an approach to governing, an expanded view of the public good that permitted and even encouraged government assistance to private enterprise in the name of the community as a whole. Would Poulson's brand of business Republicanism carry the day? As the new year of 1961 began and the outer shell of Dodger Stadium began to take shape, the direction of the city hung in the balance.

The job Jack Yount of Vinnell Constructors began just after Labor Day 1960 was one of immense proportions. He had already excavated 2 million square yards of dirt from Chavez Ravine in order to grade the future stadium's land. Now he would be tasked with moving 5.5 million more yards in order to create the "bowl" in which the ballpark could be sited.[75] He would also have to pave the 300 acres of land on which Dodger Stadium, its parking areas, and the recreation area would be built. On Yount's advice, O'Malley paid an additional $1.50 a cubic yard for special lightweight, high-strength concrete that was stronger even than that used for highway bridges.[76] There would be approximately 45,000 yards of concrete used in total.[77] The 23,000 concrete pieces, all precast, were numbered and assembled in a preplanned order.[78] Dirt excavation proved more complicated than anticipated, and three months were lost solidifying the structural foundation before the first concrete pieces could be installed.[79] In a unique arrangement, Yount built a casting yard on-site to accommodate the size and weight of the concrete blocks, which could not be transported long distances. A specially built crane placed the blocks in their designated spaces.[80]

By early 1961 the basic form of the stadium skeleton was visible from the air. Sunken into the ground, it could not be appreciated horizontally. Using cantilevers, curved steel beams that could bear heavy weights without external support, all stadium decks would offer unobstructed views. This was probably the most important departure from the architecture of the traditional stadiums of the East and Midwest and the single most significant change from a fan's standpoint. Football stadiums such as the Coliseum, on the other hand, were constructed as oval bowls. They contained no pillars in the stands and thus offered unobstructed sightlines, but were built back from the playing field in order to keep the structure upright. What spectators gained in uninterrupted views they lost in distance; it was no coincidence that binoculars were de rigueur in the football fan's game kit. But Dodger

Stadium would use cantilevers to combine clear sight lines and physical proximity.

In addition, the lower stands would be fixed in place and would not be movable to create a football configuration, ensuring that spectators would enjoy a baseball-specific experience.[81] Seventy percent of the seats would be within the infield area, and all seats would be angled toward home plate.[82] Aisles would be wider and more plentiful than at any other major league ballpark, and those above field level would include a dividing banister to prevent bottlenecks and accidents.[83] No deck would contain more than twenty-odd rows, bringing spectators on every level as close to the field as possible.[84] Vertical climbing would be kept to a minimum by the use of these relatively shallow decks.[85] After considering potential ticket demand and cost, it was decided not to enclose the stadium. Instead two bleacher-style pavilions would be constructed in the outfield, each with a roof to shield against the sun. The option to build a grandstand in that area would be left open.[86]

O'Malley had waited for decades for the chance to build his own stadium. Now he made the most of his opportunity, involving himself in virtually every aspect of its planning and effectively acting as an architect without formal portfolio. Early on he understood the potential of the Chavez Ravine site, with its downtown and mountain vistas. A 1959 Dodger promotional brochure promised fans "a sweeping sky-high panorama of the Los Angeles area."[87] O'Malley instructed Emil Praeger to examine the plans for Candlestick Park and had Dick Walsh visit it when it was completed in 1960.[88] "See if there is any feature they have that we should consider," he told Praeger. "Naturally, we do not want them to scoop us."[89] After learning that Candlestick's stadium club charged 50 cents for a cup of coffee and $1.90 for a hamburger, O'Malley commented that both were too high. He was especially concerned with the price of coffee everywhere in the stadium, since "it reaches so many little people."[90] O'Malley also instructed that the price of peanuts be reduced from the 25 cents per bag charged at most other ballparks to 15 cents a bag.[91]

These directives were consistent with an attention to detail uncharacteristic of owners whose teams played in publicly owned stadiums. O'Malley truly made Dodger Stadium his own creation. Nothing was too small to escape his attention. He consulted with Praeger on the wood used in the stadium seats.[92] He cautioned against building the pitcher's mound too high, since it could block views from some box seats.[93] He insisted that stadium deck facades be built at slight upward angles so that foul balls would not bounce directly down on patrons sitting below.[94] He asked for auxiliary scoreboards to be installed on the grandstand for the convenience of pavilion spectators who would be seated below and in front of the two main boards.[95]

O'Malley ordered that the stadium's top deck, with cheaper tickets, should contain concession stands and not a restaurant, since he predicted that fans on that level would be more likely to purchase hot dogs and soda.[96] In the restaurant on the club level, O'Malley wanted all tables to provide a view of the field.[97] He told Praeger to make sure that the sight lines from the corner seats in the last rows of the outfield pavilion—the proverbial worst seats in the house—were not obstructed.[98] O'Malley specified that dugouts be soundproofed and that bullpen mounds have the same elevation and direction as the mound on the playing field.[99] Noting that the prevailing winds in the Chavez Ravine area came from the west, he ordered the stadium configured so that they would flow into the stands and field, avoiding a hot-box effect.[100] O'Malley selected the colors of the stadium seats to reflect an earth-to-sky pattern, with yellow on the field level ranging upward to orange, turquoise, and a blue top deck.[101] He even specified the type of seat cushion he wanted available for rental at the stadium.[102]

O'Malley combined this concern with the ground-level micro operations of his new ballpark with careful attention to its larger functions. He intended that the act of attending Dodger Stadium would be as important as the outcome of the game played there. There would be, as one observer put it, "a dispassionate accent on Dodger Stadium and the larger experience rather than on the Dodgers and how they [were] doing."[103] While there would of course be more and less expensive tickets, O'Malley was determined to offer every customer the same enjoyable basics. This meant that even fans on the top stadium deck would be the beneficiaries of low

Dodger Stadium construction, September 20, 1961. University of Southern California, USC Digital Library, *Los Angeles Examiner* Photographs Collection. Photographer: AP.

ticket prices (general admission was only $1.50), beautiful mountain and skyline vistas, unimpeded bird's-eye views of the field, and high-quality, inexpensive concessions.[104]

It also meant that season boxholders on the field level, in addition to proximity to the action and a chance to see and be seen with Hollywood celebrities seated nearby, could enjoy the benefits of a stadium club second to none in amenities and services. As O'Malley planned it, the club would contain an upscale dining facility, the Diamond Room, and an adjacent bar. The food and drink options would be comparable to those in the city's best restaurants. Tables would look out on the field, and there would also be club-level ticketed seating a few steps away, affording the high-end fan the ultimate experience in ballpark luxury. Reinforcing the "club" concept, a meeting room for private functions would also be available.[105] O'Malley understood his adopted city well enough to know that, as an observer once put it, Los Angeles was "a city of stars accustomed to special treatment, and even more important . . .

those who aspired to be treated like stars even though they weren't."[106]

For both types, Dodger Stadium would need to be "an experience just a little more special, a little more exclusive, than simply going to watch a ballgame."[107] The stadium club would accomplish this goal by encouraging members to think of themselves as better situated than nonmembers. Indeed, some club members could take advantage of separate stadium entrances, to avoid interacting with average fans. O'Malley sensed that different Dodger fans would expect different things from Dodger Stadium. For some, the diehards, a Dodger victory was all that mattered. Others, and likely most stadium club members, viewed the game as an opportunity to go out for an event. It would be wonderful if the Dodgers won, of course, but if the meal was good, the atmosphere elegant, and, say, Cary Grant was seated a few tables down, the night would be a success even if the home team lost. The stadium club would reinforce the distinction between fan and customer. Dodger Stadium would offer a place, comfortable and welcoming, to both.

The stadium scoreboards would also build on the atmosphere of spectacle and entertainment. They would be the largest and most technologically sophisticated in American sports history. The left-field board would contain an unprecedented amount of space for typed-in messages, a total of eight separate rows with a capacity of 31 characters each. In contrast, Yankee Stadium's message board, considered state-of-the-art, had room for eight characters on each of its eight rows. The two Dodger Stadium main boards would utilize seventeen thousand lights, drawing enough power to light two hundred houses.[108]

But over and above its impressive physical features, the Dodger Stadium left-field message board would create a new relationship between the team and its fans. In addition to providing detailed game information, it would make spectators part of the action on the field, as when the posting of "Go . . . Go . . . Go" on the board served as a signal for fans to chant the same words to Maury Wills as he prepared to steal another base. The board would also be used to communicate special greetings to visiting groups and to individuals in the stands.[109] A Dodger public relations assistant would gather data in advance, and during the game there would appear a personalized mention of a fan's birthday, anniversary, graduation, or other significant life event. Groups would be mentioned by name, as in "A Dodger Stadium welcome to . . ." or "The Dodgers welcome . . ." Thus a major part of the ballpark experience for many fans would involve their explicit recognition *as* fans. The traditional barrier between team and spectator would be permeated, encouraging an ever-deeper identification. Giveaway, photograph, and autograph days would further enhance the idea that the fans were part of the Dodger family.

These types of connections offered the team's on-field performance a degree of insulation from harsh scrutiny, separating the stadium experience from individual game outcomes. Winning would still matter greatly, of course, but strengthening the bond between team and fan through such devices as stadium club memberships and scoreboard acknowledgments shifted the ground from competition to entertainment. Losses would occasion feelings of disappointment and commiseration with "our" Dodgers rather than the anger and disgust characteristic of most defeated fans. Loyalties would be ongoing. They would survive the errors, strikeouts, and lost leads that are the bête noir of a baseball team's supporters. The personal would replace the institutional. The Dodger fan base would be groomed for the long term.

Another link between fan and team would be forged through the sale of Dodger merchandise at the new stadium. "We want this park to be a public attraction even when no events are scheduled," O'Malley wrote in his Dodger Stadium planning notes.[110] He planned for an on-premises team store, which would be adjacent to the advance ticket office in order to create a synergy between the two.[111] Upon arriving in Los Angeles, O'Malley had hired Danny Goodman, a veteran concessionaire, as the organization's vice president for advertising. He charged Goodman with promoting the Dodger brand through an array of products bearing the team's logo. These ranged from T-shirts and hats to key chains, flashlights, and even transistor radios. Goodman plastered the blue

Dodger logo script on eighty separate items and circulated them effectively through his game-day concessions operation at the Coliseum.[112]

The new Dodger Stadium would offer a new set of opportunities for the resourceful Goodman. Expanded in-stadium concession facilities plus outside sales through arrangements with area retailers would allow him to blanket Los Angeles with merchandise and keep the Dodger name in the public eye 365 days a year. Thanks to Goodman, Dodger Stadium concessionaires would sell more logo items in more varieties than any other major league ballpark, another form of bonding between fan and team that nurtured feelings of proprietorship and even intimacy. Long before Dodger manager Tommy Lasorda coined the term "Dodger Blue" in the late 1970s to refer to the team's unique mystique, there was a culture of ownership among fans encouraged and abetted by the personal touches of club memberships, scoreboard greetings, and logo branding.

A game-day operation that stressed customer service and polite efficiency would contribute to the culture of "our" Dodgers that permeated the new stadium's atmosphere. Dodger Stadium would be the first ballpark built with the aim of creating a fan partnership as opposed to a mere spectatorship, one that would survive the inevitable lost games and unsuccessful seasons. As such, it would be a model for the modern ballpark of the twenty-first century, a place where the mention of a fan's name on the scoreboard was almost as important as the game result it reported.

Dodger Stadium would be a combination of a secular church where devoted Dodger fans came together in a common spirit and a theme park offering entertainment, fulfillment, and connection. Like a church or a theme park, it would present the world not as it was but as it could be imagined, in harmony and common purpose. It would be a sanctuary for Angelenos who wished to escape the stress and stridency of the city around them. Dodger Stadium would be a place where music played, people smiled, mountains beckoned, and life was better. Life was even better if the Dodgers won, of course, but still good even with a loss.

The new stadium would continue the Coliseum's relatively inexpensive $3.50/$2.50/$1.50 pricing scheme (the limited number of club and dugout box seats were $5.50) in order to attract families, which were O'Malley's target audience. Families meant children (who were admitted for 75 cents), and children who got into the habit of going to Dodger Stadium with their parents would grow into lifelong fans who as adults would take their own children to games, ensuring an ongoing and unwavering base of Dodger customers. The stadium thus had to be a venue in which families felt comfortable, one that made them want to return again and again. It would have to be spotlessly clean, reliably safe, and, in contrast to Ebbets Field, reasonably decorous. It would also need to appeal to women, who were expected to constitute a significant proportion of Dodger Stadium patrons. The family unit was consequently the focus of the team's ticket marketing plan for the new stadium. A devoted family man himself, O'Malley approached the task of filling his new stadium from this perspective. Children represented future customers. Women were half the area's population. The presence of both would almost guarantee that of fathers and husbands. O'Malley would thus realize his full market potential.

The design and setting of Dodger Stadium would be crucial to reaching that potential. Unlike quirky Ebbets Field, Dodger Stadium would feature clean, predictable sight lines. It would offer no unpleasant surprises. No poles. No backbreaking climbs to upper decks. No asymmetry. No pushy, panhandling ushers. No rude employees. No filthy, menacing corridors or restrooms. No aggravating searches for parking spaces on city streets. No dearth of Dodger-themed souvenirs designed to appeal to young fans. Family life was often inconvenient; Dodger Stadium would offer convenience. Families were often filled with stress; Dodger Stadium would offer relaxation. Family life could be filled with ennui and boredom; Dodger Stadium would offer entertainment that was exciting but not chaotic. At Dodger Stadium, everything would be pleasantly predictable, except for the outcome of the game itself. It would be a perfect family venue. This does not imply that it was racially exclusionary. O'Malley wanted every resident of the Los

Angeles metropolitan area to be a Dodger fan. He wanted his stands full every night. His team was popular in the African American community and had made attracting Latino fans a priority. O'Malley desired family groups of all racial backgrounds in his ballpark because they were good for business.

There is no indication that families of color sought a different type of experience at Dodger Stadium than did white families. There is, similarly, no evidence that O'Malley spurned minority customers. Had he wished to exclude them, he could have raised his lowest ticket prices, which were $1.50 for top-deck general admission and the pavilion, to less affordable levels. This would have ensured an overwhelmingly white audience. But O'Malley wanted minority fans as he did all fans. Dodger Stadium would thus offer a culturally unifying experience that, at least for the time it took to play a ball game, tied the elements of a disparate metropolitan area together. Dodger Stadium would reify the Dodgers as a commonly held civic culture.

But even if the team and stadium represented a common experience for a culturally diverse group of fans, there still would be class-based divisions in the stands themselves. Club memberships marked the most elite season box seat holders' territory. There would also be season box customers who were not club members. There would be opportunities to purchase reserved seats on a season basis, although to O'Malley's chagrin relatively few of these were sold.[113] Box ($3.50) and reserved ($2.50) seats were available in advance and at the gate on an individual basis, and upper-deck unreserved general admission and outfield pavilion tickets ($1.50) were sold on game days. This meant the stadium could accommodate all classes but in locations that varied by income level. This hierarchy of space separated out the business class—which presumably would predominate in club memberships—and working-class fans in the pavilions.

But there were an enormous number of seats in between these best and worst categories, all of which featured enough amenities to blur distinctions and make minor differences more palatable. Dodger Stadium would be above all a middle-class venue. Unlike Ebbets Field, it would have middle-class standards and sensibilities. These were broad enough to accommodate broad segments of the Los Angeles metropolitan population. Dodger Stadium would serve as a civic magnet for enough of Los Angeles to offer it a lodestar of cultural meaning.

As the stadium construction continued, so did the planning for the access roads that would be essential for bringing fans to Chavez Ravine.[114] There would be five such roads, each exiting off a freeway or major roadway, configured like spokes in a wheel.[115] City officials contended that, contrary to commonly held expectations, traffic flow would not present a major problem. "Our department is very optimistic about the access-road plan, that it will be far more successful than is anticipated," said a deputy city engineer. He predicted that a Dodger Stadium crowd of 25,000 would be able to exit within a half hour of the end of a game.[116] With the anticipated completion of the Golden State Freeway by the time of the stadium's April 1962 projected opening date, there would be three major highways that ran near the ballpark.[117] Under the terms of the stadium contract Los Angeles County would pay $2.74 million to construct the access roads up to the Dodgers' property line; the team would be responsible for all interior arteries.[118]

One road, however, was planned to cut through a section of Elysian Park, the city's oldest, which abutted Chavez Ravine. It would connect the Pasadena Freeway to Riverside Drive and then in turn to the Dodger Stadium parking lots.[119] Holland objected, claiming that the road was effectively a gift of public property. A dissenting commissioner of the city's Department of Recreation and Parks, which had authority over the road, labeled it "a giveaway to private enterprise."[120]

Another critic of the Elysian Park road during the spring of 1961 was a candidate in that year's mayoral election. Sam Yorty was running, as he customarily did, as an outside-the-establishment gadfly. It was one theme in his campaign against the Downtown interests responsible for the contract with the Dodgers that had led eventually to this road, paid for in part by city taxpayers. The fifty-one-year-old Yorty had run for office almost a dozen times previously in a political career that was then in its third decade, losing about as many times as he had won. He had served as a

state assemblyman for five years and a congressman for four more
without achieving great distinction. He had begun as a left-of-center
Democrat during the New Deal but had moved steadily to the right
thereafter. By 1961, he was a Republican in all but name—he
had supported Richard Nixon for president the year before—but
retained a nominal Democratic designation. Los Angeles's nonpartisan electoral system actually boosted Yorty's chances in the mayoral
race, since he had alienated most of the local Democratic organization over the years. Yorty's reputation was that of an unpredictable "maverick." He viewed the label as a high compliment.[121]

Yorty entered the 1961 mayoral campaign essentially as a man
without a party. He was indeed an inveterate outsider. Yorty had
no substantial ties to either Downtown or the Westside, both of
which were sources of strong support for the Dodger contract and
the Chavez Ravine project. These constituencies, separated for so
long by divides of ethnicity, religion, culture, and ideology, had
come together in the cause of building Dodger Stadium. But Holland and Roybal, the two most vociferous critics of the stadium
deal, represented constituencies that were excluded from the developing Downtown-Westside rapprochement. During the mayoral
campaign of 1961, Sam Yorty would speak for them as the champion of outsiders who felt left behind by expansion and growth.

Yorty's natural voting base had traditionally been among the
Folks. He was in fact one of them, having migrated to Los Angeles
from Nebraska in 1927. Yorty had always represented white middle-
class areas of the city, and made his home in the relatively déclassé
San Fernando Valley. Yorty now sought to add the votes of minorities to those of his Folks. Both groups were estranged from the
Downtown and Westside power centers. Moreover, minorities were
simmering with resentment toward William Parker, the notoriously
aggressive police chief, and his almost all-white force. Yorty was
thus in a position to combine the strength of the city's two major
"out" groups, Folks and minorities, in a coalition of the marginalized that would have the potential to complicate O'Malley's
Dodger Stadium plans.

While by the spring of 1961 it would be difficult to halt work
on the ballpark itself, there could be delays on permit applications,

time-consuming inspections, and lengthy contract reviews. The proposed Elysian Park access road, which had already elicited harsh criticism, was particularly vulnerable since if elected mayor Yorty would almost certainly scrutinize it closely. O'Malley, a close associate both of Poulson, the symbol of Downtown business Republicanism, and Wyman, the Westside government activist liberal, was an inviting target for Yorty. Sam Yorty had been in city politics for almost thirty years, always on the fringes of power, perennially underfinanced, dismissed as a small-timer, an opportunist, even a crank. The 1961 mayoral race would present this perpetual underdog with a final chance to settle up with the city's establishment classes.

10

THE RISE OF
SAM YORTY

Sam Yorty's electoral coalition would partially resurrect that of the 1958 Dodger contract referendum and the 1959 Arechiga eviction controversy. Downtown and Westside had allied in the cause of getting Dodger Stadium built and removing squatters from its site. They were opposed in each instance by the white homeowners and small businessmen of the city peripheries, as well as by the portions of the Latino community offended by the manner and scope of the removal process. Yorty would seek to reassemble this coalition of "the rest of us" in his mayoral campaign, broadening his outreach to include African Americans, whose humiliations at the hands of William Parker's police force would be a major element of his appeal for votes.

The policy issues that underlay the Dodger Stadium project were central to the Yorty campaign. Should the well-connected, the wealthy, the established, enjoy their own special form of state assistance? Could their gains be justified by the public benefits they produced? Yorty, the outsider's advocate, answered no to both questions. His position aligned with those of Holland and Roybal, who also answered these questions in the negative. Holland viewed undertakings such as Dodger Stadium and Bunker

Hill as public assistance to big business that drove up the taxes of his middle-class constituents. Roybal saw them as mechanisms to push the minority poor out of their homes for renewal projects that primarily benefited the rich. Yorty's mayoral candidacy raised the possibility that an interracial alliance of the marginalized could change the direction of the city.

Historian Don Parson has chronicled the rise of "corporate modernism" in post–World War II Los Angeles, which he describes as a political and social impulse that united both Downtown and Westside behind an agenda of construction, growth, and renewal.[1] Notwithstanding the ethnocultural and geographic rivalries between the two establishments, they agreed on the need for a vital and robust downtown worthy of a world-class city. This would often require the relocation of poor people, people of color, or both. Chavez Ravine and Bunker Hill were illustrative cases. Both Downtown and Westside viewed the destruction of these communities as unfortunate occurrences but necessary preconditions for the creation of a modern Los Angeles. Holland, Roybal, and their constituencies believed that this destruction, along with the attendant expenditures and resource transfers, was too high a price to pay for a modern city that would primarily benefit those who were already successful and well-off.

Of course, few public officials or candidates for office would say they did not wish Los Angeles to be a modern city, just as Holland and Roybal never said they did not want a major league baseball team in the city. The opposite of "modern," however it was defined, carried too many retrograde connotations to be politically palatable. But for Holland's and Roybal's constituencies, the practical implications of a modern Los Angeles in the hands of Downtown and Westside leadership were dispiriting. Grand plans for structures and institutions that would realize the dreams of others. Projects that would dislocate them. Redevelopment that would increase their tax burdens. Civic undertakings that would diminish and in some instances destroy their communities. In the spring of 1961 Holland and Roybal held out from different ideological perspectives against the advent of modern Los Angeles. As the mayoral campaign began, it appeared that Yorty shared their fears

Sam Yorty. *Valley Times* Collection/Los Angeles Public Library. Photographer: Unknown.

and was prepared to make the case for an alternative vision of the city's future.

Making the electoral choices more difficult was the presence of Patrick McGee in the primary race. McGee had been Holland's ally in the City Council through the Dodger contract and Chavez Ravine controversies and represented the anti-Downtown San Fernando Valley. Smooth, articulate, and charismatic, he presented a sharp contrast in style to the more rough-edged Yorty and promised to compete with him for the same voters. McGee was a relatively fresh face on the city's political scene, while Yorty had been around, running for one office or another, since the 1930s. Thanks to his well-publicized criticisms of the Dodger contract, McGee was in fact more closely identified with the city's anti-Downtown forces than Yorty, who was better known for his feuds with the statewide Democratic Party apparatus. It appeared that Yorty would take a backseat even within his own voting constituency.

Poulson himself seemed formidable as he began his campaign for a third term. That he was in the race at all was a surprise. After some cajoling and arm-twisting, Poulson's Downtown supporters had persuaded him to reverse his retirement announcement of May 1960 and run again on a platform of modernization and civic growth. Poulson was assembling a powerful base of support for his run, including establishments in media (the four metropolitan daily newspapers, most notably the *Times*), labor (the Los Angeles AFL-CIO), business (the Chandler empire and real estate, construction, legal, retail, insurance, and financial interests), the local Republican Party organization, and even significant elements of its Democratic counterpart. Poulson had also engaged the services of Baus and Ross, the region's premier political consulting firm, which had engineered his 1953 and 1957 mayoral victories and whose strategies had been instrumental in winning the Proposition B campaign in 1958. Notwithstanding his initial hesitancy about running, Poulson was the clear front-runner as the mayoral race began. But Yorty would have three important advantages: an emotional campaign issue, a powerful media tool, and in time, the physical illness of his opponent. Combined, they would shift the ground under the election and make Yorty, who heretofore had been considered a marginal candidate, into a serious one.

The seemingly prosaic issue of trash removal made many Angelenos, especially in the San Fernando Valley, fighting mad. In 1957, the Poulson administration had supported and city voters had approved a ballot proposition mandating the separation of different types of refuse—cans and bottles, dry (combustible) garbage, and wet (noncombustible) garbage.[2] Trash burning in private homes was prohibited and the city would now be responsible for pickup, replacing commercial sanitation firms.[3] Yorty had represented some of these firms as an attorney and opposed the ballot initiative unsuccessfully. His clients' losses were thus his as well.[4] In 1961, he decided to make what he termed "the oppression of the housewife" a central campaign issue.[5] City trucks were making three different pickups, one for each type of refuse, forcing homeowners—and in Yorty's articulation, housewives—into the time-consuming and messy task of accommodating them. This was an especially emotional issue in the San Fernando Valley, an area that was closely identified with the small householder and which was the epicenter of Yorty's electoral base. It also fit perfectly with

Yorty's anti-Downtown message. What better symbolized the tyranny of City Hall and the city establishment generally than requiring the Folks to pick through their garbage for the convenience of better-situated elites?

Yorty, an extrovert who once claimed he would "rather make a speech than eat," also was quick to recognize television's potential to raise his profile and spread his message.[6] Television could enable him to bypass the four metropolitan daily newspapers, all of which opposed him, and offer a direct and unmediated opening to the people of Los Angeles. The perennially cash-strapped Yorty received a windfall of free airtime when a local television personality named George Putnam proposed that the mayoral candidates appear on his KTTV show every night for a one-minute interview during the two weeks leading up to the April 4 primary election. McGee appeared the first two nights, then decided his time could be put to better use elsewhere. It would be a critical error. Yorty continued on Putnam's show, unopposed and uninterrupted, in what amounted to a series of free campaign commercials.[7] On primary day Poulson led as expected, with 179,273 votes. But Yorty narrowly edged out McGee for second place, 122,478 to 115,635.[8] Yorty owed his 7,000-vote margin to George Putnam's television program, which was aired, in an irony certainly not lost on Norman Chandler, on a station owned by the pro-Poulson *Times*.[9] Yorty and McGee had combined to hold Poulson's primary vote total to 39.7 percent, well below the 50 percent needed to avoid a runoff.[10] It would be the mayor against the self-styled maverick in the general election on May 31, 1961.

Yorty then became the beneficiary of the adage that it is better to be lucky than good. If McGee retired voluntarily from the airwaves, Poulson would do so involuntarily. He came down with a severe case of laryngitis that prevented him from speaking clearly and often from speaking at all during the runoff campaign.[11] Yorty enjoyed almost complete control of the airwaves, while Poulson's infrequent appearances "left the impression," in the words of *Time* magazine, "that he was a sick and tired old man."[12] Poulson's enforced absences left Yorty free to attack the Downtown establishment and business Republican interests almost at will. Yorty was positioned to exploit what historian Mike Davis has called "an accumulation of anti-elite resentments in the electorate."[13] This meant stoking the grievances of the same taxpayer Republican Folks who had felt excluded by the Dodger contract and the Bunker Hill redevelopment and who resented the use of "their" money to realize windfalls for the wealthy.

A Yorty supporter criticized what he considered the Chavez Ravine "giveaway," predicting that property taxes would never recoup the monies lost on the land deal and pointing to the municipal expenditures for police, fire, sewage, and rubbish collection the new stadium would require. The Bunker Hill redevelopment, he claimed, was another money loser in which the city sold property for some $20 million less than it paid for it.[14] It would take a long time before tax revenues were sufficient to offset the bond debt the city had incurred on the project.

Yorty's backer linked the Poulson administration to the main rhetorical targets of the Yorty campaign: high taxes and favoritism for the wealthy. "Do you recall the rubbish promises given by Mr. Poulson?" he asked. "How he promised there would be no added cost to the taxpayer? How he would save them money over private pickup costs? Now there is considerable talk about so much per month for rubbish pickup and even taxes for sewage connection. . . . The Bunker Hill giveaway will raise rents there, and stick the taxpayers with a bill that will require still higher taxes to pay off the bonds and interest. And all for the benefit of private corporations and wealthy people."[15] Chavez Ravine, he argued, could instead have been the site of a municipal hospital and a city jail. While the Yorty supporter admitted that his man was no "mathematical genius"—a sarcastic reference to Poulson's accounting background—Yorty did know "how to figure simple interest and tax revenue."[16] Downtown's numbers did not add up, and Sam Yorty's taxpaying Folks would be left footing the bill for expensive flights of civic fancy.

The pent-up resentments of those who felt excluded from the important decisions in Los Angeles, involving land, construction, taxes, and even refuse, were now coming together in the Yorty challenge to the Downtown establishment. The city's peripheries, its communities, had battled Downtown on a host of issues, more often than not unsuccessfully. Now through the candidacy of one of their own the Folks were seeking to shift the balance of power in the city, outsiders forcing their way inside.

Another group of outsiders drawn to Yorty were African Americans. Long antagonized by the roughhouse tactics of Parker's police, and with virtually no presence in city government, they were a potential source of votes for a candidate who identified with their marginalization. Yorty promised to open City Hall and the political system generally to black Angelenos. His campaign received a crucial boost in the African American community after a Memorial Day altercation in Griffith Park between blacks and police that Parker described as a "race riot."[17] Yorty immediately criticized the commissioner for his remarks and his department's actions, promising that Parker would have to undergo "schooling" in race relations if he wished to retain his job in a Yorty administration.[18] There was no better way for the candidate to demonstrate that he was on the side of the city's black community than to publicly take on the hated Parker. Thanks to the Griffith Park confrontation's proximity to the date of the runoff election, Yorty's remarks were bound to resonate strongly with his intended audience.

In April, the Dodgers began circulating a scale model of the completed stadium for display at local businesses. One of its first stops was Glendale's Valley National Bank, on whose board of directors former Yankee manager Casey Stengel, O'Malley's friendly rival, served.[19] On the stadium work site itself, as Melvin Durslag of the *Examiner* observed, "the isolation of Chavez Ravine is almost eerie, especially when you envision it at night. Aspiring above the hills is the City Hall tower. In terrestrial distance, it is only two miles away, but in spirit infinitely more. There is a loneliness to these hills, linked with civilization by a network of winding roads." Rising out of the darkness, Durslag imagined "an image of the Roman Colosseum itself," a fitting public venue for a city ready to meet the world.[20]

Still, there were many who did not share that vision, including John Holland. The expansion Angels debuted in April 1961, playing home games in the now city-owned Wrigley Field. At an April 26 welcoming luncheon for the team and with O'Malley in attendance, Holland proclaimed, in a sharp dig at the Dodgers, "I'm for the Angels, because it didn't cost the city anything to get them."[21] The next day, during a council session, Holland again contrasted the Angels (along with the Coliseum-renting Rams football team) with the Dodgers: "Like the Rams, the Angels came here without asking us for anything."[22] Joined by Patrick McGee and Phill Silver, Holland traveled to Wrigley Field after the council session for the Angels' home opener.[23]

The significance of the expansion team's future as a tenant of the Dodgers was not lost on Holland, who viewed the arrangement as yet another unearned gain for O'Malley. For his part, Yorty excoriated "the $30 million in city property handed to Walter O'Malley" by Poulson, "in addition to . . . several million dollars for grading and access roads to be built at taxpayer expense."[24] Yorty also opposed the idea of the Angels renting Dodger Stadium in 1962, arguing that they should play at the Coliseum instead.[25] He accused O'Malley of seeking to keep the Angels out of the Coliseum in an attempt to force them into a tenancy deal. Poulson, Yorty charged, was perpetually "looking out for O'Malley." The city of Los Angeles, Yorty said, had "given the Dodgers enough."[26] He maintained that public officials should treat Angels owner Gene Autry "with the same consideration they do O'Malley, Poulson's pal and campaign contributor. The Coliseum is a publicly owned property and no private individual should be able to dictate public policy relating to it. O'Malley has a perfect right to shut off television broadcasts of Dodger games, since he owns the team and operates it purely for profit. But he does not own the Angels and he does not own the Coliseum."[27]

Looming over the mayoral election was the issue of Dodger Stadium. Yorty had made it clear that if he was elected, everything associated with Poulson and Downtown would be subject to review and revision. This might even include the Dodger Stadium contract itself. Certainly Yorty would have allies in the City Council if he wished to revisit the stadium deal. It fit perfectly with his anti-insider campaign rhetoric. Even with the stadium half built, Yorty would conceivably be able to delay or disrupt the process.

Union Oil was relying on a 1962 opening date that would allow it to begin recouping its investment. How completion delays would affect the attitude of O'Malley's primary financier was anyone's guess. The Dodger owner thus was deeply invested in a Poulson victory. But the mayor's general election campaign was shaping up as a disaster. Still hamstrung by voice issues, distracted by a libel suit filed against him by his opponent after accusing Yorty of maintaining mob ties, and ambivalent about continuing in office at all, Poulson's effort was uninspired.

Compounding his difficulties was an ill-considered strategic decision to sideline the Baus and Ross consulting firm, whose work had been so effective in prior campaigns. After the primary election, Baus and Ross advised Poulson to downplay party affiliations in the run-off with Yorty and to emphasize instead the traditional nonpartisan nature of the mayoral race.[28] The firm's principals counseled that in a city in which Democrats enjoyed a 60 percent to 40 percent registration advantage, it would be folly to highlight Poulson's Republican background through appeals to Democrats to desert Yorty.[29]

But the mayor chose to ignore this advice and indeed to shunt Baus and Ross aside altogether during the run-off election campaign, choosing instead to rely on another firm, the Democratic-leaning Snyder-Smith Advertising. Working with state Democratic Party leaders who viewed Yorty as a renegade who had not even supported John F. Kennedy in the 1960 presidential race, Snyder-Smith sought to persuade Los Angeles's Democratic voters to support a Republican.[30] Poulson ads argued that Yorty's election would be a "disgrace to the Democratic Party" and claimed that "under [Poulson's] administration, the Democratic Party has thrived in Los Angeles."[31]

This approach offered Yorty the perfect opportunity to reemphasize one of his perennial campaign points: that the Democratic Party in Los Angeles was "bossed." The only true nonpartisan in the race, according to Yorty, was Sam Yorty. Poulson's wrongheaded general election strategy did as much to promote his opponent as anything Yorty said or did. It effectively negated the Poulson campaign's fifteen-to-one spending advantage and gave Yorty a stature he could not have achieved on his own.[32]

On Election Day, May 31, Baus and Ross's warnings against transforming a nonpartisan contest into a partisan one were borne out. Only 11 percent of the city's Democrats cast ballots for Poulson. This combined with Yorty's strong showing in the African American community to cost Poulson the election.[33] The final total gave Yorty 276,106 votes and Poulson 260,381, a margin of just under 16,000 votes.[34] Yorty carried all three majority African American council districts.[35] A shift of 20,000 votes in those districts after the primary election had provided his margin of victory.[36] Yorty also won all four San Fernando Valley council districts as well as San Pedro, in the extreme south of the city.[37] Wyman's liberal Westside went for Poulson, but it was not enough.[38]

So Yorty's coalition of white homeowners and minorities had won.[39] The victorious candidate lost no time in proclaiming that the days of the "vicious Downtown clique that has long dominated City Hall" were over.[40] "I'm sure the people who voted for me are just as tired of this Downtown clique as I am," he announced the day after the election. "Believe me, they are not going to crawl back in by the back door, either. They're out and they're going to stay out."[41] Yorty pledged to support a redistricting plan that would add another city council position from the San Fernando Valley.[42] He also demanded the resignation of the city's white police commissioners, vowing to replace them with an African American, a Mexican American, and a Valley resident.[43] While he would retain Parker as police chief for the time being, Yorty would expect him "to enforce the law and stop making remarks about the minority groups in this community, because the police have very bad public relations with [them]. . . . We're not living in the South and I expect everyone to be treated equally and fairly."[44] To O'Malley's relief, Yorty said he saw "no point" in repudiating the Dodger contract "unless it develops there is some evidence of outright bribery or fraud."[45] But he did not offer any words of support for the Elysian Park access road, which was crucial to the stadium's success, and indeed, promised a review of all existing city contracts.[46] Disappointed by Poulson's defeat, O'Malley warily awaited what a Yorty administration would bring.

His concerns were borne out when Mayor-elect Yorty asked for a delay in approving the Elysian Park road contract. "There may be ramifications in the contract," he warned, "of which the public is unaware."[47] Yorty asked that appropriations for the road, which were to come from the Los Angeles County gas tax fund outlay of $2.7 million, be held up.[48] O'Malley responded cautiously. "Certainly Mayor-elect Yorty should be given a reasonable opportunity to familiarize himself with all phases of the Dodger contract, and we will be pleased to cooperate," he stated. "We are confident he will be the first to encourage the speedy completion of the work so that the stadium will be ready for the opening of next season. He will find the contract has been litigated and has received the approval of the California and U.S. Supreme Courts as well as the approval of the people of Los Angeles in a referendum."[49]

But the issue was tailor made for Yorty's throw-out-the-insiders appeal. The access road would cut through the largest section of level land in Elysian Park.[50] Yorty said that if an alternative route "would save valuable city property, it should be considered," and he agreed with the assertion of a parks commissioner opposed to the road that it was "a plan for a private enterprise that would ruin our park."[51] Taking its cue from Yorty, the Recreation and Parks Commission on June 30 delayed action on approval of another Dodger Stadium access road, this one leading to Riverside Drive and the Golden State Freeway.[52]

Once sworn into office on July 1, Yorty appointed four new Department of Recreation and Parks commissioners. His single holdover was the one commissioner who had opposed county funding for the access roads.[53] The new mayor asked the new commissioners to study alternative routes for the Elysian Park access road. He promised to "protect the city's interest in Chavez Ravine and Elysian Park. We will not destroy any more of that area than is absolutely necessary to keep the commitment already made—that I would not have made, but which was made before I came into office."[54] If the study determined that the road was not the optimal route, Yorty vowed, "we will try to stop it."[55]

There matters stood on July 24 when O'Malley went to City Hall to speak with the new mayor, a meeting arranged by a Dodger ally, county supervisor Ernest Debs.[56] O'Malley made the case that work on the stadium had progressed too far to alter course. As a self-proclaimed foe of the status quo and established interests, Yorty was expected to stand firmly in the Dodger owner's path. O'Malley had been a close ally of the defeated Poulson. To Yorty, O'Malley's Dodger Stadium deal was Poulson's business Republicanism epitomized. Gains produced by the stadium would come at the expense of the neighborhoods, the peripheries Yorty claimed to represent.

Yet, in the first of what would become a pattern of rapprochement with the same forces he inveighed against during the campaign and for the better part of his political career, Yorty reached an agreement with O'Malley. He emerged from their meeting with a surprising announcement: while he would not explicitly endorse the Elysian Park access road, neither would he stand in its way.[57] The mayor would let the road go through without his formal signature, turning the matter over to the City Council, which he predicted would "approve the route as planned."[58] The candidate who had been so concerned about potential loss of public property was markedly less exercised and more accommodating once installed in office. "It is too late to change," announced Yorty, "and as I came into office after the fact, I will not take a position of sabotaging the ball park."[59]

O'Malley had not been the only interested party at the meeting with the mayor. Debs had attended, as had city attorney Roger Arnebergh, his deputy Bourke Jones, police chief Parker, city traffic manager Sam Taylor, and recreation and parks director George Hjelte.[60] All were supporters of the Dodger Stadium project. Arnebergh and Jones had defended it in court against the Ruben and Kirshbaum taxpayer suits. They may well have nudged the mayor toward a pragmatic decision. The alternative to the proposed route through Elysian Park would have shifted the access road alongside the Dodger Stadium property line and was simply not feasible in Yorty's eyes. It would have given O'Malley one thousand feet of valuable land fronting on the road leading into the stadium property.[61] "We have to proceed on what is best now and not on what would be ideal," Yorty averred.[62]

In the time-honored tradition of blaming difficult decisions on one's predecessor in office, Yorty had the luxury of claiming he would not have agreed to the Elysian Park access road in the first place.[63] But deeds trump words, and when he had to make a decision Yorty chose to accommodate the very power structure he had come into office denouncing. It would not be the last time he would do so. Elected as a nominal Democrat by a makeshift coalition of taxpayer Republicans and minority groups, Yorty would govern as a business Republican. His growth-oriented, modernist civic vision would hew remarkably closely to that of the same Downtown leadership that had supported Poulson and greeted Yorty's election victory with expressions of horror.[64] By the time he ran for a second term in 1965 Yorty would have the endorsement of the *Times* and the Downtown establishment.

Yorty's volte-face can be explained largely by his political personality. He was less an ideologue than a power seeker. Indeed, this perennial outsider had sought power in Los Angeles almost from the moment he stepped off the train from Nebraska in 1927. Once installed in office, Yorty realized he needed the support of the Downtown interests, whose power drew him like a moth to a flame. He was well aware that his 1961 victory had been a near thing, the result of the bad decisions and even the bad health of his rivals. Yorty began planning to win a second mayoral term before he had even started his first. He made a pragmatic decision to jettison his supporters among the Folks on issues affecting the development of Los Angeles's downtown core. But he also made a pragmatic decision to ally with them on racial issues. Yorty would reward his white homeowner supporters among the Folks by joining them in a rearguard action against a black population they viewed as threatening. While Yorty brought some African American officials into city government, his racial rhetoric tracked that of middle- and lower-class whites. He soon earned a reputation as the "white folks" mayor. Yorty had threatened to fire the police chief during the 1961 mayoral campaign, thereby winning African American votes. But once inaugurated he aligned with the hard-nosed Parker and his department, cementing the perception among the Folks that he was "their" mayor.

Yorty thus played a brilliant political double game, throwing over his white middle-class homeowner constituency for the Downtown power structure on economic and development issues but retaining their allegiance as a quid pro quo for his positions on race. Out of apparently contradictory elements Yorty would create a winning coalition, a piece of master political craftsmanship from a man who had spent decades seeking power and did not intend to give it up easily.

Yorty's meeting with O'Malley on July 24 was thus an early signal of what was to come in his administration. It did not mark the ascendency of the Folks in Los Angeles municipal politics, as many had assumed in the wake of Yorty's victory. Yorty was instead more sympathetic to the goals and aspirations of the modernist center than anyone hearing his 1961 campaign rhetoric would have imagined.

But John Holland continued to fight for his own, very different goals. He cast the only dissenting vote when a joint committee of the City Council sent the Elysian Park access road measure to the full body.[65] There Holland continued to argue against it, but the council gave its approval in early August.[66] Holland was losing more than council votes. His vision of a neighborhood-centered Los Angeles living within its financial means and focused on the delivery of basic services was losing out as well. Dodger Stadium, Bunker Hill, and the later Music Center, Disney Concert Hall, Staples Center, and Museum of Contemporary Art projects all involved ambitious and expensive alterations of the downtown landscape. More than merely changing the built environment, they also redirected the civic culture, presenting the face of modernizing growth to the nation and world.

John Holland was not interested in civic baubles of power and sophistication. His Los Angeles was a quieter, less ambitious place. It protected its citizens, paved its streets, educated its children, and collected its trash. It kept taxes low and spent money only when necessary. Its plans were limited and quotidian. It was a city of white middle-class Folks with small homes and visions that extended no further than their immediate neighborhoods. This Los Angeles, however, was being overtaken by one with greater aspirations. Dodger Stadium was its leading edge. Yorty, ostensibly the mayor for the Folks, could have made a stand against this vision of Los Angeles and what it represented. But in the first test of his commitments he chose not to do so. His decision to let the Dodger Stadium project go through undisturbed with an access road cutting through a major public park symbolized his administration's accommodation to the modernizing impulse in the city. By the end of his time in office in 1973, the Los Angeles of the Folks was no more. The city of white midwestern Protestant migrants had been supplanted by one with grand civic dreams, as exemplified by a downtown core deemed worthy of building, renovating, and saving.

It would also be a Los Angeles whose local politics began to reflect its changing demography, as African Americans and Latinos, often allied with liberal Westside forces that were themselves gaining in power and influence, challenged both Downtown and the Folks in legislative halls, boardrooms, government agencies, community organizations, and sometimes the streets. As they did so, John Holland's Los Angeles of localized dreams was fading into memory and nostalgia. When he died in 1970, Holland was eulogized as "the watchdog of the city treasury" and for "his concern about taxpayer money."[67] But by then Dodger Stadium was up, running, and successful, as was the Music Center. The Bunker Hill redevelopment had removed thousands from the neighborhood around the Civic Center, as office towers, upscale housing, and a significantly wealthier clientele began to appear in their places. Holland's vision for the city had been pushed aside by a modernizing tide of building, spending, and taxing. Holland spent most of his political career in City Hall downtown, but his real home lay elsewhere, miles away on quieter streets and sidewalks. His failure to stop the construction of Dodger Stadium encapsulated his failure to steer the city's trajectory inward toward those streets and sidewalks. Los Angeles would now open outward to the nation and world.

11

THE MODERN STADIUM

With the resolution of the access road issue by summer's end, it was clear
the Dodger Stadium project would not be derailed by government
action. It was now up to O'Malley to get the job done. The clock
was ticking inexorably toward April 1962, with no realistic alternative in the event of a missed deadline. By late August, according
to a newspaper account, "earth movers [were] as common as bags
of concrete" on the stadium work site.[1] Dick Walsh admitted, "We
are ahead of schedule on some aspects and behind on others."[2] In
an effort to put the roads issue to rest, the Dodgers agreed to construct and pay for the road that circled the stadium property as
well as all interior arteries. These would permit access to Elysian
Park and the nearby Police Academy.

O'Malley continued to sweat the details, consulting with UCLA
agronomists on the proper strain of grass for the playing field and
insisting that the south-facing parking lots "should overlook the
city" to afford dramatic views.[3] He planned for flowers to be planted
on the slopes surrounding the stadium.[4] He ordered seats with
widths of 19 to 22 inches, befitting the dimensions of the modern
fan.[5] Painfully aware of one of the most publicized shortcomings of
his former Brooklyn home, he planned for an abundance of restrooms—there would be forty-eight in all—to be maintained to the
highest standards of cleanliness.[6] Clean restrooms, O'Malley would

come to believe, were the benchmark of a well-run stadium. The issue of water fountains was also addressed, with O'Malley requesting their placement behind home plate and on each stadium level.[7]

Increasing the pressure on O'Malley to get the stadium finished was the occasion of what was scheduled to be the Dodgers' last home game in the Coliseum, on September 20, 1961. Before the opening pitch Rosalind Wyman presented the Dodger owner with a decorated cake. Sandy Koufax then defeated the Chicago Cubs 3–2 in a thirteen-inning complete-game performance.[8] The team now had paid almost $2 million in rent to the Coliseum Commission over the course of their four-year stay, the largest such sum in sports history.[9] The commission's concessions revenue from Dodger games was also the highest ever recorded for any such period.[10] O'Malley was determined never to write out another rental or concessions check again, but that would depend on the pace of the Dodger Stadium work.

His plans suffered a blow on September 27 when a crane collapsed on the site and damaged a portion of the stands.[11] The next day a replacement crane also collapsed. Work was delayed into mid-October. On a more positive note, the $250 annual memberships for the planned stadium club sold out in a matter of days, and O'Malley was planning to expand the venue's capacity before it even opened officially.[12] By late October, five and a half months prior to opening day 1962, the Dodgers had taken in over $3 million in advance ticket sales, the largest such sum in baseball history.[13]

This gave O'Malley more financial breathing room as he faced the possibility of cost overruns on the stadium. The city of Los Angeles had demanded an expenditure of $1.8 million for water line installations underneath the property and landscaping around it.[14] O'Malley viewed the city's landscaping requirement as an opportunity, albeit an expensive one, to create a parklike environment for the stadium. He was an amateur horticulturalist himself and envisioned the areas surrounding Dodger Stadium awash with lushness and color. He contracted with a landscaping firm to plant trees and flowers on both the stadium grounds and the overlooking hills. O'Malley intended them to become synonymous with the experience of attending a Dodger game, a way to attract families and especially female fans. Wherever possible, he wished to soften the edges of his new venue to make it attractive to a more decorous audience than that in Brooklyn or other existing ballparks. The idea of flowers and trees would have been risible at Ebbets Field, where a largely masculine and working-class fan base held forth passionately and aggressively. But for a different type of constituency in Los Angeles, one O'Malley hoped would be built around fathers, mothers, and children, it would be entirely appropriate. The stadium landscaping program progressed throughout the 1962 season and became an ongoing project for the organization.

By late October 1961 the outside wall of the completed stadium was in place. O'Malley began to encourage site visits from media to report on the progress being made. A United Press International writer noted, "Where last February there had only been a hill and a few pilings standing, today the semi-circular stadium nestles. . . . If all goes well, in the next few weeks the seats can start moving into the stadium."[15] The writer praised the structure's "modernistic look," singling out the column-supported sunshades that adorned the stadium's uppermost deck.[16] He quoted a confident Walsh as predicting, "All we have to fear is for torrential rains within the next couple of months. And a six-month long-range weather forecast we obtained says there shouldn't be really heavy rains until around February or March."[17]

On the other side of the country, another stadium was breaking ground. After the Dodgers' departure from New York, Robert Moses had redoubled his efforts to build a municipally owned stadium in Flushing Meadows, Queens, and on October 28 he spoke at the groundbreaking of the structure he had hoped the Dodgers would occupy. O'Malley was clearly on Moses's mind, and he used the occasion to engage in some rhetorical score settling with the departed Dodger owner. "At [O'Malley's] threat of piracy," he intoned, "the entire nation stood aghast. . . . Walter O'Malley's rendering of Tosti's Goodbye made the first cornettist in Sousa's band look like a national guard bugler. . . . From Walter O'Malley's angle,

there was, to be sure, no gold to be had in tham thar Corona hills. . . .
How could we compete with an entire arroyo in California?"[18]

Moses clung to the idea that his publicly funded stadium, soon
to be named after William Shea, the New York lawyer instrumental
in creating the National League expansion New York Mets, was
superior to O'Malley's ballpark in design and philosophy. Unlike
Dodger Stadium, it would accommodate a variety of sports. Moses
described it as "an all-purpose municipal athletic field" and a part
of "the future Flushing Meadow Park."[19] Moses was confident that
the public sector—under his direction, of course—could provide
for the needs of the city's sports fans more efficiently than businessmen such as O'Malley could. "The folklore of baseball," he predicted, "will cling like ivy over this stadium, encrust it with tradition,
mellow it with the lurid colors of fiction, invest it with the visions
of boyhood and the dreams of age, challenge the giants of Homer,
Rabelais, Bret Harte, Mark Twain, and Daudet and put Paul Bun-
yan to shame."[20]

In Los Angeles, O'Malley read Moses's overheated remarks
with a mixture of bemusement and defiance. He was as convinced
as his old rival that his own way—the entrepreneurial way—was
best for his fans, his city, and of course himself as well. Writing to
a New York friend, O'Malley observed, "It seems more popular
today to be a Socialist and want the public to spend its tax money
for your facilities. After all, it has been a long time since 1923
when the last baseball stadium to be built with private money was
called Yankee Stadium. Since that time, and you can tick them all
off, stadiums have been built on public tax-exempt land with public funds. It is a hell of a shock to find oneself to be old fashioned
but it is darn satisfying."[21]

O'Malley's sentiments would not have been shared by John Holland, who certainly would have argued that the advantages of the
favorable Wrigley Field–Chavez Ravine trade and the financial
benefits of city and county outlays for roads and infrastructure
were forms of public funds. But O'Malley's "old-fashioned" insistence on building his own stadium on his own terms—his risk, his
reward—was indeed a manifestation of a culture that was individ-
ualist and competitive and which privileged the value of freedom

over that of equality. O'Malley prized his independence over all else. Had he accepted Moses's plan to build a public stadium, O'Malley would have forfeited that independence. That he could not abide.

It was this desire to be his own boss that, more than anything else, drove O'Malley to Los Angeles. With the exception of some intervals early in his career, O'Malley had never worked for someone else. He had clients in his law firm, of course, and partners in running the Dodgers, but he was essentially in charge of his own destiny. Renting a municipal stadium in New York from Robert Moses would have made him beholden to the imperious power broker as well as to a shifting cast of local politicians with agendas of their own. Dodger Stadium had put O'Malley into debt. It had forced him into a contentious referendum battle, a costly series of lawsuits, and a racially divisive eviction controversy. It had required him to spend four seasons as a tenant in an expensive and misaligned football stadium. But the structure taking shape in Chavez Ravine belonged to him. Every penny of revenue it generated from tickets, concessions, souvenirs, parking, advertising, and radio and television rights was his. For O'Malley, who once described himself only half jestingly as a "Tory," his "old-fashioned" way of building his stadium was the American way.[22]

It was not, to be sure, an entirely self-reliant way. The fortuitous availability of the Chavez Ravine land had been essential to realizing his plans. Unlike the parcel at Atlantic and Flatbush in Brooklyn, it was already owned by the city of Los Angeles and was made available to him on affordable terms. Even with the money he spent out of his own pocket on properties the city did not acquire, O'Malley was not priced out of the project before it could begin. There was a difference, O'Malley would argue, between government assistance and government ownership. Dodger Stadium benefited him, but it also benefited the people of Los Angeles through job generation, tax payments, and general civic uplift. O'Malley believed that he, a private businessman, could do a better job than any governmental bureaucrat. While the ballpark would not bear O'Malley's name—in November it was officially announced that it would be called Dodger Stadium—his name would define everything that occurred there.[23] O'Malley would be accountable for every inconvenience, every design flaw, and every dissatisfied customer. There would be no hiding behind elected officials or government agencies if the Dodger Stadium experience went awry.

O'Malley thus had the incentive to build and operate a stadium to which fans would return over and over. For this to occur he needed control over his surroundings. He needed to own his stadium. To O'Malley, it was a logical circle. The groundbreaking for Moses's public stadium was a reminder of where he had been and the road he had been unwilling to take.

Shea Stadium, like San Francisco's Candlestick Park, would confirm O'Malley's suspicions about the efficacy of municipally constructed and operated sports venues. Opened in 1964, it was a soulless concrete hulk. Poorly maintained by the city, it accommodated both baseball and football awkwardly. Originally budgeted at $12 million, Shea Stadium's $25.5 million final price tag exceeded that of Dodger Stadium.[24] Few lamented its demolition after the 2008 baseball season. Moses's verbal pyrotechnics in New York and even the barbs Moses directed at him carried the air of vindication for O'Malley. His model of stadium construction would work. New York's would not. He was exactly where he should be.

Dodger Stadium continued to rise and O'Malley continued to be deeply involved in details that most owners would have left to subordinates. In late September he received a letter from one of his subcontractors, Allied Maintenance, regarding the installation of water fountains. "I am very pleased that you agree that public water fountains are part of a ballpark," Allied's representative wrote, "and that they will not interfere with the concession sales. In following your suggestion of locating these fountains behind home plate at each level, additional fountains might be located in the left and right field areas on each level, or perhaps near the rest room facilities where the public could be easily directed."[25]

A few weeks later, O'Malley personally walked the distance between a parking lot location and its designated stadium gate to see for himself whether the distance involved would be too great for the average patron.[26] He memoed Walsh that the stalls in the women's restrooms contained hooks instead of the shelves that O'Malley believed would better accommodate handbags.[27] He asked the city's Traffic Department to label freeway exit signs "Dodger Stadium" instead of "Elysian Park," writing half sarcastically that "they can call any of the roads anything they want to as long as they also have signs indicating that the poorest kept secret in the world is open for business and its name is Dodger Stadium."[28] Water fountains, walking distances, women's restrooms, and highway signs—O'Malley had his hand in everything, large and small.

There were things he could not control, however. Heavy rains in December mocked the long-range weather forecast Walsh had touted, slowing progress.[29] "Every time it rains," complained one of the contractors, "[it] turns into a sea of mud."[30] The crucial access road from the Golden State Freeway was behind schedule and crews were laboring six days a week from dawn to dusk in order to make up time.[31] In the midst of this, O'Malley was forced to borrow more money, with Union Oil again playing the role of bank. The company advanced the Dodgers an additional $3 million against advertising revenues, to be repaid with 5 percent interest by December 31, 1970.[32] Annual payments on this debt were scheduled to begin in January 1963, after revenues began to flow from the new stadium.[33] While the Dodger–Union Oil partnership would prove financially beneficial to both parties, O'Malley was now heavily leveraged as he raced to complete his stadium.

By late December seats were going in and parking areas were being blacktopped. The installation of elevators had begun.[34] Battling the rains, workers were grading the playing field. After the New Year, O'Malley wrote to Walt Disney, inviting him to view the stadium: "I know you've been keenly interested, and if you would like to come up and go over the layout with me, I'd be delighted to get your reactions, good and bad."[35] Already observers were comparing the new stadium to a theme park, with visiting reporters "so overwhelmed by the project that they believe O'Malley's new ballpark will be a showpiece comparable to Disneyland and Knott's Berry Farm."[36]

O'Malley considered comparisons of Dodger Stadium to Disneyland praise of the highest order. The Orange County amusement park was his ideal and model. Walt Disney had mastered the art of moving large numbers of guests from highways to parking lots to ticket windows to entry gates to concession stands to attractions and then back out the way they came, all while offering an entertainment experience that replaced life as it was with an image of life as it could be imagined. Disneyland was a constructed myth, a happy escape to a better place.[37] Walt Disney was a salesman and a marketer. He wished to bring as many guests through his park as he could. He offered streamlined, packaged, and efficient entertainment in an environment in which his guests were controlled and managed but largely unaware of it. Disney sold commercialized fantasy. O'Malley hoped to sell it as effectively in his new stadium as the master of the craft did at the nation's premier theme park.

To that end, O'Malley dispatched Dick Walsh and other top front office personnel to Disneyland for an in-depth study of its operations.[38] They came away with a blueprint for what they wanted their own park to be. Disneyland's guest services were obsessively focused on courtesy, safety, and cleanliness. So would Dodger Stadium's. An amusement park differs from a ballpark in its greater control of guest outcomes—there was, of course, no final score in Disneyland. But levels of convenience, efficiency, and atmosphere could be controlled at Dodger Stadium, and O'Malley was determined they would be. Everything he had planned for his showpiece would advance those goals. Dodger Stadium would match Disneyland and perhaps surpass it as a destination for entertainment, excitement, and escape.

Just before the New Year, O'Malley assembled a stadium dedicatory committee to coordinate the formal activities surrounding opening day, April 10, 1962. His larger purpose in organizing such a group was to mend old wounds and at last present a united public front on the stadium issue to the people of Los Angeles. O'Malley got his wish. The committee, according to the *Sporting News*, "embraces a blue-ribbon membership list of the city's business, communications, religious, sports, financial and entertainment industries."[39]

O'Malley was most interested in political rapprochement. At the committee's December 1961 organizational lunch, Yorty, its honorary chair, reached out to Poulson, his defeated rival, posing amicably with him for photographers while shaking his hand.[40] "I appreciate the great job Norris did in helping bring major league baseball to Los Angeles," said Yorty, in a far cry from the Downtown establishment-bashing of his mayoral campaign. John Holland was also at the lunch along with thirteen of the other fourteen City Council members. Acknowledging that events had moved past him, Holland said: "The fighting is all over. I'd oppose the Dodgers again if I thought the city was getting the worst of it, but I'm a baseball fan."[41] Harold McClellan, the local businessman who had negotiated the Dodger contract on behalf of the city, tried to bring the civic curtain down on the stadium battle and project an image of unanimity. "There are men here today," he told a reporter, "who had differences of opinion regarding the advent of major league baseball in Chavez Ravine, but now we are all pulling together for this community, and it bodes well."[42] Reporting on the lunch, the *Sporting News* remarked on "a new community spirit" in Los Angeles.[43]

The theme of the Dodgers as civic unifiers was now on everyone's minds. *Herald-Examiner* editor Franklin Payne exulted that "the Dodgers have done more to pull this great community together into one unit than any one thing I can think of."[44] At a January 1962 B'nai B'rith dinner honoring O'Malley as Man of the Year, actor Edward G. Robinson told the audience of thirteen hundred that the team had "unified" Los Angeles.[45] It was true, of course, that the closer the stadium came to completion, with its grandstands and light towers visible over Chavez Ravine, the more it became an accepted fact. For many Angelenos who had been on the fence throughout the stadium battle, its looming presence also retroactively validated the process by which it had come to be. The project now possessed a quality of inevitability that blunted the edges of the struggle to build it.

But the civic argument over Dodger Stadium left a residue of bitterness in portions of the city that celebratory unity lunches and awards dinners could not heal. Latinos, even those who were Dodger fans, mourned the loss of a community at Chavez Ravine. The Folks on the city peripheries, John Holland's people, would cheer for the Dodgers but were still not reconciled to the transfer of public resources to an entrepreneur. As the stadium work ground on toward opening day, it carried along with it a city with a fragile unity. O'Malley's new ballpark represented a modern Los Angeles, but not all of Los Angeles. Dodger Stadium's legacies would include a Latino community that supported both the Dodgers and a burgeoning 1960s Chicano movement built on the metaphorical ground of Chavez Ravine. It would also include a disgruntled white homeowner population suspicious of government-sponsored spending projects for the benefit of the "undeserving," a term that could easily morph from the favored businessman to the minority poor. For those who felt left behind by the city's modernist turn, Dodger Stadium offered only the facade of civic unity. These outsiders would neither forget nor forgive.

O'Malley's major problem in late January and February 1962 was rain, tons of it. Early in the month, just as the playing field was ready for sodding, it poured torrentially, forcing a ten-day delay while the area was dried and reconditioned.[46] Then as the sod was being installed it rained again for five more days, washing away the field's topsoil. The rains also delayed the blacktopping of the parking lots.[47] In all, the rains caused $500,000 in damages, including the costs of clearing away debris caused by the downpours.[48]

After seventeen inches of rain fell during the first three weeks of February, a desperate O'Malley used helicopters, hovering overhead with blades rotating, to dry the field.[49] He even rented a jet airplane engine to blast hot air from a truck.[50] Amid speculation the stadium would not be ready for opening day, O'Malley held firm: "I wouldn't even consider anything other than Chavez Ravine for April 10 and every day thereafter. I am a stubborn man. We will hit the target date no matter what the weather."[51] When the rains finally tailed off in March, O'Malley was left with about a month for the race to the finish line. Paying overtime for close to round-the-clock work, he made up for lost time.[52]

In the meantime, he received some good news from Yorty, who rejected a proposal for a sporting event admissions tax to help close the $11.5 million budget gap that he had inherited from Poulson.[53] O'Malley had fought unsuccessfully against such a tax in New York, and the idea had been put forward by Rundberg after he switched sides in the stadium battle. O'Malley had prevailed on Poulson to reject the tax, but Yorty, with his anti-Downtown campaign rhetoric, threatened to be another story. However, the new mayor continued to conciliate the same business interests he had criticized so harshly as a candidate. Yorty now voiced the hope that property tax revenues on new construction in Los Angeles would cover the budget shortfall without the necessity for a ticket tax—indeed, without the need to raise taxes on existing real estate at all.[54]

Yorty thus moved closer to the positions of the Downtown business establishment represented by Poulson. During the mayoral campaign Yorty had denounced "the $30 million worth of city property handed to Walter O'Malley" and Poulson's gift of "several million dollars for grading and access roads to be built at taxpayer expense."[55] But by early 1962 Mayor Yorty had reconciled with his erstwhile opponent as well as with Poulson's modernist vision for the city. As an integral component and perhaps the most prominent symbol of that vision, Dodger Stadium was now the object of Yorty's beneficence. Yorty the mayor opposed the same ticket tax that Yorty the candidate would have supported as part of his attack on the "Downtown clique." Yorty had made his peace with the Downtown establishment. All political roads now led to Chavez Ravine.

By mid-March, work was proceeding rapidly. Almost all of the stadium's fifty-six thousand seats were installed, the light towers were being put in place, and the scoreboard was on the way from its Des Moines, Iowa, manufacturer.[56] With drier weather, construction of the access roads moved forward again, and by late March five of the six, including the crucial seven-lane Elysian Park connection, were either complete or nearly so.[57] Walsh advised motorists to plan out their itineraries to the new stadium in advance. "There are enough roads to get a capacity crowd in and out in an hour—if the public is familiar with the area," he told the *Herald-Examiner*. "This is a whole new travel experience for everybody in Southern California, a new system of roads. But like anything else of the kind, it can be learned."[58] In the same story, *Herald-Examiner* columnist Bob Oates enthused that the view from the stadium's top deck "provides the best baseball view in America for $1.50."[59] The authoritative Jim Murray of the *Times* described Dodger Stadium as it neared completion as a "gorgeous triumph of high-rise architecture in living Technicolor with levels of ocher, aqua, coral and sky-blue, with umbrellas of concrete escarping a perimeter that looks on the mountains of San Gabriel. It will be the Taj Mahal of sport."[60]

On April 9, the day before the season was to begin, with last-minute preparations and adjustments under way up the hill at Chavez Ravine, grand opening ceremonies were held for Dodger Stadium on the steps of City Hall. Baseball commissioner Ford Frick commended O'Malley's "courage, imagination, and stamina to move a mountain. When you see that thing out there, that stadium, then you will visualize the answers to some of those crybabies who say baseball is dying."[61] County supervisor and former councilman Ernest Debs, a stadium contract supporter from the beginning, ceremonially offered O'Malley his own personal copy of the Los Angeles County budget for 1962 and remarked pointedly, "We are looking forward to taxes from the Dodger Stadium to help balance the budget."[62]

From City Hall a noon motorcade transported O'Malley, Dodger players, and public and team officials to the new stadium, where some two thousand invited guests ate lunch and watched master of ceremonies Vin Scully introduce a succession of speakers, including Frick; Cardinal James McIntyre of the Archdiocese of Los Angeles; chief Dodger contract negotiator Harold McClellan; prominent local rabbi Edgar Magnin; Yorty, who offered words of praise for Poulson; and O'Malley himself.[63] The ceremonies dragged on for six hours, and the audience drifted away while workers scurried to complete last-minute details. A large crane lifted and assembled pieces of the left-field message board.[64] The field, which had not fully recovered from the rains of February, had to be colored with green dye for aesthetic effect.[65] Arguments over the exact shade of the paint color on the outfield fences continued throughout the day until Jack Yount made a unilateral decision. His men finished the job after darkness had fallen.[66]

But the stadium was ready to open, and his financial obligations notwithstanding, all of it belonged to Walter O'Malley. "I am not a socialist and am strong for private property," O'Malley had told a Pasadena newspaper before the stadium's opening ceremonies. "I feel that stadiums should be built by private enterprise although in this age it is almost impossible to do so. At the same time, however, we did build our own stadium."[67]

John Holland, of course, would have disagreed, as he had from the moment the Dodger Stadium contract was proposed. He could not reconcile himself to state-sponsored dispensations employed in the service of a private undertaking. But O'Malley had tethered his stadium to growth-oriented, corporate modernist impulses that were more powerful than the constituencies Holland represented. These impulses crossed lines of party, ideology, race, ethnicity, and geography. They even had attracted Mayor Yorty, who had been elected just a year earlier on a platform of opposition to them. On April 10, 1962, Los Angeles would have a ballpark that epitomized a modern city, a showplace to match its dreams. It would be a unique accomplishment, made possible by the work and investment of a private individual. But it would not be the work of free enterprise alone. O'Malley instead effected a partnership with the state for the resources he needed. He then employed those resources along with those of his own to build a stadium that would help him immeasurably, but would help the city of Los Angeles as well.

But how to balance the two? At what point did the magnitude of individual gain outweigh public benefit enough to skew that balance unjustly? Norris Poulson and Rosalind Wyman offered different answers to these questions than did John Holland and Edward Roybal. The stadium that was about to open was proof that in this instance Poulson and Wyman's answers would be the determining ones. The stadium also expressed Downtown and Westside's agreement to employ public resources—taxpayer resources—to cast Los Angeles in the image of growth and progress, building an institution befitting a world-class city. Holland and Roybal represented different understandings of what Los Angeles could be, with plans for the city pitched on smaller scales. Holland's Folks and Roybal's Latinos may have had more in common than they realized. Both stood on the geographic, social, and economic peripheries of the city. Both desired a modest piece of economic security—a house, a job, a business. Their dreams lay closer to the ground, in communities and streets. Their vision of Los Angeles did not require it to be a world-class city. It did not even require Dodger Stadium. But other visions did, and there it was on April 9, 1962, gleaming and waiting, in a city of no little plans.

Fittingly, Poulson and Wyman were special guests when Dodger Stadium opened the next day. April 10 dawned warm and sunny, with cars out early on the roads to the new ballpark. The police chief, fearing massive tie-ups, had advised fans to carpool and to leave extra time for traffic delays.[68] But the flow was relatively smooth. Dodger starting pitcher Johnny Podres, heeding Parker's warning about arriving early, caught a cab in front of his downtown hotel just before 9:00 A.M. He was at the stadium's players' entrance gate in only ten minutes.[69] While not everyone fared nearly as well, there were few traffic-related complaints on opening day. At the pregame ceremonies O'Malley's wife, Kay, received the honor of throwing out the ceremonial first pitch, as the city's political, business, and entertainment establishment looked on.[70] Shortly thereafter, visiting Cincinnati Red shortstop Eddie Kasko had the honor of getting the stadium's inaugural hit, a first-inning double off Podres, as well as that of scoring its first run on a Vada Pinson single.[71] The Reds went on to win, 6–3.

There were a number of relatively minor stadium glitches— misspelled signs, malfunctioning turnstiles, lack of security in the Dodger offices—but one of them threatened to become a major one in the local media.[72] The original plans, which O'Malley had approved, called for the installation of water fountains on each of the stadium's levels and in the outfield pavilions.[73] But they were missing on opening day, and the story quickly grew to conspiratorial dimensions, with O'Malley portrayed as subsidizing his beer and soft drink sales through the omission. The State of California's Division of Labor Law Enforcement then became involved, ordering their immediate installation. O'Malley had thirteen fountains operating in the stadium by the end of April.[74] Still, the incident lingered among O'Malley's critics, who continued to maintain this oversight was deliberate. While there was no proof that the missing water fountains were anything other than a builder's mistake, they lived on as a form of urban legend in the minds of those critics.

Water fountains aside, reviews of the new stadium were enthusiastic and in some instances ecstatic. The *Times*'s Jack Smith rhapsodized that Dodger Stadium "seems unique and marvelous to me because it couldn't have happened in any other time and place in civilization, and it most likely [will] never happen again. In 100 years, I predict, Dodger Stadium will be as great a curiosity as the Colossus of Rhodes and the Hanging Gardens of Babylon."[75] A visiting sportswriter from Albuquerque called the new ballpark "the baseball stadium of the future. You're going to have to give John Q. Public something beside a hard-seat bench, a greasy hot dog, and an ice-filled cup that passes as a soft drink. O'Malley went a bit further than most because his revolutionary plant offered many, many new items. He keeps you engrossed."[76] Another out-of-town writer described Dodger Stadium as "Disneyland with a baseball diamond."[77] To Jim Murray, the city's sports tastemaker, it was "the Taj Mahal, the Parthenon, and Westminster Abbey of baseball."[78]

Dodger Stadium would be a rousing success in 1962, attracting 2,755,184 fans and shattering all-time Dodger and major league attendance records. Team income on the year was slightly over $13 million, of which approximately $7.5 million represented ticket sales.[79] Net profit totaled $1,177,000.[80]

The stadium's look, operation, and culture were distinctively modern. Its lines were sleek and symmetrical. They opened out to their surroundings rather than closing inward, as did more traditional parks. Views were unobstructed and theater-like in their positioning of seats on direct angles to the stage of home plate and mound. It was efficient, funneling fans in, through, and out in a manner worthy of Disneyland. While heavy automobile traffic would always present challenges, the number of access roads and adjacent highways, combined with the size and layout of the stadium parking lots—sixteen thousand individual spaces leveled according to seat location and coordinated from a rooftop command post—made travel to the stadium, if not always the most pleasant of experiences, still more convenient than travel to most other Southern California entertainment attractions.[81] Ballpark employees, like their counterparts at Disneyland, were trained to be unfailingly courteous and pleasant. Dodger Stadium ushers, many of whom were full-time team employees, quickly gained a reputation as the friendliest in baseball. Even parking lot attendants, traditionally among the surliest of ballpark workers, were civil. In a first, the Dodgers stationed a fan relations representative on each level of the stadium to offer assistance and guidance.[82]

Dodger Stadium also resembled Disneyland in the quality of its entertainment values. From the game's biggest and most sophisticated scoreboard to its elegant stadium club to numerous giveaway days and even to the iconic "Dodger Dog" frankfurter, the fan experience in the new ballpark was designed to stand independent of the game itself. If this gave the Los Angeles Dodger fan the reputation of having less outward passion and sophistication than the Brooklyn Dodger fan, there were many more of them, and thus more profits for the team. Dodger Stadium fans continued to sit in the stands with transistor radios listening to Vin Scully describe what they were seeing with their own eyes. Los Angeles Dodger fans also settled into the habit of responding to cheering cues orchestrated by the house organist and the scoreboard operator. It was, to be sure, a more controlled form of spectatorship than that displayed at Ebbets Field, where the crowds were known for their quirky spontaneity.

Dodger Stadium was a family-oriented venue, structured and organized for the comfort and convenience of parents and children. It probably attracted a higher proportion of female fans than any other major league ballpark. The team had enjoyed strong African American support from its beginnings in Los Angeles, and this carried over to Dodger Stadium, where the 1962 Dodger roster featured five black players, each of whom enjoyed local celebrity status. O'Malley's outreach to the Latino community also paid off with significant fan interest. While the Arechiga evictions had not been forgotten, they did not appear to affect loyalty to the Dodgers among Los Angeles Latinos. Politics and culture, at least when it came to sitting in the Dodger Stadium stands, appeared to be severable for much of the city's Latino population. Latinos represented a foundational element of the Dodger customer base in 1962 and remained so afterward.

Dodger Stadium, in fact, was probably Los Angeles's most diverse cultural institution, one of the rare patches of common ground for a city stratified along lines of class and race. The $3.50/$2.50/$1.50 ticket price structure was a relatively reasonable one, and particularly so for a city the size of Los Angeles. The price point differential between each ticket level was small enough to permit generally integrated seating patterns. Tickets were available on a day-of-game basis in all price categories. While box seats obviously attracted fans with higher income levels, their $3.50 cost was not so far removed from those of reserved or general admission tickets as to make them unaffordable.

As a result, customers at Dodger Stadium represented a cross section of classes and races. The chances that the fan in an adjoining seat was of a different background was higher there than in almost any other public venue in the city. Stadium club boxes and dugout-level seats, which were of course price-exclusionary and thus class and race-stratified, represented only 3 to 4 percent of the available seating at Dodger Stadium.[83] The stadium's atmosphere, with its emphasis on efficiency, standardization, and control, may have epitomized midcentury American middlebrow culture in a sports setting. Dodger Stadium's culture differed from more traditional spectator experiences, where winning alone was the measure of a good day at the ballpark. Dodger Stadium fans were entertained win or lose, and if this diminished the significance of the final score, it also made the game accessible to a broader audience that traversed lines of class, race, and gender.

The Dodger Stadium experience was less emotionally intense than at other ballparks, but it was more inclusive and diverse. Its combination of low ticket prices and entertainment-oriented game presentations drew in guests from the city in all of its breadth. What they saw may indeed have been middlebrow in character, but it was not exclusionary. Indeed, it was calculated to attract as many customers from as many parts of Los Angeles as possible. For the hundreds of thousands of Latinos, African Americans, and women who attended Dodger home games in 1962 and afterward, the Dodger Stadium stands were one of the few safe public spaces in Los Angeles.

While the 1962 season at Dodger Stadium was a successful one if measured by attendance, fan satisfaction, and aesthetics, it was less so on the playing field. The year saw the emergence of left-handed pitcher Sandy Koufax as baseball's best hurler and short-stop Maury Wills as the game's premier base stealer. But Koufax was sidelined with a circulatory injury to his index finger in July and was lost for over two months.

Koufax's absence was ultimately too much for the Dodgers to overcome in 1962. Ahead of the pursuing San Francisco Giants by four games with only seven left to play, they lost six of them and allowed their bitter rivals to tie them on the last day of the regular season. After splitting the first two games of a best-of-three pennant playoff with the Giants, the Dodgers carried a 4–2 lead into the ninth inning of the deciding game at Dodger Stadium. Before a disbelieving home crowd the Dodgers unraveled, allowing four Giant runs on four walks, a wild pitch, and an error. The Giants' improbable 6–4 victory sent them to the World Series.

The Dodgers and their fans were left with the accumulation of terrible ifs that haunts the dreams of the losers of excruciatingly close games. Comparisons to the 1951 season, when the Dodgers had also lost a substantial late-season lead to the Giants and carried a three-run advantage into the last inning of the final playoff game only to lose to the Giants on Bobby Thomson's home run, were inevitable. In some ways the 1962 loss was even more painful. The Dodgers had needed only one victory in their last three regular-season games, all played at home, to clinch the pennant.

They lost all of them and were shut out in the last two. Their melt-down in the ninth inning of the final playoff game was a messy, ugly affair played out before Dodger Stadium fans, in contrast to the dramatic 1951 loss, which had come at the Giants' Polo Grounds on an iconic home run. It was also agonizingly clear that a healthy Koufax during the second half of the regular season would have meant the pennant.

There would, however, be better years. Koufax put together spectacular seasons in 1963, 1965, and 1966, leading the Dodgers to National League pennants all three years and to world champi-onships in 1963 and 1965. The quality of baseball on the field was thus never an issue during the first five years of Dodger Stadium's operation. But the stadium may have been even more successful as an entertainment venue, cultural unifier, and civic state of mind. It served as a symbol for a modern Los Angeles that strove to be more than the sum of its individual neighborhoods, a city with a core and a center. UCLA chancellor Franklin Murphy, a leading growth advocate, understood Dodger Stadium's symbolic meaning and importance for the city's future. Congratulating O'Malley on the ballpark's completion in April 1962, he wrote: "As a citizen who believes strongly that Los Angeles is in the process of growing from just a big city to a great city, I want you to know that I think you have contributed as much in accelerating this change as any man in this vast center of population. . . . You have forced the people of Los Angeles to think in big-league and big-city terms. In the process the city has gotten a beautiful stadium and major league baseball, but I think the symbolism of your effort is even more important. By stimulating the people to think in large terms you have made the Music Center, the new art museum and other impor-tant facilities more easily obtainable."[84]

Dodger Stadium was indeed the first in a line of civic undertak-ings that would transform the identity of Los Angeles from a neigh-borhood city to a world metropolis. At issue in the struggle over the stadium were arguments over the nature and function of a city. What were its purposes? Simply to provide for the everyday needs of its citizens—policing, education, sanitation, and social services? Or something broader—to elevate, to uplift, to leave monuments

World Series game at Dodger Stadium, 1965. *Los Angeles Herald-Examiner* Collection/Los Angeles Public Library. Photographer: Ben White.

in its wake? John Holland and Edward Roybal had fought against the vision of Los Angeles that Dodger Stadium represented. But their Los Angeles—a city with limits on its grander dreams, one that strove to assist the everyday people, whether Holland's homeowners or Roybal's minority poor—was not the Los Angeles of Dodger Stadium, nor of the Music Center, which was completed in 1964. Nor was it the Los Angeles of the Bunker Hill redevelopment project, which over a period of decades beginning in the 1960s replaced a working-class neighborhood with high-rise office buildings, luxury apartments, upscale restaurants, and cultural institutions.

Whatever their partisan political differences may have been, Westsider Democrat Rosalind Wyman and Downtown Republican Norris Poulson agreed that institutions such as Dodger Stadium and the Music Center would define modern Los Angeles.[85] Even Sam Yorty, champion of the Folks, came to share this vision. The

Los Angeles of the 1960s would be built in the image of sleek and modern Dodger Stadium. The new ballpark served as the reflection of an ambitious and modern city.

Given Los Angeles's Progressive-influenced political structure, O'Malley's success in constructing Dodger Stadium becomes all the more impressive. Like many Western states in the early twentieth century, California used the negative example of machine-dominated eastern and midwestern cities to adopt a system of power devolution that sought to decenter the weight of political influence and bring it as near ground level as possible.

The state of California came as close as any other to enacting the Progressive legislative agenda in its entirety, including the referendum device, which played such an important role in the Dodger Stadium battle. This, combined with Los Angeles's nonpartisan electoral system, made it almost impossible for a political boss to wrest enough concentrated power to dominate the city. Nor could an unelected administrator like New York's Robert Moses amass the bureaucratic power to personally control its built environment. While the Chandler family continued to wield substantial influence over political and economic life in Los Angeles during the 1950s and 1960s, even Norman Chandler could not have cleared the way for Dodger Stadium with a stroke of his pen, as Moses could have in New York. In Los Angeles, Chandler and the city's other power brokers had to sweat out an uncomfortably close referendum on the stadium contract; they could affect the popular will through the work of firms such as Baus and Ross but not dictate it. In Los Angeles, John Holland, a provincial city councilman without a city-wide power base, was able to delay the Dodger Stadium project for more than four years and nearly derailed it. In New York, had he chosen to approve a new Dodger baseball stadium, Robert Moses would have squashed Holland like a bug.

But Los Angeles's decentered, anti-machine political system, for all its good intentions, had the practical effect of creating a disorganized civic environment in which it became more difficult for men of no little plans like O'Malley to get things done. It made the route to Dodger Stadium's opening day in April 1962 a circuitous and even tortuous one. The average Angeleno, including the Folks of John Holland's Eagle Rock district and the homeowners of the San Fernando Valley, possessed individual voices that carried loudly and powerfully. It was impossible to simply brush those voices aside in the manner of the boss of an eastern or midwestern political machine or even a self-styled good-government power broker like Moses.

O'Malley succeeded in building his stadium, of course. But to do so he had to travel down different avenues. He was forced to rely on a consulting firm in the Proposition B referendum, something that would have been unnecessary in cities such as New York and Chicago, where party organizations would have brought out the requisite voters. It forced him to deal with a chaotic host of disparate administrative boards and agencies—regulating zoning, traffic, highways, public safety, education, housing, and health—on a piecemeal basis, slowing the process of building the stadium. He was even forced to appeal directly to the voters through a television program—Dodgerthon—that also would have been superfluous in cities where political power was more centralized. Thus, in an irony that O'Malley would have ruefully appreciated, the very Progressive-influenced structure that gave average citizens in Los Angeles more power than they had in New York repeatedly threw up roadblocks to the successful completion of his ballpark.

Direct democracy is often the bane of those with no little plans. In Los Angeles it substituted the advertising techniques of Baus and Ross for the brute dictates of Robert Moses and the power of the media for that of the party apparatus. Thanks to the efforts of Hiram Johnson and the California Progressives of the early twentieth century, the age of the all-powerful boss—such as Richard Daley, James Michael Curley, Tom Pendergast, and in his own way, Robert Moses—largely bypassed Los Angeles. Civic leaders promoted an image of the city as clean and uncorrupted, free from the taint of machine politics. But decentralized and unbossed cities were often challenging places in which to push through major projects, as O'Malley discovered when he stepped off the plane from New York in 1957.

The battle to build Dodger Stadium was waged by Downtown and Westside leaders who wished to halt their city's decentering momentum and impose a common identity through a core of civic institutions. Los Angeles's Progressive heritage made this task harder, not easier. But to John Holland and Edward Roybal, who questioned the wisdom of that undertaking in the first place, that may not have been a bad thing. A regime of referendums, undergirded by advertisers and media, would ensure that in Los Angeles centralizers and civic institution builders would not go unchallenged. Their victories, when they came, would be hard-won.

The Dodgers made good on their promise to augment the city's economy through tax revenues, although not without more controversy. In 1963 the Los Angeles County assessor set the Dodger Stadium property tax bill at double the $345,000 figure O'Malley maintained had been agreed upon during his negotiations to move from New York. O'Malley appealed to the County Board of Supervisors.[86]

He received little sympathy there. "Mr. O'Malley will be expected to pay his fair share of property taxes, just like any other private enterprise," said supervisor Ernest Debs, who as a city councilman had strongly supported the Dodger contract.[87] Another contract supporter, Kenneth Hahn, asserted that the Dodgers were "a virtual gold mine."[88] Supervisor Frank Bonelli thundered, "It is almost sacrilegious for the Dodgers to be before this Board on an errand like this before the paint is dry on the stadium."[89] O'Malley was unable to convince a majority of the supervisors that the $345,000 yearly tax bill promised in 1957 had been anything more than a nonbinding estimate.[90] The Board of Supervisors upheld the assessment on Dodger Stadium, and by 1965 the team was paying $800,000 annually to the county.[91] Over the course of the succeeding decade the Dodgers would pour an additional $7 million in property tax revenue into the local economy, for a post-1962 total of almost $10 million—a sum considerably greater than the amount of rent collected by any other city operating a municipal stadium.[92]

Los Angeles's investment in the Dodgers had paid off with financial benefits for both city and team. By this measure the Dodger Stadium deal was a model of public-private cooperation. O'Malley believed deeply in the ethos of free enterprise. He opposed what he considered "socialistic ideas" in the baseball business. In 1963, he criticized baseball commissioner Ford Frick's plan to divide national television and radio revenues equally and to increase the visiting team's share of the road game gate receipts.[93] "Let us consider the effect of this," O'Malley argued, referring to his own team, "on a club that has built its own ballpark with its own funds and has developed a cash flow program for retiring its debts. The proposals would probably be disastrous. . . . [They are] bound to appeal to the 'have-nots' who are more numerous than the 'haves.' "[94] He continued in a sarcastic vein:

> If we go partially socialistic why not go all the way. . . . Let's equalize all investments in baseball, give credits on such items as real estate taxes, which vary from a high of $750,000 (Dodgers) to $20,000 per year in different clubs, let's share concessions, equalize front office salaries, scouting expenses . . . pension and profit sharing plans, let's make everybody line up and do the same. Let's demand that everybody have the same seating capacity, same ticket prices, let's each have the same degree of maintenance and painting, equalize the major league salaries, then we can all sit and draw lots for the different franchises and see what can be done when everybody is his brother's socialistic palsy walsy.[95]

In time many of O'Malley's fears of "socialism" in baseball were realized, including a player draft, shared television revenues, and taxes on teams that paid excessive salaries. O'Malley's own orientation, and that of Peter O'Malley, his son and successor as Dodger president, remained entrepreneurial and individualistic, with Dodger Stadium itself standing as the embodiment of their free enterprise principles. Yet their successes were not so much examples of the unfettered market at work as they were the fruits of a government-business cooperative arrangement that had more to do with Henry Clay than Adam Smith and where public aligned with private in the interest of the common good.

But who would make such judgments? On what basis? Did the size of O'Malley's bank account matter as long as the people of Los Angeles could enjoy a beautiful, affordable, entertaining baseball stadium? In the wake of City Council votes, a referendum, and a series of court rulings, not to mention millions of Dodger Stadium fans, it was clear that to many Angelenos, perhaps most, it did not. But there were still those in Los Angeles who would not let go of the idea that O'Malley had received a gift of public resources. No matter how many cheering Dodger fans packed their way into the ballpark on sunny summer afternoons or how many pennants and World Series the home team won, to that group the stadium deal would always exemplify a version of capitalism in which the state bestowed its favors selectively. Theirs was a populist vision that might well have animated Andrew Jackson at an earlier time in the nation's history.

One did not need to be a leftist or even a liberal Democrat like Edward Roybal to hold this view. John Holland was a business-man and a conservative Republican. But he too believed in a level field of economic play devoid of state-sponsored favoritism. To Holland, public resources belonged to all the people of Los Angeles. They should not be diverted, even to those proposing to use them to advance the public good.

But this view now lay in the shadow of the completed Dodger Stadium. As for Los Angeles itself, from here on it would base its identity on growth, spectacle, and ambitious dreams. Los Angeles had attracted Walter O'Malley because it appeared willing to give him what New York would not: land obtainable at an affordable cost on which he could construct his ballpark. But more broadly, O'Malley sought a city willing to assist him in the service of his entrepreneurial plans. He sought a civic culture in which his per-sonal gains would not be perceived as outweighing the public ben-efits of a new team and stadium. Los Angeles, a city seeking to forge a new image—sleek, efficient, and modern—was such a place. It was the place O'Malley needed, a city to meet his dreams. It would remain his home for the rest of his life. At his death in 1979 the Dodgers were the most profitable franchise in baseball thanks in large measure to Dodger Stadium, which was regarded as the model major league ballpark. Today it remains Los Angeles's most beloved sports venue.

Dodger Stadium made downtown Los Angeles possible. Downtown Los Angeles in turn made modern Los Angeles possible. There were, to be sure, other civic undertakings crucial to its growth. The Los Angeles Aqueduct gave the city its lifeblood—water—in 1913. City Hall, erected in 1928, offered a tangible locus of power projecting outward from the central core, as well as an iconic symbol of the city itself. The Los Angeles Memorial Coliseum, completed in 1923 and home to the 1932 Olympic Games, announced the city to the world. In 1939, with the opening of Union Station, Los Angeles had a transportation hub that connected it to regional and national networks of commerce and social movement.

Downtown Los Angeles, 2000. Los Angeles Neighborhoods Collection/ Los Angeles Public Library. Photographer: Marissa Roth.

But even as these structures took shape, Los Angeles's downtown declined. By 1957, when the Dodgers arrived, downtown was a place in which thousands of Angelenos worked by day and from which they fled at night. Retail trade was declining and property values stagnating. Even Union Station—which itself could have been described as an "embark-and-flee" entrepôt—had not affected this state of affairs appreciably. Downtown Los Angeles appeared much the same as it did in 1939, when Union Station was completed. But it became a very different place in the wake of Dodger Stadium's opening in 1962. The stadium began the process of change that created Los Angeles's modern downtown. It foregrounded everything that came afterward. By the 1990s, downtown Los Angeles was almost unrecognizable, no longer the drab collection of low-rises that had defined it four decades earlier. Dodger Stadium was the gateway that transformed downtown and created a modern Los Angeles.

A modern Los Angeles, of course, does not necessarily equate to a fairer Los Angeles. By the 1990s the pendulum of power had swung even further away from the Folks and from Angelenos of color toward the corporate boardrooms, real estate offices, and money center headquarters of the Downtown/Westside nexus. Ironically, it was an African American mayor, Tom Bradley, who presided over much of this shift in power relations between 1973 and 1993. Had Dodger Stadium not been built or had it not been built in Chavez Ravine, it is likely that Los Angeles's development would have taken another direction. Certainly its downtown would not have appeared the way it did in the 1990s and does today. Whether Dodger Stadium receives the credit or the blame for this, of course, is for the people of Los Angeles to decide. It may yet be too early to tell.

EPILOGUE

DODGER STADIUM AND MODERN LOS ANGELES

The story of Dodger Stadium in Los Angeles defies conventional urban historical narratives. Reformers do not struggle to take their city back from the bosses. Liberals and conservatives do not wage battle across sharply demarcated lines of class or ideology. There are, indeed, no official party designations to mark our way across its terrain. Nor is Dodger Stadium a straightforward story of the marginalization of people of color. It is instead a tale of both exclusion and inclusion, as Latinos exiled from Chavez Ravine nonetheless became a crucial element in Los Angeles's defining civic experience.

The two most prominent supporters of the Dodger Stadium project were a conservative Republican, Norris Poulson, and a liberal Democrat, Rosalind Wyman. Its two most prominent opponents were also a conservative Republican, John Holland, and a liberal Democrat, Edward Roybal. Wyman was an ally of organized labor, Poulson a pillar of the Downtown business establishment. Roybal was a supporter of activist government, Holland a believer in free enterprise capitalism.

On the surface, these alignments seem counterintuitive. But they may offer an alternative way of understanding the history of American cities, one that deemphasizes political ideology, party labels, and even the trope of "the people versus the interests." It instead foregrounds competing views of the broader purposes of a city and the ways in which those purposes would be reflected in the patterns of its growth. What is a city for? Poulson and Wyman and Holland and Roybal answered that question in contrasting ways. Wyman and Poulson may have differed on issues relating to labor, race, and policing, but they shared a vision for Los Angeles that was national and global in scope. Their vision required major institutions such as Dodger Stadium that would open outward and mark their city's newly acquired position of financial, commercial, and cultural leadership. A vital, vibrant downtown, one that could measure up to those in more established cities, was essential to that vision.

Wyman and Poulson also agreed that state assistance was necessary for their vision to be realized and that private capital and entrepreneurship by themselves would not be enough to bring to fruition the civic monuments and cultural initiatives that cities of no little plans required. Westside and Downtown, growth-oriented Democrats and business Republicans—all could put partisan and ideological differences aside and work together for a Los Angeles with the public institutions to match its status and prestige. For them, Dodger Stadium was the start of their city's rise to greatness.

But for John Holland and Edward Roybal and those they represented—the Folks, the working class, and the working poor—cities served different purposes. Theirs were the voices of the peripheries and margins, of all races, those to whom gleaming structures downtown meant little. Their Los Angeles was an everyday, workaday city. It provided basic, efficient municipal services. It cleaned the streets, taught the children, and protected the citizenry. Quality of life, for Holland and Roybal, was measured in the quotidian, not the grand gesture. This vision united them despite their obvious race- and class-based differences. Neither man believed it was appropriate for the city of Los Angeles to transfer property from one private owner to another even in the service of a great civic undertaking. Their vision even united them in the face of their differences over *levels* of government spending. However much was available, it should not be distributed on a preferential basis, even to an entrepreneur who could get things done.

The Dodger Stadium battle thus pitted the small-property-owning middle class, the working class, and the poor of Los Angeles's margins—geographic margins, economic margins, racial margins, sometimes all three—against a civic class located closer to the loci of political, economic, and cultural power. One group's dreams were localist and limited, the other's national and global. Dodger Stadium—and for that matter Bunker Hill—would not be the last time these dreams would clash in modern Los Angeles. Virtually every civic project in the city for the rest of the twentieth century, especially those sited downtown, became a field of competition between those two dreams. Mayors Sam Yorty (1961–73), Tom Bradley (1973–93), and Richard Riordan (1993–2001) all supported or came to terms with the agenda of civic growth even as opponents argued that every dollar spent downtown was one less dollar for East Los Angeles, Echo Park, or the San Fernando Valley. These arguments sometimes divided along racial lines, but not always. Like the first of those battles—Dodger Stadium—they could also separate Angelenos along markers of civic vision and ambition that defied simple racial arithmetic.

Almost every American city would reach a point in its development when its citizens would be required to set the arc of its civic trajectory. In many eastern cities, these decision points came in the nineteenth century, as their people argued over their dreams and ambitions and how to realize them.[1] Los Angeles and other western cities reached them in the years following World War II, as they pondered the civic undertakings that would serve as their announcements to the nation and world.[2] In Los Angeles, that undertaking was Dodger Stadium.

Those arrayed against the stadium and what it represented came tantalizingly close to victory. A contract offer was approved by one vote in the City Council. A referendum was decided by 25,000 votes out of 675,000 cast. Taxpayer lawsuits reached the highest courts in the state and nation. There was also the brief period between the evictions of the Arechiga family and the revelation of the other homes they owned when it seemed possible that a cross-race alliance of small property holders—Folks and Latinos, the San Fernando Valley and East Los Angeles—could alter the direction of the city, away from Downtown and Westside and Poulson and Wyman and their Los Angeles of no little plans.

But even in defeat, the stadium opponents underscored the power of an alternative urban vision based not in office suites but in neighborhoods and streets. This vision continues to be relevant to every American city struggling to decide what to be and where to go. It suggests another path for urban development, one that could move across demarcations of race and class toward broader identities and common dreams. In many respects, it resembles the vision of the urban theorist and activist Jane Jacobs, legendary opponent of Robert Moses in New York, in its understanding of cities as human places built around contact and community, not edifice and spectacle.[3] Despite battles fought and lost over the years, its time is not past.

Dodger Stadium's emergence as the physical manifestation of a new downtown did not mean that the dreams of its advocates would inevitably be realized. More than a half century after the stadium opened, downtown Los Angeles remains a work in progress. It now possesses many of the structures and institutions associated with the downtowns of great cities, including a world-class music center (1964) and concert hall (2003), a multiuse sports arena (1999), and two contemporary art museums (1986 and 2015) to go with the now-iconic baseball stadium on the overlooking hill. The Bunker Hill area is a hive of luxury apartments, stylish stores, and expensive restaurants. Figueroa Street boasts some of the most prestigious commercial real estate in the United States. A long-planned subway system is making downtown more attractive to those planning a night out.

But viable downtowns are more than collections of buildings, plazas, and civic monuments. With comparatively few permanent residents and a less-than-robust sidewalk culture, contemporary downtown Los Angeles appears to amount to less than the sum of its parts. In addition, as urban historian Mike Davis has observed, it is filled with privatized spaces that wall off "outsiders"—notably members of minority groups—and inhibit the diversity and variety of pedestrian traffic that characterize vibrant downtown areas all over the world.[4] Los Angeles is also now a city of peripheral downtowns that offer alternatives to the older and more traditional one at its core.

Yet the fact that downtown Los Angeles is less than it could be today does not mean it will not be all it can be tomorrow. The planning and construction of Dodger Stadium set Los Angeles on a course of modernization and growth in which downtown would matter as a site and symbol of civic, social, and cultural ingathering and unity. Dodger Stadium's critics argued that the cost of that unification project, assuming it could even be realized, did not justify the rewards. They charged that the ravaged communities of Chavez Ravine and Bunker Hill and resource-deprived peripheral neighborhoods were too high a price to pay for the ostensible benefits of a revitalized downtown. While they were unable to prevent the construction of Dodger Stadium, their argument lived on in the civic discourse over the fifty years following the ballpark's gala opening day. The proponents of modernization and downtown expansion thus cannot be considered to have achieved any final and permanent victory. But Dodger Stadium, looming above downtown, marks the spot where modern Los Angeles began. Its legacy is a city of contested visions and dreams, past, present, and future.

NOTES

PREFACE: OPENING DAY
IN LOS ANGELES

1. Davis, *City of Quartz*, 119.

CHAPTER 1: ROADS WEST

1. D'Antonio, *Forever Blue*, 26; Shaplen, "O'Malley and the Angels."
2. McGee, *The Greatest Ballpark Ever*, 38–67.
3. Ibid., 76–136.
4. McCue, *Mover and Shaker*, 43–48.
5. Ibid., 81–82.
6. See Sullivan, *The Dodgers Move West*, 29.
7. The roster of major league owners, in fact, was a veritable who's who of American industry. O'Malley's National League colleagues included a Du Pont heir (Robert Carpenter, Philadelphia Phillies), a chewing gum millionaire (Philip Wrigley, Chicago Cubs), a beer baron (August Busch Jr., St. Louis Cardinals), and a major property developer (John Galbreath, Pittsburgh Pirates). Del Webb, co-owner of the American League Yankees, owned one of the nation's leading construction companies.
8. O'Malley's role in Robinson's signing was obscured by Rickey's position as the public face of the team. As the partnership's "baseball" man, responsible for acquisitions, promotions, and trades, it was logical that Rickey would be the Dodger official to offer Robinson a contract. Obviously a transaction of this

magnitude could not have gone through without the support of the other partners.

9. D'Antonio, *Forever Blue*, 117.

10. See McCue, *Mover and Shaker*, 75–77.

11. Ibid., 121; D'Antonio, *Forever Blue*, 119.

12. "This Month in Walter O'Malley History: October 14" (hereafter "This Month" plus date), Walter O'Malley: The Official Website, accessed July 1, 2011, www.walteromalley.com/thisday_10_14.php.

13. D'Antonio, *Forever Blue*, 133–35.

14. McCue, *Mover and Shaker*, 81–82.

15. Ibid., 78–83; D'Antonio, *Forever Blue*, 132–36.

16. Generally regarded as the greatest baseball announcer of all time, Scully concluded his sixty-seven-year career as voice of the Dodgers in 2016.

17. The Yankees had previously defeated the Dodgers in the World Series of 1941, 1947, 1949, 1952, and 1953.

18. "New York Yankee Quotations," Baseball Almanac, accessed June 30, 2016, www.baseball-almanac.com/teams/yankquot.shtml.

19. Fred Stein, "Bill Terry," Society for American Baseball Research, accessed June 30, 2016, sabr.org/bioproj/person/4281b131.

20. See Prager, *The Echoing Green*; Marzano, *New York Baseball in 1951*.

21. "1951 New York Giants: Schedule and Results," BaseballReference.com, accessed June 30, 2016, www.baseball-reference.com/teams/NYG/1951-schedule-scores.shtml.

22. *New York Daily News*, October 5, 1955.

23. Ballparks of Baseball, accessed June 15, 2015, www.ballparksofbaseball.com.

24. Ibid.

25. Ibid.

26. Povletich, *Milwaukee Braves*, 53.

27. Ibid., 21. The Braves' initial rental terms called for a nominal $1,000 per year, which the team voluntarily increased; ibid., 13, 32.

28. Ibid., 23.

29. Major league baseball did not institute an amateur player draft, ending the bidding war for new players, until 1965.

30. Ballparks of Baseball.

31. "Year-by-Year Baseball History," Baseball Almanac, accessed June 15, 2015, www.baseball-almanac.com/yearmenu.shtml.

32. Ibid.

33. Ibid.

34. See generally Caro, *The Power Broker*; Joel Schwartz, *The New York Approach*.

35. *New York Times*, August 10, 1979.

36. Podair, *The Strike That Changed New York*, 11. See also Williams, *City of Ambition*; Freeman, *Working-Class New York*.

37. McGee, *The Best Ballpark Ever*, 7; Sullivan, *The Dodgers Move West*, 28–29.

38. D'Antonio, *Forever Blue*, 269; McCue, *Mover and Shaker*, 152.

39. "Biography: Walter O'Malley: Building a Dream," Walter O'Malley: The Official Website, accessed July 1, 2015, www.walteromalley.com/biog_ref_page3.php.

40. McCue, *Mover and Shaker*, 143.

41. "This Month," October 11.

42. *Los Angeles Times*, March 29, 1988.

43. See Sullivan, *The Dodgers Move West*, 126.

44. Quoted in ibid., 126.

45. See Murphy, *After Many a Summer*.

46. Ballparks of Baseball.

47. "This Month," May 28.

48. Sullivan, *The Dodgers Move West*, 134–35.

CHAPTER 2: WALTER O'MALLEY'S LOS ANGELES

1. See Meyer, "The Political Insider," 114–15.

2. Ibid., 115.

3. D'Antonio, *Forever Blue*, 273–74.

4. "Wyman's Historic Efforts Bring Dodgers to Los Angeles," 10, Walter O'Malley: The Official Website, accessed July 1, 2011, www.walteromalley.com/feat_wyman_page10.php.

5. Ibid.; Meyer, "The Political Insider," 114–15.

6. See Sullivan, *The Dodgers Move West*, 136.

7. Abraham Lincoln, letter to Albert G. Hodges, April 4, 1964, accessed July 15, 2011, www.abrahamlincolnonline.org/lincoln/speeches/hodges.htm.

8. See Murphy, *After Many a Summer*, 309.

9. Ibid., 311.

10. Ibid., 309, 310.

11. *New York Times*, October 9, 1957.

12. Victor G. Devinatz, "Communist Party of the United States of America (CPUSA)," *Encyclopedia Britannica* online, accessed July 25, 2011, www.britannica.com/topic/Communist-Party-of-the-United-States-of-America.

13. "United States Presidential Election, 1932," accessed July 25, 2011, *Wikipedia*.

14. See generally Williams, *City of Ambition*.

15. "New York City Mayoral Election, 1957," accessed July 25, 2011, *Wikipedia*.

16. McCue, *Mover and Shaker*, 156.

17. *Sporting News*, October 23, 1957.

18. Sullivan, *The Dodgers Move West*, 138.

19. See Blum, *American Lightning*; Irwin, *Deadly Times*; Gottlieb and Wolt, *Thinking Big*; McDougal, *Privileged Son*, 45–64.

20. See Mulholland, *William Mulholland and the Rise of Los Angeles*; Gottlieb and Wolt, *Thinking Big*; McDougal, *Privileged Son*, 64–69, 105–12.

21. See Mitchell, *The Campaign of the Century*.

22. Ibid., 577.

23. Ibid., 31.

24. Quoted in ibid., 571.

25. Parson, *Making a Better World*, 163.

26. Ibid., 93–135.

27. Starr, *Material Dreams*, 131–34. The term was first employed by the author Louis Adamic in the 1920s; ibid., 132.

28. U.S. Census Bureau: 1960 Decennial Census.

29. *Los Angeles Times*, August 20, 1951; Normark, *Chavez Ravine, 1949*, 18.

30. "Great Migration (African American)," accessed July 25, 2011, *Wikipedia*.

31. Schelling, *Micromotives and Macrobehavior*, 143.

32. Podair, "'Haven of Tolerance,'" accessed July 10, 2016.

33. Ibid.

34. *Los Angeles Tribune*, May 30, 1958.

35. *Los Angeles Sentinel*, October 15, 1959, quoted in Avila, *Popular Culture in the Age of White Flight*, 178.

36. Ibid., 168–69.

CHAPTER 3: FIGHTING THE DODGER DEAL

1. "This Month," October 25.

2. Ibid.; quoted in McCue, *Mover and Shaker*, 164.

3. *Eagle Rock Sentinel*, October 17, 1957.

4. Ibid.

5. *Highland Park News-Herald and Journal*, October 20, 1957.

6. Citizens Committee to Save Chavez Ravine for the People, "Fact Sheet," October 30, 1957, Walter O'Malley Archive, Los Angeles, CA (hereafter "O'Malley Archive"). In reality, the combined city-county contribution in Los Angeles totaled less than $5 million.

7. Ibid.

8. Ibid.

9. Ibid.

10. Ibid.

11. Ibid.

12. Ibid.

13. John Holland, "Citizens Awake! The Time Is Short!," November 6, 1957, O'Malley Archive.

14. Jim Murray, "Chavez Ravine," November 29, 1957, O'Malley Archive.

15. McCue, *Mover and Shaker*, 194.

16. "This Month," November 11.

17. Ibid.

18. Walter O'Malley to Kenneth Hahn, November 8, 1957, O'Malley Archive.

19. "This Month," November 11.

20. Ibid.

21. "This Month," November 6.

22. Ibid.

23. Ibid.

24. Ibid.

25. Jim Murray, "Chavez Ravine," November 27, 1957, O'Malley Archive.

26. Ibid.

27. Text in Taxpayers' Committee for "Yes on Baseball," "Why Taxpayers Support City-Dodger Contract," May 1958, O'Malley Archive.

28. See Findlay, *Magic Lands*; Mott, "From Bush-League Hamlet to Major-League Metropolis"; Halle, "The New York and Los Angeles Schools," 7–15.

29. Mott, "From Bush-League Hamlet to Major-League Metropolis," 74.

30. See Avila, *Popular Culture in the Age of White Flight*, 20–105, 158–61, 206–14.

31. See Parson, "'This Modern Marvel,'" 333–50; Parson, *Making a Better World*, 137–86; Alexander and Bryant, *Rebuilding a City*.

32. Quoted in Mott, "From Bush-League Hamlet to Major-League Metropolis," 90.

33. Quoted in ibid., 87.

34. *New York Times*, December 7, 1957.

35. McCue, *Mover and Shaker*, 165.

36. "Walter F. O'Malley Issues," n.d., 4, O'Malley Archive.

37. *Los Angeles Examiner*, December 16, 1957.

38. *Los Angeles Times*, December 21, 1957.

39. Ibid.

40. Ibid.

41. "This Month," December 30; *Los Angeles Times*, December 30, 1957.

42. Holland, "Citizens Awake!"

43. *Sporting News*, October 30, 1957.

44. Committee for Public Morality, "Do You Want to Endanger *Your* Home—*and Freedom*?" January 1958, O'Malley Archive.

45. Ibid.

46. Ibid.

47. Quoted in Bennett, *They Play, You Pay*, 50.

48. "This Month," December 19.

49. McCue, *Mover and Shaker*, 174.

50. *The Independent*, January 11, 1958.

51. "This Month," December 19; "Obstacle Notes," January 13, 1958, O'Malley Archive; McCue, *Mover and Shaker*, 175.

52. *Los Angeles Times*, January 14, 1958.

53. McCue, *Mover and Shaker*, 175; "Walter O'Malley: Timeline of Achievements 1903–2003" (hereafter "Timeline"), 1957–58, Walter O'Malley: The Official Website, accessed July 1, 2011, http://www.walteromalley.com/biog_time_index.php.

54. "This Month," January 12.

55. *Los Angeles Mirror News*, January 14, 1958.

56. "This Month," January 8; *Sporting News,* January 8, 1958.

57. Vincent Flaherty to Walter O'Malley, November 11, 1957, O'Malley Archive; *Los Angeles Times,* December 11, 1957.

58. Sullivan, *The Dodgers Move West,* 141–42.

59. Walter O'Malley to Los Angeles Coliseum Commission, January 17, 1958, O'Malley Archive; "Dodger Stadium Obstacles," 1958, O'Malley Archive; "This Month," January 17; D'Antonio, *Forever Blue,* 284.

60. McCue, *Mover and Shaker,* 175–79.

61. Ibid.; "This Month," January 17.

62. *New York Journal-American,* January 20, 1958.

63. Ibid.

64. "We have it in our power to begin the world over again": Thomas Paine, *Common Sense* (1776).

65. Sullivan, *The Dodgers Move West,* 142; McCue, *Mover and Shaker,* 127, 319–20.

66. Ballparks of Baseball, accessed June 15, 2015, www.ballparksofbaseball .com.

67. Sullivan, *The Dodgers Move West,* 144.

68. See Avila, *Popular Culture in the Age of White Flight,* 178–80.

69. "Wyman's Historic Efforts Bring Dodgers to Los Angeles," Walter O'Malley: The Official Website, www.walteromalley.com/feat_wyman_page11.php; "Timeline," 1957–58.

70. See Powell, "Is Big League Baseball Good Municipal Business?" 111–13, 162; Noll and Zimbalist, eds., *Sports, Jobs, and Taxes.*

71. Taxpayers' Committee for "Yes on Baseball," "General Committee" and "Lawyers Committee," n.d., O'Malley Archive.

72. Baus and Ross, "Top Performance Wins Campaigns," 1959, O'Malley Archive.

73. W. B. Ross to "Dear Editor," February 17, 1958, O'Malley Archive.

74. W. B. Ross to Walter O'Malley, February 7, 1958, O'Malley Archive.

75. Ibid.

76. Ibid.

77. Ibid.; Walter O'Malley to Herbert Baus, February 11, 1958, O'Malley Archive.

78. *San Francisco Chronicle,* January 12, 1958.

79. Proceedings, Recessed Meeting of Los Angeles Memorial Coliseum Commission, January 14, 1958, 125–26, O'Malley Archive.

80. Ibid., 132–33.

81. *Hollywood Torch-Reporter,* February 1958.

82. Ibid.

83. Letter, Bessie Smith, *Hollywood Torch-Reporter,* February 1958.

84. Ibid.

85. See Buntin, *L.A. Noir.*

86. "This Month," January 24.

87. McCue, *Mover and Shaker,* 176.

CHAPTER 4: THE REFERENDUM

1. Taxpayers' Committee for "Yes on Baseball," Press Release, February 26, 1958, O'Malley Archive.

2. W. B. Ross to Stephen Gavin, March 26, 1958, O'Malley Archive.

3. Ibid.

4. *Wall Street Journal*, March 13, 1958.

5. Ibid.

6. Ibid.

7. Ibid.

8. Ibid.

9. Shaplen, "O'Malley and the Angels."

10. W. B. Ross to Walter O'Malley, April 25, 1958, O'Malley Archive.

11. Shaplen, "O'Malley and the Angels."

12. Ibid.

13. Ibid.

14. The quote is attributed to St. Francis Xavier (1506–1552).

15. Shaplen, "O'Malley and the Angels."

16. Ibid.

17. Creamer, "Who Called That Bum a Smodger?"

18. *New York Times*, April 19, 1958.

19. "This Month," April 17.

20. *New York Times*, April 19, 1958.

21. Ibid.; "Welcome to LA," Walter O'Malley: The Official Website, accessed October 20, 2016, www.walteromalley.com/phot_detail.php; "History in the Making: First Major League Game in Los Angeles," Walter O'Malley: The Official Website, 4, www.walteromalley.com/feat_firstlagame_page4.php.

22. *New York Times*, April 19, 1958.

23. Ibid.

24. "This Month," April 17.

25. "History in the Making," 5.

26. Ibid.

27. "History in the Making," 4.

28. Ibid., 5.

29. Ibid., 7.

30. Ibid., 7–8.

31. Sullivan, *The Dodgers Move West*, 147–48.

32. D'Antonio, *Forever Blue*, 289.

33. Accessed October 21, 2016, www.baseball-almanac.com/teams/laatte.shtml; Sullivan, *The Dodgers Move West*, 148.

34. Sullivan, *The Dodgers Move West*, 51.

35. Ibid., 150; Povletich, *Milwaukee Braves*, 181.

36. *Los Angeles Times*, April 19, 1958.

37. Quoted in Sullivan, *The Dodgers Move West*, 154–55.

38. Los Angeles Superior Court, Case No. 687210, April 19, 1958.

39. See Bob Timmerman, "Vote No on B? Why? Looking Back 50 Years," *The Griddle* (blog), Baseball Toaster, March 10, 2008, http://griddle.baseballtoaster .com/archives/920926.html.

40. Shaplen, "O'Malley and the Angels."

41. Ibid.

42. *Hollywood Torch-Reporter*, April 1958.

43. W. B. Ross to Walter O'Malley, April 28, 1958, O'Malley Archive.

44. *Los Angeles Herald and Express*, May 24, 1958.

45. *Los Angeles Times*, May 15, 1958.

46. *Los Angeles Mirror News*, May 16, 1958.

47. Sullivan, *The Dodgers Move West*, 154.

48. "Timeline," 1957–58.

49. Ibid.

50. Ibid.

51. Ibid.

52. Statement of Mayor Norris Poulson to the California State Assembly Interim Committee on Government Efficiency and Economy, May 16, 1958, O'Malley Archive.

53. Ibid.

54. *Los Angeles Times*, May 17, 1958.

55. *Los Angeles Examiner*, May 16, 1958.

56. Ibid.

57. *Los Angeles Times*, May 16, 1958.

58. Downtown Business Men's Association to California State Assembly Governmental Efficiency and Economy Committee, May 15, 1958, O'Malley Archive.

59. Ibid.

60. *Los Angeles Examiner*, May 16, 1958.

61. *Los Angeles Times*, May 17, 1958.

62. Ibid.

63. Ibid.

64. Ibid.

65. Ibid.

66. Ibid.

67. Ibid.

68. *Los Angeles Examiner*, May 16, 1958.

69. Barry Popik, "You Can't Beat Somebody with Nobody," *The Big Apple* (blog), December 8, 2010, www.barrypopik.com/index.php/new_york_city/entry /you_cant_beat_somebody_with_nobody.

70. Sullivan, *The Dodgers Move West*, 158.

71. Baus and Ross, "Memorandum," May 1958, O'Malley Archive.

72. Poulson later claimed that he had contacted Giles and urged him to announce that the Dodgers' future in Los Angeles was contingent on the outcome of the June 3 vote. Sullivan, *The Dodgers Move West*, 156–57.

73. See Sullivan, *The Dodgers Move West*, 155–57; New York *Daily News*, May 23, 1958.

74. *New York Post*, May 22, 1958.

75. Ibid.

76. Ibid.

77. Ibid.

78. Ibid.

79. Walter O'Malley, "For Immediate Release," May 26, 1958, O'Malley Archive.

80. Ibid.

81. Ibid.

82. Walter O'Malley, Interview, May 1958, O'Malley Archive.

83. Walter O'Malley, "For Immediate Release," May 26, 1958, O'Malley Archive.

84. Norris Poulson, "Who Would Have Ever Dreamed?" 205, Norris Poulson Papers, UCLA Library Special Collections, Charles E. Young Research Library, University of California at Los Angeles (hereafter "Poulson Papers").

85. *New York Journal-American*, May 20, 1958.

86. *New York World-Telegram and Sun*, May 24, 1958.

87. Bureau of Industrial Service, "Survey of Public Opinion on Proposition B—The Baseball Ballot," May 1958, O'Malley Archive.

88. Ibid.

89. Ibid.

90. Ibid.

91. Ibid.

92. Ibid.

93. *Los Angeles Times*, May 28, 1958.

94. *New York Mirror*, May 27, 1958.

95. *Los Angeles Examiner*, May 28, 1958.

96. Ibid.

97. Ibid.

98. Ibid.

99. *Los Angeles Times*, May 27, 1958.

100. Patrick McGee, "I propose that the city of Los Angeles . . . ," May 28, 1958, O'Malley Archive.

101. Ibid.

102. Ibid.

103. Ibid.

104. Sullivan, *The Dodgers Move West*, 158.

105. Ibid.

106. Ibid.

107. Ibid.

108. *Los Angeles Times*, May 24, 1958.

109. Taxpayers' Committee for "Yes on Baseball," "Why Taxpayers Support City-Dodger Contract," May 1958, O'Malley Archive.

110. *Los Angeles Examiner*, May 29, 1958.

111. Ibid.

112. Taxpayers' Committee for "Yes on Baseball," "'B' Is for Baseball," May 1958, O'Malley Archive; Taxpayers' Committee for "Yes on Baseball," Press Release, May 28, 1958, O'Malley Archive.

113. Baus and Ross, Proposition "B" Fact Sheet, May 29, 1958, O'Malley Archive.

114. Taxpayers' Committee for "Yes on Baseball," Press Release, May 30, 1958, O'Malley Archive.

115. "Radio Schedule—Yes on Baseball," May 29, 1958, O'Malley Archive.

116. *Los Angeles Mirror News*, May 31, 1958.

117. *Los Angeles Examiner*, June 1, 1958.

118. See Sullivan, *The Dodgers Move West*, 159; *Los Angeles Times*, June 1, 1958.

119. Ibid.

120. W. H. Daum to Karl Rundberg, May 23, 1958, Edward R. Roybal Papers, UCLA Library Special Collections, Charles E. Young Research Library, University of California at Los Angeles, Box 6, Folder 1 (hereafter "Roybal Papers").

121. Sullivan, *The Dodgers Move West*, 159–60; "This Month," June 1.

122. Accessed October 21, 2016, www.baseball-reference.com/teams/LAD/1958-schedule-scores.shtml.

123. Citizens Committee to Save Chavez Ravine for the People to Ronald Reagan, June 1, 1958, O'Malley Archive.

124. *Los Angeles Times*, June 2, 1958.

125. "Chavez Ravine Fact Book, Which Comprises the Untold Story of the O'Malley–Chavez Ravine Deal That Mayor Poulson Did Not Tell," April 9, 1962, O'Malley Archive.

126. "L.A. Dodger Telethon: Show Routine," June 1, 1958, O'Malley Archive.

127. *Los Angeles Times*, June 2, 1958.

128. Ibid.

129. Ibid.

130. Ibid.

131. "This Month," June 2.

132. "Timeline," 1957–58.

133. "Referendum Vote Returns—June 3, 1958," O'Malley Archive.

134. Ibid.

135. "This Month," June 3.

136. Ibid.

137. "This Month," June 4.

138. "This Month," June 5.

139. *Los Angeles Herald and Express*, July 2, 1958.

140. *Huntington Park News Herald and Journal*, June 11, 1958.

141. "Counter," July 1, 1958, O'Malley Archive; *Los Angeles Times*, July 2, 1958; W. B. Ross to Walter O'Malley, July 7, 1958, O'Malley Archive.

142. *Los Angeles Times*, July 2, 1958; *Los Angeles Herald and Express*, July 2, 1958.

143. Ibid.

144. Ibid.

145. Ibid.

146. *Los Angeles Tribune*, July 11, 1958.

147. *Los Angeles Times*, July 2, 1958; *Los Angeles Herald and Express*, July 2, 1958.

148. See Avila, *Popular Culture in the Age of White Flight*, 180.
149. Ibid., 169–70; Acuna, *Occupied America*.
150. *Los Angeles Mirror News*, June 5, 1958.
151. Ibid.
152. Ibid.
153. Ibid.
154. Ibid.
155. *Los Angeles Metropolitan Area Newsletter*, July 5, 1958.
156. See Mott, "From Bush-League Hamlet to Major-League Metropolis."
157. Ibid.

CHAPTER 5: IN THE COURTS

1. Sullivan, *The Dodgers Move West*, 165; *Los Angeles Times*, June 20, 1958; "Timeline," 1957–58.
2. See "Chavez Ravine Fact Book," O'Malley Archive; Sullivan, *The Dodgers Move West*, 162–67.
3. "Chavez Ravine Fact Book," O'Malley Archive; Sullivan, *The Dodgers Move West*, 163–64.
4. See Sullivan, *The Dodgers Move West*, 162–67, 221; "Chavez Ravine Fact Book," O'Malley Archive.
5. See Sullivan, *The Dodgers Move West*, 162.
6. Walter O'Malley, "For Immediate Release," May 26, 1958, O'Malley Archive; *Los Angeles Times*, May 27, 1958; "Chavez Ravine Fact Book," O'Malley Archive. Some sources set the Chavez Ravine valuation at $2,289,204 but that of Wrigley Field at $2,225,000. See Baus and Ross, "Questions and Answers on the City-Dodger Baseball Contract," May 1958, O'Malley Archive; Taxpayers' Committee for "Yes on Baseball," "Why Taxpayers Support City-Dodger Contract," May 1958, O'Malley Archive. The *Los Angeles Times* reporter covering the Praeger trial listed the valuations as $2,179,203 for Chavez Ravine and $2,000,000 for Wrigley Field; *Los Angeles Times*, June 25, 1958.
7. *Los Angeles Times*, June 25, 1958; Sullivan, *The Dodgers Move West*, 166–67.
8. *Los Angeles Mirror News*, June 21, 1958; *Los Angeles Times*, June 21, 1958; *Los Angeles Examiner*, June 21, 1958; Sullivan, *The Dodgers Move West*, 164.
9. Sullivan, *The Dodgers Move West*, 164.
10. *Los Angeles Times*, June 21, 1958.
11. Sullivan, *The Dodgers Move West*, 163.
12. *Los Angeles Mirror News*, June 21, 1958.
13. Sullivan, *The Dodgers Move West*, 166–67.
14. Ibid.
15. Ibid.
16. Ibid.
17. Ibid.; *Los Angeles Times*, June 25, 1958.
18. Sullivan, *The Dodgers Move West*, 167.

19. Ibid.
20. Ibid.
21. *Los Angeles Times*, June 25, 1958.
22. Ibid.
23. Ibid.; Sullivan, *The Dodgers Move West*, 166–67.
24. Sullivan, *The Dodgers Move West*, 167.
25. Walter O'Malley to Emil Praeger, June 30, 1958, O'Malley Archive.
26. Walter O'Malley, Memorandum, June 1958, O'Malley Archive.
27. Ibid.
28. Ibid.
29. Disneyland was clearly on O'Malley's mind. In an August 1958 letter to Walt Disney, he wrote, "A long time ago I had an idea that there might be something in the ultimate development of Chavez Ravine that would bring into the picture some of your imagination and good taste. You might recall I wrote you a letter to that effect last year." Disney responded with an invitation to meet and discuss the proposed stadium. Walter O'Malley to Walt Disney, August 4, 1958, O'Malley Archive; Walt Disney to Walter O'Malley, August 7, 1958, O'Malley Archive.
30. See *Los Angeles Daily Journal Report Section*, August 25, 1958, 22–27; *New York Times*, July 14, 1958; Sullivan, *The Dodgers Move West*, 168–71.
31. *Los Angeles Daily Journal Report Section*, August 25, 1958, 25.
32. Ibid., 26.
33. Ibid., 27.
34. Ibid., 24.
35. Ibid., 27.
36. "Timeline," 1957–58.
37. *Washington Post*, July 15, 1958.
38. Ibid.
39. *Los Angeles Mirror News*, July 14, 1958.
40. Quoted in Avila, *Popular Culture in the Age of White Flight*, 166.
41. *Studio City Graphic*, July 16, 1958.
42. Ibid.
43. *New York World-Telegram and Sun*, July 15, 1958.
44. O'Melveny and Myers, "Analysis of Judge Praeger's Opinion in the Kirshbaum and Ruben Cases," July 1958, O'Malley Archive.
45. Although, of course, the matter did not end there. The 1953 Los Angeles mayoral race between incumbent and public housing proponent Fletcher Bowron and Norris Poulson, whose primary motivation for running was opposition to "socialistic" housing policies, was effectively another referendum on this question. Poulson's victory sealed the fate of public housing in Los Angeles. The new mayor reached an agreement with Washington officials to halt work on projects that had not been completed, which included Chavez Ravine. In 1955 the federal government sold the Ravine property to the city of Los Angeles. The deed contained the "public purpose" clause that was to play such an important part in the battle over the construction of Dodger Stadium. See Don Parson, *Making a Better World*, 103–86.
46. See "Chavez Ravine Fact Book," O'Malley Archive.

47. *Newsday*, July 14, 1958.

48. "This Month," August 15; *Sporting News*, August 27, 1958.

49. "This Month," August 15.

50. Quoted in Mott, "From Bush-League Hamlet to Major-League Metropolis," 89.

51. Sullivan, *The Dodgers Move West*, 171–72.

52. Ibid., 228; accessed October 21, 2016, www.baseball-almanac.com/teams/laate.shtml.

53. W. H. Nicholas, "Baseball Revenue—1958 Baseball Season—Los Angeles Dodgers," September 30, 1958, O'Malley Archive. This figure excluded concessions from nine home games which under the lease terms were payable to the Coliseum Commission.

54. McCue, *Mover and Shaker*, 246.

55. A. E. Patterson to Walter O'Malley, September 26, 1958, O'Malley Archive.

56. Ibid.

57. Ibid.

58. Ibid.

59. Ibid.

60. Ibid. It took another two decades, but Patterson's goal was realized. In 1978, the Dodgers became the first major league baseball team to draw over 3 million fans. Sullivan, *The Dodgers Move West*, 228.

61. W. B. Nicholas to Walter O'Malley, October 1, 1958, O'Malley Archive.

62. Sullivan, *The Dodgers Move West*, 171.

63. *Sporting News*, November 19, 1958.

64. Ibid.; Harry Walsh to Kay O'Malley, October 16, 1958, O'Malley Archive.

65. *Sporting News*, November 19, 1958; McCue, *Mover and Shaker*, 228, 230–31.

66. *Ruben v. City of Los Angeles*, Supreme Court of the State of California, L.A. Nos. 25238 and 25239, Opening Brief of Appellant Los Angeles Dodgers, Inc., 18.

67. Ibid.

68. Ibid., 12–18, 22–24.

69. Ibid., 23.

70. For all the controversy about ownership of what lay beneath the surface of Chavez Ravine, nothing of significant value was ever discovered there.

71. *Ruben v. City of Los Angeles*, Opening Brief of Appellant Los Angeles Dodgers, Inc., 17.

72. Ibid., 9.

73. Ibid.

74. Ibid., 9–10.

75. Ibid.

76. Ibid., 10–11.

77. Ibid., 11.

78. Ibid., 12–15.

79. Ibid., 12–13.

80. Ibid., 12–15, 22–24.

81. Ibid., 17.

82. Ibid.

83. Ibid., 7–8.

84. *Sporting News*, October 11, 1958.

85. "This Month," July 16.

86. See Sullivan, *The Diamond in the Bronx*, 114–15.

87. "This Month," July 16.

88. *City of Los Angeles v. Superior Court of the County of Los Angeles,* 51 Cal.2d 423 (1959); Sullivan, *The Dodgers Move West*, 172–75.

89. *City of Los Angeles v. Superior Court of the County of Los Angeles,* 51 Cal. 2d 423 (1959).

90. Ibid.

91. Ibid.

92. Ibid.

93. Ibid.

94. Ibid.

95. Ibid.; Sullivan, *The Dodgers Move West*, 172–75; Henderson, "Los Angeles and the Dodger War, 1957–1962," 280.

96. Sullivan, *The Dodgers Move West*, 172–75.

97. Ibid., 178; *Ruben v. City of Los Angeles* and *Kirshbaum v. Housing Authority of the City of Los Angeles,* 51 Cal.2d 857, 337 P.2d 825 (1959).

98. *Ruben v. City of Los Angeles* and *Kirshbaum v. Housing Authority of the City of Los Angeles,* 51 Cal.2d 857, 337 P.2d 825 (1959).

CHAPTER 6: WHOSE LAND?

1. Sullivan, *The Dodgers Move West*, 172–75.

2. "This Month," January 13.

3. Norris Poulson, quoted in Sullivan, *The Dodgers Move West*, 174.

4. Los Angeles Dodgers, Inc. to City of Los Angeles, Attn.: Roger Arnebergh, City Attorney, 1959, O'Malley Archive.

5. Sullivan, *The Dodgers Move West*, 175.

6. *Los Angeles Mirror News*, January 29, 1959.

7. *Highland Park News-Herald and Journal*, February 19, 1959.

8. Ibid.

9. *Los Angeles Herald and Express*, February 19, 1959.

10. *Highland Park News-Herald and Journal*, February 19, 1959.

11. Ibid., February 22, 1959.

12. *Los Angeles Herald and Express*, February 19, 1959.

13. *Highland Park News-Herald and Journal*, February 5, 1959.

14. E. J. Burns to Walter O'Malley, January 19, 1959, O'Malley Archive.

15. Bank of America to Walter O'Malley, February 2, 1959, O'Malley Archive.

16. E. J. Burns to Walter O'Malley, January 19, 1959, O'Malley Archive.

17. Ibid.

18. Walter O'Malley to California Bank, February 16, 1959, O'Malley Archive.

19. Bank of America to Walter O'Malley, February 13, 1958, O'Malley Archive.

20. Ibid.

21. Cuff, *The Provisional City*, 307–9; Parson, *Making a Better World*, 67, 91, 110, 146–47, 154–55, 170, 197; *Los Angeles Herald and Express*, April 8, 1955; *Hollywood Citizen-News*, November 25, 1954.

22. See Parson, *Making a Better World*, 103–35.

23. *Los Angeles Herald and Express*, April 8, 1955; Parson, *Making a Better World*, 146–47, 154–55.

24. *Hollywood Citizen-News*, November 25, 1954.

25. Fritz Burns to Edward Roybal, March 25, 1955, Roybal Papers, Box 4, Folder 1.

26. *Los Angeles Mirror News*, January 15, 1959.

27. Ibid.

28. C. A. Owen to Los Angeles City Council, November 19, 1958, Roybal Papers, Box 4, Folder 3.

29. Apartment Association of Los Angeles County to Los Angeles City Council, August 6, 1958, Roybal Papers, Box 4, Folder 3.

30. Edward Roybal to Grant Beach, April 8, 1959, Roybal Papers, Box 4, Folder 1.

31. Downtown Community Association, "Resist the Rape of Our Downtown Community," 1954, Roybal Papers, Box 4, Folder 1.

32. *Los Angeles Times*, May 13, 1959; Dick Walsh to Walter O'Malley, March 12, 1959, O'Malley Archive.

33. Los Angeles Dodgers, Inc. to City of Los Angeles, Attn.: Roger Arnebergh, City Attorney, 1959, O'Malley Archive.

34. Normark, *Chavez Ravine, 1949*, 18.

35. Ibid.

36. *Los Angeles Times*, August 20, 1951.

37. Ibid.

38. Normark, *Chavez Ravine, 1949*, 12.

39. Ibid., 18.

40. Ibid., 81.

41. *Los Angeles Times*, August 20, 1951.

42. Ibid.

43. Special Report, "Public Housing and the Brooklyn Dodgers," *Frontier*, June 1957.

44. Hines, "Housing, Baseball, and Creeping Socialism," 132.

45. Housing Authority of the City of Los Angeles to the Families of the Palo Verde and Chavez Ravine Areas, July 24, 1950, California State University at Los Angeles library website, www.calstatela.edu/library/image/evictionnoticebig.jpg.

46. Ibid.

47. See Special Report, "Public Housing and the Brooklyn Dodgers."

48. Hines, "Housing, Baseball, and Creeping Socialism," 138.

49. Ibid.

50. *Highland Park News-Herald and Journal*, May 10, 1959.

51. See Cuff, *The Provisional City*, 236–51.

52. Ibid., 236.

53. Ibid., 240.

54. Ibid., 251.

55. Ibid., 22.

56. Ibid., 21.

57. Parson, *Making a Better World*, 112, 114.

58. Ibid., 117–26, 203–8.

59. Ibid., 114.

60. Ibid., 130.

61. Ibid., 130–35.

62. Cuff, *The Provisional City*, 295–96.

63. Ibid., 277–79; *Los Angeles Times*, August 20, 1951.

64. Roger Arnebergh, Statement to Los Angeles City Council, May 11, 1959, Roybal Papers, Box 5, Folder 6.

65. Poulson, "Who Would Have Ever Dreamed?" 208–12, Poulson Papers.

66. Normark, *Chavez Ravine, 1949*, 21.

67. "Chavez Ravine Fact Book," O'Malley Archive.

68. Ibid.; Parson, *Making a Better World*, 171, 257 n. 22; Hines, "Housing, Baseball, and Creeping Socialism," 140; Norris Poulson to Council of the City of Los Angeles, July 20, 1959, O'Malley Archive.

69. *Los Angeles Times*, May 14, 1959.

70. Poulson, "Who Would Have Ever Dreamed?" 209, Poulson Papers.

71. *Los Angeles Herald and Express*, April 13, 1959; Ransom S. Callicott, "City of Los Angeles Resolution Regarding the Arechiga Property in Chavez Ravine," May 13, 1959, O'Malley Archive; Edward Roybal to Bourke Jones, August 20, 1957, Roybal Papers, Box 6, Folder 1.

72. *Wilshire Press*, April 16, 1959.

73. Ibid.

74. Parson, *Making a New World*, 174.

75. Rosalind Wyman to Walter O'Malley, September 1, 1955, O'Malley Archive.

76. Edward Roybal to Bourke Jones, August 20, 1957, Roybal Papers, Box 6, Folder 1.

77. *Highland Park News-Herald and Journal*, April 23, 1959.

78. Ibid.

79. Ibid.

80. *Los Angeles Mirror News*, April 29, 1959.

81. Ibid., May 6, 1959.

82. Ibid.

83. "Biography: 1959: A Year of Change," 61, Walter O'Malley: The Official Website, www.walteromalley.com/biog_ref_page61.php; "This Month," May 7.

84. "This Month," May 7.

85. See Avila, *Popular Culture in the Age of White Flight*, 169–70.

CHAPTER 7: THE ARECHIGA DISPOSSESSIONS

1. *Los Angeles Times*, May 9, 1959.

2. Avila, *Popular Culture in the Age of White Flight*, 167; Laslett, *Shameful Victory*, 115.

3. Editorial, KFWB, Los Angeles, May 11, 1959, Roybal Papers, Box 5, Folder 7.

4. Laslett, *Shameful Victory*, 115; Parson, *Making a Better World*, 174; Sullivan, *The Dodgers Move West*, 179.

5. Avila, *Popular Culture in the Age of White Flight*, 167; Editorial, KFWB, Los Angeles, May 11, 1959, Roybal Papers, Box 5, Folder 7; Henderson, "Los Angeles and the Dodger War," 282; Parson, *Making a Better World*, 174; Sullivan, *The Dodgers Move West*, 179.

6. *Los Angeles Times*, May 9, 1959.

7. Henderson, "Los Angeles and the Dodger War," 282.

8. "Biography: 1959: A Year of Change," Walter O'Malley: The Official Website, 63, www.walteromalley.com/biog_ref_page62.php.

9. *Los Angeles Mirror News*, May 9, 1959.

10. Laslett, *Shameful Victory*, 117–20; Parson, *Making a Better World*, 177.

11. "Black Friday in Chavez Ravine! A Day That Will Live in Infamy!" May 8, 1959, O'Malley Archive.

12. Sullivan, *The Dodgers Move West*, 179.

13. Ibid.

14. KFWB, Los Angeles, News Bureau Editorial, May 9, 1959, O'Malley Archive.

15. Ibid.

16. "Black Friday in Chavez Ravine!" May 8, 1959, O'Malley Archive.

17. *Highland Park News-Herald and Journal*, May 10, 1959.

18. Ibid.

19. Joseph Babando to Edward Roybal, May 10, 1959, Roybal Papers, Box 6, Folder 10.

20. Alice Ingersoll to Edward Roybal, May 11, 1959, Roybal Papers, Box 6, Folder 1; Avila, *Popular Culture in the Age of White Flight*, 167.

21. William Hagan to Edward Roybal, May 11, 1959, Roybal Papers, Box 6, Folder 1.

22. Edgar Poe to Edward Roybal, May 12, 1959, Roybal Papers, Box 5, Folder 8.

23. See Avila, *Popular Culture in the Age of White Flight*, 169.

24. Una Urhelburt to Edward Roybal, May 14, 1959, Roybal Papers, Box 5, Folder 8.

25. H. R. Ratliff to Edward Roybal, May 14, 1959, Roybal Papers, Box 5, Folder 8.

26. Meyer Jacoby to Edward Roybal, May 10, 1959, Roybal Papers, Box 6, Folder 1.

27. *Los Angeles Herald and Express*, May 12, 1959.

28. Ibid., May 11, 1959.

29. Ibid., May 12, 1959.

30. Ibid.

31. Ibid., May 11, 1959.

32. Ibid.

33. Ibid.

34. Ibid.

35. Ibid.

36. Ibid.

37. *Los Angeles Mirror News*, May 13, 1959.
38. *Los Angeles Herald and Express*, May 13, 1959.
39. Ibid.
40. Ibid.
41. *Los Angeles Examiner*, May 14, 1959.
42. Ibid.
43. *Los Angeles Herald and Express*, May 13, 1959.
44. Ibid.
45. *Los Angeles Examiner*, May 14, 1959.
46. Ibid.
47. Ibid.
48. Ibid.
49. Ibid.
50. Edward Roybal to Mary Cummings, May 25, 1959, Roybal Papers, Box 5, Folder 6.
51. Ibid.
52. *Los Angeles Examiner*, May 14, 1959.
53. Ibid.
54. Ibid.
55. Ibid.
56. *Los Angeles Mirror News*, May 14, 1959.
57. Ransom S. Callicott, "City of Los Angeles Resolution Regarding the Arechiga Property in Chavez Ravine," May 13, 1959, O'Malley Archive.
58. Ibid. Voting as a bloc, Holland, Roybal, Rundberg, and McGee defeated both the resolution and the proposed investigation of the Arechigas. *Los Angeles Times*, May 15, 1959.
59. *Los Angeles Herald and Express*, May 13, 1959.
60. *Los Angeles Times*, May 15, 1959.
61. *Los Angeles Examiner*, May 15, 1959.
62. Ibid.
63. *Los Angeles Mirror News*, May 15, 1959.
64. *Los Angeles Examiner*, May 17, 1959; "Biography: 1959: A Year of Change," 63.
65. Ibid.
66. *Los Angeles Examiner*, May 19, 1959.
67. Ibid.
68. Mrs. Oliver Babcock to Edward Roybal, May 12, 1959, Roybal Papers, Box 5, Folder 8; H. A. Garza to Edward Roybal, May 13, 1959, Roybal Papers, Box 6, Folder 1.
69. Mary Cummings to Edward Roybal, Roybal Papers, Box 5, Folder 6.
70. Mrs. Lee Bell to Edward Roybal, May 29, 1959, Roybal Papers, Box 6, Folder 1.
71. Mrs. John Galvin to Edward Roybal, May 13, 1959, Roybal Papers, Box 6, Folder 1.
72. Mrs. L. Brown to Edward Roybal, May 19, 1959, Roybal Papers, Box 6, Folder 1.

73. Ibid.

74. S. J. Anderson to Edward Roybal, May 13, 1959, Roybal Papers, Box 5, Folder 8.

75. Al Hill to Edward Roybal, May 14, 1959, Roybal Papers, Box 6, Folder 1.

76. Edward Breslin to Edward Roybal, May 15, 1959, Roybal Papers, Box 5, Folder 8.

77. Erma Dutton to Edward Roybal, May 14, 1959, Roybal Papers, Box 6, Folder 2.

78. "Biography: 1959: A Year of Change," 62.

79. *Los Angeles Examiner*, May 17, 1959; "Biography: 1959: A Year of Change," 63.

80. Sullivan, *The Dodgers Move West*, 179.

81. Avila, *Popular Culture in the Age of White Flight*, 169.

82. Ibid., 170.

83. *Los Angeles Times*, May 5, 2012.

84. Ibid. See generally Laslett, *Shameful Victory*, 159–78; Avila, *Popular Culture in the Age of White Flight*, 169–70.

85. *Los Angeles Times*, May 5, 2012.

86. Ibid.

87. *Los Angeles Times*, May 15, 1959; McCue, *Mover and Shaker*, 235.

88. *Los Angeles Times*, May 15, 1959.

89. *Los Angeles Mirror News*, May 19, 1959.

90. *Los Angeles Times*, May 12, 1962; Parson, *Making a Better World*, 179.

91. *Los Angeles Times*, October 17, 1971.

92. Ibid.

93. Henderson, "Los Angeles and the Dodger War," 285.

94. Normark, *Chavez Ravine, 1949*, 81.

CHAPTER 8: PRIVATE GAIN, PUBLIC GOOD? THE BUSINESS OF BASEBALL IN LOS ANGELES

1. "Statement of John S. Gibson, President, Los Angeles City Council," June 3, 1959, O'Malley Archive.

2. Agreement by and between the City of Los Angeles and Los Angeles Dodgers, Inc., June 3, 1959, O'Malley Archive.

3. Ibid.

4. Ibid.

5. Ibid.

6. Ibid.

7. *Los Angeles Times*, June 5, 1959.

8. "This Month," August 5.

9. *Highland Park News-Herald and Journal*, June 7, 1959.

10. Ibid.

11. Ibid.

12. *St. Louis Post-Dispatch*, June 7, 1959.

13. Norris Poulson to Council of the City of Los Angeles, July 20, 1959, O'Malley Archive.

14. Press Release, Civic Center News Agency, n.d., O'Malley Archive.

15. *Los Angeles Times*, May 23, 1959.

16. Ibid.

17. Walter O'Malley, Memorandum, May 26, 1959, O'Malley Archive.

18. *Los Angeles Times*, May 23, 1959.

19. List of Chavez Ravine Properties, n.d., O'Malley Archive; "Statement by H. C. McLellan," 1959, O'Malley Archive; H. C. McClellan, "Fact Sheet: Obstacles to Completion of Dodger Chavez Ravine Stadium," 1959, O'Malley Archive.

20. Henry Walsh, Memorandum, July 10, 1959, O'Malley Archive.

21. *Los Angeles Mirror News*, July 14, 1959.

22. *Wilshire Press*, August 6, 1959.

23. Ibid.

24. Ibid., August 13, 1959.

25. Ibid.

26. Ibid.

27. Ibid.

28. *New York Times*, October 23, 1959; McCue, *Mover and Shaker*, 250–51.

29. *Los Angeles Mirror News*, October 21, 1959.

30. Ibid.

31. *New York Times*, October 23, 1959.

32. Ibid.; McCue, *Mover and Shaker*, 250–51.

33. *New York Times*, October 23, 1959.

34. Ibid.

35. Ibid.

36. *Los Angeles Herald and Express*, October 12, 1959.

37. Ibid.

38. *New York Times*, October 23, 1959.

39. *Los Angeles Herald and Express*, October 16, 1959.

40. Ibid.

41. Ibid.

42. Ibid., October 14, 1959.

43. *New York Times*, October 23, 1959.

44. "Biography: Curveball Right Down the Middle," 57, Walter O'Malley: The Official Website, www.walteromalley.com/biog_ref_page57.php.

45. *Los Angeles Herald and Express*, November 5, 1959.

46. Ibid.

47. Press Statement, Walter O'Malley, October 23, 1959, O'Malley Archive.

48. Ibid.

49. *Los Angeles Examiner*, November 5, 1959.

50. Ibid.

51. *Los Angeles Examiner*, November 7, 1959.

52. "H. C. McClellan: O'Malley Shabbily Treated by Dodger Obstructionists," November 9, 1959, O'Malley Archive.

53. *Los Angeles Herald and Express*, November 6, 1959; *Los Angeles Examiner*, November 5, 1959.

54. *Los Angeles Herald and Express*, November 6, 7, 1959; Los Angeles City Council Ordinance No. 114,949 (Zoning Map), November 10, 1959, O'Malley Archive.

55. Norris Poulson to Council of the City of Los Angeles, July 20, 1959, O'Malley Archive.

56. Ibid.

57. Ibid.

58. *Los Angeles Times*, September 17, 1959.

59. *Highland Park News-Herald and Journal*, January 17, 1960.

60. Ibid.; Parson, *Making a Better World*, 171.

61. *Highland Park News-Herald and Journal*, January 17, 1960.

62. Ibid., February 14, 1960.

63. Ibid. The Dodgers themselves had delivered their own such agreement in December 1959. Press Release, Housing Authority of the City of Los Angeles, January 4, 1960, O'Malley Archive.

64. *Highland Park News-Herald and Journal*, February 14, 1960.

65. Ibid., August 6, 1959; McCue, *Mover and Shaker*, 255.

66. Walter O'Malley to G. William Shea, September 11, 1959, O'Malley Archive.

67. *Highland Park News-Herald and Journal*, August 9, 1959.

68. Ibid., August 6, 1959.

69. Ibid.

70. *Gardena Valley News*, October 1959.

71. *Beverly Hills Reporter*, October 1959.

72. Ibid.

73. Harold Kennedy to Roger Arnebergh, September 28, 1959, O'Malley Archive.

74. Ibid.

75. *Los Angeles Times*, September 30, 1959.

76. Ibid.

77. Ibid.

78. Sullivan, *The Dodgers Move West*, 187.

79. "This Month," October 8.

80. "This Month," October 9.

81. *New York Journal-American*, October 15, 1959.

82. *Beverly Hills Reporter*, October 1959.

83. *Los Angeles Herald and Express*, October 2, 1959.

84. *Los Angeles Examiner*, October 21, 1959.

85. Quoted in Sullivan, *The Dodgers Move West*, 188.

86. *New York Times*, October 23, 1959; *Gardena Valley News*, October 1959; *New York Journal-American*, October 23, 1959; *Los Angeles Times*, December 3, 1959.

87. *New York Times*, October 23, 1959.

88. *Los Angeles Herald and Express*, October 2, 1959.

89. *Los Angeles Examiner*, October 21, 1959.

90. John Gibson to Walter O'Malley, September 16, 1959, O'Malley Archive.

91. "Aftermath, 1959," Walter O'Malley: The Official Website, www.waltero malley.com/57-58_aftermath.php.

92. Ibid.

93. *Los Angeles Examiner*, September 18, 1959.

94. *Los Angeles Mirror News*, July 10, 1959.

95. *New York Journal-American*, August 25, 1959.

96. "Building O'Malley's Dream Stadium: Unveiling Plans," Walter O'Malley: The Official Website, accessed July 1, 2011, www.walteromalley.com/stad_hist _page5.php.

97. Ibid.

98. *Los Angeles Mirror News*, May 23, 1960; H. C. McClellan, "Fact Sheet: Obstacles to Completion of Dodger Chavez Ravine Stadium," 1959, O'Malley Archive.

99. Dick Walsh to Walter O'Malley, March 26, 1960, O'Malley Archive.

100. Emil Praeger to Jack Yount, March 16, 1960, O'Malley Archive.

101. "Statement by H. C. McClellan," 1959, O'Malley Archive.

102. H. C. McClellan, "Fact Sheet: Obstacles to Completion of Dodger Chavez Ravine Stadium," 1959, O'Malley Archive.

103. Ibid.

104. Ibid.

105. Ibid.

106. List of Chavez Ravine Properties, n.d., O'Malley Archive; *Los Angeles Examiner*, February 13, 1960.

107. "This Month," February 12; List of Chavez Ravine Properties, O'Malley Archive.

108. Dick Walsh to Emil Praeger, February 9, 1960, O'Malley Archive.

109. See Maynard, *Woodrow Wilson*, 125.

110. *San Francisco Chronicle*, January 15, 1960.

111. This perception would soon change when the many deficiencies of Candlestick Park, perhaps the worst-sited and most weather-challenged stadium in baseball history, became apparent.

112. *Wilshire Press*, February 1960; *Highland Park News-Herald and Journal*, February 21, 1960.

113. Ibid.

114. Ibid.

115. *Los Angeles Examiner*, May 4, 1960.

116. Ibid.

117. Ibid.

118. Ibid.

119. *Los Angeles Mirror News*, May 16, 1960.

120. See Moore, *Daniel H. Burnham*, 147.

121. Walter O'Malley to August Busch Jr., January 28, 1960, O'Malley Archive.

122. Walter O'Malley to Frank Schroth, March 25, 1960, O'Malley Archive.
123. Dick Walsh to Walter O'Malley, March 20, 1960, O'Malley Archive.

CHAPTER 9: BUILDING THE DODGER STADIUM EXPERIENCE

1. Transcript of Interview, Jack Yount, 1971, O'Malley Archive.
2. Walter O'Malley to Jack Yount, April 11, 1960, O'Malley Archive; Jack Yount to Walter O'Malley, April 11, 1960, O'Malley Archive; "This Month," April 13; *New York Times*, April 14, 1960.
3. Walter O'Malley to Jack Yount, April 11, 1960, O'Malley Archive.
4. Jack Yount to Walter O'Malley, April 11, 1960, O'Malley Archive.
5. Walter O'Malley to Jack Yount, April 11, 1960, O'Malley Archive.
6. *New York Times*, April 14, 1960.
7. *Los Angeles Examiner*, April 6, 1960.
8. See "PPIE: The City That Knows How," San Francisco Public Library website, sfpl.org/index.php?pg=2000141201.
9. *Los Angeles Examiner*, April 19, 1960; *Los Angeles Herald and Express*, May 18, 1960.
10. Walter O'Malley to Emil Praeger, May 19, 1960, O'Malley Archive.
11. Ibid.
12. Walter O'Malley to A. L. Carr, April 27, 1960, O'Malley Archive.
13. *Film Daily*, April 29, 1960; *Motion Picture Daily*, April 29, 1960.
14. *Los Angeles Mirror News*, May 4, 1960.
15. "This Month," June 15.
16. *Los Angeles Herald and Express*, May 3, 1960.
17. Ibid.
18. Ibid.
19. Ibid.
20. *Los Angeles Mirror News*, May 16, 1960.
21. *Citizen-News*, May 25, 1960.
22. *Los Angeles Herald and Express*, May 26, 1962. This last warning would prove prescient. While buses ran to the new stadium, they never accounted for a significant proportion of spectators and "beating the traffic" quickly became the goal of automobile-dependent Dodger fans. A direct rail link to the stadium has never been built.
23. *Citizen-News*, May 25, 1960; *Los Angeles Herald and Express*, May 26, 1960.
24. *Citizen-News*, May 25, 1960.
25. Ibid.
26. *Los Angeles Herald and Express*, May 18, 1960; *Wilshire Press*, May 19, 1960.
27. Ibid.
28. *Los Angeles Mirror News*, May 16, 1960.

29. *Los Angeles Examiner*, April 19, 1960.

30. Ibid.

31. *Citizen-News*, May 26, 1960.

32. *Los Angeles Mirror News*, May 16, 1960.

33. Ibid.

34. Ibid., June 1, 1960; *Los Angeles Herald and Express*, May 25, 1960.

35. *Life*, June 20, 1960; Walter O'Malley to Kay and Peter O'Malley, June 15, 1960, O'Malley Archive.

36. Walter O'Malley to Kay and Peter O'Malley, June 15, 1960, O'Malley Archive.

37. Ibid.; Union Oil Company to Los Angeles Dodgers, Inc., June 16, 1960, O'Malley Archive; Memorandum of Discussion Between Jack Smock et al., re the Los Angeles Dodgers, Inc., June 14, 1960, O'Malley Archive; Union Oil Company to Los Angeles Dodgers, Inc., June 17, 1960, O'Malley Archive; Promissory Note, Los Angeles Dodgers, Inc., September 15, 1960, O'Malley Archive; D'Antonio, *Forever Blue*, 312–13; McCue, *Mover and Shaker*, 246, 416.

38. Walter O'Malley to Kay and Peter O'Malley, June 15, 1960, O'Malley Archive.

39. Check, Union Oil Company to Los Angeles Dodgers, Inc., September 15, 1960, O'Malley Archive.

40. See Wolfe, "Candlestick Swindle."

41. Ibid.

42. *Wilshire Press*, June 30, 1960.

43. Ibid.

44. Ibid.

45. *City News*, June 30, 1960.

46. *Wilshire Press*, July 7, 1960.

47. Ibid.

48. Ibid.

49. Ibid.

50. Ibid.

51. Ibid.

52. Ibid.

53. Ibid.

54. Ibid.

55. Ibid.

56. Harry Walsh, Memorandum, August 16, 1960, O'Malley Archive; "This Month," August 19.

57. *Los Angeles Times*, January 3, 1961. The city's fiscal year ended each June 30.

58. Ibid.

59. Ibid.

60. *Wilshire Press*, July 14, 1960.

61. Huber Smutz to Walter O'Malley, August 4, 1960, O'Malley Archive.

62. *Wilshire Press*, July 14, 1960.

63. Ibid.

64. "Building O'Malley's Dream Stadium: Unveiling Plans," Walter O'Malley: The Official Website, www.walteromalley.com/stad_hist_page5.php.

65. "Building O'Malley's Dream Stadium: Concrete Ideas," Walter O'Malley: The Official Website, www.walteromalley.com/stad_hist_page6.php.

66. Ibid.

67. *San Francisco Chronicle*, August 25, 1960.

68. "This Month," August 27.

69. "This Month," October 3.

70. See Avila, *Popular Culture in the Age of White Flight*, 178–81.

71. Walter O'Malley to Emil Praeger, June 29, 1960, O'Malley Archive; Walter O'Malley to Dick Walsh, March 15, 1962, O'Malley Archive.

72. *San Francisco News-Call Bulletin*, February 7, 1962.

73. Opposed by many of the same groups that had opposed Dodger Stadium, the Chavez Ravine World Zoo project was blocked in court and eventually abandoned.

74. See Starr, *Golden Dreams*, 153–54, 156–60, 162–63.

75. Jack Yount, Transcript of Interview, 1971, O'Malley Archive.

76. Ibid.; "This Month," August 25.

77. Jack Yount, Transcript of Interview, 1971, O'Malley Archive; "This Month," August 25.

78. Jack Yount, Transcript of Interview, 1971, O'Malley Archive.

79. Ibid.

80. Ibid.

81. "Great Ideas at Dodger Stadium (That Never Made It to First Base!)," 7, Walter O'Malley: The Official Website, www.walteromalley.com/feat_walsh_page7.php.

82. "Dodger Stadium Construction Facts," 2, Walter O'Malley: The Official Website, accessed July 1, 2011, www.walteromalley.com/stad_facts_page2.php.

83. "Great Ideas at Dodger Stadium," 2.

84. "Dodger Stadium Construction Facts," 2.

85. Walter O'Malley to Emil Praeger, June 8, 1960, O'Malley Archive.

86. O'Malley's decision not to exercise this option—the stadium was never enclosed—would prove fortuitous. The view of the San Gabriel Mountains from the Dodger Stadium grandstand, which became one of the ballpark's signature "looks," would have been obstructed or lost by a deck erected in the outfield.

87. Los Angeles Dodgers, "Dear Dodger Fan," 1959, O'Malley Archive.

88. Harry Walsh to Walter O'Malley, January 21, 1959, O'Malley Archive.

89. Walter O'Malley to Emil Praeger, May 3, 1959, O'Malley Archive; Dick Walsh to Walter O'Malley, May 15, 1961, O'Malley Archive.

90. Walter O'Malley to Dick Walsh and E. J. Burns, April 13, 1961, O'Malley Archive; Walter O'Malley to Frank Stevens, April 13, 1961, O'Malley Archive.

91. Walter O'Malley to Dick Walsh and E. J. Burns, April 13, 1961, O'Malley Archive.

92. Walter O'Malley to Emil Praeger, June 29, 1960, O'Malley Archive.

93. Walter O'Malley to Emil Praeger, July 12, 1960, O'Malley Archive.

94. Ibid.

95. Dick Walsh to Emil Praeger, August 12, 1960, O'Malley Archive.

96. Ibid.

97. Ibid.

98. Walter O'Malley to Emil Praeger, July 12, 1960, O'Malley Archive.

99. "Building O'Malley's Dream Stadium: The Drawing Board," Walter O'Malley: The Official Website, www.walteromalley.com/stad_hist_page4.php; Walter O'Malley, Dodger Stadium Planning Notes, June 1958, O'Malley Archive.

100. Walter O'Malley, Dodger Stadium Planning Notes, June 1958, O'Malley Archive.

101. "Dodger Stadium Construction Facts," 2.

102. Dick Walsh to Emil Praeger, March 2, 1961, O'Malley Archive.

103. Stout, *The Dodgers*, 405.

104. These included what was to become known as the "Dodger Dog," generally regarded as the nation's best-tasting ballpark frankfurter.

105. Walter O'Malley, Dodger Stadium Planning Notes, June 1958, O'Malley Archive.

106. Stout, *The Dodgers*, 261.

107. Ibid.

108. "Building O'Malley's Dream Stadium: World's Largest Scoreboards," Walter O'Malley: The Official Website, www.walteromalley.com/stad_hist_page8 .php.

109. Ibid.; author communication with Brent Shyer and Robert Schweppe (former Los Angeles Dodgers front office staff), August 23, 2016.

110. "Building O'Malley's Dream Stadium: The Drawing Board."

111. Walter O'Malley, Dodger Stadium Planning Notes, June 1958, O'Malley Archive.

112. *Sporting News*, May 10, 1961; McCue, *Mover and Shaker*, 237, 240–41.

113. Walter O'Malley to Emil Praeger, September 29, 1961, O'Malley Archive.

114. *Los Angeles Times*, February 13, 1961.

115. Ibid.

116. Ibid.

117. Ibid.

118. Ibid.

119. "This Month," June 14.

120. *Los Angeles Mirror*, June 15, 1961.

121. See Ainsworth, *Maverick Mayor*; Bollens and Geyer, *Yorty*.

CHAPTER 10: THE RISE OF SAM YORTY

1. See Parson, *Making a Better World*; Parson, "'This Modern Marvel.'"

2. Bollens and Geyer, *Yorty*, 115–22.

3. Ibid.

4. Ibid.

5. Davis, *City of Quartz*, 126.

6. *Los Angeles Times*, June 6, 1998.

7. Bollens and Geyer, *Yorty*, 125–26, 147.

8. Ibid., 122; accessed October 20, 2016, https://en.wikipedia.org/wiki/los _angeles_mayoral_election,_1961.

9. Phelan, "Trouble in Happyland," 82.

10. Bollens and Geyer, *Yorty*, 122.

11. Mayo, "The 1961 Mayoralty Election in Los Angeles."

12. Bollens and Geyer, *Yorty*, 125.

13. Davis, *City of Quartz*, 126.

14. Democratic County Central Committee, "Mayor Poulson's Bus Rides," n.d., O'Malley Archive.

15. Ibid.

16. Ibid.

17. Bollens and Geyer, *Yorty*, 132.

18. Ibid.

19. "This Month," April 2.

20. *Los Angeles Examiner*, April 26, 1961.

21. *Long Beach Independent*, April 28, 1961.

22. *Highland Park News-Herald and Journal*, April 30, 1961.

23. Ibid.

24. *Los Angeles Herald and Express*, May 4, 1961.

25. *Los Angeles Examiner*, May 2, 1961.

26. Ibid.

27. Ibid.

28. See Mayo, "The 1961 Mayoralty Election in Los Angeles."

29. Ibid.

30. Ibid.

31. Ibid., 334.

32. Ibid., 332.

33. Ibid., 337.

34. Bollens and Geyer, *Yorty*, 133.

35. Sonenshein, "The Dynamics of Biracial Coalitions," 340.

36. Ibid., 337.

37. Bollens and Geyer, *Yorty*, 134.

38. Sonenshein, "The Dynamics of Biracial Coalitions," 340.

39. Saltzstein and Sonenshein, "Los Angeles: Transformation of a Governing Coalition," 194.

40. *Los Angeles Mirror*, June 2, 1961.

41. Ibid.

42. Ibid.

43. Ibid.

44. Ibid.

45. Ibid.

46. *Los Angeles Examiner*, June 2, 1961.

47. *Los Angeles Mirror*, June 14, 1961.

48. Ibid., June 15, 1961.

49. Ibid.; "This Month," June 15.

50. *Los Angeles Examiner*, June 15, 1961.

51. Ibid.
52. *Highland Park News-Herald and Journal*, June 30, 1961.
53. *Los Angeles Examiner*, July 14, 1961.
54. Ibid.
55. Ibid.
56. *Los Angeles Times*, July 25, 1961.
57. *Los Angeles Examiner*, July 25, 1961.
58. Ibid.
59. Ibid.
60. Ibid.
61. *Los Angeles Examiner*, July 25, 1961.
62. *Los Angeles Times*, July 25, 1961.
63. *Los Angeles Examiner*, July 25, 1961.
64. Phelan, "Trouble in Happyland," 82.
65. *Los Angeles Times*, August 9, 1961.
66. Walter O'Malley to Arch Field, August 14, 1961, O'Malley Archive.
67. *Highland Park News-Herald and Journal*, March 12, 1970; *Los Angeles Times*, March 12, 1970.

CHAPTER 11: THE MODERN STADIUM

1. *Los Angeles Tribune*, August 29, 1961.
2. "This Month," August 23.
3. Ibid.; Walter O'Malley to Emil Praeger, August 25, 1961, O'Malley Archive.
4. Walter O'Malley to Emil Praeger, September 29, 1961, O'Malley Archive.
5. Stout, *The Dodgers*, 260–61.
6. "Building O'Malley's Dream Stadium: Visit to Disneyland," Walter O'Malley: The Official Website, walteromalley.com/stad_hist_page7.php.
7. Dick O'Connor to Walter O'Malley, September 25, 1961, O'Malley Archive.
8. "This Month," September 20; Don Zminda, "A Home Like No Other: The Dodgers in L.A. Memorial Coliseum," in *The National Pastime, Endless Seasons: Baseball in Southern California* (Phoenix: Society for American Baseball Research, 2011), 84–86.
9. *Los Angeles Examiner*, September 24, 1961.
10. Ibid.
11. Walter O'Malley to Frank Schroth, September 28, 1961, O'Malley Archive.
12. *The Tidings—Los Angeles*, March 30, 1962.
13. Walter O'Malley to Frank Schroth, October 23, 1961, O'Malley Archive.
14. Ibid.; File Memo, October 25, 1961, O'Malley Archive.
15. Alex Kahn, United Press International, October 28, 1961, O'Malley Archive.
16. Ibid.
17. Ibid.
18. "Remarks of Robert Moses at the Groundbreaking of the Flushing Meadow Park Municipal Stadium," October 28, 1961, O'Malley Archive.
19. Ibid.

20. Ibid.

21. Walter O'Malley to Joe Williams, November 1, 1961, O'Malley Archive.

22. See Kahn, *The Boys of Summer*, 426.

23. "This Month," November 10.

24. Akers, "Selling Shea."

25. Dick O'Connor to Walter O'Malley, September 25, 1961, O'Malley Archive.

26. Walter O'Malley to Emil Praeger, November 3, 1961, O'Malley Archive.

27. Walter O'Malley to Dick Walsh, March 15, 1962, O'Malley Archive.

28. Walter O'Malley to Roger Miller, March 12, 1962, O'Malley Archive.

29. *Sporting News*, December 27, 1961.

30. Civic Center News Agency, January 4, 1962, O'Malley Archive.

31. "This Month," December 25.

32. Henry Walsh to File, January 2, 1962, O'Malley Archive.

33. Agreement between Los Angeles Dodgers, Inc. and Union Oil Company, January 5, 1962, O'Malley Archive; Promissory Note, Los Angeles Dodgers, Inc. to Union Oil Company, January 5, 1962, O'Malley Archive.

34. *Sporting News*, December 27, 1961.

35. Walter O'Malley to Walt Disney, January 10, 1962, O'Malley Archive.

36. *Los Angeles Mirror*, November 24, 1961.

37. Starr, *Golden Dreams*, 160–61.

38. Ibid.; "Building O'Malley's Dream Stadium: Visit to Disneyland."

39. *Sporting News*, December 27, 1961.

40. Ibid.

41. Ibid.

42. Ibid.

43. Ibid.

44. Franklin Payne to Walter O'Malley, January 19, 1962, O'Malley Archive. The *Herald and Express* and *Examiner* were consolidated in January 1962 to form the *Herald-Examiner*.

45. "This Month," January 28.

46. "Building O'Malley's Dream Stadium: Visit to Disneyland."

47. *Daily Signal* (Huntington Park, CA), February 1, 1962.

48. "Building O'Malley's Dream Stadium: Visit to Disneyland"; Walter O'Malley to Emil Praeger, January 29, 1962, O'Malley Archive.

49. "Building O'Malley's Dream Stadium: Visit to Disneyland."

50. Ibid.; "This Month," February 22.

51. "Building O'Malley's Dream Stadium: Visit to Disneyland"; "This Month," February 21.

52. *Los Angeles Times*, March 4, 1962.

53. *Highland Park News-Herald and Journal*, February 22, 1962.

54. Ibid.

55. *Los Angeles Herald and Express*, May 4, 1961.

56. "This Month," March 22.

57. *Los Angeles Herald-Examiner*, March 22, 1962.

58. Ibid.

59. Ibid.

60. *Los Angeles Times*, January 29, 1960.

61. "This Month," April 9.

62. *Sporting News*, April 18, 1962.

63. "This Month," April 9.

64. "Building O'Malley's Dream Stadium: Opening Day Preparation," www .walteromalley.com/stad_hist_page9.php.

65. Ibid.

66. Jack Yount, Transcript of Interview, 1971, O'Malley Archive.

67. *Pasadena Independent Star-News*, April 8, 1962.

68. "Building O'Malley's Dream Stadium: Opening Day Preparation."

69. Ibid.

70. Ibid.

71. "Building O'Malley's Dream Stadium: Opening Day Preparation."

72. *Los Angeles Herald-Examiner*, April 11, 1962.

73. Jack O'Connor to Walter O'Malley, September 25, 1961, O'Malley Archive.

74. *Los Angeles Herald-Examiner*, April 25, 1962; Walter O'Malley to Frank Schroth, May 1, 1962, O'Malley Archive.

75. "Building O'Malley's Dream Stadium: Lasting Impressions," Walter O'Malley: The Official Website, www.walteromalley.com/stad_hist_page11.php.

76. Ibid.

77. "This Month," April 24.

78. Sullivan, *The Dodgers Move West*, 228.

79. Los Angeles Dodgers, Inc., Statement of Income, October 31, 1962, O'Malley Archive.

80. Ibid.

81. *Los Angeles Herald-Examiner*, April 8, 1962; "Dodger Stadium Construction Facts," 1, Walter O'Malley: The Official Website, www.walteromalley.com /stad_facts_index.php.

82. Walter O'Malley to Dick Walsh, April 16, 1962, O'Malley Archive.

83. Author communication with Robert Schweppe (former Los Angeles Dodger front office staff), November 5, 2015.

84. "This Month," April 25.

85. Norris Poulson's loss to Sam Yorty in the 1961 mayoral election marked the end of his time in public life. He spent his last years as a partner in an accounting firm and died in 1982. In his memoirs, Poulson linked his defeat to his association with Dodger Stadium. See Poulson, "Who Would Have Ever Dreamed?" 199, 205, Poulson Papers. After a series of feuds with Yorty, Rosalind Wyman lost her bid for a fourth term on the City Council in 1965. Like Poulson, she attributed her rejection at the polls to a backlash against the stadium project. Wyman continued her active career in the California State Democratic Party as a strategist and adviser to younger candidates but did not run for public office again. Edward Roybal was elected to Congress in 1962 and spent thirty years in the United States House of Representatives. He served on that body's Appropriations Committee, chaired the Congressional Hispanic Caucus, and retired in 1993 as one of the most honored elected officials in California history. He passed away in 2005.

86. "This Month," July 16; McCue, *Mover and Shaker*, 280–82.

87. "Stadium Tax Chronology," July 22, 1962, O'Malley Archive.

88. Ibid.

89. Ibid., July 20, 1962.

90. Ibid., July 22, 1962; "This Month," July 16.

91. "Stadium Tax Chronology," July 22, 26, 1962; Lipsitz, "Sports Stadia and Urban Development," 9.

92. "Stadium Tax Chronology," May 14, 1975; Lloyd A. Menveg to Norris Poulson, May 14, 1975, O'Malley Archive; Baim, "Net Accumulated Value Calculations for 14 Stadiums."

93. Walter O'Malley to Jim Mulvey et al., January 2, 1963, O'Malley Archive.

94. Ibid.

95. Ibid.

EPILOGUE: DODGER STADIUM AND MODERN LOS ANGELES

1. See Burrows and Wallace, *Gotham*; Maggor, *Brahmin Capitalism*.

2. See Findlay, *Magic Lands*.

3. See Jacobs, *The Death and Life of Great American Cities*; Flint, *Wrestling with Moses*.

4. Davis, *City of Quartz*, 223–63.

BIBLIOGRAPHY

Abu-Lughod, Janet L. *New York, Chicago, Los Angeles: America's Global Cities*. Minneapolis: University of Minnesota Press, 1999.

Acuna, Rudolfo. *Occupied America: A History of Chicanos*. New York: Harper and Row, 1988.

Ainsworth, Ed. *Maverick Mayor: A Biography of Sam Yorty of Los Angeles*. Garden City, NY: Doubleday, 1966.

Akers, W. M. "Selling Shea." *Sports on Earth*, September 26, 2014. www.sportsonearth.com/article/96537676/shea_stadium_construction_1960s_robert_moses.

Alexander, Robert E., and Drayton S. Bryant. *Rebuilding a City: A Study of Redevelopment Problems in Los Angeles*. Los Angeles: Haynes Foundation, 1951.

Avila, Eric. *Popular Culture in the Age of White Flight: Fear and Fantasy in Suburban Los Angeles*. Berkeley: University of California Press, 2004.

———. "Revisiting the Chavez Ravine: Baseball, Urban Renewal, and the Gendered Civic Culture of Postwar Los Angeles." In *Velvet Barrios: Popular Culture and Chicana/o Sexualities*, ed. Alicia Gaspar de Alba, 125–39. New York: Palgrave Macmillan, 2003.

Baim, Dean. "Home Field Advantage: Municipal Subsidies to Professional Sports Teams." PhD dissertation, University of California, Los Angeles, 1988.

———. "Net Accumulated Value Calculations for 14 Stadiums." Appendix to "Sports Stadiums as 'Wise Investments': An Evaluation," Policy Study no. 32, Heartland Institute, November 1, 1990.

Banfield, Edward C., and James Q. Wilson. *City Politics*. Cambridge, MA: Harvard and MIT University Presses, 1963.

Banham, Reyner. *Los Angeles: The Architecture of Four Ecologies.* New York: Harper and Row, 1971.

Barraclough, Laura. *Making the San Fernando Valley: Rural Landscapes, Urban Development, and White Privilege.* Athens: University of Georgia Press, 2011.

Bavasi, Buzzie, with John Strege. *Off the Record.* Chicago: Contemporary Books, 1987.

Behrens, Earl C., and Dan Fowler. "California Politics: New Faces, New Power." *Look,* September 29, 1959, 33–35.

Bennett, James T. *They Play, You Pay: Why Taxpayers Build Ballparks, Stadiums and Arenas for Billionaire Owners and Millionaire Players.* New York: Copernicus Press, 2012.

Bernstein, Shana. *Bridges of Reform: Interracial Civil Rights Activism in Twentieth-Century Los Angeles.* New York: Oxford University Press, 2010.

Blum, Howard. *American Lightning: Terror, Mystery and the Birth of Hollywood.* New York: Three Rivers Press, 2008.

Bollens, John C., and Grant B. Geyer. *Yorty: Politics of a Constant Candidate.* Pacific Palisades, CA: Palisades Publishers, 1973.

Bottles, Scott. *Los Angeles and the Automobile: The Making of the Modern City.* Berkeley: University of California Press, 1987.

Boxerman, Burton A., and Benita W. Boxerman. *Ebbets to Veeck to Busch: Eight Owners Who Shaped Baseball.* Jefferson, NC: McFarland, 2003.

Brook, Vincent. *Land of Smoke and Mirrors: A Cultural History of Los Angeles.* New Brunswick, NJ: Rutgers University Press, 2013.

Buntin, John. *L.A. Noir: The Struggle for the Soul of America's Most Seductive City.* New York: Three Rivers Press, 2009.

Burrows, Edwin G., and Mike Wallace. *Gotham: A History of New York City to 1898.* New York: Oxford University Press, 2000.

Campanella, Roy. *It's Good to Be Alive.* Boston: Little, Brown, 1959.

Carney, Francis. "The Decentralized Politics of Los Angeles." *Annals of the American Academy of Political and Social Science* 353 (May 1964): 107–21.

Caro, Robert A. *The Power Broker: Robert Moses and the Fall of New York.* New York: Vintage, 1975.

Catalena, Mark, and Peter Jones, dirs. "Inventing LA: The Chandlers and Their Times." PBS, 2009.

Caughey, John, and LaRee Caughey, eds. *Los Angeles: Biography of a City.* Berkeley: University of California Press, 1977.

Champlin, Charles. "Los Angeles in a New Image." *Life,* June 20, 1960, 74–90.

Claire, Fred, with Steve Springer. *Fred Claire: My 30 Years in Dodger Blue.* Champaign, IL: Sports Publishing, 2004.

Cohane, Tim. "The West Coast Produces Baseball's Strangest Story." *Look,* August 19, 1958, 50–58.

Connolly, N. D. B. *A World More Concrete: Real Estate and the Remaking of Jim Crow South Florida.* Chicago: University of Chicago Press, 2014.

Creamer, Robert. "The Transistor Kid." *Sports Illustrated,* May 4, 1964, 96–108.

———. "Who Called That Bum a Smodger?" *Sports Illustrated,* March 24, 1958, 14–19, 59.

Cuff, Dana. *The Provisional City: Los Angeles Stories of Architecture and Urbanism*. Cambridge, MA: MIT Press, 2000.

D'Antonio, Michael. *Forever Blue: The True Story of Walter O'Malley, Baseball's Most Controversial Owner, and the Dodgers of Brooklyn and Los Angeles*. New York: Riverhead Books, 2009.

Davis, Margaret Leslie. *The Culture Broker: Franklin D. Murphy and the Transformation of Los Angeles*. Berkeley: University of California Press, 2007.

Davis, Mike. *City of Quartz: Excavating the Future in Los Angeles*. London: Verso, 1990.

———. *Ecology of Fear: Los Angeles and the Imagination of Disaster*. New York: Metropolitan Books, 1998.

Dawson, Jim. *Los Angeles's Bunker Hill: Pulp Fiction's Mean Streets and Film Noir's Ground Zero!* Charleston, SC: History Press, 2012.

De Wit, Wim, and Christopher James Alexander, eds. *Overdrive: L.A. Constructs the Future, 1940–1990*. Los Angeles: Getty Research Institute, 2013.

Dorinson, Joseph, and Joram Warmund, eds. *Jackie Robinson: Race, Sports, and the American Dream*. Armonk, NY: M. E. Sharpe, 1998.

Durslag, Melvin. "A Visit with Walter O'Malley." *Saturday Evening Post*, May 14, 1960, 31, 104–6.

Ellsworth, Peter. "The Brooklyn Dodgers' Move to Los Angeles: Was Walter O'Malley Solely Responsible?" *Nine: A Journal of Baseball History and Culture* 14 (Fall 2005): 19–40.

Evanosky, Dennis, and Eric J. Kos. *Lost Los Angeles*. London: Pavilion, 2014.

Fetter, Henry D. *Taking on the Yankees: Winning and Losing in the Business of Baseball, 1903–2003*. New York: W. W. Norton, 2003.

Fimrite, Ron. "They're Beginning to Sound Like a Broken Record." *Sports Illustrated*, September 26, 1977, 36–41.

Finch, Frank. *The Los Angeles Dodgers: The First Twenty Years*. Virginia Beach, VA: Jordan, 1977.

Findlay, John M. *Magic Lands: Western Cityscapes and American Culture After 1940*. Berkeley: University of California Press, 1993.

Flint, Anthony. *Wrestling with Moses: How Jane Jacobs Took On New York's Master Builder and Transformed the American City*. New York: Random House, 2009.

Foner, Eric. *Free Soil, Free Labor, Free Men: The Ideology of the Republican Party Before the Civil War*. New York: Oxford University Press, 1970.

Ford, John Anson. *Thirty Explosive Years in Los Angeles County*. San Marino, CA: Huntington Library Press, 2010.

Freeman, Joshua B. *Working-Class New York: Life and Labor Since World War II*. New York: New Press, 2001.

Fulton, William. *The Reluctant Metropolis: The Politics of Urban Growth in Los Angeles*. Baltimore: Johns Hopkins University Press, 2001.

Gelfand, Mark I. *A Nation of Cities: The Federal Government and Urban America, 1933–1965*. New York: Oxford University Press, 1975.

Gottlieb, Robert, and Irene Wolt. *Thinking Big: The Story of the Los Angeles Times, Its Publishers and Their Influence on Southern California*. New York: G. P. Putnam's Sons, 1977.

Gutierrez, David. *Walls and Mirrors: Mexican Americans, Mexican Immigrants, and the Politics of Ethnicity.* Berkeley: University of California Press, 1995.

Halberstam, David. *The Powers That Be.* New York: Knopf, 1975.

Halle, David. "The New York and Los Angeles Schools." In *New York and Los Angeles: Politics, Society and Culture—A Comparative View,* ed. David Halle, 1–46. Chicago: University of Chicago Press, 2003.

Hayden, Dolores, "Model Houses for the Millions: Architects' Dreams, Builders' Boasts, Residents' Dilemmas." In *Blueprints for Modern Living: History and Legacy of the Case Study Houses,*" ed. Elizabeth A. T. Smith, 197–212. Cambridge, MA: MIT Press, 1989.

Helyar, John. *Lords of the Realm: The Real History of Baseball.* New York: Villard Books, 1994.

Henderson, Cary S. "Los Angeles and the Dodger War." *Southern California Quarterly* 62 (Fall 1980): 261–89.

Hines, Thomas S. "Housing, Baseball, and Creeping Socialism: The Battle of Chavez Ravine, Los Angeles, 1949–1959." *Journal of Urban History* 8 (February 1982): 123–43.

Hirsch, Paul. "Walter O'Malley Was Right." In *The National Pastime, Endless Seasons: Baseball in Southern California,* 81–83. Phoenix: Society for American Baseball Research, 2011.

Hise, Greg. *Magnetic Los Angeles: Planning the Twentieth-Century Metropolis.* Baltimore: Johns Hopkins University Press, 1997.

Holland, Gerald. "A Visit with the Artful Dodger." *Saturday Evening Post,* July 1968, 24–25, 56–58.

Horne, Gerald. *Fire This Time: The Watts Uprising and the 1960s.* Charlottesville: University of Virginia Press, 1995.

Hunt, Darnell, and Ana-Christina Ramon, eds. *Black Los Angeles: American Dreams and Radical Realities.* New York: New York University Press, 2010.

Irwin, Lew. *Deadly Times: The 1910 Bombing of the Los Angeles Times and America's Forgotten Decade of Terror.* Guilford, CT: Lyons Press, 2013.

Jacobs, Jane. *The Death and Life of Great American Cities.* New York: Random House, 1961.

Kahn, Roger. *The Boys of Summer.* New York: Harper and Row, 1972.

Keane, James Thomas. *Fritz B. Burns and the Development of Los Angeles.* Los Angeles: Historical Society of Southern California, 2001.

Klein, Norman. *The History of Forgetting: Los Angeles and the Erasure of Memory.* London: Verso, 2008.

Klein, Norman, and Martin J. Schiesl, eds. *Twentieth Century Los Angeles: Power, Promotion, and Social Conflict.* Claremont, CA: Regina Books, 1990.

Kurashige, Scott. *The Shifting Grounds of Race: Black and Japanese Americans in the Making of Multiethnic Los Angeles.* Princeton: Princeton University Press, 2008.

Lanctot, Neil. *Campy: The Two Lives of Roy Campanella.* New York: Simon and Schuster, 2011.

Langill, Mark. *Dodger Stadium.* Charleston, SC: Arcadia Publishing, 2004.

Lankevich, George J. *American Metropolis: A History of New York City.* New York: New York University Press, 1998.

Laslett, John H. M. *Shameful Victory: The Los Angeles Dodgers, the Red Scare, and the Hidden History of Chavez Ravine*. Tucson: University of Arizona Press, 2015.

Leahy, Michael. *The Last Innocents: The Collision of the Turbulent Sixties and the Los Angeles Dodgers*. New York: Harper, 2016.

Leavy, Jane. *Sandy Koufax: A Lefty's Legacy*. New York: HarperCollins, 2002.

Lipsitz, George. "The Making of Disneyland." In *True Stories from the American Past*, ed. Norman Graebner, 179–96. New York: McGraw Hill, 1993.

———. "Sports Stadia and Urban Development." *Journal of Sport and Social Issues* 8 (Summer-Fall 1984): 1–18.

Long, Julia Grant. *Public/Private Partnerships for Major League Sports Facilities*. New York: Routledge, 2012.

Longstreth, Richard. *City Center to Regional Mall: Architecture, the Automobile and Retailing in Los Angeles, 1920–1950*. Cambridge, MA: MIT Press, 1997.

Lowenfish, Lee. *Branch Rickey: Baseball's Ferocious Gentleman*. Lincoln: University of Nebraska Press, 2007.

Mackenzie, Kent, dir. "The Exiles." Milestone Films, 1961.

Maggor, Noam. *Brahmin Capitalism: Frontiers of Wealth and Populism in America's First Gilded Age*. Cambridge, MA: Harvard University Press, 2017.

Marzano, Rudy. *New York Baseball in 1951: The Dodgers, the Giants, the Yankees and the Telescope*. Jefferson, NC: McFarland, 2011.

Maynard, W. Barksdale. *Woodrow Wilson: Princeton to the Presidency*. New Haven: Yale University Press, 2008.

Mayo, Charles G. "The 1961 Mayoralty Election in Los Angeles: The Political Party in a Non-Partisan Election." *Western Political Quarterly* 17 (June 1964): 325–37.

McCue, Andy. *Mover and Shaker: Walter O'Malley, the Dodgers, and Baseball's Westward Expansion*. Lincoln: University of Nebraska Press, 2014.

McDougal, Dennis. *Privileged Son: Otis Chandler and the Rise and Fall of the L.A. Times Dynasty*. Cambridge, MA: Perseus Publishing, 2001.

McGee, Bob. *The Greatest Ballpark Ever: Ebbets Field and the Story of the Brooklyn Dodgers*. New Brunswick, NJ: Rutgers University Press, 2005.

McGirr, Lisa. *Suburban Warriors: The Origins of the New American Right*. Princeton, NJ: Princeton University Press, 2001.

Mechner, Jordan, dir. "Chavez Ravine: A Los Angeles Story." PBS, 2005.

Merwin, John. "The Most Valuable Executive in Either League." *Forbes*, April 12, 1982, 129–32, 134, 138.

Meyer, Richard E. "The Political Insider." *Los Angeles*, July 2010, 110–15, 147.

Miller, Robert. "Baseball, Politics, and Urban Renewal: The Dodgers Move to Los Angeles." *Perspectives: A Journal of Historical Inquiry* 17 (1990): 25–45.

Mitchell, Greg. *The Campaign of the Century: Upton Sinclair's Race for Governor Of California and the Birth of Modern Media Politics*. New York: Random House, 1992.

Moore, Charles. *Daniel H. Burnham, Architect, Planner of Cities, Vol. 2*. Boston: Houghton Mifflin, 1921.

Mott, Michael. "From Bush-League Hamlet to Major-League Metropolis: Los Angeles, the Dodgers and Proposition B." *Ex Post Facto* 14 (Spring 2005): 73–93.

Mulholland, Catherine. *William Mulholland and the Rise of Los Angeles.* Berkeley: University of California Press, 2000.

Murphy, Robert. *After Many a Summer: The Passing of the Giants and Dodgers and a Golden Age in New York Baseball.* New York: Union Square Press, 2009.

Murray, Jim. *Jim Murray: The Autobiography of the Pulitzer Prize Winning Sports Columnist.* New York: Macmillan, 1993.

———. "Walter in Wonderland." *Time,* April 28, 1958, 58–64.

Nadeau, Remi. *California: The New Society.* New York: David McKay, 1963.

Needham, Andrew. *Power Lines: Phoenix and the Making of the Modern Southwest.* Princeton: Princeton University Press, 2014.

Nicolaides, Becky M. *My Blue Heaven: Life and Politics in the Working-Class Suburbs of Los Angeles, 1920–1965.* Chicago: University of Chicago Press, 2002.

Noll, Roger G., and Andrew Zimbalist, eds. *Sports, Jobs, and Taxes: The Economic Impact of Sports Teams and Stadiums.* Washington, DC: Brookings Institution Press, 1997.

Normark, Don. *Chavez Ravine, 1949: A Los Angeles Story.* San Francisco: Chronicle Books, 1999.

Parrott, Harold. *The Lords of Baseball.* New York: Praeger, 1976.

Parson, Don. "Los Angeles' Headline Happy Public Housing War." *Southern California Quarterly* 65 (Fall 1983): 251–85.

———. *Making a Better World: Public Housing, the Red Scare, and the Direction of Modern Los Angeles.* Minneapolis: University of Minnesota Press, 2005.

———. "'This Modern Marvel': Bunker Hill, Chavez Ravine, and the Politics of Modernism in Los Angeles." *Southern California Quarterly* 75 (Fall–Winter 1993): 333–50.

Phelan, James. "Trouble in Happyland." *Saturday Evening Post,* May 25, 1963, 78–82.

Pitt, Leonard, and Dale Pitt. *Los Angeles A to Z: An Encyclopedia of the City and County.* Berkeley: University of California Press, 1997.

Plaut, David. *Chasing October: The Dodgers-Giants Pennant Race of 1962.* South Bend, IN: Diamond Communications, 1994.

Podair, Jerald. "'Haven of Tolerance': Dodgertown and the Integration of Major League Baseball Spring Training." Historic Dodgertown website, http://historicdodgertown.com/history/haven-of-tolerance.

———. *The Strike That Changed New York: Blacks, Whites, and the Ocean Hill–Brownsville Crisis.* New Haven: Yale University Press, 2002.

Polner, Murray. *Branch Rickey: A Biography.* New York: Atheneum, 1982.

Poulson, Norris. "The Untold Story of Chavez Ravine." *Los Angeles,* April 1962, 14–17, 50.

———. "Who Would Have Ever Dreamed?" UCLA Library Special Collections, Charles E. Young Research Library, University of California at Los Angeles.

Povletich, William. *Milwaukee Braves: Heroes and Heartbreak.* Madison: Wisconsin Historical Society Press, 2009.

Powell, Douglas S. "Is Big League Baseball Good Municipal Business?" *The American City*, November 1957, 111–13, 162.

Prager, Joshua. *The Echoing Green: The Untold Story of Bobby Thomson, Ralph Branca and the Shot Heard Round the World*. New York: Pantheon Books, 2006.

"Public Housing and the Brooklyn Dodgers." *Frontier*, June 1957, 7–9.

Rampersad, Arnold. *Jackie Robinson: A Biography*. New York: Knopf, 1997.

Regalado, Samuel O. "Dodgers Beisbol Is on the Air: The Development and Impact of the Dodgers' Spanish Language Broadcasts, 1958–1994." *California History: The Magazine of the California Historical Society*, Fall 1995, 281–89.

Rice, Christina, and Emma Roberts. *Bunker Hill in the Rearview Mirror: The Rise, Fall, and Rise Again of an Urban Neighborhood*. Los Angeles: Los Angeles Public Library, 2015.

Riley, Dan, ed. *The Dodgers Reader*. Boston: Houghton Mifflin, 1992.

Roberts, Myron. "When the Cleat Was on the Other Foot." *Los Angeles*, October 1982, 154–60.

Saltzstein, Alan J., and Raphael J. Sonenshein. "Los Angeles: Transformation of a Governing Coalition." In *Big City Politics in Transition*, ed. H. V. Savitch and John Clayton Thomas, 189–201. Newbury Park, CA: Sage Publications, 1991.

Sanchez, George J. *Becoming Mexican American: Ethnicity, Culture, and Identity in Chicano Los Angeles, 1900–1945*. New York: Oxford University Press, 1993.

Sayre, Wallace, and Herbert Kaufman. *Governing New York City: Politics in the Metropolis*. New York: Norton, 1965.

Schelling Thomas C. *Micromotives and Macrobehavior*. New York: W. W. Norton, 2006.

Schwartz, Joel. *The New York Approach: Robert Moses, Urban Liberals and the Redevelopment of the Inner City*. Columbus: Ohio State University Press, 1993.

Self, Robert O. *American Babylon: Race and the Struggle for Postwar Oakland*. Princeton: Princeton University Press, 2003.

Shapiro, Michael. *Bottom of the Ninth: Branch Rickey, Casey Stengel, and the Daring Scheme to Save Baseball from Itself*. New York: Times Books, 2009.

———. *The Last Good Season*. New York: Doubleday, 2003.

Shaplen, Robert. "O'Malley and the Angels." *Sports Illustrated*, March 24, 1958, 62–70.

Shermer, Elizabeth Tandy. *Sunbelt Capitalism: Phoenix and the Transformation of American Politics*. Philadelphia: University of Pennsylvania Press, 2013.

Sides, Josh. *L.A. City Limits: African American Los Angeles from the Great Depression to the Present*. Berkeley: University of California Press, 2006.

Sitton, Tom. *Los Angeles Transformed: Fletcher Bowron's Urban Reform Revival, 1938–1953*. Albuquerque: University of New Mexico Press, 2005.

Smith, Curt. *Voices of the Game*. New York: Simon and Schuster, 1992.

Soja, Edward W. *My Los Angeles: From Urban Restructuring to Regional Urbanization*. Berkeley: University of California Press, 2014.

Sonenshein, Raphael J. "The Dynamics of Biracial Coalitions: Crossover Politics in Los Angeles." *Western Political Quarterly* 42 (June 1989): 333–53.

———. *Politics in Black and White: Race and Power in Los Angeles.* Princeton: Princeton University Press, 1993.

Stark, Milton. "L.A. Renaissance." *California Highways and Public Works,* September–October 1961, 1–17.

Starr, Kevin. *The Dream Endures: California Enters the 1940s.* New York: Oxford University Press, 1997.

———. *Endangered Dreams: The Great Depression in California.* New York: Oxford University Press, 1996.

———. *Golden Dreams: California in an Age of Abundance, 1950–1963.* New York: Oxford University Press, 2009.

———. *Material Dreams: Southern California Through the 1920s.* New York: Oxford University Press, 1990.

Stout, Glenn. *The Dodgers: 120 Years of Dodger Baseball.* Boston: Houghton Mifflin, 2004.

Sullivan, Neil J. *The Diamond in the Bronx: Yankee Stadium and the Politics of New York.* New York: Oxford University Press, 2008.

———. *The Dodgers Move West.* New York: Oxford University Press, 1987.

Thompson, Fresco. *Every Diamond Doesn't Sparkle: Behind the Scenes with the Dodgers.* New York: David McKay, 1964.

Travers, Steven. *A Tale of Three Cities: The 1962 Baseball Season in New York, Los Angeles, and San Francisco.* Dulles, VA: Potomac Books, 2009.

Ulin, David L., ed. *Writing Los Angeles: A Literary Anthology.* New York: Library of America, 2002.

Waldie, D. J. *Holy Land: A Suburban Memoir.* New York: St. Martin's, 1996.

Waldinger, Roger, and Mehdi Bozorgmehr, eds. *Ethnic Los Angeles.* New York: Russell Sage Foundation, 1996.

Weaver, John D. *Los Angeles: The Enormous Village, 1781–1981.* Santa Barbara, CA: Capra Press, 1981.

Williams, Mason B. *City of Ambition: FDR, La Guardia, and the Making of Modern New York.* New York and London: W. W. Norton, 2013.

Wolfe, Burton H. "Candlestick Swindle." 1972. Shaping San Francisco's Digital Archive @ Found. www.foundsf.org/index.php?title=Candlestick_Swindle.

Zimbalist, Andrew. *Baseball and Billions.* New York: Basic Books, 1992.

Zminda, Don. "A Home Like No Other: The Dodgers in L.A. Memorial Coliseum." In *The National Pastime, Endless Seasons: Baseball in Southern California,* 84–86. Phoenix: Society for American Baseball Research, 2011.

INDEX

Note: Page numbers in italic type indicate photographs.